THE HATFIELD-MCCOY FEUD
Tug Valley

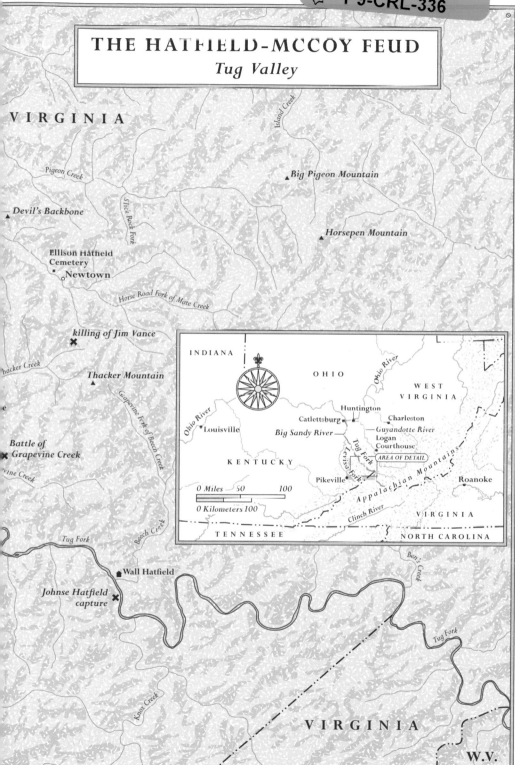

THE FEUD

ALSO BY DEAN KING

AUTHOR

Unbound

Skeletons on the Zahara

Patrick O'Brian: A Life Revealed

A Sea of Words

Harbors and High Seas

EDITOR

*Every Man Will Do His Duty: An Anthology
of Firsthand Accounts from the Age of Nelson, 1793–1815*

THE
HATFIELDS &
McCOYS
THE TRUE STORY

DEAN KING

LITTLE, BROWN AND COMPANY
New York Boston London

Little, Brown and Company
Hachette Book Group
237 Park Avenue, New York, NY 10017
littlebrown.com

First Edition: May 2013

Little, Brown and Company is a division of Hachette Book Group, Inc.
The Little, Brown name and logo are trademarks of Hachette Book Group, Inc.

The publisher is not responsible for websites (or their content) that are not owned by the publisher.

The Hachette Speakers Bureau provides a wide range of authors for speaking events. To find out more, go to hachettespeakersbureau.com or call (866) 376-6591.

Library of Congress Cataloging-in-Publication Data

King, Dean.
    The feud: the Hatfields & McCoys, the true story / Dean King. — First edition.
    pages cm
  Includes bibliographical references and index.
  ISBN 978-0-316-16706-2
    1. Hatfield-McCoy Feud.   2. Vendetta — Kentucky — History — 19th
century.   3. Vendetta — West Virginia — History — 19th century.   I. Title.
  HV6452.K42H355 2013
  975.4'404 — dc23   2012049512

10 9 8 7 6 5 4 3 2 1

RRD-C

Printed in the United States of America

For my parents, Bill and Betsey,
and

For my niece Liza
September 27, 1984–October 8, 2012

All different things brought it on.

—Andrew Chafin,
Devil Anse Hatfield's nephew
and messenger

*The human varmint is the most coorious
an' cunningist varmint thar is.*

—Devil Anse Hatfield

*Mountains make fighting men. No matter where
in the world you go, you'll find that's true.*

—Ralph Stanley

CONTENTS

~

PART I
BAD BLOOD,
1854–1882

PART II
THE RAGE AND THE OUTRAGE,
1882–1887

Contents

AUTHOR'S NOTE

~

In 1865, as our nation began to recover from its cataclysmic civil war and to forge a more perfect union, there were yet the inevitable aftershocks. The conflict not only reunited the thirty-six states (two had been added since the start of the war), but also launched a new era of economic growth, urbanization, and industrialization, one that would sweep the land, like the railroads, from coast to coast. But not all Americans were equally prepared to rise on the tide of modernity.

In an isolated pocket of the southern Appalachian Mountains, two Old World families, suspended in geographic convolutions as ancient as time, in ridges and hollows that seemed to stop clocks (and where today cell phones and GPS devices are of little use), continued the bloodshed over matters of passion and honor.

Before the war, Hatfields (of English blood) and McCoys (of Scots-Irish roots) lived on both sides of the Tug River, which separates West Virginia and Kentucky, in relative harmony, intermarrying and working and trading together. After the war, a West Virginia faction of the Hatfield family and a Kentucky branch of the McCoy family found themselves at each other's throats. Their hostilities would stretch over the course of three decades—from 1865 to 1890.

The fighting grew so bitter and became such a threat to public safety that it almost brought the two Civil War border states back to war. In 1889, the governors of West Virginia and Kentucky carried the dispute all the way to the Supreme Court of the United States. The resulting decision paved the way for one man to go to the gallows and sparked a bounty hunters' war in the Tug Valley.

America was riveted by the violence, which headlined newspapers nationwide. At the height of the feud, a chagrined New York City journalist, T. C. Crawford, declared after visiting the Tug Valley: "I have been away in Murderland."

In an age of feuds, the Hatfields and McCoys' was neither the longest nor the bloodiest, yet it captured our national imagination, etched itself in our psyche, and became a defining moment in the American experience, a reflection of something essential in our fierce, liberty-loving character. "Fighting like Hatfields and McCoys" became a catchphrase. Over the decades, the story of these two families and their vendetta has drawn us back again and again, as newspapers, magazines, books, movies, and, most recently, a block-buster miniseries in 2012 spun the history—murky even as it unfolded—into legend, into myth.

Having family roots in West Virginia, I knew the story all too well—or thought I did. When in the summer of 2008 my brother-in-law Morgan Entrekin, the publisher of Grove/Atlantic Press, suggested that I take a second look at the feud and consider a new retelling of it, I was skeptical at first. Interestingly, it was John F. Kennedy Jr. who had brought the idea to Morgan; before Kennedy's tragic death, in 1999, they were planning a publishing partnership between Kennedy's magazine, *George,* and Grove/Atlantic. Kennedy, from one of America's iconic families, was fascinated by the iconic Hatfield-McCoy feud and by the fact that there were still pockets of the eastern United States outside governmental control so late in the nineteenth century. At a time when he was seeking more his-torical narrative for *George,* Kennedy felt this story in which local politics and states' rights were determined over the barrel of a Winchester was a natural.

As I read about the feud, I began to realize that the story was far more complex—at once more brutal and more heartrending—

than I knew. The true story and what it says about humanity had been lost for me, like for most, in the legend. As I investigated, I became convinced of two things: that the tale of the troubles between these two isolated American families had much to tell us about who we are as Americans and that the story needed to be rebuilt from the ground up using records, original documents, and early accounts whenever available, while corroborating as much of the story as possible on-site in the West Virginia and Kentucky border country where it happened.

OVER THE YEARS, I found, the telling of the feud story caused almost as many arguments as the feud itself. Some accounts ignored elements of the story that clashed with myth; others narrated it from afar, scratching the surface but going no deeper. Such reluctance is understandable. The McCoys and Hatfields have their own differing versions of every feud clash.

After I embarked on the research, I discovered that many truths of the feud lay hidden away, languishing like forgotten keepsakes in a dusty attic, and thus our interpretation of this vital episode of American history was incomplete and often askew. For instance, I found an unpublished novel about the feud by a local judge who personally witnessed a feud event and faithfully recorded original court documents, but it had been stowed in a trunk in a barn for seventy years. The account of a secret murder witnessed by a boy who served as a feud messenger surfaced in a home recording that had sat for decades without being transcribed. A misplaced confession turned up in the wrong folder in a museum. And the forgotten journal of a niece of one of the feud principals—Devil Anse Hatfield—emerged from a farmhouse near the Tug River.

Until now, pages and pages of firsthand reporting had been lost in newspaper archives. One account described the never-before-revealed (and since forgotten) details of Devil Anse's distilling operation. Another, by James Creelman, one of the most influential newspaper correspondents of the day, went undiscovered by previous historians because it carried no byline.

These contemporary journalists knew that in order to best tell this story there would be no substitute for getting to know the Tug Valley and the Hatfields and McCoys in person. The same is true today. On my first trip, in the summer of 2009, with the help of two forest rangers and my daughter Hazel, I bushwhacked down to the mouth of Thacker Creek on the Tug Fork of the Big Sandy River to see the place where Jeff McCoy had been shot and killed in 1886. We had not been there fifteen minutes when some locals let it be known in feud-worthy fashion that they did not appreciate my snooping around. As gunshots sprayed the river surface near us — making me, as far as I know, the second chronicler of the feud (Creelman being the first, in 1888) to be warned off with rifle fire while researching the story — we beat a hasty retreat up the riverbank.

I returned in the fall, this time with a Hatfield guide, Scotty May, who lives on Mate Creek and whose Chafin clan intermarried with the Hatfields. Now things went much more smoothly, and I was soon riding up on the ridges with a slew of Hatfields — armed with chain saws, pistols in hip holsters, and jars of corn liquor — to the family hideouts. Family members took me to hidden cemeteries and produced journals, deeds, and other documents, all the while imploring me to correct the record on this point or that one.

Likewise, when I visited with the McCoys, they welcomed my research, providing me with interviews, tours of feud sites, and rare family photographs. Betty Howard, a genealogist who lives in Pikeville, Kentucky, and is related to the McCoys and others involved in the feud, including the lawman "Bad" Frank Phillips, was as generous with her voluminous research on the feud as she was unbridled in her pro-McCoy beliefs.

Using such resources, documents, and past accounts, I have attempted in these pages to correct the record, to deflate the legends, to check the biases, and to add or restore accurate historical detail. Like every feud historian, I have occasionally had to rely on oral tradition, one that is often contradictory since many versions of each event have surfaced over time and since quite a few of those directly involved kept silent or told lies because warrants for their arrests stayed on the books for decades.

Of the fatalities in the feud, three McCoys (two women and a boy) were said to have died of a broken heart. While this malady dates back to biblical times—insults caused King David to suffer from a broken heart, and Shakespeare's feudist Lady Montague died of it ("Grief of my son's exile hath stopp'd her breath," says her husband)—it is only recently that science has attempted with some success to quantify and explain such a phenomenon. It appears that emotional distress, if not broken-heart syndrome, did play a role in these deaths (and they are thus marked among the "killed" in the charts that help you keep track in this book).

Parts of the feud remain shrouded in mystery and probably always will. Still, this powerful true saga of love, lust, greed, and rage that ensnared three generations of two families on what was then an isolated and relatively lawless American mountain frontier is graphic enough. Its lessons are about what happens when society's safeguards are absent or fall apart, when men—armed as they please—are left to their own devices to enforce "justice," and when family ties determine right and wrong and tribalism prevails. Our self-reliant, wilderness-dwelling forebears often had to grapple with a foe more potent and more relentless than external enemies: their own demons.

—*Dean King*

The Hatfields

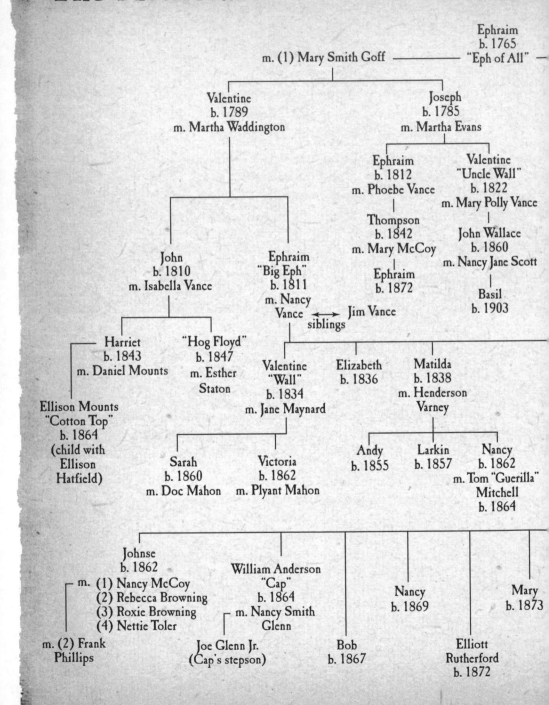

Ephraim
b. 1765
"Eph of All"

m. (1) Mary Smith Goff

Valentine
b. 1789
m. Martha Waddington

Joseph
b. 1785
m. Martha Evans

Ephraim
b. 1812
m. Phoebe Vance

Valentine
"Uncle Wall"
b. 1822
m. Mary Polly Vance

Thompson
b. 1842
m. Mary McCoy

John Wallace
b. 1860
m. Nancy Jane Scott

John
b. 1810
m. Isabella Vance

Ephraim
"Big Eph"
b. 1811
m. Nancy
Vance ⟷ Jim Vance
siblings

Ephraim
b. 1872

Basil
b. 1903

Harriet
b. 1843
m. Daniel Mounts

"Hog Floyd"
b. 1847
m. Esther
Staton

Valentine
"Wall"
b. 1834
m. Jane Maynard

Elizabeth
b. 1836

Matilda
b. 1838
m. Henderson
Varney

Ellison Mounts
"Cotton Top"
b. 1864
(child with
Ellison
Hatfield)

Sarah
b. 1860
m. Doc Mahon

Victoria
b. 1862
m. Plyant Mahon

Andy
b. 1855

Larkin
b. 1857

Nancy
b. 1862
m. Tom "Guerilla"
Mitchell
b. 1864

Johnse
b. 1862
m. (1) Nancy McCoy
    (2) Rebecca Browning
    (3) Roxie Browning
    (4) Nettie Toler

m. (2) Frank
Phillips

William Anderson
"Cap"
b. 1864
m. Nancy Smith
Glenn

Joe Glenn Jr.
(Cap's stepson)

Nancy
b. 1869

Mary
b. 1873

Bob
b. 1867

Elliott
Rutherford
b. 1872

A Selective Genealogy

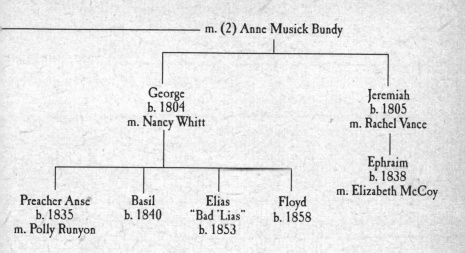

— m. (2) Anne Musick Bundy

George
b. 1804
m. Nancy Whitt

Jeremiah
b. 1805
m. Rachel Vance

Ephraim
b. 1838
m. Elizabeth McCoy

Preacher Anse
b. 1835
m. Polly Runyon

Basil
b. 1840

Elias
"Bad 'Lias"
b. 1853

Floyd
b. 1858

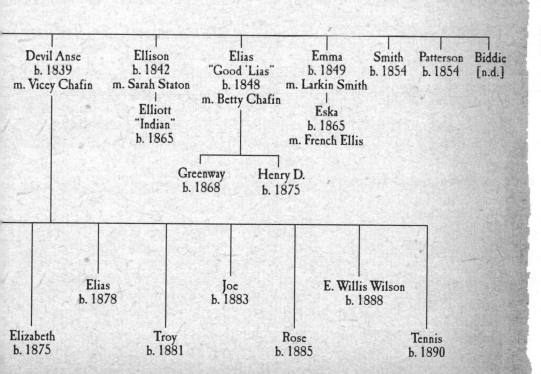

Devil Anse
b. 1839
m. Vicey Chafin

Ellison
b. 1842
m. Sarah Staton

Elias
"Good 'Lias"
b. 1848
m. Betty Chafin

Emma
b. 1849
m. Larkin Smith

Smith
b. 1854

Patterson
b. 1854

Biddie
[n.d.]

Elliott
"Indian"
b. 1865

Eska
b. 1865
m. French Ellis

Greenway
b. 1868

Henry D.
b. 1875

Elias
b. 1878

Joe
b. 1883

E. Willis Wilson
b. 1888

Elizabeth
b. 1875

Troy
b. 1881

Rose
b. 1885

Tennis
b. 1890

The McCoys

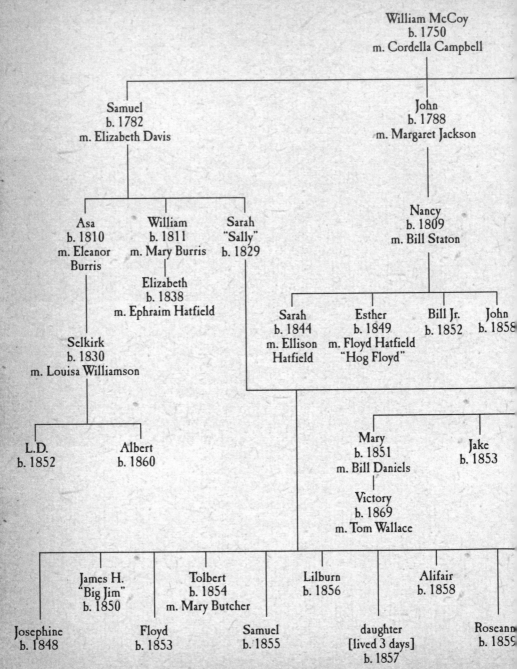

William McCoy
b. 1750
m. Cordella Campbell

Samuel
b. 1782
m. Elizabeth Davis

John
b. 1788
m. Margaret Jackson

Asa
b. 1810
m. Eleanor
Burris

William
b. 1811
m. Mary Burris

Sarah
"Sally"
b. 1829

Nancy
b. 1809
m. Bill Staton

Elizabeth
b. 1838
m. Ephraim Hatfield

Sarah
b. 1844
m. Ellison
Hatfield

Esther
b. 1849
m. Floyd Hatfield
"Hog Floyd"

Bill Jr.
b. 1852

John
b. 1858

Selkirk
b. 1830
m. Louisa Williamson

L.D.
b. 1852

Albert
b. 1860

Mary
b. 1851
m. Bill Daniels

Jake
b. 1853

Victory
b. 1869
m. Tom Wallace

James H.
"Big Jim"
b. 1850

Tolbert
b. 1854
m. Mary Butcher

Lilburn
b. 1856

Alifair
b. 1858

Josephine
b. 1848

Floyd
b. 1853

Samuel
b. 1855

daughter
[lived 3 days]
b. 1857

Roseann
b. 1859

A Selective Genealogy

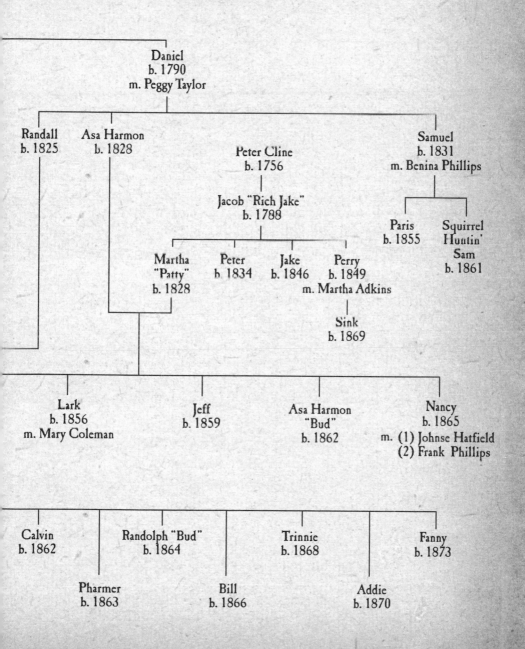

THE FEUD

~

The Fate of Cotton Top Mounts

February 18, 1890

I t was February, a time when the locals usually hunkered down in smoky cabins on the brink of stir-craziness, quietly riding out the long, brutal months of an Appalachian winter, subsisting on cured razorback pork and venison, stored in smokehouses in hollowed-out tree trunks they called meat logs, and on cornmeal and bear grease. But this year, a quarter century after the end of the war that had scarred them all deeper than they even knew and deposited a black feud in their midst, like a miasma trapped in the hills, the bloodthirst in their veins had worked on them like spring, thawing their deep inner reserve, bringing forth in their minds words that needed to be uttered and images that needed to be seen. And so they came, in droves, in some cases, entire families, as if it were Election Day or a revival, to satisfy their inescapable urge to behold a man hang by his neck.

Not that the cold would have stopped them. These mountain people, of British descent mostly, were inured to it. They left their cabins lightly chinked to let air circulate and even in winter closed their doors only at night. They rarely wore coats—if they had them—and routinely did chores barefoot in the snow. The men often waded in icy rivers while fishing and logging and, on bear hunts, slept on the ground without blankets.[1]

On this day, they emerged on foot from the hollows, where their cornfields lay at such an incline that one visiting newspaper reporter said their places "looked like farms stood on their edges." Many traveled on trails, breathing again hope in the crisp air of the Cumberland Plateau, where the hills were covered in magnificent trees, descended from the great swath of first-growth wilderness. Here oaks bulged to twenty feet around, and tulip poplars soared two hundred feet in the sky. Lean and long-legged, these mountain people were accomplished walkers, used to covering distances with burdens that city dwellers could hardly imagine. They thought nothing of shouldering a two-bushel sack of corn, weighing 112 pounds, for a ten-mile trip to a mill and then turning back again with the milled corn the next day, or covering twenty miles in a night to hunt a bear, only to return home for breakfast and chores.[2]

Others set out for the hanging on mules or horses. Some drove carts pulled by oxen on roads that were nothing more than ruts across rock and packed soil. Still others boated the Levisa Fork of the Big Sandy, up- or downriver to the bend where the Pike County seat, Pikeville, a town of nearly five hundred souls, stood watch. Pikeville was without benefit of either train tracks or telegraph wires, less a town than a sort of fortress in the wilderness, a place for a hanging.

They came to see the curse of the hostilities vanquished. They came to bury the bad name. They came to bear witness to justice meted out the old-fashioned way, in the light of day, official and tangible. There were those in the throng who knew that for the Big Sandy Valley, this hanging was also the down payment on railroad tracks, jobs, and, for some, riches. Out would go timber. Coal would be king.

IT HAD BEEN TWO YEARS since a New York City newspaperman had come down and written a story about the feud, dubbing the valley Murderland for the entire world to read. Now news of the looming execution of Devil Anse Hatfield's half-witted, bastard, albino nephew Cotton Top Mounts had spread through the bleak winter hills around the tributaries of the Big Sandy with the snap and crack of wildfire.[3]

Strictly speaking, the execution was not to be public, as public executions had been banned in Pike County for four decades. But the fence being erected around the gallows on the edge of town was a sham. Since the scaffold had been built in a notch on a small hillside, the fence would not block the view for spectators sitting on the hill, nor was it meant to. As eager as anyone to alter the fortunes of their region, local officials had bucked the spirit of the law, if not the letter, for something altogether bigger: the greater good of the people. They welcomed a public spectacle to spread the message — that feuding and wanton killing would no longer be tolerated — in the most graphic and profound way.

Everyone was curious: Would a member of the Hatfield gang really swing? And was it true that Cap Hatfield, Cotton Top's cousin, or his uncle Wall who was rumored to have seven wives and fifty-five children, had bribed him to confess with the promise of a new saddle? Would one more death mean the end of three decades of killing? Would the stain, the blight on their community, finally be removed? Or would Devil Anse ride again, this time to save Cotton Top and, in so doing, make certain the further flow of blood?

PIKEVILLE SHERIFF HARMON MAYNARD HAD his hands full. The town had swelled tenfold with a volatile mixture of rough mountain folks, bounty hunters, Union and Confederate army veterans (both regulars and irregulars), moonshiners, swindlers, and journalists, the last coming from as far away as Louisville. Maynard understood the gravity of the situation and was taking no chances. He had sworn in twenty deputy sheriffs to make sure the execution took place. In addition, he had called up a citizens' guard of more than fifty heavily armed men, whose guns were equipped with bayonets for riot control and close fighting. It was an impressive show for far-flung Pikeville. The town was ready.[4]

Maynard, a former schoolteacher and first-term sheriff better known as Harm, scoured the streets with beady black eyes that peered out above his woolly brown beard as if from behind a bush. The threat of a Hatfield raid, the impositions of scurrilous reporters, and the demands of state militia officers, judges, and the governor himself — not to mention the keeping of the most high-profile prisoners in the state — had taxed his reserves.

His compact jail in the center of town was considered extremely secure, but Cotton Top was locked up with Charley Gillespie, who had more than a few tricks up his sleeve. When the jail's sewage system mysteriously backed up, it had looked like the two of them would have to be moved to a less secure part of the jail. Then one of the other inmates suggested that the sheriff take a good look in the sewer pipe. He did and found that it had been stuffed with pieces of blanket. Gillespie and Cotton Top stayed right where they were.

When the inevitable trouble arrived, it came from an unexpected quarter. Former deputy sheriff Frank Phillips, a killer and cuckolder of Hatfields, and Bud McCoy, the son of the first man killed in the feud, had been drinking all night. As the crowd grew that morning, the two men strutted through the streets. With a loaded revolver in each hand, Phillips, a small, fastidious man with dark hair and fine features who looked younger than his forty-eight years, periodically fired into the air. He aimed to stop the hanging, he shouted, although he never said why; perhaps he did not think it a fitting end to his own death-defying efforts to subdue the violent West Virginia clan. Though remorseless, Cotton Top — whose father was murdered in the feud — was taking a fall for the rest of the Hatfields.

The McCoys themselves claimed that while Mounts was in the Pikeville jail, he admitted that Cap Hatfield had promised him five hundred dollars, a rifle, a saddle, and immunity if he would take the murder charge. Apparently unaware of how little money he would be needing in the near future, Mounts had complained to them that he had received the saddle and the rifle but only a few of the dollars.[5]

Cotton Top Mounts.

Phillips declared that *he* had run the Hatfields down, and now he aimed to run Pikeville. Backed by his deputies and carrying the burden and will of his hundred first cousins in the area, not to mention his wife, Arminta, the daughter of a legendary Confederate spy, Sheriff Maynard had other ideas. He and his men stopped the rogue lawman and told him to quit making trouble. Phillips responded that the schoolteacher could try to stop him. Maynard— emboldened by the fact that he already had—threatened to put Phillips in jail. Phillips punched him. Then in a flash he kicked hard to Maynard's rib cage, snapping four ribs like dry sticks. Maynard drew a pistol and pulled back the hammer. But before he could shoot, his officers jumped on Phillips, took his guns, and began to beat him. Bud McCoy drew his weapon and leveled it just as Phillips's other friends dove into the fray. They managed to wrestle him, nearly unconscious from the whiskey and the beating, away from the lawmen. Bent in pain, Maynard now rose and summoned more guards. Two dozen men wielding bayoneted rifles gained control of the situation and dispersed the mounting crowd.[6]

The officers dragged Phillips partway into the jail. It would not do to actually lock him up: in addition to being a former deputy sheriff, Phillips was a wealthy and influential citizen from an old local family, with formidable friends like Colonel Dils and Perry Cline. He had married into the McCoy clan and was a father supporting seven children and stepchildren. To many, he was also a hero for fearlessly riding down the Hatfields. So instead, the officers left him sprawled on the floor, his body in the cell and his feet outside. His alcoholic coma would keep him out of trouble until the execution was over, and even then, they had ensured that he would not feel much like causing trouble.[7]

By MIDMORNING, the hillsides surrounding the gallows—a natural amphitheater—were teeming with people. Rumors raced through the crowd that the Hatfields were coming and that the McCoys had sent guards to defend the two passes leading to town. Nerves were on edge. Pregnant Eliza Tibbs was so overwhelmed that she fainted. Later, when her son Oscar was born, he turned out to be a deaf-mute, yet another tragedy that would be chalked up to the feud.[8]

If others seemed restless or unnerved by the proceedings, Cotton Top did not. He came from stock that had the dubious distinction of displaying great equanimity on the scaffold, dating back to his great-great-grandfather Abner Vance, a hunter and a preacher who lived near Abingdon, Virginia. Seventy years previously, Vance, before being strung up for the murder of Lewis Horton, calmly composed a ballad lamenting his plight. He had shot Horton, a doctor, for an affront of a sexual nature to his daughter and fled to the west. After many months on the run in the wilds of the Tug River Valley, he had returned to face the charges against him, hoping for leniency given the circumstances. But the frontier was not big on nuances. On the scaffold, the doomed man crooned his ballad, which became known as "Vance's Farewell," bidding good-bye to his wife, whom he called "my old sweetheart." He then immortalized the perfidy of his foes, who "a lie against me swore." Naturally, he pined for vengeance:

> *But I and them shall meet again*
> *When Immanuel's trumpet shall blow.*
> *Perhaps I'll be wrapped in Abraham's bosom*
> *When they roll in the gulf below.*

Vance's ballad also expressed his love for the land to the west, along the Virginia-Kentucky border, that he had discovered while a fugitive, some of which he had staked claim to:

> *Green are the woods through which Sandy flows.*
> *Peace dwells in the land.*
> *The bear doth live in the laurel green.*
> *The red buck roves the hills.*[9]

Before meeting his fate, Vance had not only composed his ballad but also parceled out his claim to his children. They went there to start a new life. Vance, a violent man who hoped for better for his family, had thus directed them to a place where, contrary to his lyrics, peace did not dwell. In fact, it was a place of reduction and extraction, and violence was as much a part of life as childbirth and homemade spirits. The seminomadic Cherokee, Shawnee, Delaware, and Mingo had used this territory as a hunting ground for buffalo, bear, elk, deer, and, eventually, white men. In turn, white men would kill the Indians, the bears, and one another for more than a century before the day that Cotton Top Mounts was to be hanged, a killing that could be seen in these parts as not a retribution but a partial atonement for the whole cycle of slaughter.

Vance was not the only one of his kin who had performed nobly in the proximity of death. In 1885, his Kentucky cousin Ransom Hatfield had served as a special guard to a man about to be hanged in Catlettsburg and had "exhorted the doomed man to exert every power of mind and muscle, as well as to call on God for help, to enable him to meet his end with becoming fortitude." He had so bolstered the man that he faced his execution with "heroic composure." [10] But Ransom had not been the one with the noose around his neck.

Just after noon, Harm Maynard, for whom one term as sheriff would be enough to propel him back to the farm, repaired to the jailhouse and in a gruff voice read the death warrant. Cotton Top, who had been feeling ill for several days and whose left arm still troubled him, had not slept at all the previous night. Despite his bad behavior in stuffing up the pipes, he was granted a last request. As last requests go, his lacked the flair of Red Fox's just two years later. Sentenced to hang for the quadruple murder of a family near Pound Gap, Virginia, twenty miles south of Pikeville, the mystical red-haired charlatan doctor would be granted his unusual wish: Before he died, he wanted to dress in the white linen robes that he planned to don in heaven and preach his own funeral sermon; afterward, he wished his body to remain unburied for three days so that he could rise up to preach again before continuing on to the pearly gates. Cotton Top, who had confessed to his feudist sins in multiple documents on multiple occasions, merely asked for a cigar, which he puffed on, occasionally blowing smoke rings. [11]

The battered Maynard would not preside over the execution; Deputy Sheriff Harry Weddington would have that honor. The Reverend Dr. J. W. Glover, a scowling, mustachioed Methodist preacher, said prayers with the condemned man before he was conveyed on a wagon the half mile to the execution ground. He rode atop his own coffin. [12]

GUARDS SCANNED THE CROWD TO detect any signs of opposition, but it was as quiet as a jury. Cotton Top was now firmly clamped in the jaws of justice—or partial justice, anyway—and of history and lore. There needed to be a definitive end to this story of feuding and murder. Cotton Top—a love child of the war, a violent simpleton—apparently was it.

That is, unless, as was still expected by many, his uncle Devil Anse and a gang of Hatfields wielding Colts and Winchesters were just over the hill ready to storm the execution ground and free him.

Standing on the gallows, his time dwindling, Cotton Top felt the urge to sing, like Abner Vance before him, but not in a musical way like Abner. Instead, at the penultimate moment of his life, the twenty-five-year-old sang, like the desperate fall guy he was, a croaked and anguished plaint: "The Hatfields made me do it!" [13]

PART I

~

BAD BLOOD

1854–1882

Chapter 1

~

War Comes to the Big Sandy

1854–1862

Prior to the Civil War, the Tug River Valley essentially ignored calendars and resisted progress. There were no roads, no rails, no schools, and no churches in the area. The transcontinental telegraph system, which crossed the nation in 1861, bypassed the region. Telegraph service would not arrive in the valley for three more decades. Barricaded as they were in mountainous cul-de-sacs, locals spoke a dialect barely recognizable to outsiders, a tongue more Elizabethan than modern Victorian, using *yit* for *yet*, *mought* for *might*, *seche* for *such*, and the word *allow* to mean "figure." They added *es* to form plurals like *nestes*. They *afeared* witches and haints. Questions from outsiders made them *techeous* (a state in which they were best avoided). The forest that enveloped them and, along with the hills, shaped their lives — a part of what the botanist-explorer William Bartram dubbed the sublime forest — was still dense, vast, and virginal.[1]

One day in the fall of 1854, when he was fifteen, Anse Hatfield went out in the forest to bag some squirrels for the stew pot, something he had done many times before. Gangly, on his way to six feet, Anse, whose mother called him Ansie, was always on the move, slipping adroitly through the trees, already with the signature Hatfield slouch in his gait. His hawk-nosed intensity and nasal twang were cut by a penchant for practical jokes and a raucous and infectious laugh. Like his father, Big Eph (pronounced "Eef"), he liked to wrestle, but not more than he liked to hunt. Wearing a buckskin coat and carrying a rifle, powder, and balls, he set loose his pack of hounds, led by three trustworthies named Rounder, Fife, and Drum. No sooner had he let the dogs go than they scared up a large spike-horn deer.[2]

The trio went tearing off after it. As the buck topped the ridge of Big Pigeon Mountain, Anse took into account the distance and the rise, leveled the barrel of his gun considerably above it, and squeezed the trigger. But his prey was too far away. It disappeared over the ridge with the dogs in hot pursuit. Anse was concerned. This buck had legs and might lead his dogs beyond return. There was plenty of trouble to get into among the intricate bends and folds of the woods here, almost no stretch of which was flat. Boulders, roots, and rocky streams hid beneath the leaf cover and behind rotting logs. In slicks, where lightning strikes and landslides had felled the trees, grew thick snarls of laurel, myrtle, huckleberry, and rhododendron that could trap a hell-bent hound like a steel cage. It was easy to get lost here, no matter how acute one's sense of smell or direction. Anse, worried yet confident in his mastery of the place, set off at a fast trot.[3]

He raced through the undulating wilderness, past trees festooned in ghastly hues of old-man's beard. Here and there antler lichen clung tombstone-like to trunks living and dead. The Mingo chief Logan, like many of the Indian tribes that had once roamed the place, had welcomed white traders and settlers to his tribe's vast sacred hunting ground, until 1774, when they murdered his family. Then Logan had attacked white settlements with ferocity. "When the good soul had the ascendant, he was kind and humane," the chief later explained, "and when the bad soul ruled, he was perfectly savage and delighted in nothing but blood and carnage."

By 1824, the Indians were gone, and the Virginia General Assembly created Logan County, which would eventually form nearly half of the state of West Virginia. Within a year, the last known bison in the county (and, indeed, in all of Virginia) were killed. Still, young Anse stalked a stretch of the Great Forest where elk roamed and where wolves and wildcats — the latter called variously cougars, catamounts, pumas, panthers (pronounced "painters"), or mountain lions by the locals — prowled.[4]

When Anse did not return home for supper, his mother, Nancy — the illegitimate daughter of the scandalized daughter of Abner Vance — began to worry. She told Big Eph that she was afraid that Anse was hurt. He told her not to worry: the boy was every bit as "stout as a bear." Big Eph, a six-foot-tall, dark-complected, blue-eyed, Bunyanesque man of 250 pounds who had once treed and killed a wildcat with a butcher knife he carried in a scabbard, was a shrewd judge of these things. He laughed when Nancy suggested that a bear might have attacked Anse. "If a bear even gets a glimpse of a man in the woods, then he goes the other way," he assured her. "Besides, Ansie has hunted so much, he's a dead shot." The boy was used to pursuing not only deer and squirrels but raccoons, possums, and groundhogs, along with grouse, wild turkeys, and ducks. He even knew how to shoot a swimming turtle in the head so that it would not sink. "No bear is going to get in speaking distance of him," Big Eph declared. And then he added, "Why, I seen him shoot a squirrel's eye out in the top of a tall hickory when I couldn't even see the squirrel before it fell." Anse, he knew, could do a man's work and could fend for himself.[5]

But the next day, Nancy was even more worried that a bear might have gotten Anse, who, no matter how stout and sure of shot, was still just a boy. Nancy, like her son, was tall, strong, and smart. She was graced with her mother's features: a high forehead, a thin nose, and a square chin. Only ten of her eighteen children would survive childhood, but those who did were, like her, sturdy and intelligent. Able to read and write, she owned a medical book and served as the area's midwife, which yielded her a wide network of friends. Between her tutoring and the will of the family to improve its lot, eight of her grandchildren would go on to become doctors.[6]

Now Nancy decided something must be done to find her boy. Big Eph and their oldest son, seventeen-year-old Wall, rode over to Ben's Creek, to the east, where two Hatfield uncles lived, to see if Anse had stayed there or stopped by for a meal. He had not.

In fact, as the stag thrashed off through the woods, Anse had set out too fast, stumbling to his knees before he even made it up Big Pigeon. Cursing, he jumped up and moved his gear back in place as he made his next stride. But a breathtaking mile later, when he gained the top of the ridge, the buck had vanished. Stopping to consider his next move, Anse sensed that something was not right. He reached down to his shot pouch—it was too light. When he stumbled, he realized, the shot had all fallen out.

"There I was with my gun shot empty, bullets lost, and that spike buck aleadin' every dog I had clean out of the county," he would recall. He decided he could not afford to go back, for if he did, he might never see his hounds again. He had to stay on their heels.

Following the buck's and dogs' trail along the top of the ridge, Anse lost track of time. It might have been an hour or two later when he looked down and saw something that stopped him cold: about sixty yards below the ridge, curled up on a carpet of leaves, lay a colossal black bear. Anse's eyes grew big. This was a rare chance to bag a monster that would keep the family in bear steaks and grease for months to come. Then the truth of his predicament caught up with him: His bullets lay in the dirt several miles back. His pack of hounds was running wild after the spike-horn. He was standing before this incredible prize with no way to claim it.

Anse's frustration turned to rage. "The longer I stood," he later said, "the madder I got." He cursed the god who would do this to him and, after leaning his now worthless gun against a black pine, ran down the slope of the mountain yelling and waving his arms. The startled bear awoke and scrambled to its feet after a maniacal Anse planted a boot in its backside. The bear tore off down the slope, covering twenty paces to get to a chestnut oak large enough to climb. It shinnied up the tree, lodged in a fork thirty feet off the ground, and stared down at its pursuer. Breathing hard and still in a rage, Anse stared back. Then he stripped off his jacket and shirt and began flailing the tree with them, all the while shouting at the animal above.

The bear decided to wait it out aloft. Caught between his missing dogs and his spilled shot, Anse did the same below.

Two hours later, the dogs found him. They had given up on the buck and circled back. Now they got wind of the treed bear and started howling. Anse stood watch all night as the passing moon lit the woods around him.

He stayed in the same spot through the next day. He had nothing to eat and nothing to drink, and his mouth grew drier and drier, but he refused to stand down.

It was sometime after midnight on the second night when he looked up and saw on the ridge what he recognized as the light of a pine torch. He hooted like an owl, a Hatfield family signal. A hoot came in return. Hearing the call of their clan, the dogs began to bay. Soon Wall and a neighbor, Peter Brooks, stood next to Anse. When they asked him if he was hurt, he responded, "Hurt? The devil! The only one that got hurt here is a four-year-old bear. I kicked his behind so hard with my boot that he took to a tree."

They gave Anse a slab of venison that his mother had sent for him. He divided it among his hungry dogs, having decided that he would eat nothing until he took his prey. The only problem was that Wall and Brooks had brought neither guns nor shot. They tried to convince Anse to come back with them, but he refused. Realizing it was futile, Wall finally asked Brooks to go get bullets for Anse's gun. Before he could return, however, Big Eph and a gang of men showed up. They handed Anse a gourd full of water. He pulled out the corncob stopper, tilted his head back, and gulped it down. Then, taking the bullets they offered him, he loaded his gun, took aim, and bagged his first bear.

A short time later, after he returned home with a panther he had shot, Nancy declared her boy "not afeared of no kind of varmint nor of the devil hisself!" She called him Devil Anse after that. The nickname would prove apt to friend and foe.[7]

A CONTEMPORARY OF DANIEL BOONE, who pushed through the Cumberland Gap in 1775, opening up the "West" to settlement, Devil Anse's great-great-grandfather Joseph Hatfield was considered one of the ablest scouts and woodsmen on the western frontier. The family had arrived in western Virginia from England by 1770, building forts for protection against the Indians and hunting bears in the Alleghenies. Intermarried with Dutch, French, and Germans, the Hatfields were a staunch blend, "tall and muscular, with a good share of brains and will-power," according to an observer in 1887. "They are a high-spirited family, but are kind, neighborly, and just to all who treat them just."[8]

In 1776, some Hatfields, along with the Bromfield family, were living by the New River near Big Stony Creek. One night, unbeknownst to each other, a Bromfield and a Hatfield both went to the same salt lick. One — though it is not known which — took the other for a bear moving in the brush and shot him dead.

In the years to come, as neighbor turned against neighbor, not every killing would be so accidental.

Of the four sons of Joseph Hatfield's son Eph (known as "Eph of All"), three — Joseph, George, and Jeremiah — lived on the Kentucky side of the Tug, mostly in Pike County. Only one, Valentine, Devil Anse's grandfather, settled on the West Virginia side. Eph of All's four sons would sire more than fifty children, and brothers, sisters, aunts, uncles, and cousins would move across the Tug with ease — on foot where it was shallow.

Likewise, the McCoys, who had reached Kentucky by 1804, lived on both sides of the Tug and came and went as they pleased. The families were on good terms with each other and were intermarried on both sides of the river. In fact, Tug Valley dwellers in general were so intertwined that in 1849 they petitioned to move the Virginia-Kentucky state line so that the entire valley would lie within Virginia. "The present line," they noted, "divides neighborhoods, friends and relations." Among the signers were more than a dozen McCoys and Hatfields, families linked together by business and politics, in addition to marriage.[9]

This same year, Randall and Sarah McCoy fell in love and married. They were first cousins descended from William McCoy, who in 1804, having been awarded two hundred acres of land in Virginia (now part of Kentucky) for service in the Revolutionary War, had settled in the Tug Valley. Four of his ten sons eventually continued west, but the others and two daughters had planted the McCoy seed on both sides of the river. Like John Knox, the dogmatic founder of Scottish Presbyterianism, the Scots-Irish McCoys had strong traits. They were socially democratic, believing intensely in the equality of all men. They were austere, like their forebears, who had lived in turf huts in the Scottish Lowlands, hardened to discomfort, and adept at survival. While they might accept a friendly hand from a neighbor they could repay, they turned their backs on charity. They would starve before they would beg.

One thing you did not do lightly was cross a McCoy. The family had a fierce streak beyond most. "The McCoys had a reputation for being hospitable to strangers," Jim McCoy, a nephew of Randall, the family patriarch during the feud, would later say, "but a person better look out if he ever stole anything from them." As an example, Jim cited his cousin Leland, who had a prized plum tree in his backyard. "Once every day for a week, he found plums missing from that tree," Jim recounted. "Finally he decided he was gonna fix whoever it was who was taking those plums. So, he put poison on the tree." The fruit was never stolen again. The thief died.

By 1850, William's son Sam had become wealthy, owning 1,500 acres of prime land. Living outside Stringtown, Kentucky, he and his wife, Elizabeth, reared eighteen children, including Sarah, better

Randall McCoy.

known as Sally. Sam's younger brother Dan was less fortunate. Unsuccessful in business, he was considered quarrelsome and shiftless by his neighbors. He and his wife, Peggy, moved their children (there would be thirteen in all), including Randall, their fourth child, born in 1825, to Logan County, Virginia, when Randall was a boy. But Dan could not make a go of it there either. To help pay for their farm, Peggy raised and sold hogs; she also sold a snakebitten horse that she had rescued. When Dan lost the farm in a lawsuit after he had been timbering on their neighbor's property, she decided that she would be better off without him and took the then-unusual step of divorcing him.

Cousins Randall and Sally started out in Logan County but after a while moved across the river to Pike County, where they set out to build a life and a family on property given to them by her father.[10]

DESPITE THE GENERATIONS OF HARMONY, the warm feelings that united the two sides of the Tug evaporated in the spring of 1861 when Virginia seceded from the Union. The Big Sandy River and the Tug Fork became part of the Confederacy's western border and a fault line in the division among the states. On one bank was Kentucky, which stayed neutral but would go Union the next year. On the other was a portion of Virginia that would become part of West Virginia and a Union state in 1863, although many of its people would remain fiercely Confederate. Mixed sentiments persisted on both sides of the river, but it was a decisive border, cutting families like a saber. Almost all of the Hatfields and McCoys on the Virginia side of the river stood with the Confederacy, and almost all of the Hatfields and McCoys on the Kentucky side went with the Union. Randall McCoy was an exception. His Virginia ties ran deep. He chose the Confederacy.

By the fall of 1861, when Union colonel and future president James A. Garfield maneuvered his Eighteenth Brigade into the Kentucky side of the Tug Valley to secure strategic troves of salt, iron ore, timber, and coal, the larger conflict had rent the social fabric of this section of the Appalachians. Here, in the nation's oldest mountains, amid some of its most convoluted and confounding terrain, the war was personal and ignited rampant raiding and feuding. The families on either side *knew* the enemy, and more than any patriotic feeling, their own honor was at stake, because in these parts a man simply did not allow another man to tell him what to do or take anything from him. Here, where most people lived hand to mouth, his family's survival was at stake.

The men who lived in these mountains had learned to fight from the Indians and had honed their craft of wilderness warfare — defending, tracking, ambushing, killing — and used it against them, until they had secured the place for themselves. They had a shoot-first, ask-questions-later mentality. They wrestled and fought for fun. Now they turned their sights on each other, and they excelled at the bloodletting.

Shocked by the bitter, remorseless killing, Garfield described his mission as rooting out the "infernal devil that has made this valley a home of fiends and converted this war into a black hole in which to murder any man that any soldier from envy, lust, or revenge hated." Yet not even the future president, who earned a promotion to brigadier general for briefly securing the region that winter, could gain a real grip on the place.

Serving under Garfield in the Big Sandy Valley was a prophetic man who, seeing longtime neighbors stalking and killing one another "among the interminable hills," understood the place on a deep level. "Long after the war is closed, men will bear here the old grudge toward each other," Ohio captain Charles Henry observed; "the bitter gall of hatred will still course their veins, the feudal flames will be yet unquenched.

"A simple declaration of peace," he declared, "will never do."[11]

As Garfield occupied the rebellious valley, the men along Peter Creek in Pike County, Kentucky, organized a Union home guard. Among its members was Randall McCoy's strapping six-foot-three brother Asa Harmon McCoy, called Harmon, who was thirty-three years old when he signed up in February 1862. Tight-lipped, with curly dark brown hair and a broad handsome face, Harmon left two slaves behind to take care of his farm and his family: his wife, Martha, better known as Patty, and their four children. Patty was the daughter of a wealthy landowner named Jacob Cline (whose father gave Peter Creek its name), and her brother, also Peter, joined the same company as Harmon. Peter Creek, emboldened by Garfield's presence, was quickly becoming a Union stronghold.

Just four days after enlisting, Harmon found himself in a skirmish. He took a bullet in the chest. Without much delay, word went out that it was Devil Anse Hatfield, a crack shot, who had wounded him.[12]

Having married a neighborhood girl, nineteen-year-old raven haired Vicey Chafin, a couple of days after the battle at Fort Sumter and set up a home on Cline family land by the Tug Fork, Devil Anse, who like the rest of his immediate family sided with his state and the South, found himself just a stone's throw away from a hornet's nest of Union sympathizers. Peter Creek, with some twenty homes whose men had chosen or would choose blue over gray, was almost a straight shot—at least for these parts—from Devil Anse's, just around a bend on the opposite bank of the Tug and up a creek. Groups of partisans on both sides struck each other, at first usually at night, in preemptive attempts to save their own. Like others in the area, when he was not working on his farm or fighting, Devil Anse, now a powerful and wily young man who bore a remarkable resemblance to the Confederate general Stonewall Jackson, hid in the woods near his house to keep from being captured or shot at night. To some extent, life went on. nine months after marrying, he and Vicey had their first child, a boy, Johnse (pronounced "Joncee"). But not long afterward, with Devil Anse absent, Vicey and Johnse were burned out of their cabin in the middle of the night.

Eventually, the region being deemed remote and of marginal significance, Garfield moved on. The fledgling Union home guard's hundred or so men, led by Captain Uriah Runyon and William "Yankee Bill" Francis, were left to fend for themselves. Devil Anse's double cousins (cousins on both sides) James, Joseph, and Thompson Hatfield were among the Peter Creek men who rode with Francis and Runyon, as were Peter Cline and his brother Jake, joined by Harmon McCoy—who had survived his chest wound—and his cousin Pleasant McCoy.[13]

If Devil Anse, a for-profit moonshiner, ever had any doubts about which side of the conflict he was on, the federal government helped clear them up in 1862, when it passed a law making it illegal to distill whiskey without a federal license, rendering all home craftsmen outlaws. He and his brothers Ellison and Elias and their father, Big

Devil Anse Hatfield. *(Dr. Coleman C. Hatfield Collection, courtesy of Dr. Arabel E. Hatfield)*

Eph, now fifty-one, volunteered for the Virginia State Line cavalry, joining a regiment made up of Logan County men and led by officers of a former company known as the Logan County Wildcats.

Major John B. Floyd, whose home and business were in War-field, had organized the Virginia State Line to defend this western portion of the state. Floyd was from an old Virginia family and was a former governor of the state; he had also served as U.S. secretary of war under James Buchanan. A tour in the State Line lasted only a year, as opposed to the three-year stint of the regular army. Devil Anse was commissioned a lieutenant, which made sense: known for his physical prowess, the twenty-three-year-old—although also something of a prankster—was a natural leader.[14]

In February 1862, Floyd had been part of the Confederate debacle at Fort Donelson, on the Cumberland River in Tennessee. Leaving Simon Bolivar Buckner in command, Floyd had slipped out with his men before the infamous surrender to General Ulysses S. Grant that gave the rising Union star his nickname, Unconditional Surrender, and earned him a promotion to major general. Buckner, who would be one of the governors of Kentucky during the feud years, went to a military prison. With this victory, Grant opened up Tennessee to federal troops and guaranteed that Kentucky would remain in the Union. For his part, Floyd now took an aggressive stance along the Tug. He regularly dispatched State Line raiders into Kentucky, where they battled Union home guard forces while seizing horses and other livestock in the name of the cause. Not surprisingly, what was considered confiscation by one side was viewed as theft by the other, and Union forces struck back as opportunity allowed.

In the fall, Yankee Bill and his riders, including his son James, Peter Cline, and, some say, Harmon McCoy, inexplicably struck the Pike County farm of fifty-eight-year-old George Hatfield, whose four sons fought for the Union. Yankee Bill took what he wanted from the house, along with fifteen head of cattle, twenty-five hogs, fifteen sheep, and a yoke of oxen.[15]

Shortly thereafter, he and his men crossed the Tug and stormed the farm of a man named Moses Cline, a cousin of Peter and of Harmon's wife, Patty. When the home guard declared that they were requisitioning Cline's livestock, he resisted. The men shot him in the chest and made off with the animals, leaving him for dead and the farm in shambles. As Cline teetered on the verge of death, his family summoned his good friend Devil Anse Hatfield to say good-bye. Devil Anse swore to his friend that he would hunt down the men who had attacked him and avenge this crime.

In fact, Devil Anse had other scores to settle with Francis and his home guard, whom he blamed for burning his cabin and for putting a bull's-eye on his back. Though the lines separating vigilante justice, feuding, and warfare were thin and often crossed, Devil Anse went up the chain of command and obtained orders to kill or capture Francis. However, when the State Line routed the Union home guard at Warfield, Virginia, in October, Francis and Runyon vacated the area and attached their battered companies to the Union 167th Militia in Wayne County, Virginia, on the Ohio River, abandoning the Tug and Big Sandy valleys to Floyd's forces. Yankee Bill had escaped — for now.

In early December 1862, the Virginia State Line cavalry, including Devil Anse, raided Union supply boats in Prestonsburg, Kentucky. As they returned, the riders sacked farms and swept up two dozen of their antagonists. Among them, the ill-fated Harmon McCoy was captured at his home and marched off to a prison in Richmond. Another of the captives warned Devil Anse that a price of twenty-five dollars had been put on his head by Mose Cline, a well-known slave of the Jacob Cline family. On his deathbed, Jacob Cline had charged Mose with taking care of his two younger sons: thirteen-year-old Perry, the youngest, and Jake Jr., sixteen. Mose had patrolled with Peter and in one instance had helped fight off a Rebel raid, clubbing several attackers with his rifle butt.

When Devil Anse reported this threat to his superiors, according to the Hatfield version of the story, one of them instructed him to kill Mose. U.S. deputy marshal Dan Cunningham, who would become a nemesis of Devil Anse, told it differently. According to him, Devil Anse and a comrade "entered Mose's house without any provocation and shot him dead on the floor."

In the broader scheme of the war, Mose's killing was not a particularly notable event. However, in regard to the Hatfield-McCoy feud, it was an aggravating circumstance, a precursor to the animosity that would embroil the families. The Clines and the McCoys had many ties. Mose was a loyal defender of the Cline family, the guardian of two of its sons. He had threatened Devil Anse, and now he was dead. The hostility had been born. These deeds would come to haunt all of them.[16]

In late December, the State Line cavalry moved to Saltville, Virginia, about forty-five miles southeast of Pikeville, to protect the massive saltworks there. But in early March of 1863, word spread that the State Line was about to be absorbed by the Confederate Army and moved south to the Tennessee line. Floyd's soldiers asked for little, but they were the last line of defense for their own families and homes and did not want to leave the area. Floyd furloughed his men, and they vanished overnight.[17]

Not long after, Devil Anse led a group of men across the river into the Peter Creek basin. Several versions of the killing of Yankee Bill Francis have surfaced over time. The most common of these says that Devil Anse and his companion in arms Randall McCoy stalked the Union home guard leader on his farm, watching from the woods and strategizing their attack as he moved in and out of his house doing chores. They decided that Devil Anse would shoot first and Randall would back him up. But while Francis, a shopkeeper in peacetime, was inside, Randall had second thoughts about killing him and told Devil Anse that he did not want to do it.

Before they could discuss it further, the moment arrived. Francis came to the door with his wife. He was preparing to go out, and she was tying his necktie in the waning light of the afternoon. Devil Anse leveled his rifle and squeezed the trigger. Bill Francis's blood spattered his wife's face, and he tumbled from her grasp.

The Hatfields tell another, perhaps more plausible version. In their account, Francis (who would have been unlikely to go about his chores so blithely) was hiding out in the woods when Devil Anse and his men arrived. But they knew the area as well as he did, and once they picked up his trail, he could not shake them. Finally, he doubled back to his cabin on the Left Fork to make a last stand. The

Rebel contingent followed him there and stormed the cabin. Devil Anse, leading the way, burst through the door. Cornered, Francis blazed away. Devil Anse shot back. Francis was hit and killed.

Years later, those who heard the story of Yankee Bill's death would reflect less on the differing accounts than on a shared detail that, with the passage of time, seemed almost preposterous: side by side as executioners were Randall McCoy and Devil Anse Hatfield, future patriarchs of the warring families.[18]

Chapter 2

~

Un-Civil Warfare

1863–1865

A blood feud, in the vein of the Hatfields versus the McCoys, or the Montagues against the Capulets of Shakespeare fame, is essentially a state of warfare between two families. Feuds do not always have neat beginnings and ends. A feud can be anything from a revenge killing that occurs many years after the original crime to a complex brew of conditions, grievances, and affronts resulting in violence and retribution.

The first mistake people make regarding the Hatfield-McCoy feud is in arguing over when it began, a disagreement that arose even before the feud ended—though exactly when it ended is also a matter of dispute. Was the feud sparked by the senseless murder of Harmon McCoy at the end of the Civil War? Was it ignited fourteen years later, when Harmon's brother Randall accused Floyd Hatfield of stealing his razorbacks? Or was it Johnse Hatfield's misbegotten love affair with Roseanna McCoy that caused a fury so fierce that it raged out of control?

The answer to these questions is simply: yes. Like a bonfire lit from three different sides, the conflagration grew out of these events—though they occurred over a span of decades—and gained strength from their accumulation.

*   *   *

AT THE OUTSET OF THE WAR, while Kentucky was still neutral, John Dils, a Pikeville merchant and ardent Unionist, was surprised when a Confederate officer recruiting men in the area accosted him over his anti-Confederate rhetoric. He was even more surprised when the officer arrested him and dispatched him to Libby Prison in Richmond. Soon released from captivity, the indignant Dils traveled to Washington, DC, the following February and offered his services directly to President Lincoln. Commissioned a colonel in the U.S. Volunteers in September 1862, Dils raised the Thirty-Ninth Kentucky Mounted Infantry regiment to defend the eastern part of the state from Confederate attack. More than two hundred men answered his recruiting call on the first day. The Pikeville and Peter Creek men formed Company H. Paroled from a Confederate prison in the spring of 1863 and hoping to return to the fight, Harmon McCoy was examined by a Union surgeon on April 6 at the U.S. General Hospital in Annapolis, Maryland. Though the doctor recommended he be discharged from service, Harmon broke his parole and joined the Thirty-Ninth's Company H instead.

Over the next year and a half, Dils's men fought in many battles in Kentucky, Virginia, and Tennessee. They also culled property from the region's Confederate homes to great effect, sweeping up, among other things, many hundreds of horses. In the summer of 1864, however, a company of black soldiers joined the regiment at its Louisa, Kentucky, headquarters. Despite serving on the side that would end slavery, the men of the Thirty-Ninth proved to be unenlightened. Many packed up their guns and gear and left in a fit of anger; among them were Tug Valleyites Jake Cline and Asbury Hurley. It was a bad decision on more than one count. Leaving aside their prejudice, they were now fugitives of the regular army as well as vulnerable to the home guard on both sides.[1]

In the spring of 1863 came a momentous shift in the dynamics of the war in this region: the western part of Virginia realized its tumultuous effort to secede from the rest of Virginia and became an independent state. In April, President Lincoln signed a proclamation admitting the new state of West Virginia, loyal to the Union, as of June 20. (The only other state created during the Civil War was Nevada.) Although the legality of the move would be argued in court after the war, the confusion that this rift added on the ground was real and immediate. That May, Devil Anse and his brothers Ellison and Elias enlisted in the Forty-Fifth Battalion Virginia Infantry of the Confederate Army. Ellison was made a second lieutenant and Anse probably a first lieutenant. However, by December, when the Forty-Fifth went into winter camp in Virginia, Devil Anse and Elias had skipped out. While Ellison stuck around, his two brothers had served their last stint as regular soldiers. Once more they headed back to their families on the Tug, where Devil Anse, along with his uncle Jim Vance and brother-in-law Johnson McCoy, who was his best friend and the namesake of his son Johnse, helped establish a home guard. They called themselves the Logan Wildcats, perhaps in homage to the former unit of that name under General Floyd, who had recently died of stomach cancer.

Closely associated with the Wildcats were the forces of Rebel Bill Smith, whose son Larkin would marry Devil Anse's younger sister Emma during the war. Smith led the combined force of four hundred Logan County irregulars on a series of cross-border raids. Major Devil Zeke Counts also sometimes led these irregular Rebel forces on border raids, teaming up at times with Lieutenant Colonel Vincent Witcher. The latter, known as Clawhammer because of the dark swallowtail coat he wore in battle, had a reputation for brutality and for summarily executing men of fighting age who were not enlisted in the Confederate ranks. Riding with these men, Devil Anse earned a reputation for being fearsome and fearless.[2]

The Logan Wildcats returned from these raids with more than just rations and supplies. When Devil Anse and his fellow partisans came calling, former Union soldiers had a choice: enlist as Confederates at the end of a gun barrel, or die. Jake Cline decided to enlist. In

October, as Union troops from the Big Sandy Valley joined an attack on Saltville, depleting the valley of blue uniforms, Rebel Bill and Devil Anse stormed the town of Peach Orchard, a Union outpost upriver of Louisa. Ellison and Elias Hatfield, Johnson McCoy, and Cline, their former enemy, took part in the raid that targeted, among other places, stores and warehouses owned by Colonel Dils. In the end, the raiders' loot included $3,500 worth of clothing, boots, and hats. They torched the warehouses on their way out of town.[3]

Asbury Hurley, a relative by marriage to the Mounts and Cline families who had moved across the river to Pike County during the war, skirmished with Devil Anse and his men. After abandoning the Thirty-Ninth, Hurley and his twenty-one-year-old son, Flem, returned home and laid out in a rock house, one of the area's many shallow caves, which had provided temporary homes to early settlers and were still used by hunters for camping. One day they discovered that one of their cows was missing and set out on its trail. The route led to a group of Rebel irregulars, headed by Devil Anse, who were butchering the animal in the woods. The Hurleys started to shoot. The Rebels scattered, but not before one was fatally shot.

Killing one of Devil Anse's men was not a good idea. Threats soon arrived, demanding that Asbury and Flem surrender. Instead, they decided to run for it and return to the Thirty-Ninth. But it was too late. Devil Anse's men closed in, and the father and son negotiated their surrender as prisoners of war. After the two laid down their arms, the Rebels took them to a large flat rock, stripped off their clothes, and bound them. According to one account, Devil Anse backed up thirty paces, fixed a rest out of logs, placed his gun on it, and shot them both, Asbury twice, Flem three times.[4]

U.S. deputy marshal Dan Cunningham had a low opinion of Devil Anse and would later call him "no soldier at all," just a "murderer" and a "bush-whacker." Cunningham accused Devil Anse and his cohorts of preying on the Union men of Peter Creek for personal gain. According to him, Devil Anse was involved in the shooting of Reuben Dotson as he picked pawpaws beside a creek, which left him a cripple. He and his men ambushed John Poss as he walked along a path near the mouth of Grapevine Creek. Charlie Mounts, a farmer and miller who rode with Runyon and was a cousin of the Cline brothers, took his bullet through the heart while making sorghum molasses. He fell into the fire and had to be pulled out by his children before he was incinerated.[5]

BY NOVEMBER 1864, the Confederacy teetered on collapse. In Logan Courthouse, the charred remains of the once proud county courthouse — burned six months earlier by Union troops from Ohio to avenge the death of a company captain — testified to the bleak reality. Confederate deserters swelled the home guard ranks and grew increasingly brazen. The Hatfields took part in another raid on Peach Orchard, this time overrunning an election precinct and attempting, somewhat absurdly, to cast votes in the Abraham Lincoln–George B. McClellan presidential election of November 8. Remarkably, some thirty Rebel irregulars voted to reelect Lincoln, reasoning that "they could whip" him "but did not know about whipping McClellan," the former commander of the Army of the Potomac and general in chief of the Union Army. The attempt failed. The Rebel votes were disallowed, and after the war, the raiders would be indicted for voter fraud. Devil Anse and his brother Wall were accused of theft as well for having made off with the horse and saddle of a Union militia captain during the raid.[6]

How Randall McCoy was captured is unknown, but at this juncture he was serving time in a Union prison camp, so he was not around when a fatal clash between the McCoys and the Hatfields took place. A week before Christmas, Devil Anse's brother Ellison finally abandoned the now miserable Forty-Fifth Virginia Infantry, which was holed up in the Shenandoah Valley. The unit had dwindled to fewer than thirty men, tattered enough to be described as "nearly naked" and said to have only a single blanket among them. Conditions at home were severe but, Ellison reckoned, better than this. The most consistent of the Hatfield fighters, he returned a hero to his family and neighbors.[7]

On the day before Christmas, Harmon McCoy, who had been captured at his home almost exactly two years earlier, was honorably discharged from the Thirty-Ninth Kentucky Mounted Infantry. All he wanted to do at this point was make his way upriver to his home beside the Tug Fork to see his wife, Patty. Having already been shot in the chest, he now had a broken leg from a buggy accident to show his five children, including Mary, thirteen; Jacob, eleven; and Lark, eight. As much as anyone, Harmon had earned some family time. He barely knew the youngest two: Jeff, who was five, and Bud, two.

But this brutal war gave no respite to the weary, certainly not to those on the Kentucky–West Virginia line. After reaching his home on Peter Creek, Harmon soon found himself under siege. As he fetched water from his well one morning, the crack of a gun sounded from the woods, and a shot whizzed past him. He scurried for cover, but the message had been received. Patty urged him to take refuge in the woods.

Though reluctant to leave his bustling home yet again and hampered by a persistent soldier's hack in addition to a leg still not right from multiple fractures, Harmon set out. To evade his pursuers, he waded in and across frigid Peter Creek and took a circuitous route for several miles before holing up in a hideout, a rock house about a mile from home, where he would have access to food from his family. Exhausted, he burrowed into his cave just in time to beat a winter storm. A bitter rain poured down, obscuring the half-moon, and after dark it began to snow, bringing an eerie, cold, and—for a man used to camp life and now the joyous sounds of family—lonely hush to the forest.

Several nights later, after Patty and the children had gone to bed, a gang of men pounded on their cabin door and then burst in. Among them were Devil Anse and someone even more frightening: his uncle and compatriot Crazy Jim Vance. The jittery-eyed

Asa Harmon McCoy. *(Big Sandy Heritage Center)*

Confederate roughrider, who also went by Bad Jim, had ridden with Witcher, terrorizing the Shenandoah Valley on raids. Crazy Jim — the illegitimate son of the disgraced daughter of Abner Vance and a married preacher — was no man to mess with. Worse, he had a score to settle. Fighting in the Virginia State Line, his brother Richard had been shot and mortally wounded near the mouth of Little War Creek. Some said Harmon McCoy did it.[8]

Patty told them that Harmon was not there. They searched the place and left.

Before dawn, young Mary slipped out of the house to go warn her father that the gang had come looking for him. Her intentions were good, but fatal: Later that morning, the Hatfields followed Mary's trail in the snow to the rock house. There they found evidence of Harmon's stay and tracks leading away from the cave.

Clearly, Harmon had realized the danger he was in from Mary's footprints. The snow that had calmed the night hours had now set a dreadful snare.

With his ailments, Harmon could make little headway, and the men, easily deciphering his attempted deceptions, caught up with him in Caney Branch Hollow. They took him without a fight, stripped off his clothes, laid him out naked on a frozen log, and lashed him to it. Though no one has ever proven it, it is believed that Crazy Jim Vance, with his demonic stare — caused by a lateral nystagmus, which in times of stress made his irises dance back and forth — was the one who shot Harmon McCoy in the head.[9]

It took the family three days to find Harmon's body. Getting him out of Caney Branch Hollow and across the risen Peter Creek was a treacherous affair, which Patty attended to herself with the help of Pete, one of the family's slaves. Patty, who was pregnant again, was determined to see Harmon to his final resting place, and eventually, at no small risk to herself and Pete, they managed to get him home. Even then, the difficulties continued: the ground was frozen, and they had a hard time burying him.

Later generations would claim that the McCoys would have avenged Harmon's death at the time but for the fact that with Randall incarcerated, there was a leadership void in the family.

Some historians have misinterpreted the circumstances surrounding Harmon McCoy's death and misjudged its impact on the feud. The notion that he was considered a traitor is widespread but false, based on the mistaken belief that he was an anomaly fighting for the Union. He was in good company among his Peter Creek neighbors. The fact that there was no immediate retaliation has also been interpreted to mean that the McCoys did not take deep offense, but this too is a misreading. It is not unusual in a feud to see a decade or more pass between events as sons come of age and avenge the killings of fathers.[10]

After the war's end, in the spring of 1865, it would take time for matters to sort themselves out while the combatants struggled to reestablish their lives, their broken families, and their means of survival. Certain retaliations had taken place during the war, and certain repercussions would follow it, both inside the courthouses and outside their purlieu. The postwar years allowed little time to grieve. Lives had to move on. There was work to be done and business to conduct. McCoys and Hatfields spoke to one another when they met and then passed on. However, for Patty and the children, who were now destitute, the pain endured. As they sat around the fire on a bitter winter's night, the talk would turn to Harmon, and they cursed the West Virginia Hatfield clan.[11]

Lark was particularly haunted by the murder. His father had appeared like a Christmas gift, only to be snatched away again forever. Some came to regard Harmon's death as a war incident, best forgotten for the good of all. "Everyone was so scared, they wouldn't do anything," Lark later recalled. But Lark McCoy would not forget. Though only eight years old, he pledged to kill the man who had killed his father.

His family would have its revenge. Wrong would be returned for wrong.

Chapter 3

~

Timbering the Sublime Forest

1865–1877

At the end of the war, Devil Anse Hatfield still lived amid his brothers in the dense woods on the bank of the Tug River, about five miles and ten bends above Mate Creek, named after Mate, a hunting dog that died there along with the bear it was chasing when both fell through the winter ice. The mouth of Mate Creek, where the Tug could be easily crossed, was a focal point of the area. And Randall McCoy still lived just across the Tug on Blackberry Fork, a tributary of Pond Creek in Kentucky.

In the aftermath of the prolonged struggle, it was to the rugged, primordial forest that the men and their families retreated to start again, perhaps to be cleansed of their sins by the grand and remorseless natural world around them, but definitely to turn a profit. The alluvial soils, cool climate, and remoteness of the Cumberland Plateau provided an ideal environment for trees. The intricately intertwined hills were covered in magnificent hardwoods, behemoths descended from the Great Forest that once covered the region before the continental plates separated.

The Tug Valley was still mostly virgin forest, virtually untouched and a haven for wildlife, helped by the fact that the locals heated their homes with the soft coal they could pick from seams all around them. These woods would save the men economically, speeding their

The Great White Mingo Oak, believed to be the largest white oak in the world, stood at the head of Trace Fork of Pigeon Creek. It was cut down in 1938, following its death, at which time it was calculated to be 577 years old. *(West Virginia and Regional History Collection, West Virginia University Libraries)*

recovery from the war, but in the process, the forest would be wiped out. Later, Devil Anse's nephew, Governor Henry D. Hatfield, would declare that "the ruthless destruction of one of the greatest forests in the world has taken place within our state." By then — 1913 — almost sixteen million acres of woodland had been reduced to fewer than a million and a half.[1]

Winter was the toughest season here. The craggy heights of the southern Appalachians were cold and windswept, with a climate closer to Canada's than the Carolinas'. Some said the Tug River got its name during the French and Indian War, when a party of Virginians and Cherokee fighting the Shawnee were snowed in and had to eat buffalo hide, which they roasted in thin strips, or tugs, to survive. Others say English trappers had found the Tug in winter and, snowed in as well, had been forced to eat the tugs from their boots. Either way, a man living in the Tug Valley had to be prepared to be shut in at times and to provide for himself and his family always.[2]

Each spring, torrential rains in March and April transformed the rocky wooded slopes of the river valley. As streams of water plunged off ledges and rushed down steep and narrow hollows (pronounced "hollers") to fuel a now raging Tug, foliage leafed out along the riverbanks, trees budded, and violets blanketed the hills. The Tug Valley once again became, to its modest inhabitants at least, a land of plenty. Along the river's lush banks, the women filled baskets with blueberries, blackberries, and pawpaws. Wild grapevines provided small purple possum grapes, if you could beat the possums to them. The locals knew when and where to find edible young pokeberry plants, as well as nettle weed and dandelions. They harvested wild mint to make fragrant tea. They turned the bark of sassafras roots into a sort of coffee, tapped maples for syrup, and collected honey from beehives, either wild or cultivated in hollowed-out gum trees. They dried gourds to fashion drinking cups, ladles, sugar dishes, and scoops for livestock feed. They made fabric from flax and dyed it with madder root for scarlet, black walnut hulls for brown, and hickory bark for yellow.

Also resourceful, the men made gunpowder from saltpeter and bartered for lead to make their own shot. They fished, hunted for wild game and fowl, kept semiwild hogs, and distilled their own alcohol, an art practiced by their Old World ancestors for centuries and an act signaling neither rebellion nor depravity, simply a way of life. Distilled spirits, when properly employed, were considered both salubrious and medicinal.[3]

The river itself yielded them bass, trout, several varieties of catfish — channel, blue, and yellow (or mud) — frogs, and snapping and leatherback turtles. Redtail suckerfish ran in the spring, so bony that locals simply pounded them with a mallet, fried them crisp in lard, and ate them whole. Catfish roe was another spring treat.

The mountains receded from the river in hierarchical waves of green and blue. Many peaks were so close together that you could throw a rock from one slope to another. In the narrow hollows between them — or etched into their sides by seasonal streams — the locals felled trees and planted corn, wheat, sorghum, cotton, and flax, though only a third of the unsparing terrain was arable, and filled their cabins with as many children as the seasons allowed.[4]

With the South eagerly rebuilding after four years of bitter destruction, timber was in great demand, and the Tug River Valley had it in spades. Indeed, there was not only a seemingly inexhaustible expanse of timber, but also an easy way to transport it: logs could be floated down brooks, streams, and rivers — the Levisa and Tug forks of the Big Sandy and the Guyandotte River in West Virginia to sawmills on the Ohio River, and from there the lumber could be shipped around the nation.

Giant tulip trees — native only to the East Coast and China and, at two hundred feet, North America's tallest trees — blossomed in spring, catching sunlight in brilliant lanterns. The mountain men, who called them yellow poplars, put them to the ripsaw and ax. They also felled and floated other hardwoods — steely hickories, dense elms, and sprawling walnuts — on westward rafts. Sawmills on the Ohio hummed, turning these trees into the lumber that was building America. At the international Centennial Exposition in Philadelphia in 1876, the state of West Virginia would proudly display at its much-visited exhibit samples of its wide array of commercial lumber: from cedar, spruce, and white walnut to chestnut, sugar maple, white ash, and black cherry.

To construct a raft of logs, the loggers floated or sledded their timber to a cofferdam in a river bend. There they interspersed

Loggers prepare to fell a giant tree. *(West Virginia and Regional History Collection, West Virginia University Libraries)*

Timber crew posing on a downed tree. *(West Virginia and Regional History Collection, West Virginia University Libraries)*

floaters—logs of lighter wood, like poplar, chestnut, basswood, or sometimes pine—with those of the denser ash, oak, hemlock, hickory, maple, or walnut to keep them buoyant. Once the logs were in line, they fastened oak or hickory binders to the ends with hardwood pegs. Over time, metal chain dogs, wedge-shaped steel points joined together by short chains, replaced the wooden pegs. Then the men attached rigging made from ropes or grapevines.

With a good tide, it took four or five days to reach Catlettsburg. The raft was an unwieldy beast and, even in the best conditions, difficult to steer using long stern and bow oars swiveling within forked stanchions or locks. There was little uniformity in the size of the rafts. Those that were launched on the creeks were often under sixteen feet wide and forty feet long, containing from ten to twenty thousand board feet, while the rafts that floated on the wider and more navigable sections of the Big Sandy were much larger. Once a raft was adrift and caught in a racing flood tide, its fate was more in the river's control than the crew's. Some years, the tide faltered, and rafts were stranded in bends and on sandbars. These were left to rot or were retrieved the following year, when they were worth less than those of new wood. In good years, after they reached the lower stretches, rafts were amassed and lashed together in fleets, which could sometimes travel as far as Cincinnati or Louisville before feeling the bite of the saw.

When the waterways became filled with timber, the river runs were treacherous. It was cold, wet, dangerous work. Men could be crushed, drowned, or overcome by hypothermia, and, as if that were not enough, they had to be on guard against robbers and thus kept rifles and pistols strapped to the driest places on their bodies as they maneuvered their payloads downstream. The last spring tide in April, when the briars had greened and budded and the snowball bushes had already lost their blooms, was the best time to set out. But some farmer-loggers, relying on folk weather prognostications or desperate for supplies or money, launched on the freshets of February or the March thaws. These voyages often fell victim to flash storms of sleet and snow. It was not unheard of for a sleeping rafter to wake up plastered to his raft by a coat of ice.[5]

Sections of the "inexhaustible" first-growth forest near streams or rivers were much prized. Loggers argued over property claims, boundaries, and the logs that often got jumbled on the crowded waterways or that were stolen by timber pirates. Using either branding irons or hammers with brands raised on their faces, the lumberjacks marked their log ends with symbols that, like livestock brands, could be registered in a courthouse. Still, the shores were rife with audacious thieves and "salvagers," who snared runaway logs. Instead of restoring branded logs to their owners or sending them down to the mill booms, where buyers tallied the logs, they "dehorned" branded logs, sawing off their ends. When raftsmen resorted to side branding, the thieves responded by chiseling off the sometimes deep marks, albeit leaving suspicious dents.

Most rafts carried at least one experienced man who knew the river's quirks. He would ride at the bow on the lookout for eddies, sucks, rocky shoals, narrows (or "na'rrs," as the mountain men said), and hazardous debris. "Pull her to the left!" he would shout, or "Hold the stern tight!" as the need arose. "Everybody walk outside!" meant it was time to lighten the load by jumping in the water. Above the mill sites, log booms could back up the tide of timber for miles.[6]

Perils could be found on land too. Following cold, wet, week-long, nearly sleepless journeys, loggers often indulged in drunken binges and trysts with prostitutes. Men with guns and money and nothing but another year of hard labor to look forward to did not always make wise decisions; gambling sometimes stripped them of an entire winter's earnings in a night or two. Likewise, armed robberies and murders occurred at an alarming rate. All too often, the much-anticipated return home of the loggers with cooking supplies, store-bought clothes and tools, and news of the outside world was a moment not of joy, but of regret.

*   *   *

RANDALL McCoy's SONS BIG JIM and Tolbert took advantage of the good times. They were two of the most able timbermen in the area. A timber merchant could harvest land he owned, or he could buy trees for a dollar apiece, or two dollars for an especially good specimen (though the most prized wood, walnut, cost up to ten dollars per tree). The price of the labor to fell the trees, peel them—all logs were floated to the mills without their bark—haul them to a waterway, build the raft, and then float it to the mill was a dollar a day per man.

High-quality poplar brought sixteen cents a cube (twelve inches in length by eighteen in diameter). Oak and sycamore and many other species brought in ten to twelve cents. Top walnut went from twenty cents to a dollar a cube. Walnut was so valuable that men would go back and dig up the stumps to sell for veneer.

Those selling timber had their tricks, sometimes concealing rotten cores with solid pegs. Logs with bad knots or holes were locked into rafts with the blemishes facing down to avoid detection. Buyers had their own stratagems: some were known to squeeze their calipers together when measuring logs to trim an inch here and there, which, when compounded across a raft, added up.[7]

Shrewd men, like Big Jim, Tolbert, and Devil Anse, knew what to be on the lookout for and were able to make good money. They also knew how to protect what was theirs, or what they presumed to be theirs.

The brothers Perry and Jake Cline worked on Devil Anse's timber crew. Perhaps they were trying to learn the business to better exploit their landholdings. It was a strange partnership. The Clines were brothers-in-law of the murdered Harmon McCoy. It was their slave Mose—charged with looking after them by their dying father—who had put a price on Devil Anse's head and who died for it. In the end, things would not work out harmoniously.

According to Perry Cline, in 1870, Devil Anse started logging on land along Grapevine Creek that belonged to Cline. However, Devil Anse claimed a right to the land based on a survey by Big Eph and even started building cabins there. The two settled their differences in a trade, or so they thought. Cline received property in Pike County. But something went amiss. In 1872 Devil Anse filed a lawsuit against both Clines claiming that they had trespassed on his property and cut timber. The suit never went to trial.

In the spring of 1877, Perry Cline officially signed over half of the five thousand acres that he and his brother Jake inherited from their father to Devil Anse. It was prime property situated along Grapevine Creek and the Tug and included the Clines' Old Home Place. Devil Anse, Vicey, and their children now flourished in the Cline family's ancestral house.[8]

Chapter 4

~

The Importance of Razorbacks

1878–1880

By July 1866, Congress had reduced the army to a peacetime level of just over 54,000 men. By 1876, the number had dropped by half again, to 27,000. That year, America's centennial celebration took a blow when the news hit the week before the Fourth of July that General George Custer had suffered a devastating defeat at the hands of two thousand Lakota and Cheyenne, under Sitting Bull, in the Montana Territory. Custer had been dispatched to open the Black Hills to gold prospectors, which the Indians, whose land it now was, hotly opposed, and to make a statement that would hit newspaper front pages from coast to coast during the presidential political conventions. Instead, Custer's Last Stand shocked the nation.

The disputed election of Ohio Republican Rutherford B. Hayes, a former Union general, to the presidency that fall resulted in a compromise with the Democrats that ended Reconstruction and the federal occupation of the South. Army forces were shifted to the West to fight Indians and police the frontier. As America rebuilt, laid rails, and expanded, the Indians would be pushed onto smaller and more marginal reservations in the West, and the blacks, now free but left to their own devices, would be oppressed and persecuted in the South. In southern Appalachia, the isolated hill people would be conned out of their land by wealthy northeastern industrial interests, which, as the railroads opened up the region to mass extraction, swooped in and snatched up coal and timber rights before the locals had any idea what they were worth. In little more than a decade, the industrialists would wrest almost complete economic and political control of the region from the people who lived there.[1]

IT IS NOT SURPRISING THAT the Hatfield-McCoy feud found a new spark at this juncture in history, as the strictures and safeguards of the Reconstruction era suddenly vanished. What does come as a surprise is that amid the high-risk and often turbulent work of the timbering industry, with its unbridled inebriation and rowdiness of unleashed mountain men on payday, it was a rather prosaic dispute over livestock that ignited the tinderbox of the feud.

Razorback hogs were an important part of the farm economy in Appalachia, providing most of the meat during the harsh winters, which dumped an average of two to three feet of snow on the land and required year-round preparations. With the gradual retreat of the big game, the domesticated swine got the locals through. Elm-peelers, as they were often called, because they liked to peel and eat the bark off the area's abundant elm trees, required relatively little labor since they were allowed to freely roam the densely forested slopes between farms in the summer to fatten on acorns and the mast of nut-bearing trees.

The razorback was nothing like its feedlot cousin, the four-hundred-pound porker bred to have an intestinal tract ten times its length. With half the intestines, the local hogs were, as one observer put it, "long-legged, long-snouted, long-tailed, long-bristled, razorback, slab-sided" throwbacks, built hard and wiry for speed and foraging and having a telltale raised streak of bristles down the spine. In short blasts, a razorback could run faster than a horse. A sow with a brood was considered fiercer than a wolf. And the razorbacks tended to be immune to hog cholera, which had been wreaking havoc with farm swine since before the war.[2]

There were few disputes over the razorbacks because each family earmarked its hogs with its own particular notch, a cut as distinctive as a cattle brand or a timber mark. Some even registered their cuts, like their land and other markings, with the county court. But most of all, since the pork was a critical part of the annual harvest, a mountaineer always had a feel for where his razorbacks and their broods of long-snout sucklings were hiding out.[3]

A hog was a mountain family's "money in the bank," according to John Vance, a descendant of three of the major feudists. It "was where their next meal was coming from, and it was how they could feed their children in the winter. If they were lucky enough to have one to sell or trade, the proceeds were used to acquire flour, salt, and coffee, or sometimes shoes or boots for their families. It was their mainstay for survival."[4]

The mountaineers gathered in their razorbacks and selected those for slaughter in the fall, after Thanksgiving, when it was cold enough outside to prevent the meat from spoiling. They smoke-cured the hams over hardwood fires. They rendered the belly fat into lard, which could be combined with nuts to make pies or baked with cornmeal, salt, and water to make corn pone. Sometimes they added fried skin, or pork rind, to make cracklin' corn bread. A hog's lights (or lungs), spleen, and brain found their way into dishes, as did the heart, liver, kidneys, and head, all considered delicacies. Even the feet, ears, and tail were eaten. The hooves were boiled to make glue. The bristles filled beds and pillows. The only thing wasted when they butchered a hog, the saying went, was its squeal.[5]

Here and elsewhere, hog stealing was a serious offense. In Ireland in 1843, Red Kelly, the father of the famous anticolonial Australian outlaw Ned Kelly, was commuted to Tasmania for seven years of hard labor for stealing a pair. In Kentucky, a circuit judge, noting that in his district men were acquitted of murder more often than of hog stealing, remarked that a hog seemed of more value than a human. Livestock theft was looked on as a particularly lowly crime, tantamount to stealing food out of a family's pot. Rustling a horse or cow out west might get you the rope; stealing a hog in the Appalachians was worse. It earned you and your family shame and scorn.[6]

In September 1878, according to Randall's nephew Squirrel Huntin' Sam, Randall, with the help of two brothers, Hense and John "Bushy" Scott, put his hogs up in a lot so he could castrate several of the shoats. The sow broke through the fence and escaped with six shoats and her mate. This was a nuisance, not a disaster, since the hogs ran wild all summer anyway, so the men let the animals go without a chase. Snow was a foot deep on the mountain by the time Randall—who at fifty-four was an established if still impoverished farmer, a father of sixteen children, and a grandfather of many more—got around to hunting them down one morning the following February. The hogs had wandered far searching for food in the depths of winter, and he saw no sign of them until evening, when he was crossing over a mountain at the head of a creek. There, Randall discovered a roughed-up spot where the hogs had recently been grubbing for the increasingly spare nourishment. Nearby were the tracks of a man. Randall followed them to his nephew Tom Stafford's place on the Tug. Randall checked Stafford's pen and then went to the door of the cabin. A son of Sally's older sister Ellender, Stafford, who was thirty-five and a justice of the peace, came outside. "Tom, where'd you find my hogs?" Randall asked.

"Is those your hogs, Uncle Randall?"

"Sure are my hogs."

"Well, Uncle Randall, I didn't know whose hogs they were. I brung them out with mine."

Since it was late, Randall told Stafford he would come get them the next day. But Stafford's brother-in-law Floyd Hatfield, twenty-nine, who lived about half a mile away, across the river in Logan County, showed up shortly after Randall left. He too claimed the hogs, saying that they had crossed the Tug on the ice, and he insisted on taking them, even after Stafford explained that Randall McCoy had said they were his and warned that Randall, with his hot temper, would surely resort to legal action if Floyd took them. "Why, I can prove the hogs are mine" was Floyd's response as he drove them off.[7]

When he discovered what had happened, Randall went to see Floyd, who was not only a double first cousin of Devil Anse but also married to Esther Staton, a sister of Sarah Ann, Ellison Hatfield's

Hog Floyd Hatfield in later years. *(Dr. Coleman C. Hatfield Collection, courtesy of Dr. Arabel E. Hatfield)*

wife. Randall confronted Floyd, claiming that the hogs and their brood were his. An examination of the hogs in question did not help: the earmarks were either nonexistent or too similar to each other to be distinguished. The two men argued, neither backing down at all. Randall threatened to go to the law, and Floyd told him to go ahead. With veins popping in his forehead, Randall departed, heading straight to the nearest justice of the peace, Preacher Anse Hatfield, another cousin of Devil Anse. Preacher Anse, a former Union soldier and now, at age fifty-seven, a Hardshell Baptist minister, as well as a relative of Floyd Hatfield, lived in a log house in Raccoon Hollow on Blackberry Creek. As a justice of the peace, he was a local legal officer, a man who commanded respect as a community leader and who was an arbiter of disputes.[8]

Randall wasted little time in getting to the point. He demanded a warrant of delivery for the hogs. Preacher Anse issued it. But when Randall presented it to Floyd—who would forever after be known as Hog Floyd—he was just as determined to keep the disputed swine. Instead of turning them over, he posted a bond for the delivery of the hogs on the day of trial, scheduled by Preacher Anse for the following Saturday.

Randall had taken a legitimate but aggressive tack in trying to regain what he believed to be his property. As a result, what might, in cooler and more careful hands, have been decided in a friendly manner had now become a matter of honor.

THE TRIAL WAS TO BE held at Preacher Anse Hatfield's house. The presiding judge well understood the sensitivity of a trial that pitted the two clans against each other, particularly when the charge reflected directly on a man's character. He decided to call a jury. As there were few people in the area who were neutral and none foolish enough to get involved if they were, he determined that the jury of twelve would consist of six Hatfields and six McCoys; that way he could not be accused of bias.[9]

Preacher Anse Hatfield and his wife, Polly Runyon Hatfield, after the feud. *(Dr. Coleman C. Hatfield Collection, courtesy of Dr. Arabel E. Hatfield)*

Randall's suit against Floyd for theft was the scandal of the day, and both sides showed up in force for the trial. Hatfield kith and kin—Chafins, Ferrells, Mahons, Vances, and Statons—gathered at the makeshift courthouse, as did McCoy partisans, including Colemans, Gateses, Normans, Sowards, and Stuarts.

To start things off, Preacher Anse, a man known for his oratory skills—he had been ordained in 1869 and was licensed to preach, a thing he did every Sunday at the Pond Creek Baptist Church—asked the claimant and the defendant as well as the jury to disarm. Reluctantly, they did, setting their pistols on the judge's bench as directed and stacking their rifles against the wall in a corner of the room. An impressive array of weapons filled the chamber. Those who had come to watch the trial placed their guns along the wall outside the cabin. As being away from their farms and timbering operations came at a high cost, these mountaineers were not wordy and did not cotton to lengthy explications. The trial would not drag on for days. It would be terse, intense, and settled in a sitting.[10]

What was actually testified to is now a matter of hearsay, not fact. Newspaper reporter John Spears would later write that several witnesses for Floyd swore that they recognized his hogs and that they were the same ones that he had brought to court and tied up outside under a beech tree. According to Spears, Randall "could bring no witnesses." But Squirrel Huntin' Sam claimed that Randall "proved the hogs to be his by 2 or 3 of his neighbors and also by Hense Scott and John Scott, his brother, to be the same hogs McCoy had in his pen to work on."[11]

"Evidence is of little value when witnesses are ruled by influences stronger than conscience," feud chronicler Virgil Carrington Jones later opined. "Witness after witness took a seat in the cane-bottomed chair that had been placed directly in front of the judge. They talked as their clan adherence dictated."[12] Perhaps, but one deposition stood out.

One of Floyd's witnesses, Bill Staton Sr., who was married to Nancy McCoy, was considered a McCoy by virtue of marriage but had two daughters who were married to Hatfields, including one married to Floyd himself.[13] According to George McCoy, a juryman at the trial, Staton testified that he had been present when Floyd earmarked the razorbacks. At this, Randall jumped up and launched into a furious tirade, railing against all of the Hatfield witnesses, whom he accused of lying. Staton, enraged by Randall's accusations, lunged at him. But Randall's sons were faster and seized Staton before he could strike their father. With that, the trial moved uneasily to the deliberation phase.

The jury of twelve being evenly split between Hatfields and McCoys, neither side could complain of a stacked deck, but a stalemate was all the more likely. For a while it looked like the jury would indeed be hung. George McCoy, one of the jurymen, later described the judge's charge to the panel to family historian Truda McCoy: "Gentlemen of the jury, I've swore you to be fair and square," Preacher Anse, who would later serve in the Kentucky state legislature, began. "I want you to forget that Floyd's Hatfield and Randall is McCoy. The Good Book says do unto others as you'd have em do to you. If them hogs was yourn you'd want em, wouldn't ye? Well, give em to the man you think they belong to—be he McCoy or Hatfield. That is all, Gentlemen."[14]

The jury adjourned to a back room. After considerable discussion, mostly vehement and along family lines, Leck Hatfield, the foreman of the jury, called for a voice vote to see where they stood.[15] Before the vote, he suggested that they agree that if either man won the majority of the votes, he would get the hogs. Several jurymen readily agreed. It had boiled down to that, not so much a determination of Floyd's guilt as a consideration of who had a better claim to the hogs. Leck led off by declaring for Floyd. They argued back and forth for a while until something remarkable happened.

A McCoy, Selkirk, citing Bill Staton's testimony that he actually saw Floyd brand the hogs, said that he would not contradict this. Both men had their rights, Selkirk reasoned, but it seemed to him that there was no evidence to prove that Floyd did not own the hogs, and since he possessed them, he should keep them. Thus, Selkirk McCoy sided with Floyd Hatfield, giving him the decisive edge—and arguably igniting America's most notorious feud.

Scoffed George McCoy at this unexpected turn of events, "If that wouldn't make a man puke, nothing would." It was likely lost on no one present that Selkirk, a Confederate veteran, and his two sons—Lorenzo Dom, better known as L.D., and Albert—happened to work in Devil Anse's logging outfit.[16]

In any event, Randall lost his case. When the verdict was announced, the Hatfields cheered. To add insult to injury, Randall had to pay the court costs. Glares and curses passed between the two sides after the announcement, but this skirmish was over. All parties picked up their weapons and departed without resorting to them. That should have been the end of it. But the humiliated Randall seethed long after his debacle in court. To anyone who would listen, he damned the procedure and vowed revenge.

Finally, one day in 1879, on the banks of the Tug, his angry words bore bitter fruit. Floyd and Ellison Hatfield, Bill Staton Jr., and several others of the Hatfield clan were fishing, drawing a seine through the river, when Randall and two of his sons rode up. After some passing remarks, Randall started ranting about the hogs. The Hatfields responded in kind. When Randall resurrected his accusation against Bill Staton's father, it was more than the twenty-eight-year-old Staton could stand. He grabbed a stone and hurled it at the old man's teeth, hitting him hard enough to knock him down. Randall's sons sprang to his defense, tackling Staton and beating him until Ellison pulled them apart.[17]

Another time, Staton and his brother John were poling a scow up the Tug, when a second flat-bottomed boat, drifting rapidly downstream, appeared around a bend. In it were two of Randall's sons, Floyd and Calvin. The two crews saw one another at the same time. Instinctively, they maneuvered their boats toward opposite banks. From the cover of the shore, they began firing potshots at each other. They kept it up until dark, expressing their anger and disdain for one another but accomplishing little else.

The significance of these skirmishes is that while the elder generation sought strength and power through financial means, resorting to the court system to settle disputes, their anger and resentment were effectively pushed down to the next generation, which was less prone to seek peaceful solutions.

Squirrel Huntin' Sam would later describe several fights with Staton in detail, like the day Staton met up with Lon McCoy on the road in front of Tom Stafford's house. Staton, who was strong and quick, according to Sam, "jumps on McCoy for a fight." In turn, Lon hit Staton so hard with his rifle that he broke off the stock. Staton grabbed the gun barrel and swung at Lon, but "McCoy caught the lick and hit Staton with his fist," reported Sam, "nearly knocking him down." Stafford, who happened to be a brother-in-law of Staton, intervened, putting a stop to the fight. A few days later, Staton and his friends managed to spirit off Lon's brother Lark after church and, in the words of Squirrel Huntin' Sam, "gave him a good whipping."[18]

The next Sunday, the McCoys returned the favor. After an itinerant preacher spoke at a revival meeting at the Caney schoolhouse in Logan County, several of Randall's sons and Lark and his brothers took up positions about a hundred yards apart on Staton's route home. "The first bunch jumped out of the bushes and held him till Lark McCoy gave him a good whipping and let him loose," Squirrel Huntin' Sam later wrote. "And Staton went running." As Staton reached the hiding place of the second contingent, they leaped out of the bushes and fired five or six shots at his feet.

"He soon were out of sight," Squirrel Huntin' Sam related, but Staton let it be known that the McCoys would never be safe as long as he was alive.

"Sometime after this happened, Johnse Hatfield stole Rosanne McCoy, Randall McCoy's daughter, away from home, kept her out in the mountains three or four days before the McCoys found out where they were," Sam further noted, referring to the next significant conflict between the families. "Whereupon this raised a big disturbance." Sam neglected to mention that in between the two incidents, he murdered Bill Staton.[19]

∼

IT WAS UNFORTUNATE for the younger Bill Staton that he crossed paths with Paris and Sam McCoy in a lonely stretch of woods. He knew it right off, just as he had known that at some point it was all going to come to a head one way or another. His father had been put in a tough spot, and he had done what he had to do, and nothing good was going to come of it, not for him or his family, not for the accuser who called him a liar or the accuser's family.

The Statons, of Welsh descent, had been in these parts, like the Hatfields and McCoys, since before it was safe from the terrifying raids of the Indians who used it as a hunting ground. Staton's Run, a tributary of the Kanawha River, was named for an ancestor of theirs who was ambushed and killed by Indians in 1789.

On this day, June 18, 1880, the three men encountered one another about a mile below what would later become known as Hatfield Tunnel, on the Norfolk and Western railroad, by an oxbow in the Tug Fork in Logan County. Staton certainly was not expecting to meet up with the two brothers. Fortunately for him, he was armed, and he saw them first. It was almost impossible not to see Squirrel Huntin' Sam, a six-foot-eight, 250-pound behemoth with big ears and eyes like gun sights. Hiding behind a bush, Staton raised his gun, propped it in the vee of the limbs, shut an eye, squinted down the barrel, and took a bead on one of his two cousins walking up the path.[20]

Like him, they lived in Logan County. Their father, Sam Sr., a younger brother of Randall and Harmon, had been a hard-luck man, inheriting nothing from his own hard-luck father, gaining no advantage from his marriage, and struggling as a hired farmhand living in a shack in the town of Logan Courthouse until his sudden death, more than a decade earlier. Ever since, these two brothers—Paris and Sam—and another brother had hired out as laborers and hunted to support their mother, Benina, born a Phillips, and feed the family.

With his lungs swollen with the breath that stilled his body for shooting, an inhalation of honeysuckle and deep forest scent, Staton, the eighth of Nancy McCoy and William Staton's nine children (the second was also William but had died before Bill was born, thus ceding the name to him) squeezed the trigger, firing the first accurate shot between the Hatfields and the McCoys since Harmon's death had set the two families at odds.

Ironically, this first salvo of the postwar feud was a McCoy firing at a McCoy. Though Staton was McCoy by blood, two of his sisters had married into the Hatfield family. It was just the sort of familial convolution that paradoxically added to the heat of the anger, the ripening conditions of viral feud, hatred within resentment.

Paris McCoy, the younger of the two brothers, dropped to the ground; Staton's rifle slug had pierced him through the hip. Then his adrenaline hit, and Paris, twenty, bounded to his feet, raised his own rifle, and fired back. He was a better shot than Staton, who was hit in the chest. Both men discarded their spent rifles and came at each other, spurting blood.[21]

When they collided, they fought like cornered animals or, worse, kin with a grudge, punching, clawing, and biting. Staton clenched his cousin's cheek in his teeth and slashed his face with dirt-rimmed fingernails. Blood spewed everywhere. Staton would have had Paris licked if it had not been for Sam. The twenty-five-year-old, who was also known as Big Sam because of his size, was quirky. He went barefoot summer and winter, and he liked inordinately to hunt squirrels. (Thus his more common nickname.) He would rise before dawn, melt lead in the fireplace while his coffee boiled, fill bullet molds for his muzzle-loader, and roll the balls smooth, like beads, in his big fingers. He often went hunting for three days at a time. Once, he killed a hundred squirrels in a single outing and delivered them to a church for a benefit supper. Another time, on the bank of Mate Creek, he shot Staton's rifle right out of his hand. (Elias had prevented the two from going after each other then.) On this occasion, Sam had his pistol ready but was afraid of hitting his own brother as the two cousins grappled. Perhaps he also did not want to insult him by interfering, not unless and until it seemed absolutely necessary. Only once it was clear that Paris was utterly drained of strength and failing did he squeeze the pistol aimed point-blank at Staton's head and blow his brains out.[22]

According to Logan County historian George Swain, Staton "fell back with his arms tightly wound about the body of his adversary and instantly expired. He was wrenched loose from Paris

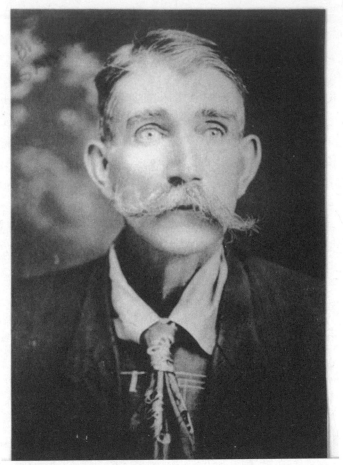

Squirrel Huntin' Sam McCoy.

McCoy and left to die in the roadway." Because the battle had happened in fairly remote parts, where razorbacks and wildcats roamed, Staton's body was not found until several days later. The McCoy brothers made themselves scarce during that time, but when they showed up again, Paris limped visibly and sported a mean gouge across his face that no amount of hunting grime could hide. When Staton's gruesome, nearly headless corpse was discovered, those who had seen the two brothers drew the obvious conclusion.[23]

On July 13, 1880, Logan County justice of the peace Wall Hat-field, Devil Anse's brother, sat for the examining trial, swore out warrants for the arrest of Paris and Sam McCoy, and appointed two special constables— one being his own brother Elias—to hunt down the suspects. Pike County justice of the peace Tolbert Hat-field, a twenty-seven-year-old second cousin of Devil Anse's, also signed the warrants, making it a cross-jurisdictional manhunt.[24]

Chapter 5

~

Moonshine and Love

1880

From Devil Anse's house beside the Tug there was virtually no evidence of his moonshining operation for a revenuer, a sheriff, or a detective to sniff out. A little below the house, a creek came down to join the Tug. Bushes and grapevines shrouded the creek, which was his "workway," the path to his still. Even if a snoop broke through this and saw that the creek was walkable, the still was a mile upstream. Overhanging brush would require him to proceed most of the way bent at the waist. All the supplies traveled up and down this stony brook to Devil Anse's outdoor distillery the same way. It was backbreaking work.

The still sat on a flat bald stretching about fifty feet across the side of the mountain. Devil Anse used a sixty-gallon boiler that he had bought from the owner of a steamer on the Big Sandy. The deal had taken place at dusk one evening near Louisa, Kentucky. They rolled the heavy boiler onto a flatboat, covered it with a tarp, and disguised it with barrels. Then Devil Anse and three men — possibly his sons, and possibly Big Jim, Randall's son, who worked for Devil Anse making moonshine (though it is hard to know for sure since the business was clandestine) — had poled it up the river. Finally, it, like everything else, had been lugged the mile up the creek to the bald on a corn sled — a wooden crate on runners for hauling corn out of sloped, rocky fields. They cut a door in the bottom of the boiler and placed it on a big square slab of sandstone that was balanced with rocks underneath its corners.

Devil Anse and his sons built a dry stone wall around the still with a roof of split boards over it. They left a hole in the wall to allow them to reach in and build a fire beneath the sandstone slab. Fresh ice-cold water was funneled to the operation via wooden troughs from an uphill spring. The wood they needed for making buckets and barrels and for fires was plentiful around the bald. All they had to haul up was the main ingredient. When they were making apple brandy, or applejack, Devil Anse's specialty, they needed three hundred bushels for a large batch, and lugging those apples up to the still on the corn sled was a major task. Up top, the men took turns mashing the apples a bushel at a time in a solid tub, using the butt of a small buckeye tree. They shoveled the apple pulp into 125-gallon vats and stirred in water to create what looked like a thin applesauce. They made about 1,300 gallons of apple mash at a time and then let it sit for ten days while it soured.

On the eleventh day, they began filling the still with the fermented apple mash. The cap was screwed onto the still, and the worm—a copper coil—onto the cap. They built an intense but low-smoke hickory-wood fire beneath the stone. By heating the stone instead of directly heating the boiler, they never burned the mash. Once the stone and still were hot, it took just a small fire to keep the batch at a low boil, just right for making moonshine. Alcohol vaporizes at 173 degrees F, and they kept it as close to that temperature as possible to avoid scalding it.

As steam rose from the simmering mash, it passed through the copper coil, which ran through a wooden barrel filled with cold spring water, and condensed. The resulting liquid trickled out into a wooden bucket. Each full bucket was emptied into a barrel. As long as the stream of liquid coming from the barrel tasted like brandy, they kept it coming, usually for about four hours. Once it got watery, they snuffed the fire, emptied the still through the door in the bottom, and started over again.

This way they made six singlings — the amount of whiskey from a full still — in a twenty-four-hour period. Each singling amounted to about ten gallons. It was intense work, and when it was finished, they were only halfway there; a man could get very drunk and very sick off singlings, but this was not the product they were after.

Once enough singlings were collected to fill the still twice, the men gave the still a thorough cleaning, then filled it with the singlings and lit the fire; the steam ran through the worm and was condensed again, this time producing an even purer whiskey, the doublings. It was about 98 percent pure alcohol. Around ten gallons were produced before it began to weaken. Then the men put the fire out, topped off the remaining liquid with more singlings, and lit the fire again.

In this way, six gallons of mash produced a gallon of singlings, and a hundred and twenty gallons of singlings yielded forty gallons of top-quality Hatfield applejack.

At other times, Devil Anse distilled corn whiskey. Made from milled corn, the corn mash fermented faster — in six to eight days — than the apple mash but also took extra preparation. To start the process, they put the shelled corn in a tow sack, soaked it in water, and left it in sawdust for about three days. They then laid it out in a loft to dry for another three days. Next, it had to be ground into a coarse meal, either at home or by a miller. The water-driven mills on the creeks in the area were frequently visited by revenue collectors trying to sniff out moonshiners.

Both kinds of liquor were kept in barrels for as brief a time as possible before being put into stoneware jugs to be transported to customers. The jugs cost between fifteen and twenty-five cents per pint, depending on the distance they had traveled and the difficulty involved in delivering them.

Distillers and customers checked the strength of white lightning — clear corn liquor — by the bead, pouring some into a glass vial and shaking it. The stronger the whiskey, the more bubbles. Hatfield whiskey beaded long and fine.[1]

Despite the fact that Devil Anse had been accused of assassinations and other crimes during the war, at this point, Randall McCoy (though not necessarily other members of the McCoy family) bore him no ill will. Big Jim was making a living working for Devil Anse in his moonshining enterprise — an endeavor that required absolute faith among participants. Indeed, Devil Anse's sons were not keen on the hard work required, and Randall — whose family was not as wealthy as Devil Anse's — was more than happy to have Big Jim fill in for them. He learned the trade inside and out.[2]

At the same time, Johnse and his younger brother William, better known as Cap, developed into prime salesmen, taking advantage of their extensive network of family and friends on both sides of the Tug. In Kentucky, they racked up dozens of trafficking indictments but avoided jail time. The indictments were something of a formality, since Kentucky law required grand jurors to issue an indictment for any legal infraction they happened to witness during the period prior to being called up. Many of the grand jurors were Hatfield customers, men who would not violate their oaths but who were not keen to prosecute either. Johnse and Cap understood the jurymen's obligation and did not take the indictments personally.

~

IN A BRASH PLAN that would profoundly affect property owners on both sides of the river, Devil Anse proposed to the authorities of Logan County in 1880 that he be allowed to dam up the Tug Fork. He chose to ignore the fact that he would be impeding traffic up and down the channel and chose to see only the benefits the dam might provide. His plan was to build a water gristmill and sawmill on his land at a shoal where the Tug met Peter Creek, which would be useful to the public, not to mention profitable to him, especially since it would allow him to mill his own corn for moonshine.

Devil Anse seems to have seen the river simply as another watercourse through the area and not as a state boundary. His great-grandfather was buried on the Kentucky side, and he had more kin there than in West Virginia. He and his brothers and sons routinely influenced Kentucky elections and showed up at the polls, even though none of them could cast a vote. Devil Anse applied to the court to appoint commissioners to study his proposal. Despite the audacity of the plan, the court duly appointed a panel that included Uriah McCoy, Dr. Elliott Rutherford — a friend of Devil Anse's — and several others to consider the proposition and report back around Election Day in October.[3]

In the isolated hills of the Tug Valley, where work went on seven days a week year-round, Election Day was a welcome diversion. Families finished their chores early and prepared for a convivial day at the polling grounds. While baptisms, ceremonial foot-washings (practiced by the Hardshell Baptists), and funerals allowed for a certain amount of socializing, Election Day was more unbridled, like a wedding but without the preacher. It also attracted a greater spread of people. In these hills, where grievances had little room to dissipate, so too the young had few chances to make new acquaintances. It was routine for cousins to marry cousins and neighbors to marry neighbors, and on Election Day, matchmakers and parents with eligible sons and daughters — boys of seventeen and up and girls of fourteen or more — kept a vigilant eye for marriage prospects. The women all wore their best dresses and bonnets. News and gossip flowed freely. Gingerbread, hickory-nut pies, and other treats were served to like-minded voters and also sold. The men bartered, traded stories and information, played fiddles and coon-gut banjos, and drank copiously.[4]

Only men twenty-one or older could vote, and that vote had a value in whiskey. The price of a man's allegiance was a healthy tot. Candidates all had to vie in this liquid manner or face losing. On this particular Election Day, in the spring of 1880, a number of Hatfields crossed the Tug to join in the excitement around the Pike County polls, which were located beneath a massive beech tree at the mouth of Hatfield Branch. The impressive tree was in Jerry Hatfield's yard near his apple orchard. Although the West Virginia Hatfields could not vote here, Eph of All's grave was on the hillside above the polling site, and the family already had an outsize presence, with three hun dred voters by name or marriage outnumbering almost all other families in the area. The West Virginia Hatfields gathered here to socialize with their cousins and to see to their interests. Together with the whiskey drinking, it could be a recipe for trouble, but on this occasion, tensions were eased by the fact that the Hatfields and the McCoys were supporting the same candidate.[5]

Devil Anse and Vicey's eighteen-year-old son, Johnse, was not eligible to vote in the election and did not much care about politics anyway. He did, however, have an abiding interest in pretty young women. He needed to look no farther than his uncle Wall, who was married but known to have fathered dozens of children with vari- ous widows and otherwise unattached women, to see an exemplar of the mountain Casanova. Weighing a lean 165 pounds, with blond hair and blue eyes and an outlaw's swagger, Johnse had the looks and charm to be an apprentice of just such a life. A bootlegger, he roamed both sides of the Tug selling his father's moonshine whiskey and always sported plenty of heat for protection. His brother Cap later described him as a great boozer, a fine shot with a pistol and a rifle, and a heartless lover. Twenty-seven arrest warrants, mostly on concealed-weapons charges (and the attendant fines, appealing to sheriffs), awaited him every time he entered Kentucky, enhanc- ing his reputation in the eyes of many of the independence-loving mountaineers.[6]

One look at the eye-catching Roseanna McCoy with her wavy auburn hair and Johnse was captivated. Surprisingly, he had never noticed this gem from Pike County before and had to ask his uncle Jim Vance who she was. Roseanna was tall and slim with creamy skin, and at twenty-one — the ninth of Randall and Sally McCoy's sixteen children — she was beguilingly older than Johnse. In this place, where girls often married before the age of sixteen, she was an unusually ripe fruit to be still on the vine. She had passed a few of her years in the elegant Pikeville home of Perry and Martha Cline, taking care of their children, and could thus be said to have seen some of the world. Crazy Jim warned Johnse not to mess with Randall McCoy's daughter, but he shrugged off the advice and wasted no time in introducing himself.[7]

If Roseanna resisted, her resistance wilted in his warm gaze. As the two chatted, Randall got wind of it and strode toward his daughter, scowling. He stopped in the shade of a tree and called her to him. He told her plainly to forget mixing it up with Johnse, and then he returned to his politicking. But Roseanna was at an age where finding a man was something of a fixation, and Johnse had her attention. She was too old to be living at home, and, Hatfield or not, he interested her. They strolled around to the back of the house, where some of the Hatfields were circled up, singing and dancing to the accompaniment of a banjo. But the couple shied away from the group and eventually walked into the woods. When they finally emerged at the end of the day, they found that Randall had left, thinking that Roseanna had gone ahead with her mother and the other women.

Now Roseanna and Johnse mounted his horse and rode toward the Tug. Fearless in their affection, they covered only several miles, but they crossed a vast distance.

When they arrived at the Hatfields' house, Devil Anse was not there. All Vicey could do was gasp and shake her head. They would have to spend the night there at least. After Devil Anse returned late that night, Vicey told him what had happened. Devil Anse decided to sleep on it.

In the morning, Johnse told his father that he intended to marry Roseanna. But Devil Anse had already been stewing on the matter and told his son that he would not allow it. Vicey urged him to let the two marry, but Anse was resolute. He did not kick Roseanna out of the house, however.[8]

Johnse knew better than to argue with his father. He and especially Roseanna were now in a predicament: If she went home, she would be the subject of her father's wrath and her brothers' scorn. She would also be separated from Johnse and would surely lose

Johnse Hatfield. (*Dr. Coleman C. Hatfield Collection, courtesy of Dr. Arabel E. Hatfield*)

him. If she stayed, she would almost certainly worsen her troubles at home but might have a chance to hold on to Johnse, since Vicey was on their side and perhaps Anse would soften.

Across the Tug, Randall at first worried about his daughter's safety, but he quickly learned from neighbors that Roseanna was at the Hatfields'. Then he became enraged. Still, there were codes, and he expected that Devil Anse would respect them. Such respect, however, was not immediately forthcoming. Marriages happened

Roseanna McCoy. *(West Virginia State Archives)*

quickly in these hills and were often consummated before a couple could exchange vows. That was acceptable enough, and Roseanna was but one of his sixteen children, far from his only concern. Much to the frustration of Sally, who begged him to forgive the couple for their rashness and accept the union, Randall wrote off his daughter. To him, she was a Hatfield now, and he declared that he would never have anything to do with her again.

Later that month, however, Randall learned that the two had in fact not married but were living in sin, sleeping together in a bed in the same room with Devil Anse and Vicey and much of the rest of the family. While Randall could begrudgingly accept losing his daughter, he could not accept this disgrace to the McCoy name.

He weighed his options, including an armed raid on the Hatfields. That would be bloody at best, though, and reclaiming his daughter that way—a daughter he had already turned his back on—might cost him a couple of sons. He decided instead to ask a friend, John Hatfield, who was half McCoy, to go to the Hatfield place and deliver a message to his daughter. It was brief: "Come home now."[9]

John delivered the message, but Roseanna refused to leave, and he was forced to return empty-handed. Predictably, Randall did not take the news well. He growled to Sally that he would bring his daughter home "if I have to kill every Hatfield in West Virginia to do it." He then sent John Hatfield back to Devil Anse's with an ultimatum for Roseanna: Return home now, or I am coming to get you, and I'll kill anyone who tries to stop me.[10]

Here, then, was the next red flag of the feud. While Johnse's behavior regarding Roseanna was reckless and possibly dishonorable, and while Devil Anse's response was peevish and vindictive, it was Randall in his fury who crossed the line: issuing an ultimatum in this circumstance was akin to declaring war.

John Hatfield, who was an officer of the law in addition to being a cousin of both families, told Roseanna that her father meant business and was ready to come in with lethal force. This time Roseanna buckled under the pressure. For the peace of the families, she decided to return home in shame. Randall did not beat her—he considered her beneath it—but he never spoke to her again. From that day forward, he acted as if she did not exist and walked away whenever she tried to talk to him. Even feud chronicler Truda McCoy, while trying to put her kin in the best light, admitted that he was an intolerant and angry man. "God forgives the sinner," she wrote, "but Randall McCoy was not so lenient."[11]

ON THE OCTOBER 12 ELECTION DAY in West Virginia, voters in the Magnolia District of Logan County reelected Wall Hatfield justice of the peace and elected Elias Hatfield constable, giving the Hatfield family two powerful positions in the community. The brothers would appear before a judge at the Logan County Courthouse to take their oaths of office, and their four-year terms would start the first of the following year. The bonds were substantial, but the Hatfields had means and were capable of forming alliances with others of wealth and power who could help them put up the money. In December, Wall, Jim Vance, and Moses Chafin would also be appointed to review a proposal for building a road from the mouth of Thacker Creek to the head of it and over to Grapevine Fork of

Beech Creek. Crazy Jim would eventually be commissioned to oversee its construction.[12]

It was sometime in the latter part of October that Roseanna moved back home. She was shunned not only by Randall but also by her brothers. With winter coming, it was a busy time. Hogs had to be collected, slaughtered, and smoked. It was a time to chop wood, can vegetables, hunt, and cure meat for the winter. Roseanna went about her chores, and in the days leading up to Christmas, she realized that she was pregnant with Johnse's baby. It was only a matter of time before her slender frame would reveal its secret. Roseanna knew she had to do something drastic or her life was going to be even more miserable. She went to see her aunt Betty McCoy for help.

Aunt Betty, who was married to Sally's brother Allen and who was sometimes called Betty Allen to further identify her among the expansive family tree, lived in Stringtown (now Burnwell), half a mile up the Tug from the mouth of the McCoy Branch. The mother of eleven children, she was a devout but tolerant woman and agreed to take in her desperate niece.

When Johnse discovered that Roseanna had moved out of her parents' house, he determined to see her again. Now, however, he was a marked man. He might get away with running moonshine, since most mountain people considered making and selling whiskey their right and agreed that the government could be damned for interfering in it, but sneaking over the border to see Roseanna was a different story. The McCoy clan, ashamed and irate over the scandal, knew Johnse would return to Kentucky to sell whiskey sooner or later. Randall's twenty-six-year-old son, Tolbert, asked Pike County sheriff Joe Radcliffe to issue a warrant for Johnse's arrest for carrying a concealed deadly weapon.[13] With an eye toward the potential income from Johnse's many fines, Radcliffe was only too happy to deputize Tolbert. He also offered a reward for Johnse's arrest.

Word soon spread among the McCoys that Johnse had been seen skulking around Allen and Betty's place. It was true. Although Aunt Betty would not let Johnse in the house, she otherwise did not object to his visits, hoping for the best between the two. Randall sent his teenage sons Bud and Bill to spy on the house and let him know when Johnse showed up again.[14]

Tolbert and his seventeen-year-old brother, Pharmer, in turn followed Roseanna. They watched her from a safe distance one day as she left the Pond Creek road and climbed up a dreen, the dry bed of a creek. The brothers quietly turned up the mountainside, gained the dreen from above, and followed it down. Rounding a stand of bushes, they came upon the couple making love. All parties were taken aback. Tolbert and Pharmer raised their guns. They cursed their sister, not for fornicating—they were not prudish but matter-of-fact people who lived close to the earth and to their livestock and were used to couples and singles sleeping in the same room—but for doing it with a hated Hatfield and betraying her family. They seized Johnse's guns and placed him under arrest. After binding his hands tight, they shoved him roughly down the gully and onto the Pond Creek road.[15]

Humiliated and afraid, Roseanna watched how roughly her brothers were treating Johnse and could only imagine what would happen when her father got ahold of him. In an instant, she made a fateful decision, one that her family would find even more unforgivable than her choice of a Hatfield suitor or her decision to have sex with him without getting married first. She knew she had to act decisively, and she hurried around the mountain near Stringtown to the farm of her cousin Tom Stafford.[16]

With no time to try to find Tom, she tore off a strip of her petticoat, tied a loop in it with a slipknot, and made a makeshift hackamore bridle. She slipped it over the nose of one of his horses, a bay. Never mind that she was several months pregnant—she threw a leg over the animal's bare back and dug her heels into its sides, lurching into a gallop.[17]

Roseanna crossed the mountain over a well-marked route, later known as Sledge Road. She topped the ridge, then sped down toward the Tug River through McGinnis Hatfield's cornfields. She forded the river in the shoals of the Hatfield bottom. On the West Virginia side, she raced on to the logging camp at Elias's, where Devil Anse and Elias and a number of other Hatfields were cutting timber.[18]

When he heard what Roseanna had to say, Devil Anse moved with the assurance of the military leader that he had been. Within half an hour, he had raised a small force, including several of his sons, his cousin Floyd, and a few neighbors.[19] Elias and his wife had been standing there when Roseanna rushed up. Elias was tall and powerfully built, though he had the sloping shoulders typical of the family, with high cheekbones and sharp features beneath a short rough mustache and sideburns. A journalist later described his face as "very decidedly English in its lines," with a "broad forehead, deep-set, clear, blue eyes, a big Roman nose, hooked, and a very determined chin." It was clear that trouble was brewing, and Elias's wife told him not to go with the group; Elias, who considered himself a man of peace, wavered. Devil Anse glared at him. "Come with me," he demanded, "or you are no Hatfield." Elias went.

Devil Anse was dead certain that his son was being taken to Pikeville to jail, and he had an idea where he could cut the party off if he and his men rode fast enough. In short order, they forded the Tug Fork and set off at a gallop, heading for the top of Stringtown Mountain. The McCoy contingent, which now also included Randall and Big Jim, was shocked when they crested the peak to find a troop of well-armed Hatfields waiting for them, not only led by Devil Anse but also possessing overwhelming force.[20]

Among the fiercest in the waiting group was Johnse's brother Cap, who was only seventeen but was soon to become one of the most vehement and hated feudists. Cap was mean-looking, snub-nosed, and wall-eyed. "Next to eating, killing was Cap's favorite sport," Truda McCoy wrote. "He loved to watch things die. When he was still small, he would dissect frogs while they were still alive, and stick terrapins with his knife. Later, he insisted on killing the chickens that his mother prepared for their Sunday dinner. He liked to see them flop all over the yard." He had yet to commit a homicide, she noted, but was eager to get his first notch.[21]

When Cap was ten, out of curiosity, he had picked up a rock and used it to hammer a percussion cap for a firearm. The charge exploded and blinded him in one eye. The other eye, left a milky blue, darted around trying to do the work of two good eyes, giving him a disturbing appearance. The accident had earned him his nickname. There was another factor that might have contributed to his antisocial behavior, though it is impossible to date: after Cap died, doctors found a fragment of a bullet inside his skull, pressing on his brain.[22]

Andy Chafin, a cousin who later served as a messenger boy for the Hatfields, would say that in his opinion, Johnse was actually the meanest of the bunch, but Cap was the dodgiest. "Cap wasn't mean," Chafin explained. "If you troubled 'em, he'd shoot ya, and he'd shoot ya mighty quick, too. . . . He was dangerous. He just, he didn't care to kill ya, that's all. But, he was one of the best neighbors you ever seen." If, that is, you were on his side.[23]

Devil Anse was in a rage and lashed out at the men who had dared to ambush his son. But he had no reason to kill anyone yet — he had the upper hand and a clear mission to accomplish, not a war to start. In fact, Anse would later express a favorable opinion of Randall McCoy, and since Big Jim worked for him making moonshine, they had a conspiratorial bond, a thing not taken lightly in these parts. As Andy Chafin explained: "They were friends before they got in this feud, you see. Anse thought a lot of the old man McCoy and his wife. Now I know he did, because I talked to him about it, talked with him. Heard him tell about it. But, uh, the boys he didn't like."[24]

It was Devil Anse's restraint that prevented a shootout or any other violence against the outmanned McCoys. However, Tolbert later filed a complaint with the Pike County sheriff: not only had Devil Anse and his gang forcibly taken Johnse, whom Tolbert had legally captured and was holding in custody, but they had detained the McCoy posse and "kept them as prisoners for a long time, cursed and abused them." Tolbert successfully prevailed upon a Pike County justice of the peace to issue warrants for the arrest of

Devil Anse and his men. He did not, however, accuse Devil Anse of attempted murder, as some would claim.[25]

In many societies, in similar situations—when the chastity of a female was violated—family honor required a retaliatory murder, leading to the classic blood feud. If the woman was suspected of being promiscuous or of initiating the act, family honor sometimes further required that she be killed by her own relatives. (A practice, sadly, not extinct.) However, in southern Appalachia, women had more control over their sexuality. They sometimes had sex before marriage and sometimes even changed husbands. Promiscuity did not necessarily dishonor the family, and in fact, where available men were few and far between, it was not only accepted but expected that a young woman or a rapidly aging one—over fifteen—would employ her wiles to secure a mate. Moreover, strong-willed women were not uncommon here, and as women were important providers in the household, their status was, in some regards, relatively high. In fact, while a husband's behavior was often brutish and a wife was expected to be subservient, the beating of women was rare.[26]

Though the seduction of a woman in this part of Appalachia might give rise, as in this case, to retaliation, it was seldom at the level of murder or an extended feud. Here, feuds were more likely to arise from theft, drunken brawls, or economic power struggles, especially in the illicit whiskey trade or, in the postwar period, between those advancing commercial interests, such as mining and timbering, and those discouraging outsiders from making inroads into perceived local domains.[27]

Like so many other Hatfield-McCoy clashes, this one and its ensuing accusations would go unresolved. Kentucky law officers ultimately refused to deal with the interstate legalities or to attempt to detain the Hatfields. Resentment from this confrontation would fuse with the gathering storm of hostility, a tempest that would eventually rain down violence upon them. However, for one person—Roseanna McCoy—the repercussions of this day were immediate and devastating.

Chapter 6

~

The Wages of Love

1880–1882

The 1880s would be a decade of both progress and turmoil in the United States. In 1881, Clara Barton established the Red Cross; the Tuskegee Institute opened its doors in Alabama; and Thomas Edison and Alexander Graham Bell formed the Oriental Telephone Company. A hurricane ravaged the southeast coast, killing seven hundred people, and a wildfire, known as the Thumb Fire, blistered more than a million acres in Michigan, killing almost three hundred people. Kansas became the first state to ban the drinking of alcohol, a watershed in the temperance movement, which would parch throats and singe collars for the next half century.

In Montana, the Sioux chief Sitting Bull surrendered to federal troops. An infamous Texas shootout, known as the Four Dead in Five Seconds Gunfight, began with a feud in El Paso over cattle rustling. In the Gunfight at the O.K. Corral, in a mere thirty seconds, thirty shots were fired in the town of Tombstone, Arizona, wounding two Earp brothers and killing Billy Clanton and two McLaury brothers. In the New Mexico Territory, the outlaw and gunslinger William Bonney, better known as Billy the Kid, escaped from a county jail, killing two men and then riding off on a stolen horse, only to be shot dead a few months later by Sheriff Pat Garrett.

The same year, on July 2, a man who believed he was called

upon to save the Republican Party and prevent another civil war stepped up on a railroad platform in Washington, DC, and shot the nation's twentieth president twice in the back with a pearl-handled .44. That president was James A. Garfield, the former general who had made his name in part by briefly taming the Tug Valley during the Civil War. Garfield, a war hero in eastern Kentucky, clung to life until mid-September and then died after having served only six months in office.[1]

And that was just 1881.

Like the rest of the nation, the Tug Valley entered a period of rapid change and economic expansion. Logan County's population, 7,300 in 1880, would grow by more than 50 percent, to 11,100, by the end of the decade. The railroad was on its way, and the arrival of trains meant the exit of coal, with the potential to turn piles of rock into piles of money.[2]

Most accounts of the feud hold that a period of tranquillity followed the contretemps surrounding the love affair of Johnse Hatfield and Roseanna McCoy. But that is overstating it by a good bit. It was undoubtedly a time of reflection for Devil Anse, who married off his two oldest sons, Johnse and Cap, which had the welcome effect of freeing up space in the cabin for more offspring. He and Vicey would have thirteen. In addition, Devil Anse's father died, at the age of sixty-nine. The family buried Big Eph in the Hatfield cemetery on a steep knoll above Mate Creek.[3]

Father and son had had their differences; Big Eph, who, unlike Devil Anse, was a quiet man, had given Anse's brothers tracts of land to launch their family lives, but he had not given any land to Anse. Did he think Devil Anse had been too ruthless during the war? Had they had a falling-out over business matters? Or had Devil Anse already taken care of himself enough that Big Eph thought it better to distribute his resources elsewhere? There is little to give us a clue.

However, designating a child as a namesake was an important aspect of Appalachian culture and an outward acknowledgment of significant ties. Devil Anse and Vicey named their firstborn Johnse, after Johnson McCoy (a nephew of Sally McCoy), who was married to Vicey's sister Sarah and who rode with Devil Anse during the war. Cap's real name was William Anderson, after Devil Anse, and they named subsequent sons after Robert E. Lee and Willis Wilson, the West Virginia governor who would later protect the Hatfields. It is telling that they did not name a son after Big Eph.[4]

In some regards, the fact that Big Eph bequeathed Devil Anse nothing worked in Anse's favor. Out of necessity, he had become a shrewd and assertive businessman, whether it came to whiskey, timber, or land.

THREE MONTHS AFTER THE HATFIELDS intervened in Johnse's arrest, Elias and Floyd were detained in Pike County and put in jail for their roles in disrupting the Kentucky legal process. From his days as a Confederate marauder, Devil Anse still lingered heavily in the psyche of Pike County, and it was widely feared that he might once more unleash his wrath to protect his kin. However, again, the conflict was defused. This time two of Tolbert McCoy's own cousins, Reuben and Sylvester McCoy, came forward to testify in defense of the Hatfields.

Roseanna was still at Aunt Betty's, and that spring she gave birth to a baby girl, whom she named Sarah Elizabeth, after her mother and Aunt Betty. She called her Little Sally. Her mother came to visit, but her stubborn father and brothers considered her betrayal unforgivable and continued their boycott.

Born under tragic circumstances, Little Sally was to know nothing else: an epidemic of measles struck the area in the winter of 1881; she caught the disease and then developed pneumonia and died. It was a crushing blow to Roseanna and would prove to be too much for her. Randall managed to set aside his bitter feelings long enough to pay his respects to his lost granddaughter. Sally tried to convince Roseanna to come home again, but she refused. Little Sally was buried in a hillside cemetery above Aunt Betty's house.[5]

Roseanna intended to stay at Aunt Betty's, but when she found out that her next older sister, Alifair, had come down with typhoid and had been calling out for her in her fever dreams, she agreed to go back. Alifair lay near death for almost three weeks, but she came around. Saved for now, she would play a tragic role later in the feud.

The vigil had helped keep Roseanna's mind off her own recent loss. Soon she was called back to Pikeville to help nurse another victim of typhoid, which was sweeping through the area. This time she went to the bedside of one of Perry and Martha Cline's daughters. The couple had four children at the time — Allen, age nine; Rocksey, six; Butler, four; and one-year-old Mamie — so Roseanna stayed on to help even after the typhoid epidemic passed.

Johnse came to see her and tried to convince her to marry him. But she had experienced too much grief, and too much had passed between them. She was caught in a purgatory somewhere between him and her own family, and she was resigned to staying there. She asked him to leave, and the two never saw each other again.[6]

JOHNSE, THE WHISKEY PEDDLER, took to the jug, and consoled himself by indulging in low company. He shacked up with a prostitute named Belle Beaver in a now unknown locale that was called Happy Hollow. Tarred and feathered and run out of North Carolina on a rail, Beaver was doing a brisk trade in West Virginia, according to feud historian Truda McCoy, but was happy to be paid by the handsomest Hatfield in squirrel meat and white lightning. The righteous local women, however, quickly recoiled at Beaver's presence in their community and sent their men to set things straight. They visited her place at night and ended Johnse's profligate pursuits, at least with her:

> The next day she was found hanging suspended
> from a rafter of the shack. Her hands were tied
> together at the wrists with ropes. Another rope was

tied under her armpits and her mother hubbard dress was gathered over her head and tied in a knot. A rope was tied well under the knot and to the rafter. Belle had been hanging there twenty-four hours naked from the armpits down.[7]

Beaver was still alive, but she decided to move on to greener pastures.

At the same time that he had been cavorting with Beaver, Johnse was courting not only Nancy McCoy but also Mary Stafford. When Stafford's family discouraged a union, Johnse turned his full attention to Nancy, a curvaceous, dark-haired fifteen-year-old living on Peter Creek. The odds were even longer here. Nancy had been the unborn child inside Patty McCoy as she searched for, found, and buried her husband, Harmon. And Patty, whose Cline relatives had grown close to Roseanna, firmly opposed the idea. Enough was being said about that scandalous affair already. She did not want her daughter mixed up with the likes of Johnse Hatfield.

Although Nancy had reached marrying age, she was still in school and had to walk two miles each way on a path that sometimes merged with a creek. Johnse, who was often abroad, would meet her and give her a ride on his horse. Before long, he persuaded her that they should get married. Support came from an unlikely quarter in her older brother Lark. In 1875, Lark, then nineteen, had married the girl next door, Bill Coleman's eighteen-year-old daughter, Mary, whose father had also been killed in the war. Although Lark carried a heavy burden and had a hot temper — he got so mad that his mouth quivered — he argued that Johnse had had nothing to do with the death of their father. Furthermore, he had not behaved dishonorably toward Roseanna because he would have married her if their fathers had not prevented it. Patty still forbade her daughter to marry Johnse. Nancy, who was known for her strong will, did it anyway, in Pikeville on May 14.[8]

As was the tradition, Hatfield family members and friends

Mary McCoy, wife of Lark. *(Courtesy of Debbie McCoy Autry)*

teamed up and built the newlyweds a home, in this case on Grape-vine Creek, across the Tug and a little downstream from the Peter Creek cabin where Nancy had grown up. The couple were a bridge between the two families, an unlikely one, to be sure, built on the silt of a mountain stream. Though they could not know it, the new-lyweds would have but a year of grace to meld and start a family; then Nancy, like Roseanna, would find herself in the most tenuous of positions, pulled in two different directions by the two opposing clans. But she was made of much sturdier material than Roseanna, even if Johnse loved her less, and she would prove to be instrumen-tal to the designs of not one, but both sides.

~

IN THE WINTER OF 1882, Squirrel Huntin' Sam was holed up in the cave where Harmon McCoy had spent his last miserable days. It was an inauspicious hiding place not only for its history but also for the fact that the Hatfields had proven that they knew where it was. Paris had been arrested the previous year by E. S. Ferrell, a friend of the Hatfields. Sam now survived by shooting winter squirrels and collecting mast like the hogs. But even a hint of smoke from his fires could be detected by a keen-eyed hunter, and with the leaves off the trees, Elias Hatfield, the constable, noticed just such a hint. On February 23, he crept up to the mouth of the cave. He waited until dark and then leveled his gun on Squirrel Huntin' Sam and ordered him to put his hands up. Sam knew the jig was up and did not resist.[9]

Elias took Squirrel Huntin' Sam across the Tug and directly to his brother Wall, the justice of the peace presiding in the case, who delivered the captive to the Logan County jail to stand trial for the murder of Bill Staton Jr. It is notable that Elias did not try to exact vigilante justice. Bail was set at $2,500, and, although Truda McCoy reported that Squirrel Huntin' Sam's uncle Randall prepared the clan to rescue him by force if he was convicted, there seems to have been no effort to raise this sum of money so that he could post bail.[10]

More than a hundred armed McCoys showed up in Logan Courthouse on the day that Sam and Paris were brought to trial. Hatfields were everywhere too. Even with a Hatfield presiding over the trial, it was an uphill battle for the prosecution. The brothers swore that Staton had fired at them first. There were no witnesses to the fight, so only circumstantial evidence could be brought against them. After Staton's corpse was found, investigators had combed the battle scene and found bushes that had been uprooted or crushed or had their limbs broken. It was clear that a violent struggle had taken place, meaning the three men had had their chances, which was about all any man could ask for under the circumstances.[11]

Wall Hatfield, who was forty-eight, was older and smaller than Devil Anse but large in authority and stature. He lived with his wife of twenty-nine years, Jane, and six of their eleven children at the mouth of Grapevine Fork on Beech Creek. He had built a sturdy cabin and barn on his property in 1861 from the logs of poplar and cucumber trees, the cold-hardiest and northernmost of the magnolias. Given the codes of the land, where carrying arms and attending to one's self-defense were expected and where assault and murder convictions were all too rare, and despite his own brother Elias's efforts to capture Squirrel Huntin' Sam, Wall had little choice but to find Sam and Paris not guilty. There was too little to contradict the defendants' claim that they killed Staton in self-defense.[12]

THE SPRING AND SUMMER OF 1882 were relatively peaceful. On the surface, relationships stabilized. Both families stuck more or less to their own realms and toiled away, planting and harvesting their crops and cutting timber for cash. But beneath the surface, tempers were simmering on each side. "When the McCoys talked about the Hatfields among themselves, it was 'them Damn-Hatfields' or 'Hog Thief Floyd' or that 'Bunch of Bushwhackers,'" wrote Truda McCoy, who was both born a McCoy and married to a McCoy. "When the Hatfields talked about the McCoys, it was 'them Damn-McCoys' or something equally bad." And just as democracy was the strength of the American nation, now just over a century old, it was in some ways the weakness of the mountaineers, who thrived when left alone. Elections demanded that they come together every two years, and all minds were now focused on the upcoming August polls.[13]

Here Truda McCoy voiced the frustrations of her clan: "It was a well-known fact that Devil Anse Hatfield tried to dominate the Pike County elections, furnishing whisky and swaying the voters to his way of thinking." A resident of West Virginia, he did not even vote in Pike County, but he did business there, in moonshine. "He came over with his clan to buy votes and put his man into office."[14] This rubbed the McCoys the wrong way.

It turned out that this day Randall McCoy and his brothers and

sons would be working for the same candidate as the Hatfields—
Tom Stafford, running for justice of the peace. Stafford was the
McCoys' neighbor who found Randall's hogs and a brother-in-law
of Ellison Hatfield.

However, on August 6, the day before the election, Randall's
twenty-nine-year-old son, Floyd, rode from house to house along
Blackberry Creek warning his brothers and cousins to come prepared for trouble. That afternoon Tolbert McCoy, then twenty-eight
and considered the toughest of Randall's sons, sat on his porch
almost within sight of the polling grounds, polishing his gun and
cleaning his knife. Tolbert, who had married Mary Butcher a year
and a half earlier, when she was sixteen, was already the father of
two. But fatherhood had done little to mellow him.[15]

SOME HISTORIANS DATE THE START of the feud to Monday, August
7, 1882. In a region where political ambition knew no bounds and
public office offered untold powers, political campaigns were noto-
riously hard-fought and corrupt. Votes were openly rewarded with
tots of "campaign" whiskey. It was common for a partisan to set up a
fifty-gallon barrel of spirits with a spigot and a tin cup and dole out
servings, just as Lonnie Lee recalled the Hatfields doing for his relatives when they ran for government offices: "They put up a sign that
said, 'If you're a Lee man, help yourself. If not, don't touch it.' "[16]

"It was the custom then, as well as now, although the law has
placed serious restrictions upon the practice, to supply voters with
copious quantities of whiskey," journalist Charles Mutzenberg would
write in 1917. "A candidate who failed to do his duty in this respect
was certain to lose many votes, if not the chance of election. On the
occasion in question, 'moonshine' liquor was plentiful. Both the
Hatfields and McCoys and their adherents imbibed freely and during the day grew boisterous and belligerent."[17]

On Election Day, drunkenness was standard, but there was nothing standard about drunkenness in these parts. As one moonshiner

put it, the taste of corn liquor was so "mild and meller" that it might "fall on you like a ton of bricks."[18] As a result, the impulse of the rabbit to spit in the face of the bulldog was never more on display. The good thing about drinking corn liquor, folks said, was that, although it would make you desperately thirsty, it would not give you a horrible hangover. The unrestrained election of 1882 was to be a little different, however. Not only would there be a hangover, but it would last a decade.

Chapter 7

~

Tumult on Election Day

August 7–8, 1882

Afather of ten, and at forty still a physically powerful man, Deacon Ellison Hatfield was not only a respected Confederate Army veteran but also a beloved church stalwart. His house of worship was not in his home state of West Virginia, however, but across the Tug in Kentucky. On one Sunday of every month, you could find Ellison at the Baptist church on Pond Creek, where his cousin Preacher Anse Hatfield presided. Big Jim McCoy went there, as did just about everyone else. On a fair day, eight hundred or more horses and mules were tied up to trees and bushes outside, and twelve hundred people were eager to hear the service, many more than could fill the pews inside the eighteen-by-thirty-foot log structure.

When the first hymn was announced, it was Deacon Ellison's sign to call in the parishioners. He went to the front door and roared, "Oh, ya-as! Oh, ya-as! Preachin' is now about to begin. You alls as kaint git to come in please move away and keep silence." When he spoke, people listened. The hundreds left outdoors shifted away from the holy edifice to continue their conversations beyond earshot, waiting for Preacher Anse to come outside, mount the horse block, and go from raising the roof to reaching for heaven.[1]

On August 7, 1882, Preacher Anse, an election official as well as

Ellison Hatfield in Confederate dress. *(West Virginia State Archives)*

a justice of the peace, felt confident that the day's balloting process would be relatively harmonious, since Tom Stafford was an overwhelming favorite.

But the preacher was wrong.

Devil Anse's brothers Ellison and Elias, who lived near the mouth of Mate Creek, crossed the Tug Fork that morning as much to socialize with their Kentucky cousins as to influence the vote. Constable Matt Hatfield and his wife, Alice, known as Maw, had a cellar in their home, on a bend in the Tug above the mouth of Blackberry Creek, where their cousins often stayed when they visited.

Maw, who was fond of a corncob pipe, which was a woman's pleasure while the men chewed, warmed her family and guests in blankets she had produced from sheep to loom.[2] She liked the West
Virginia Hatfields. They were part of the greater family she had
married into. However, Big Ellison and Good 'Lias, as they were
known, also brought baggage concerning their McCoy neighbors: It
was Elias who had hunted down and arrested Squirrel Huntin' Sam,
and Ellison who had urged a conviction. Although the case had gone
in the McCoys' favor and some family had even testified against
Sam, other McCoys resented what Elias and Ellison had done.[3]

New York Sun reporter John R. Spears, who visited the area in
1888 to report on the feud, placed the blame for the violence this
day on the local scourge — whiskey. According to Spears, by noon
"the boom for Stafford had swelled to magnificent proportions."
The candidate of choice for both families would win by a landslide —
it was as good as over — so, having reason to celebrate, the Hatfields naturally sent for more moonshine. Runners went to known
purveyor Joe Davis's place at the mouth of Blackberry Creek, and
more jugs of applejack and corn liquor soon arrived, perhaps that
made by Devil Anse himself. Locals later told Spears, "Davis ought
never to have sold both apple and corn moonshine, for the mixture
always did and always will provoke men to wrath."

There were two Elias Hatfields at the polling grounds that day.
One was Good 'Lias, who was by most accounts of upstanding
character and whose children would go on to remarkable heights,
one of them, Henry, improbably becoming a medical doctor, a
Republican politician, and West Virginia's fourteenth governor.
The other was Preacher Anse's brother, a mean drunk who had
earned himself the name Bad 'Lias.

Bad 'Lias owed Tolbert McCoy a small sum of money for a fiddle he had recently purchased, and after all had partaken of the
moonshine, Tolbert decided it was a good time to try to collect
the balance due. Spears, who reported the events of this day in the
greatest detail, claimed that Tolbert "wanted the money to buy

moonshine with, and asked for it." Bad 'Lias saw the situation differently, and in fact, according to Spears, "declared he did not owe Tolbert a cent."[4]

Tolbert did not need the money; he had a thriving business as a timber trader and a substantial interest in many rafts of logs floating down the Tug. If anything, it was a point of pride. The two began to argue. Backed up by his brothers, nineteen-year-old Pharmer and fifteen-year-old Bill, Tolbert dug in his heels.[5]

The dispute occurred about a hundred yards from the beech tree where the election was being conducted. The men were drunk and loud. Tolbert's wife, Mary, who had an infant daughter, Cora, to care for in addition to her stepson, Melvin, came to retrieve her husband. Sally also begged them to stop arguing. But Tolbert was immovable. Someone went and told Preacher Anse that trouble was brewing between his brother and the McCoys. Preacher Anse made his way to the group of bellicose men. He first admonished his brother, but, true to form, Bad 'Lias, now ornery drunk, would not heed his advice. Then Preacher Anse tried to reason with Tolbert: "Tolb," he said, "Election Day is no day for a settlement." But Tolbert, though he respected Preacher Anse, had worked himself into an explosive rage—as the McCoys had a tendency to do—and continued to insist that Bad 'Lias pay up. Finally, the McCoys were persuaded to move in the direction of the beech tree, back into the thick of the election proceedings. The spectators, however, only increased the tension.[6]

In addition to Preacher Anse, there were a number of public officials in the crowd that day, including two Pike County constables, both Hatfields, yet as Tolbert and Bad 'Lias did the inevitable dance, no one attempted to intervene. The two went after each other. Spears, who adopted a somewhat sympathetic view of Bad 'Lias, claimed that Tolbert "jumped on him to pound him into paying the money." Bad 'Lias had few friends, and fewer still who would interfere with a pigheaded drunk just to keep him from getting what he deserved. Older and more inebriated, he took the brunt of the blows.[7]

Friends, foes, and kin quickly gathered around. Good 'Lias joined the crowd, along with his brother Big Ellison, who had been lying in the shade of a tree trying to avoid the heat.

As Tolbert beat Bad 'Lias into submission, the law officers attempted to separate them, but a fever pitch had been reached, and there were multiple parties to watch. Good 'Lias showed his revolver, and Big Ellison held a nasty jackknife in his hand. Pharmer drew a pistol. Still, Constable Matt Hatfield managed to grab Tolbert while Constable Floyd Hatfield seized Bad 'Lias.[8]

Big Ellison had the habit of wearing a wide-brimmed straw hat and took the kidding for it good-naturedly. Some say that in an attempt to defuse the tension with humor, he offered Tolbert his prized hat in exchange for forgetting about the money he was owed for the fiddle; it would feed their cattle for some time, he jested. But Tolbert, who by now was hell-bent on trouble, would not be appeased. According to some sources, he glared defiantly at the former Confederate lieutenant considered a hero by many and shouted in his face, "I'm hell on earth."

Amused, Big Ellison looked Tolbert square in the eye and replied: "You're a damn shit hog."[9]

But it seems more likely that, as others claim, Big Ellison suddenly became the aggressor. "Unfortunately for all concerned, the mixture of two kinds of moonshine had so worked on the mind of good Deacon Ellison Hatfield that he was not now a peacemaker," Spears wrote, "as he had tried to be on a former occasion." Big Ellison was incensed that Tolbert, the strongest of the McCoys, had picked a fight with and humiliated Bad 'Lias, one of the weakest of the Hatfields. Mutzenberg described Big Ellison as "enraged and on fire with copious drinks of whiskey" and said he challenged Tolbert "to fight a man of his size" (although Tolbert was no more his size than Bad 'Lias was Tolbert's).[10]

The bickering continued, and Big Ellison grew more animated. He waved his jackknife in Tolbert's face." Hemmed in by the crowd and seeing that Tolbert might get stabbed if he continued to hold him, Constable Hatfield let him go.

Spoiling for a fight, Tolbert leaped back within the ring of onlookers that had formed and whipped out his own curt but fat-bladed jackknife. He and Ellison sprang at each other, the crowd surging with their violence as they tried to observe the blows yet avoid them. Tolbert, smaller and quicker, sank his knife into Ellison's side, so fiercely that it might have killed him if the blade had not been deflected by his rib cage. The towering Ellison—in Mutzenberg's description, "straight as an arrow . . . six feet six in his stocking feet and weighing considerably over two hundred pounds"—responded by slashing through Tolbert's felt hat, leaving a bloody groove from his left ear to the top of his forehead.

The two men backed away from each other for an instant. Then, in less time than it took to catch their breath, they heaved together again. In the clash, Big Ellison's blade accidentally snapped shut on his fingers, forcing him to drop it. He attacked with his massive, bleeding fists instead, pummeling Tolbert and spattering blood everywhere. One punch knocked Tolbert to the ground, and Big Ellison leaped on top of him, his left hand going for Tolbert's throat while his right fist battered his rib cage. Desperate, Tolbert, who had managed to keep a grip on his knife, focused all his power on his flailing right arm. He stabbed, pulled the blade back, and stabbed again. The broad two-inch blade shredded Ellison's side and hip, and then it did real damage, plunging into his stomach and piercing his liver. As the crowd converged, Tolbert's youngest brother, Bill, also managed to reach in and stab Ellison several times with his knife, before throwing it down and running off.

Preacher Anse, disturbed by the ferocity of the fight, tried to separate the two men, but it was beyond his powers at this point. With fire in his side and the realization suddenly upon him that this was no longer a struggle for subjection but one of life and death, Big

Ellison let go of Tolbert's neck and reached for a rock weighing no less than ten pounds. With both hands, the Civil War veteran lifted the rock overhead and then thrust downward with all his might toward Tolbert's skull.

At the same time, Pharmer, who had been braced for action and waving his revolver with the flow of the struggle, squeezed the trigger. Preacher Anse, who was crouching nearby, heard the report of the gun and then saw a slight twist of Ellison's flax shirt as the bullet entered his back, just above the right suspender button. The slug deflected up into his body.[12]

The impact of the shot jolted through Ellison's core and loosened his grip on the stone. Tolbert shifted. The trajectory of the stone hiccupped, and it missed its mark, thumping the earth beside his head.

Pharmer flung the smoking revolver to the ground and ran. Stunned by the sudden turn of events, Good 'Lias set off after the boy.

Big Ellison sat back and groaned, "I'm shot and shot for dead." Losing blood from multiple wounds, he struggled to his feet, stumbled over to a tree, squatted against it, and skidded into shock. Across the river, his pregnant wife was nursing their four-month-old son, Andy. Louis and Lydia, two and six, respectively, were running around her while Nancy, eight, and Emma Jane and Floyd, both ten, all demanded attention. His son Elliott, known as Indian, was fifteen. If their father died, he and Valentine, fourteen, would be the men of the house. Polly, twelve, would have to help her mother with the young ones.[13]

As he ran, Elias fired his revolver at the barefoot boy. Pharmer ran even faster, and Elias, who had been gulping moonshine, emptied all five chambers of the gun without hitting his mark. Matt Hatfield joined in the chase, and when Pharmer tripped and fell, the two men pounced on him. They dragged him back to the big beech tree at the polling station.[14]

Tolbert, who was battered and spent, was also arrested. Moments later, his seventeen-year-old brother, Bud, who had been exploring a nearby spring when he heard the gunshots, arrived and surveyed the bloody battleground. He picked up the knife that fifteen-year-old Bill had used to stab Big Ellison. Joe Davis, the bootlegger who had provided the now-accursed mix of apple and corn whiskey, saw Bud holding the bloody knife and seized him. According to both John Spears and Truda McCoy, Bud was mistaken for his younger brother Bill. "The officers were puzzled. Which one of the boys had done the cutting?" Truda McCoy wrote. Bill was "somewhat large for his age" and Bud "about the same size. . . . They looked so much alike that even their closest neighbors could not always tell them apart." Bud, who had not even seen the fight, protested his innocence, but when he learned that his younger brother was involved, he grew silent.[15]

ELIAS TOOK CHARGE OF HIS wounded sibling and sent a messenger to tell their brothers Anse and Wall, who were at the Peter Creek precinct, about ten miles away, that Big Ellison was near death. In the meantime, he had to act on his own to try to save his brother. He decided that he needed to get him back across the river to West Virginia. With the help of some friends, he improvised a stretcher using quilts and poles and carried Ellison across the Tug Fork to the home of Anse Ferrell in Warm Hollow. Dr. Elliott Rutherford, better known simply as Doc, examined Ellison and found twenty-seven distinct stab wounds, including one that had penetrated his right lung. "The course of the bullet could not be traced," Spears later wrote.[16]

Back at the now subdued polling site, Constable Floyd Hatfield, at age twenty-four a much younger brother of Preacher Anse, had taken possession of the three McCoys, who had been arrested at around two in the afternoon and were kept under heavy guard for two more hours while others discussed what to do with them. It was decided that Floyd should take them to the Pikeville jail, some twenty-five miles to the southwest as the crow flies but farther over winding mountain trails Since the journey would take ten hours on horseback, he decided to set out the next day. They would stay the night at his house, about two miles away.[17]

Knowing that trouble was sure to come once Devil Anse saw his brother, especially when he heard the particulars of the fight, Preacher Anse advised Matt Hatfield to help guard the McCoys. He also urged them to set out for Pikeville immediately. Floyd refused; he had no desire to be on the treacherous mountain trails with three prisoners after dark or to spend the night under the stars while trying to keep them secure.

The constables compromised with the preacher. Floyd directed the group to his place for supper. Afterward, they carried on farther up Blackberry Creek to John Hatfield's place, where they, along with the boys' father, Randall, would stay that night. Preacher Anse, in his capacity as justice of the peace, put the brothers in the charge of two Pike County deputies — more Hatfields: Tolbert and Joseph. Matt and Floyd were relieved of that duty.

Early — but as it turned out, not early enough — the following morning, Tuesday, August 8, the two deputies, several other guards, and the three prisoners and their father set out for Pikeville. By the time they began their journey, news of the fight had spread along the river and up the creeks and branches like moonshine on payday. In West Virginia, Wall Hatfield had already rounded up his two sons-in-law Doc and Plyant Mahon and their brother Sam. Doc and Sam were thirty-two-year-old twins, Plyant a year older. All three were lumberjacks who worked for Devil Anse. They set out for Kentucky at dawn, following Pound Mill Run and heading up the banks of Blackberry Creek. There they met up with Elias, who told them that Big Ellison had been moved across the river and that the McCoy boys were on their way to Pikeville. Wall and Elias powwowed and decided to send the Mahons back home and to move fast to waylay the Pikeville-bound party by themselves.[18]

After visiting Big Ellison, who was barely clinging to life at

Anse Ferrell's house, Devil Anse had spent the night with his men, including his son Johnse, in an abandoned house beside the Tug. In the morning, the Mahon brothers joined them, and they all continued on to Preacher Anse's, where they ate. Other Hatfields and their allies were headed for Blackberry Creek.[19]

THE KENTUCKY DEPUTIES TOLBERT AND Joseph Hatfield and their contingent had gone less than a mile from John Hatfield's house when Wall and Elias caught up to them. Wall, himself a justice of the peace for more than a decade, albeit in West Virginia, not Kentucky, coolly made the Hatfield case that the McCoys should be tried not in Pikeville but in the district in which the crime had occurred so that the testimony of Doc Rutherford, the doctor attending Ellison, could be heard without delay. Wall might merely have been stalling, since the crime did occur in Pike County, not Logan County, where the Hatfields intended to take the prisoners. Fearing for the safety of his sons, Randall vigorously opposed the idea. But after conferring with each other, the Kentucky constables — Wall's cousins — agreed to the request."[20]

Some maintain that Randall cut out right away to seek assistance in Pikeville. He wanted justice to take its course in the courtroom and had little confidence that the Hatfields would allow the legal process to take place at all. They would certainly hold his sons in West Virginia, not in Kentucky, and if Ellison died, they would just as certainly demand blood for blood. However, it appears that Randall stayed on a while longer, as he later testified about subsequent events that he witnessed: The party turned back, he recounted, and as he suspected, the situation began to deteriorate even more. They had gone between a quarter and a half mile when they stopped at Dials Branch. Wall was loading the three prisoners onto a corn sled when Devil Anse and a heavily armed band showed up to join them.[21]

The Hatfield lawmen were vastly outnumbered by their own

cousins from the other side of the river and their cousins' hired hands. Among Devil Anse's party were Cap and Johnse; the three roughneck Mahon brothers; Alex Messer, a gunslinging drifter and former Union soldier who also worked on Anse's timber crew; and Charlie Carpenter, the schoolteacher at Mate Creek, who was held by many to be a rabble-rouser and by some to be delusional. Once the prisoners were in the corn sled, they were pulled by a mule to their next stop. This mode of transport served the Hatfields' purposes by both speeding up their travel and further debasing the McCoys — the more helpless, in the eyes of their captors, the more detestable. Now it was only a matter of time until the pretense of the situation being in any way legal vanished entirely.[22]

The growing throng reached Preacher Anse's house before noon. They stopped for dinner, the midday meal in southern Appalachia. This is where Big Jim saw his brothers once more, but like his father, he could do nothing to help them. After dinner, Wall would later testify, he decided to have a shave. Meanwhile, Devil Anse summoned his fellow West Virginians outside to the yard, where they discussed the situation. Though most of the men were too young to have been involved in the war, which had ended seventeen years before, Anse reverted to his quasi-military ways, calling out in a commanding voice, "All friends of the Hatfields fall in line." About forty men did so. Growing increasingly uncomfortable with the proceedings, Preacher Anse told Wall and Devil Anse to leave his property.[23]

Instead, Devil Anse called for a rope and told Carpenter, who fetched one from his horse, to lash the prisoners together by their arms. The overzealous schoolteacher cinched the rope until it cut off the circulation to their hands. Pain aside, this was a distinct demotion in status. With the rope, the presumption of innocence was symbolically stripped away, and the line between security on the one hand and humiliation and torture on the other blurred. Devil Anse nodded to Preacher Anse and announced to the Kentucky officers, "We're taking charge of the murderers." Carpenter tugged on the rope and forced the McCoy brothers back onto the corn sled.

Randall could see where this was heading and knew he had no time to lose. As the group with the prisoners set out toward the Tug, he lit out for Pikeville. Before he went, Wall warned him that his boys would die if an attempt was made to take them back. "This is the last time I ever saw them alive," Randall later testified.[24]

The group headed down Blackberry Creek, Wall riding along as a guard part of the way. Big Jim accompanied them for about a mile and a half, at which point, he later testified, Devil Anse told him he had "no business further down." According to Big Jim, Devil Anse also said in his presence "that he had a notion to tell the Officers along that he had no further use for them." Big Jim, who well knew the codes of respect for elders in the area, said only, "I stopped."

At a ford near the mouth of Blackberry Creek, where William McCoy lived and with Randall's brother James and Bill Daniels, a son-in-law of Patty McCoy, watching, Wall, Cap, and Johnse Hatfield, Charlie Carpenter, and Joe Murphy loaded the brothers onto a skiff and poled it across the Tug to West Virginia. Once across the river and back in Devil Anse's territory, the group of forty men drove their prisoners about a mile up Mate Creek to Rutherford Branch. With rain threatening in the middle of the afternoon, they secured them in a dilapidated, out-of-use schoolhouse. The dismal one-room log structure now became the brothers' holding cell and the last roof they ever had over their heads.[25]

PART II

~

THE RAGE AND THE OUTRAGE

1882–1887

Casualties, 1864–1882

Hatfields

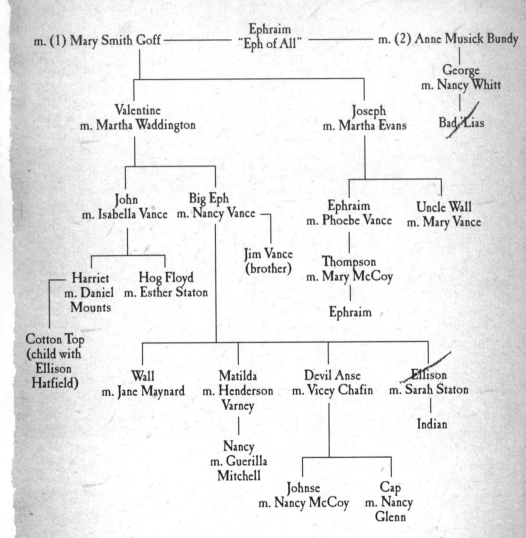

Ephraim
"Eph of All"

m. (1) Mary Smith Goff ——— m. (2) Anne Musick Bundy

George
m. Nancy Whitt

Valentine
m. Martha Waddington

Joseph
m. Martha Evans

Bad 'Lias

John
m. Isabella Vance

Big Eph
m. Nancy Vance

Ephraim
m. Phoebe Vance

Uncle Wall
m. Mary Vance

Jim Vance
(brother)

Thompson
m. Mary McCoy

Harriet
m. Daniel
Mounts

Hog Floyd
m. Esther Staton

Ephraim

Cotton Top
(child with
Ellison
Hatfield)

Wall
m. Jane Maynard

Matilda
m. Henderson
Varney

Devil Anse
m. Vicey Chafin

Ellison
m. Sarah Staton

Indian

Nancy
m. Guerilla
Mitchell

Johnse
m. Nancy McCoy

Cap
m. Nancy
Glenn

McCoys

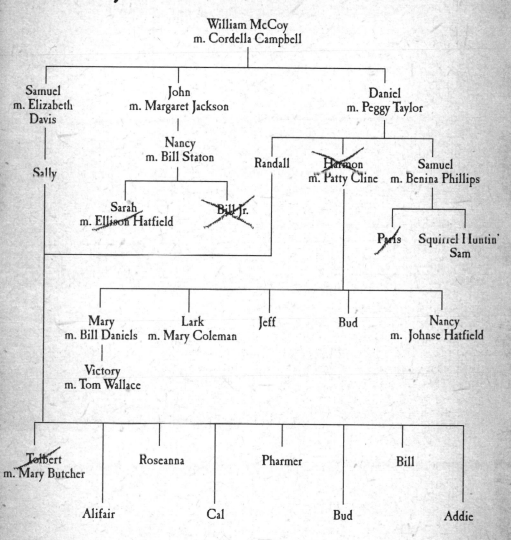

William McCoy
m. Cordella Campbell

Samuel
m. Elizabeth
Davis

John
m. Margaret Jackson

Daniel
m. Peggy Taylor

Sally

Nancy
m. Bill Staton

Randall

Harmon
m. Patty Cline

Samuel
m. Benina Phillips

Sarah
m. Ellison Hatfield

Bill Jr.

Paris

Squirrel Huntin'
Sam

Mary
m. Bill Daniels

Lark
m. Mary Coleman

Jeff

Bud

Nancy
m. Johnse Hatfield

Victory
m. Tom Wallace

Tolbert
m. Mary Butcher

Roseanna

Pharmer

Bill

Alifair

Cal

Bud

Addie

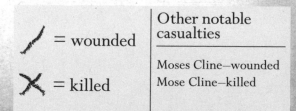

/ = wounded

X = killed

Other notable casualties

Moses Cline—wounded
Mose Cline—killed

~

Chapter 8

Mountain Justice

August 9–10, 1882

Monday's election and its agreeable result should have been a harbinger of better times for everyone. Supported by both families, Tom Stafford had been elected a justice of the peace in Pike County. If the stars had aligned differently, it might even have reinforced the notion of common cause and hinted at new possibilities for the two families. But, instead, moods on both sides of the Tug were fast souring as Big Ellison's chances of surviving his internal lacerations grew increasingly slim. The deathbed vigil continued in Anse Ferrell's house; pure corn was passed, deadening the pain but raising volatility and sharpening tempers.

Meanwhile, the various local authorities refused to get involved, and there was no state police force in either Kentucky or West Virginia to step in. In both states, if things got really out of hand, local officials might appeal to the governor to turn out the state militia, but that was done only in drastic situations and usually after an investigation by the state adjutant general. When the West Virginia Department of Public Safety—its state police—was finally created by the legislature, in 1919, it was not to address criminal activity, which abounded, but to quell violence resulting from labor unrest following World War I. Even then, West Virginia was only the fourth state to create its own police agency.[1]

*　　*　　*

TUESDAY AFTERNOON, on the banks of the Tug, a deepening tragedy was unfolding, one that would set in motion more than a decade
of heedless violence. It was mostly a time of tense waiting. The
medicine the Hatfields had access to was rudimentary, and almost
all of their resources came from nature: a buckeye, or horse chestnut, rubbed smooth in pockets warded off rheumatism; a bezoar
stone extracted poison from a venomous bite; willow bark tea alle-
viated pain; the juice from black walnut hulls tackled ringworm.
For just about any other ailment, from infants' teething pains to
depression, a dram or more of pure corn was the remedy.[2]

But even pure corn could not cure twenty-seven stab wounds
and a bullet in the back.

Men armed with rifles, shotguns, and jugs of liquor continued
to arrive at the abandoned schoolhouse where the McCoys were
being held, which lay only about a mile from Ferrell's house, on
land given by Big Eph.[3]

While Elias stayed by Ellison's bedside, messengers went back
and forth to the schoolhouse with news. Anse and Wall visited their
brother, who at times was lucid and managed to give them a whispered account of the fight, damning all three McCoys. When they
asked him what he thought they should do with the McCoys if he
died, he replied: "Give them the civil law," but the law was not necessarily what Devil Anse had in mind.

Inside the schoolhouse, which had been replaced by a newer one
on Elias's property at the mouth of Mate Creek and had sat empty for
several years now, the three brothers lay bound by the rope on a
filthy floor. Anse, Wall, Johnse, and Cap took turns standing watch.
The inside of a schoolhouse was a place they scarcely knew. In these
parts, the school year typically lasted for only two months, after
"foddering time." Girls did not enroll at all, and the boys learned all
too little from itinerant teachers who were perhaps not overly moti-
vated by their salaries, which consisted mostly of furs, bear bacon,

corn liquor, and tobacco, the last of which was designated as legal tender in Kentucky. Though clever, Randall and Devil Anse (who served as a school trustee) were almost entirely illiterate.[4]

To pass the hours, the Hatfield party threatened and bullied the three McCoys. Within their prisoners' earshot, they speculated on the most painful places to be shot, sniggering in anticipation of testing their theories. Any response from the McCoys only led to further jeering and ridicule.[5]

The three brothers were told that they would be tried the following afternoon, Wednesday, by Wall, a proposition that did not cheer them. Although Wall was unusually cool-headed and had given Paris and Squirrel Huntin' Sam a fair shake in their trial for the murder of Bill Staton, he was visibly out of sorts, pacing about grimly. Rain poured down with biblical ferocity, blackening the surrounding woods and turning the ground to mud. "Prayer to the Almighty is not only a duty, but a pleasure in time of tribulation," Wall admonished the brothers. "And it won't hurt even should Ellison's recovery permit you to escape death." In the midst of the deluge, a messenger arrived with the news that Ellison was, on the contrary, slipping away.[6]

Fearing the worst, McCoy family members were also in motion. At dusk, Sally arrived at the derelict schoolhouse to see her sons and plead for mercy. A generally well-respected woman, she was religiously devout and no patsy. She had, as most knew, publicly lambasted her own cousin for being a cow fornicator. (He had countered that she was a vicious gossip.)[7]

With Sally was Tolbert's young and attractive wife, Mary, clutching their four-month-old daughter, Cora, in her arms. Before the shocking events of the past two days, things had been proceeding well for the newlyweds. They had the new baby, and Tolbert's trade in timber was thriving. Now Mary found herself with her mother-in-law kneeling in front of Anse and Wall and, choking back sobs, begging them to allow the brothers to have a fair trial. If bringing Cora was an attempt to elicit sympathy, it did not work.

Wall Hatfield. *(Dr. Coleman C. Hatfield Collection, courtesy of Dr. Arabel E. Hatfield)*

"Yo' needn't beg and yo' needn't cry," Devil Anse coldly responded, according to Spears. "If Ellison dies, yo' boys has got to die."

While Wall and Anse were firm on this point, they were not immune to the women's suffering or their courage in coming alone to the schoolhouse. The two Hatfields let them in to see their loved ones. Still lashed together on the floor, the brothers engaged in what would be their last conversation with the two women.

Outside the schoolhouse, more Hatfield men, wet and mud-spattered, arrived; so, too, did three McCoys: Selkirk, the hog-trial juryman who tipped the balance in Floyd Hatfield's favor, and his sons L.D., thirty, and Albert, twenty-two, all timbermen who worked for Devil Anse and were loyal to him. At this point it would have required a small army to retake the three McCoy brothers.[8]

Night fell. Rain threatened again. Through the open door, the McCoys saw and tried to ignore the quasi-military guard bivouacked around a number of campfires. Having nothing else to do after pitching camp and tending to their mounts, these men idly played cards. Ribald songs and plaintive hymns, the only tunes they knew, drifted like the hickory smoke of their fires on the humid night air. Laughter was quickly stifled. Still, curses, grunts, and guffaws occasionally broke out as the ubiquitous jugs were passed. Then an argument erupted. It was not over money or cards or an insult—it was over the manner of death the brothers should be subjected to if Big Ellison passed. Some favored hanging, but they all were satisfied with the suggestion that "they make it a shooting match, with live targets."

Wall sat on the schoolhouse porch with a double-barreled shotgun across his lap. By ten o'clock, Sally's crying, praying, and pleading for mercy neared hysteria. This was irritating and set the men on edge. The schoolteacher, Charlie Carpenter, stationed in a stand of trees surrounding the clearing, told her to shut up. No one wanted to listen to her, but no one else did anything to interfere with her either, maybe out of respect or maybe out of fear of the long-term consequences.

Then someone arrived with a rumor on his tongue, and someone else shouted that Randall McCoy and a rescue party were forming across the Tug. The Hatfield men had been all too ready for something, anything, to happen, and the clack of gun breeches opening and closing punctuated the bug drone of the deep woods as the men checked their ammunition. Sally denied the news, knowing it was false because Randall had gone to Pikeville. But Wall took it seriously. He demanded that she and Mary depart, warning them that if Randall tried to interfere, the boys would pay the price.[9]

The miserable women left and felt their way through the dark, crossing rain-swollen streams and stumbling along the trail.

Sometime around midnight, bruised, brokenhearted, and shivering, they arrived at Doc Rutherford's house, where they were taken in for the night. The sixty-one-year-old doctor, who was away tending to Ellison, had close ties to both families in the feud: Not only was he a friend and financial supporter of Devil Anse's (and the namesake of his fourth son, Elliott, who, like Doc, would go on to study medicine), but Rutherford's daughter Mary was married to Sally and Randall's son Floyd. As Tuesday became Wednesday, the women huddled inside by the hearth, regaining their strength and struggling to keep their hopes alive. They determined to return to the schoolhouse in the morning.

As for Randall, he was more than thirty miles away in Pikeville, where he had gone to consult with a lawyer and wait for his sons to arrive. He was now in the company of his spurned daughter, Roseanna, who was still living at the Cline house. As the dark hours passed, and his sons did not appear, he grew more disheartened and considered heading back to the Tug at daylight.

Outside the schoolhouse, a lantern hung near the door, providing the only light, a magnet to moths and beetles. Used to sleeping in snoring groups in drafty, overcrowded cabins or on the rocky forest floor, the Hatfield guards dozed off, impervious to the warm drizzle in the buggy, smoky, snake-ridden woods, the burning thirst that trailed the passage of pure corn slowly rising inside them.

THE NEXT DAY, Wednesday, August 9, Preacher Anse and a delegation of friends crossed the Tug to see the prisoners and Devil Anse. Preacher Anse asked his cousin to turn the McCoy brothers over to the Kentucky authorities. Devil Anse was a man who knew the court system well. Since the war, he had been in and out of the courtroom on many occasions, to face charges (on his wartime activities as well as for trespassing and moonshining), to press charges, and to defend himself in civil cases, most notably against Perry Cline and against a merchant who had tried to bilk him for timbering supplies. He was aware that things could go in your favor or not, sometimes in unpredictable and illogical ways, but he was an honest businessman, and most often things went his way. He had even been to an appeals court to overturn an unfavorable decision, so he understood the mechanisms of the justice system in a relatively sophisticated fashion. But this was different. Since Devil Anse was illiterate, his way of thinking had been shaped not by school and reading but by life and its experiences. From his youth, he was a woodsman, a hunter, and a predator. In matters of money and contracts, he had learned that he could take his disputes to court. In matters of life and death and family well-being, however, he fell back on his survival instincts and his war experience. He eyed his cousin and replied tersely: "If my brother Ellison gets well, the law can handle it."[10]

People were Preacher Anse's business, and he knew a stubborn soul when he encountered one. He had encouraged his cousin to do the right thing and could only hope that he might mull it over and accede. Perhaps God in all His grace would intervene. Preacher Anse held out no great hope, though. In the meantime, three souls were teetering on the brink of their judgment day, and he went to work with fervor.

"Old Uncle Anison Hatfield," Sam McCoy later wrote, "stayed with the boys till he were told the third time to leave. They told him to leave or else." As he was getting ready to depart, Preacher Anse urged the brothers to continue to pray. According to Sam, Bud said, "Uncle Anse, I don't know how."

Preacher Anse told him, "Say, 'Lord, have mercy on me.' "[11]

That morning, Sally and Mary set out again for the Hatfield schoolhouse. When they reached the schoolyard and began pleading for mercy, some of the men, already weary of the two women, taunted them. If Ellison died, the brothers heard from inside the tumbledown schoolhouse, they were to be "filled as full of holes as a sifter bottom."[12]

By two o'clock, it was clear that Ellison was not going to recover, and Big Jim arrived to join the women and try to help his brothers.

Wall told all three to leave. When the two women resisted, he warned them that if they did not go immediately, he would physically remove them. Reluctantly, they left the cursed schoolhouse, knowing they would probably never see Tolbert, Pharmer, and Bud again.

At three o'clock on Wednesday afternoon, some forty-eight agonizing hours after the Election Day fight, Doc Rutherford pronounced Big Ellison dead. In one sense, after two decades, the circle was complete: The Hatfields had now forfeited their Confederate hero to the McCoys, compensation for the Union man that the McCoys had lost at the hands of the Hatfields. But two wrongs never add up to a right; they merely multiply, and no one recognized any balancing of the scales.

The Hatfield men had been quietly grieving this inevitable loss, and as Ellison's wife and children knelt around his bed weeping, they moved to avenge it.

Elias and Anse stalked out to the yard and dispatched a messenger to let the others know.

When they heard the galloping horse, the schoolhouse guards jumped to their feet. The sweating horse stopped with a shiver. "Ellison's done died," the messenger shouted.[13] An angry and distraught bellow rose from the shocked men, shocked even though the news had been all but a certainty. They lumbered around the schoolyard, averting their eyes from one another and regaining their bearings. Casting ominous looks inward through the chinks between the logs, they began to channel their emotions into something they could deal with — throat-ripping anger.

Elias took Ellison's body to his house and then joined the force at the old schoolhouse, where the mood was like a brooding storm before a hair-raising lightning bolt. Although this was to be mob justice, the mob was not without order. A trial was held, but the verdict had already been handed down with Ellison's last breath. The sentence: death for all three, though by now there was some question as to Bud's involvement. They would make an inquiry if possible before killing him.

The brothers, knowing that they were about to die, broke

down, tears staining their grimy faces. For Tolbert, the grief was short-lived, however. To him, there were things worse than death, like showing weakness in front of a Hatfield. Regaining his composure, he growled defiantly: "I want the man that kills me to stand right before my eyes. I want to look him right in the eye."[14]

It would be a moonless night. Anse — standing with his brothers Wall and Elias, as well as his sons Johnse, Cap, and Bob, the last just fifteen — organized his men. The family included Andy and Lark Varney, sons of Devil Anse's sister Matilda, and eighteen-year-old Tom "Guerilla" Mitchell, who was married to their sister Nancy, and was rounded out by Bill Tom Hatfield, a cousin of Devil Anse; the slow Cotton Top Mounts; and Joe Murphy, whose daughter would later marry Wall's youngest son. Charlie Carpenter served as the sergeant at arms. The three Mahons, the three crossover McCoys, the two Whitts, Dan and Jeff, and Alex Messer mustered with others in lines in front of the schoolhouse.

Devil Anse saddled up. Elias would stay behind. And although by now he had misgivings about the proceedings, Wall stood aside as Devil Anse ordered Carpenter to bring out the prisoners. In eerie silence the throng ushered the McCoys toward the river on foot. Pharmer and Bud openly wept.

When they reached the Tug, a voice spoke up. It was Wall. He had decided that he would go no farther. It was he who had assured Old Randall on Tuesday morning that his sons would be tried in the district where the fight had taken place; relying on his word, Randall had gone to get legal help in Pikeville. While Wall had his character flaws — he was reported to be a serial philanderer, for one thing — he was both a justice of the peace and a church deacon, roles he took seriously. He had decided to go against his brother and make a stand. "The Bible condemns murder," he asserted, arguing that they should turn the brothers in to the authorities and let them be tried in court.[15]

But Devil Anse would not hear it. He directed the men to keep going. They marched into the river. Overcome by fear and exhaustion, Pharmer lost consciousness. Two men took him under the shoulders and dragged him through the current. Bud sobbed. Tolbert trudged stoically, according to Spears, "erect and in silence, man fashion." When they got to the Kentucky shore, the Hatfield squad kicked water into Pharmer's face to revive him. The path picked up again on the far side of the Tug, but the party turned off it. They marched the condemned along the weed-choked riverbank.

Exasperated, Wall headed home, he later testified, by himself. Shortly after he reached the main road, he encountered his brother Elias on his way to Joe Davis's to buy whiskey. Elias invited him to come along and sent a man across the river to buy a jug. When the man came back, Davis was with him. Wall asked Davis if he had seen the boy, meaning Bud McCoy, stab Big Ellison. Davis said, "All I know is I seen him with a knife in his hand and there were blood on it."

Wall responded, "That's all I want to know."[16]

It was a chilly summer night. Stars buckshot the black sky. Several hundred feet upstream from where they had forded the river and about a quarter mile below the mouth of Sulphur Creek, the execution squad reached a depression in the bank, a sink opening onto the river, where rubbish was dumped, including, recently, the carcasses of sheep-killing dogs. They would go no farther.

At a copse of pawpaws, the men hung a lantern to cast some light and to check for snakes, which were said to prefer blackberry bushes and pawpaw trees. They shoved the trio of McCoys to the ground among the fallen green fruit, now split open and rotting, and bound them to the saplings. "Anse said that we would rest there," Dan Whitt later testified, "and the parties all joined—squatting around the McCoy boys and cocking their guns and pistols and saying they were going to have some fun or a shooting match."[17]

At this point, Doc, Sam, and Plyant Mahon and Mose Christian, who was married to Wall's daughter Octavia, left to return to the West Virginia side of the river. The others then forced the McCoys to rise to their knees. They deliberately placed Tolbert with his back toward them, in response to his insolent challenge to look him in the eye. Pharmer, in shock from fear, faced them like a treed raccoon in torchlight. Innocent Bud turned toward his brothers, who had gotten him into this and who could equally do him no good now.[18]

The firing squad—Anse, Johnse, Cap, Bob, and Bill Tom Hatfield as well as Cotton Top Mounts, Charlie Carpenter, Guerilla Mitchell, the Varneys, Joe Murphy, Alex Messer, and one or more of the Mahons, depending on whose story you believe—got into position in a line, raised their guns, and waited for a command.[19]

Big Jim, at age thirty-two the oldest of Randall's sons and himself the father of four children with another on the way, had learned of Ellison's death and now sat anxiously on the porch of his uncle Asa's cabin on Sulphur Creek. His mother had begged him not to intercede. She could see that there was little chance of taking the boys by force, and she preferred to gamble that Devil Anse might yet do the right thing and turn her sons over to the authorities than to risk losing more lives trying to free them. The night was still, and Big Jim had heard the men pass along Sulphur Creek. He went down to the bank of the Tug and later testified that he saw Wall and Elias, Cotton Top, and Doc and Plyant Mahon there.[20]

Twenty minutes later, a fusillade ripped through the languid late-summer air on the Kentucky side of the Tug. Flashes of light crackled beneath the tree canopy. After the burst of fire—fifty shots or more—several more reports rang out. Then, for maybe two minutes, silence.

At his home at the head of Mate Creek, Billy Anse McCoy, who was sitting on his porch with Sam Simpkins, heard the horrible cacophony. Although Billy Anse was not involved in the feud that bore his family's name, the volley would deeply affect his life and that of everyone in the valley.[21] Big Jim McCoy heard it too. It was like being struck by lightning.

After talking to Davis, Wall would testify, he and Elias "started back down the river bank to meet a call of nature." In the meantime, all hell broke loose on the opposite shore.[22] Wall would later take a daring stand based on his claim of innocence: He would turn himself over to the Kentucky authorities. It would cost him dearly.

The two older brothers—Tolbert, who had started the fight, and Pharmer, who had ended it by shooting Ellison—were riddled with shot. The fatal bullet pierced Tolbert's skull with such velocity that it passed straight through and kept going. Another shot also hit his head, and lead filled his torso. Pharmer was shot once in the head and multiple times in the body. But nobody had aimed at Bud, who now trembled uncontrollably as he looked down on his brothers, who were slumped in place, as if they had just dozed off. Johnse, Cap, Guerilla, and Cotton Top fired a few more shots into the two corpses out of spite. Then they turned and with the others started down the river.[23]

But Alex Messer decided to go back, saying, "Dead men tell no tales."[24] Devil Anse looked at Messer, a six-footer with dark hair and blue eyes later described as "sharp, penetrating, shifty . . . as if he was constantly gazing down a gun barrel," and agreed. "Go you," he said, nodding in the direction they had come from, and rode on.

From a broken family from Hazard, Kentucky, Messer was a Union infantryman who had served in the Fourth Regiment of the Kentucky Mounted Infantry Volunteers, which had seen action throughout the Southeast. His brother Elijah fought on the other side, serving as a sergeant in the Confederate Thirteenth Kentucky Cavalry, Tenth CSA. Alex seemed to like army life, volunteering early for three years and then re-upping for another three. However, he had become entangled with a drowning mule while crossing a river outside Macon, Georgia, and his resulting injuries cut short his service.

Messer loaded his shotgun with buckshot and returned to where the kneeling boy, still bound, awaited his fate. Now forty-four, Messer was something of a rolling stone. He had done at least one stint in the Louisville jail around 1870 and was currently on his fourth wife, who was twenty years his junior and pregnant with their first child. Messer walked up to Bud on the embankment, placed the barrels of his gun against his head, and squeezed both triggers.[25]

Jim McCoy's heart broke as his little brother's animal cry of anguish reached him from across the river. An instant later, the boom of the double-barreled shotgun thundered off the mountain walls.

THEIR WORK DONE, the reports of so many nearly simultaneous gunshots still ringing in their ears, and oblivious to the fact that this act of taking justice into their own hands would haunt them the rest of their lives, the execution squad recrossed the Tug into West Virginia. Perhaps pressured to do it by Devil Anse, Wall was waiting for them — although he would later deny it — so that he could administer an oath of secrecy. Devil Anse had his men form a row facing the justice of the peace. "Hold up your right hands," Wall commanded, as if he were in his courtroom. "You and each of you do solemnly swear never to reveal to anyone what has been done this night under the penalty of death, so help you God." It was not a question. "I do" was the only possible response.[26]

Shang Ferrell was with Elias at his house, as Ferrell later testified, when Devil Anse, Wall, Johnse, and others showed up that night around ten. Elias asked Wall what they had done with the boys. "We have sent them back to Kentucky to stand the civil law," Wall replied, in a twisted echo of Ellison's deathbed suggestion.[27]

BIG JIM AND SEVERAL OF Asa's neighbors crossed the Tug to inspect the site of the commotion. At around the same time, Randall and Roseanna McCoy arrived home from Pikeville and were met by Sally, who told them that Ellison had died but that the boys had been alive when she had seen them earlier that day.[28]

Carrying lanterns and guns, Big Jim and Anse Ferrell approached the refuse pit praying for a miracle but expecting the worst. The worst is what they found. Big Jim later described the horrific scene stoically: "My brothers was dead when I found them." Lifting their lamps, they made out the bloody, broken bodies tethered to the shrubs like animals. Pharmer was shot sixteen times. Tolbert had taken at least six shots. Bud remained in a kneeling position hanging on to the bushes with the top of his head missing.[29] The two men did not disturb the scene of the crime.

The next morning, Thursday, justice of the peace Joe Hatfield, acting as the district coroner, led a contingent of men, including a grand jury, to inspect the crime scene. They found Bud still up on his knees. According to Squirrel Huntin' Sam, one of the party picked up the top of his skull, which had flown six feet from his body, "scooped up his brains and returned them to his head."[30] Joe cut the ropes tying the bodies to the pawpaws as the twelve-man grand jury inspected the scene.

The officers who had originally arrested the three McCoys testified to the grand jury that at Preacher Anse's house, the prisoners were taken from them and bound and that Devil Anse, Wall, and Cap Hatfield had told them to "vamoose."[31] In just half an hour, Joe Hatfield and his jury produced a verdict: The three McCoys had "come to their death by shot wounds at the hands of persons to the jury unknown." The names of the alleged perpetrators—if not justice—would be produced in due time. With a jackknife, someone inscribed in the shiny bark of an old beech tree that shaded the murder grounds *The McCoy Boys, Shot in 1882,* and then scratched a crude border around his work.[32]

News of the murder spread rapidly. When he heard that the corpses were lying down by the riverbank, John Wallace Hatfield, a strapping, square-headed twenty-year-old, readied a sled with two yokes of oxen and with his brother-in-law and his father—known as Uncle Wall, to distinguish him from the other Wall Hatfield—drove to the pawpaw patch. They loaded the bodies onto the sled and then drove them to the McCoy home on Blackberry Fork. It was eleven o'clock at night before they finished their gruesome task. Between the weight of the bodies and the rocky five-mile journey, their sled was destroyed. But these Hatfields, friends of Randall and Sally, could rest easy, having delivered the McCoy brothers to their final resting place.[33]

Chapter 9

~

Life After Death

1882–1884

The three McCoy brothers, who in the midsummer heat had been laid out outside on the porch at Randall and Sally's, were photographed for posterity. In the picture, the brothers look placid, their faces shaved except for trim mustaches, their clothes clean, their arms crossed on their chests with their wrists bound to keep them in place. Three men, presumably their brothers, squat behind them, lifting their heads up to the camera. Tolbert's and Bud's skulls are held together by fresh white bandages.

Word spread from house to house, and more than a thousand mourners made their way to the head of Blackberry Fork for the funeral, which was held on Friday, August 11, the day after their bodies arrived home. A broad common grave on a hillside shelf beside the house awaited the trio. Many in the community said that the three had brought about their own downfall and would now have eternity to share one another's company, but the grief was real as friends placed each coffin on a litter and soberly carried the brothers one at a time across the stream and uphill to the grave. Here, as the Baptist preacher was about to begin his prayer, Sally fell on her knees and wailed, calling on God to witness that if her pleading on the morning of Election Day had been heeded, neither Ellison nor her boys would have suffered such tragic ends.[1]

Tolbert, Pharmer, and Bud McCoy laid out for burial at their parents' house. *(Kentucky Historical Society, Hatfield Family Photo Collection)*

Suddenly, the Tug was again a wedge between two peoples. At the best of times, men routinely carried pistols and knives, even to church. Now as they donned their Sunday best to attend Ellison Hatfield's former church, they also grabbed their rifles. At the church, on Peter Creek, home of Devil Anse's Civil War enemies, alertness was at its peak. While preparing the bread and wine for Communion, the deacons and elders leaned their rifles against the pulpit.[2]

News of the reprisal killings of the McCoy boys spread all the way to Louisville and Frankfort. However, Pike County was so remote and considered such a backwater that people who heard of the slaughter reacted with a certain detachment, shaking their heads at the barbarity of their mountain-dwelling cousins.

On September 12, a month after the McCoy boys were laid to rest in the hillside grave, if not in peace, county prosecutor S. G. Skinner filed three joint indictments, one for the murder of each brother, in open court. The indictments listed eighteen wanted men for Tolbert and Bud and twenty-one for Pharmer.[3]

On September 18, a Pike County jury, impaneled by circuit court judge George Brown, deliberated for several days and brought charges against twenty men. Devil Anse was the most prominent; his sons Johnse and Cap and his brothers Wall and Elias, as well as Ellison's illegitimate son Cotton Top Mounts, were also charged. Bill Tom Hatfield, about whom little is known, rounded out the Hatfields on the list, numbering seven in all. Then there were the three Mahon brothers, Doc, Sam, and Plyant. Also among the twenty were the three crossover McCoys, Selkirk and his sons Albert and L.D.

The governor of Kentucky posted a reward of $100 for the capture of any of the five highest-profile men on the list: Devil Anse, Cap, Johnse, and Bill Tom Hatfield and Guerilla Mitchell. While the justice system moved relatively swiftly in the safety of a courtroom, in the real world it did not. When the court next convened, months later, the sheriff reported that he had been unable to arrest any of the indicted men. Beside each name in the court records, he wrote, "Not found in this county, February 18, 1883." No one, not even the sheriff, was willing to directly confront the Hatfields.[4]

Several months later, a strange disease struck the deer population of Logan County, and hunters started finding deer corpses throughout the woods. It was as if a curse had hit the land, a variation of a biblical plague. Deer that were found alive were staggering around, their tongues swollen and black. In that, too, could be read implications: a loose tongue could have grave consequences. Usually a plentiful supply of meat, the deer would virtually disappear from the woods for years to come.

A YEAR AFTER HE WAS charged with the murders, on September 12, 1883, Johnse Hatfield, busy selling moonshine in Kentucky, was indicted for carrying a deadly weapon in Pike County. Though such a charge seemed trifling given that he was already wanted for a capital crime, a bench warrant was issued for his arrest and his bail set at $150. This was one of many concealed-weapons indictments against Johnse, and like those before it, it was probably initiated by the McCoys. Nothing would come of it.[5]

A month later, nineteen-year-old Cap married his first cousin Nancy Smith, who went by Nan and who was a niece of Devil Anse and also of the former home guard captain Rebel Bill Smith. Cap was not Nan's first choice. The seventeen-year-old had turned him down when he had courted her in previous years, instead marrying Joe Glenn, a promising young timber merchant and partner in a general store.[6]

Perhaps Cap's temper and reckless behavior had had something to do with her reluctance. One night, he and a dozen of his friends and their dates showed up at a church dance about half an hour after it started. A Dr. Reese and his friends had already filled the dance floor. When Cap asked Reese to let his friends dance, Reese told them all to come back the next night. Cap drew his pistol, but Reese was even quicker in drawing his. He did not hesitate to pull the trigger either, hitting Cap in one hip and, as he pivoted from the impact, in the other as well, blasting him to the floor. Cap's friends barely prevented the angry doctor from issuing a coup de grâce to the head.

Devil Anse claimed he tended to Cap for an entire month after that episode without even removing his own clothes for a rest. His Winchesters and pistols were loaded the whole time, as he was prepared to wreak vengeance in what he felt was the necessary and honorable way should Cap die. He admitted that his son "was in the wrong," but only the result mattered. "If he had killed my boy, I should have killed him to make it square," he said. As it turned out, the Hatfields never even lodged a complaint against Reese. "Let him go," Anse said once Cap recovered. "He did not kill, so I've got nothing to say."[7]

Joe Glenn, who was new to the area by way of Georgia, certainly appeared to have better prospects than Cap did. Nan had been fourteen at the time of their marriage. Two years later, however, Glenn was ambushed and riddled with bullets. Cap denied any responsibility for the murder, and some said the treachery was committed by a former business partner of Glenn's. Whatever the case, the second time around, Cap got his woman, the widow Nan, with three boys as interest.[8]

THE HATFIELDS ONCE AGAIN CROSSED freely into Kentucky, though the indicted men usually ventured only in numbers and well armed. The bench warrants for their arrests were repeatedly issued but just as repeatedly returned "not found." When there was an election, the Hatfields warned the Kentucky sheriffs not to bring the bench warrants to the voting precincts where they planned to show up. As these admonitions were heeded, nothing major transpired for several years.

The distress in the McCoy household, however, was palpable. Randall, who was a rapidly aging sixty-three, grew increasingly irked by the sight of the Hatfields going about their business as if nothing had happened. While Sally clenched her jaw and carried on tending to her family the way a mother had to, she was deeply distraught and occasionally in the middle of her chores broke down and convulsed in fits of grief. Tolbert's widow, Mary, who had moved in with them, comforted and cared for her mother-in-law, suppressing her own heartbreak and rage to be strong for Sally and for Melvin and Cora. To make matters worse, she was engaged in a court battle with Tolbert's business partner over the value of Tolbert's stake in their timber operation. Over time, Sally grew stronger, but Mary slept and ate less and less. She began to waste away.[9]

Always brooding, and now more than ever, Randall regularly visited Pikeville, riding more than thirty miles over a rugged trail to complain to Perry Cline, a nephew by marriage. An attorney, Cline had escaped his youth on the Tug and, after losing his inherited land to Devil Anse, moved to Pikeville to pursue his ambitions in law and politics. He gave Randall reason to hope that something might still be accomplished through the legal system.[10]

These efforts by Randall did not go unnoticed by the Hatfields, who were greatly concerned that he might stir up more trouble in Pike County. As one of the largest and most influential families in the area, they let it be known through the grapevine that they were displeased, and, according to some, "harassed the McCoy family in every possible manner"; namely, through intimidation and the constant threat of violence. They thought if they could force the McCoys to leave the area, it would alleviate the pressure to prosecute those accused of killing the McCoy trio.[11]

It was during the following summer, in June 1884, that the next significant violence broke out. The Hatfields had decided that it would be in their best interests to terminate by any means Randall's agitation of the legal authorities in Kentucky. By the family's reckoning, justice had been served. The three boys had murdered a Hatfield, and they had paid the price with their own lives. The Hatfields could recite a litany of injustices perpetrated by the courts, sheriffs, the jail system, and state and federal authorities to justify having taken matters into their own hands, and they had a good many friends and allies who saw it that way too.

They resolved to keep an eye out for an opportunity and saw it come that June. Randall had been summoned to the Pikeville courthouse to appear at a public hearing regarding Tolbert's timber interests. Randall's son Calvin, or Cal, who acted as executor of Tolbert's estate, had filed suits to establish Mary's rights. The Hatfields, who had their informants, knew about the court date. They also knew that the route that Randall and Cal would take to Pikeville and back ran through remote parts between steeply sloping hillsides that provided ample opportunities for an ambush.

They resolved to kill them both.[12]

Heavily armed, Johnse, Cap, and Bill Tom Hatfield, Cotton Top Mounts, Mose Christian, and two other men hid in the brush on a mountainside. About thirty feet below them was the route that the

McCoys would use to travel home. After everyone was in place, along came a young son of Tom Stafford, the justice of the peace who had been elected the same day that his brother-in-law Ellison Hatfield had been mortally stabbed. Cap came out of his hiding place, stopped the boy, and told him to go to the courtroom and bring back a description of the clothes Randall and Cal were wearing and the guns they were carrying and to keep mum about it all the while.

By the time the hearing ended, it was dusk. The participants filed out, and the two Scott brothers, Bushy and Hense, Randall's neighbors who had been called as witnesses, were among the first to leave. The Scotts belonged to a well-liked family, one of the few in the area considered friends by both the Hatfields and the McCoys, and they would be traveling along the same route as Randall and some of the other McCoys. In fact, they set out on the road — actually just a bridle path — with Randall's son Sam.[13]

At the site of the planned ambush, the Hatfield faction was antsy, their nerves on a hair trigger from waiting and watching all day. The light grew dim as the sun sank below the ridgeline. When they spied three men in the distance who seemed to fit the boy's description, they presumed them to be the two they wanted — Randall and Cal — plus another. When the trio reached the predetermined spot, about fifty yards away, Cap gave the signal, and the Hatfields opened up. The travelers were riding three abreast, which made the firing angles more difficult. The horses were shot and killed. Sam had his hand on Hense's right shoulder, and when a bullet pierced the shoulder, Sam felt the impact of flesh and bone bulge into his hand. In shock, the two men leaped together over the lower side of the slope and hid. Hense cried out that he had been hit. Bushy fired his rifle at the ambushers, and the shot whizzed across Cap's chest, penetrating just enough to make it ooze blood. Bushy reloaded his gun and stepped to a scrub tree. As he raised the rifle, a slug drilled his right knee. He fell, writhing on the ground, dangerously wounded and bleeding profusely. Settling in the dust and clenching his eyes tight, he groaned in pain. More slugs exploded around him, covering him in dirt and dust. Biting his tongue, he lay as still as he could.[14]

As Truda McCoy told the story, Cal McCoy heard the shooting and came running on the double. He fired his two pistols to let his brother know that help was on the way. When the would-be assassins heard the shots, they fled in the dark.

They thought they had killed Randall, but in reality they had crippled Bushy for life, an injustice that not only caused more grief and resentment in the area but also raised the pressure on the Hatfields to get Randall, the primary instigator of opposition to them.[15]

This was not the only case of mistaken identity in the Hatfields' efforts to be rid of Randall. In another incident, Cap shot Uncle Wall, not his own uncle but the Kentucky cousin who went by Uncle Wall. Spotting him from a distance of about two hundred feet and thinking he was Randall, Cap stepped behind a giant chestnut tree and fired. According to Uncle Wall's grandson Basil Hatfield, "He shot grandpa, aimed to kill him, but some way or another the rifle made a long fire." Instead of killing Uncle Wall, Cap shot him through the kneecap.

When he went to inspect the damage he had done, he found, instead of a wounded McCoy, an enraged Hatfield, kin by blood and marriage, wielding a buck knife. When Cap saw the deadly blade and the intent, he dodged back. "You cowardly thing!" Uncle Wall bellowed after hearing Cap's fast attempt at an apology. "If you wanted to shoot [Randall] McCoy why didn't you walk up to him like a man an tell him you was going to shoot. Why'd you hide like a hound dog and shoot somebody for?" Like Bushy Scott, Uncle Wall was crippled for life.[16]

SEVERAL MONTHS AFTER THE FAILED ambush of Randall and Cal, friends of both the Hatfields and the McCoys decided they should have a rendezvous to settle their differences — or, as Squirrel Huntin' Sam put it, to "make friends and forget about it." The plan was to meet at the Caney schoolhouse in Logan County and attempt to hash things out. Both parties were wary but willing to give it a go. The Hatfields arrived first at the schoolhouse, which was in West Virginia. Randall and his friends pulled up at the far side of the Tug, choosing to feel things out before crossing over.

Squirrel Huntin' Sam, whose wife, America, had just given birth to their firstborn, Sam Jr., on July 2, 1884, was with the Hatfields. Although a McCoy, the new father had friends in both families, and he made it known that he would not talk about either side to the other. But what he saw now made him incredulous and mad: Johnse had his rifle — a cylinder six-shot cap and ball — resting in the fork of a pawpaw. He was sighting it across the river at where the McCoys were gathered.[17]

"Johnse, what are you doing there?" asked Sam, towering over the preoccupied young man.

"Oh, I'm sighting across the river," Johnse replied nonchalantly, as if there were no McCoys at the other end of the barrel.

"Now," Sam said, "you put that gun up. Supposing you fire that gun and kill somebody, then you'd hang or be penitentiared for life."

Johnse's uncle Elias came over. Sam told him that he was trying to get Johnse to put his gun down. "Johnse, set that gun up against the schoolhouse," Elias told his nephew, "or I'll slap the damn face off you. Go on."

Johnse grinned and put down the gun. His barely restrained desire to shoot was typical of the feelings on both sides. The two groups shouted to each other across the river, but emotions were still too raw and nerves too jangled for any type of reconciliation.

The McCoys rode away again, never having crossed the river.

Chapter 10

~

Taking Names and
Keeping a List

1884–1886

W hile Devil Anse's sons had stepped into the maelstrom of family hatred and now apparently had taken the lead, Devil Anse, to be sure, still quietly led from the rear.

Of the men who would eventually attempt to ride the Hatfield clan into the ground, two would be raised to superhero level by W. B. Lawson in his 1894 dime novel *The Hatfield-McCoy Vendetta.* One of these men was Kentucky Bill, who is lightly disguised as Kentuck in the work of fiction.

In 1892, the real-life Kentucky Bill Napier would take part in a classic arrest that the press tied to the feud, though it was unrelated. After searching for three murder suspects in the hills of western Virginia, the dashing and clever detective and his partner tracked them down to a farm. They went to the house pretending to be lawyers and promised to get the fugitives off if they were tried. The outlaws then described the murders in detail to the detectives, who persuaded the trio to accompany them into town. They were locked in a jail cell in Covington, Virginia, before they realized they had been had. Clever it was, but nothing compared to Kentucky Bill's exploits in the feud.[1]

The other man in Lawson's novel, whom he calls the Man from 'Frisco, is based on Dan Cunningham, who would be called by one reporter "the detective who rode herd on the Hatfields." In so doing, he believed, perhaps not without reason, that he had divine assistance: his achievements earned him a place in *Ripley's Believe It or Not* as the only man shot at more than a hundred times without being hit.[2]

The first dozen or so of the bullets aimed at Cunningham were the result of another clash, the Jackson County feud. In 1846, the heirs of Matthias Bruen, a wealthy merchant of New York City, had inherited 266,000 acres from a 1796 land grant, most of which lay in what had become Jackson and Roane counties of West Virginia. The Bruen family had previously sold some of the massive tract, originally surveyed by George Washington, to various settlers. Newcomers from the Clinch River Valley of southwestern Virginia had moved onto tracts bordering Bruen land, sometimes squatting on Bruen property. Poor land records, flawed surveys, and overlapping titles led to continual disputes, which were compounded by conflicting allegiances during the Civil War.[3]

One of the Clinch Valley men, Joe Kiser Jr., would confess on his deathbed to his role in the land war that resulted. First, he helped another Clinch Valley man, Cain Counts, set Dan Cunningham's brother Nathan's barn on fire. Then he and Counts led a gang of men in ambushing him.

Nathan and Dan's father, Joel Cunningham, had settled in the southern part of Jackson County around 1840. After hewing a cabin out of the forest, Joel went to fetch his wife near the Ohio River, but by the time he returned with her, Clinch Valleyites had squatted in the cabin. To keep the peace, he let them have it and built another one nearby, where he started a farm and a family and went on to become a leading citizen and justice of the peace, with a 488-acre tract of former Bruen land. Clinch Valley men, hard up for opportunities, continued to flow west from Virginia's former frontier to this new one. Some were of the lowest nature, illiterate, clannish scofflaws who had been forced out of the valley. Among them, the intermarried Skean, Counts, and Kiser families squatted on the Bruen expanse and started causing trouble. They resisted the building of schools and the laying of a road to Charleston — any public improvements that might encourage landholders to evict them.[4]

By the time the 1861 elections rolled around, when Dan was eleven, the Cunninghams and other pro-Union families had grave differences with the pro-Confederate Clinch Valley clans, who had formed an alliance called the Consolidated Band to pursue their interests. The Band was "out for theft, murder and gain," Dan later wrote. As a justice of the peace, Joel Cunningham had convicted Band member Joe Skean of the vicious killing of a neighbor's yearling colt. (After a dispute with the neighbor, Skean had lashed the colt to a tree and slit its throat.) Joel sentenced Skean to jail. The Consolidated Band vowed revenge. On Election Day, the Band, armed with guns and clubs, staked out the polls in the town of Kentuck and defied the Union men to vote. Frank Skean clubbed one opponent in the head so hard that he had to be carried away on a stretcher. Skean and Ab Kiser drew guns on Joel and Nathan. Joel refused to be cowed. He and Nathan voted.[5]

The next day, as Nathan was working in his garden, one of the Skeans came rushing at him with a knife. Nathan lunged, grabbed his gun, squeezed the trigger, and wounded his attacker. They wrestled and traded blows until they were exhausted. Nathan took refuge at his parents' house, a mile away. By dawn, the house was surrounded by gunmen. Night after night, Dan watched the Clinch Valley clansmen lurking around their house with weapons drawn. He was scared and haunted by them.

When the war came, Joel organized a company of state troops while the Band set about looting the county, carrying off sides of bacon, barrels of flour, dry goods, and groceries from stores and mills, pillaging Union men's houses down to taking the sheets off their beds. Joel and his men arrested gang members but released them on their promise to take the oath of allegiance to the Union. They never did; instead, they ambushed Joel's company on a trail near the town of Jeffreys, killing one man and wounding others.[6] The company escaped and eventually joined the regular army, but in January 1862, Joel, exhausted and sick, died in a military camp at Buffalo, West Virginia. He had been run into the ground. Dan was twelve.

Left unchecked, the Band rampaged. Devil Zeke Counts led raids on the Kentucky border, teaming up with the notorious Colonel Vincent Witcher and Rebel Bill Smith. (In 1864, Counts was among the eighty guerrillas who, along with Devil Anse Hatfield, commandeered the polls in Lawrence County, Kentucky, so that they could vote for Abraham Lincoln.) In their unholy alliance, Devil Anse of Logan County and Devil Zeke of Roane County rode together in the war, along with Crazy Jim Vance, Wall Hatfield, and Cain Counts, both in the Virginia State Line and afterward in irregular actions. None of this would escape Dan Cunningham, who was soaking it all in, taking names and keeping a mental list. In a war of this nature, as in a feud, often a young boy who witnesses the events will return a decade or more later to avenge a father's murder, or in this case a brother's. Dan was that boy.[7]

Toward the end of the war, Nathan Cunningham came home on furlough. At dawn a few days after his arrival, a dozen men — the Band now claimed to be Confederates of Jenkins Cavalry — rushed into his house and shot him. The slug passed right through his lung. Nathan snatched up his rifle, fought his way outside, and, trailing blood, ran a mile to his family's home, where Dan and their other siblings still lived with their mother. With each breath that Nathan took, the fabric over the wound was sucked in and out of the bullet hole.

Like Harmon McCoy, Nathan Cunningham had returned home only to find that he had been safer in the war.

Demonstrating his family's uncanny resistance to death when being shot at, however, Nathan survived. During Reconstruction, he became a deputy U.S. marshal and an agent for the Bruens in a survey of their vast landholdings. Both positions put him in opposition to the Band, and, according to Dan, "Secessionism" would be in them "all their natural lives." It was after Nathan arrested Band members for distilling liquor in violation of Internal Revenue laws that Joe Kiser and Cain Counts set his barn and stables on fire. He caught them in the act. The case was scheduled for the September 1877 term of the circuit court, around the same time that litigation over the Bruen land was coming to a head. As a Bruen agent, Nathan informed many Clinch Valley settlers that they had to move. In early August, the Band, determined to hold on to its land by any means, met in a tobacco barn to plot his murder.[8]

Returning from a trip to Charleston, Nathan and his eleven-year-old son, Joel, were ambushed by members of the Band partway up a long hill. They shot Nathan twice, blasting him off his horse. One slug hit him in the chest, another in the stomach. The fingers on his left hand were shot off. Joel helped his father onto his feet and held his right hand as they tried to get away. Counts and his cohorts followed the two like jackals.

Three more shots rang out.

"Go home and tell mother that Wade Counts has killed me," Nathan told Joel. Then he shouted, "Wade Counts, you have killed me. Don't kill my boy . . ."

Pierce Skean pulled father and son apart and held Nathan's arms behind his back as Joel ran for home. Joe Skean, the infamous colt-throat-slitter, struck Nathan in the temple with the butt of a rifle to settle that old score. Nathan fell to his knees. Then Kiser and Cain Counts smashed his head with rocks, and they all left him to die.

Dan Cunningham called them "heartless demons."

The trial of Wade Counts and Joe Kiser in Judge Starcher's court at Kentuck was a farce. The day after the murder, Cunningham, by this time a schoolteacher, had investigated the ambush site. Behind the boulder where the gang had hidden, he had found apples and tracks. He picked up the apples and followed the tracks through the woods. They led to John Kiser's place, where he found the tree the apples came from and signs of a recent gathering. The tracks continued to the Counts family farm, where the accused all swore they had spent the entire day deadening timber, girdling the bark with axes to stop the flow of sap and thus kill the large trees, a technique used in the Appalachians (especially by moonshiners preparing to plant corn) that left a grim landscape of dying trees. But when Cunningham went back to examine Counts's place on the sly, he found no signs of recent deadening.

Among the eight witnesses Cunningham summoned to the trial, one had seen Joel Skean ride up the creek before the murder, and Nathan's son Joel identified Pierce Skean as the man who pulled him away from his father. But when Cunningham went to discuss the case with county prosecutor V. S. Armstrong, a former Confederate Army officer, his evidence was ignored. Instead, Armstrong told him, "If we really try to convict those fellows, the Band will make a slaughterhouse of the county."[9]

"Then there's no help from the law?" Cunningham asked incredulously.

"Well, there's other ways. You know a gun when you see one."

The likelihood of prosecution became even slimmer when Judge Starcher saw fit to chastise Cunningham for being pushy and threatened to make him pay the witnesses' expenses. After dismissing the charges, Starcher and Armstrong rode off with Counts and Kiser and other members of the Band.[10]

Cunningham was stunned by this injustice against his dead brother — who by the age of thirty-eight had not only fought for his country but served in public office for eighteen years. The Consolidated Band, which Cunningham referred to by many names, including the Regulators (a reference to the war's rapacious homefront militias), had driven his father from his home, killed his brother, and bullied and robbed the citizens of Jackson County, a county shaped by his grandfather, who was its first high sheriff. Cunningham loathed the shady prosecutors and crooked judges who protected the Band either out of cowardice or for profit. Livid, he packed up his books and rode away, leaving Armstrong and the rest to think that they had defeated him.

Cunningham spent the next few years as an itinerant teacher but also followed his brother into law enforcement, training with pistol and rifle. At six feet tall and possessing a farm-strong, chiseled frame, he was powerful and cat-quick in a fight. He neither drank nor used tobacco in any form. In 1884, he was hired for the position of deputy U.S. marshal. He knew there was only one kind of justice, and that was justice by the book. "Cunningham is a one-ideaed man; a fighter of one weapon," a reporter would later write. "A mission of revenge dominates his life, and his weapon is the law." Some would dismiss him as "a revenuer," since it was these deputy U.S. marshals who were called on to enforce bootlegging statutes for the Internal Revenue Service, but it was a job he took to. He would serve during the terms of three successive marshals.[11]

His wanderings took him east into Roane County, Devil Zeke Counts's home turf, a place of wilderness and hardscrabble homesteads and mountaineers even more isolated than those in Jackson. Named for a state supreme court justice, Roane County had, ironically, become known for lawlessness and crooked officials. In the fall of 1884, some friends of Peter Cook, a constable murdered there, hired Cunningham, who had already earned a reputation for being shrewd and single-minded, to help solve the crime. Cook had been riding to the county courthouse through the woods near Big Sandy Creek on the day he was killed. It was an area, noted Cunningham, where "Secessionists lived," which to him meant mayhem, even two decades after the end of the war. Two shots had been fired from a height of about thirty yards above the road, but Cook was hit with twelve slugs. Afterward, Cunningham would show that one of the weapons used was a musket loaded with multiple small slugs of lead.

Cook had been carrying evidence for a sensitive and racially explosive case involving a black man named George who had had a long courtship with a white woman whom Cunningham called only

Disaway Ledsome's girl. George had abandoned her and moved to Charleston, where he married another woman. The trouble started when he moved back to Big Sandy Creek with his new wife. An angry Ledsome and her sister, Lil Hall, decided to take revenge. One night when George and his wife went to a church meeting, the two women robbed their house and then burned it down. Cook later caught them with George's possessions and arrested them.

Then things went from bad to worse. Prior to her trial, Ledsome married a man named Reynolds, and her father advised his new son-in-law and Lil's husband, Curtis, that the only way to keep their wives from going to prison was to kill Cook.

The two men spent the night before the shooting at Hall's father's house. A neighbor was having a party that evening, and after dark, Reynolds and Hall stashed a musket and a revolver in a hollow tree near the neighbor's place and then joined the party until late at night. In the morning, they passed by the neighbor's unarmed and told him they were going out to find some missing hogs. After retrieving their weapons, they crossed the mountain and then lay in ambush all day. Around four o'clock, having just decided to give up and head home, they saw Cook coming. When he reached a point directly below them, Hall fired the musket and Reynolds the revolver. Cook fell, mortally wounded, staring with shock at his murderers and locking eyes with Reynolds as he died.

It was that stare that helped Cunningham convict the pair. It troubled Reynolds so much that one foggy day while he was chopping timber in a deep hollow, he saw Cook's ghost sweeping toward him in the gloom. On the day of the trial, when Cunningham, who had pieced together the crime, grilled Reynolds, he broke down and confessed: "I even saw the whites of his eyes," he lamented, "and that look haunts me in my sleep."

IN THE SPRING OF 1886, Cunningham set out to tackle a Roane County crime spree. Abe Looney had operated a prosperous general store and post office for decades. He was a generous man, good to his eponymous town, Looneyville, and its people. Just across a ridge, two men had built a rival store. However, they soon found that competing against Looney and his legacy of goodwill was a losing battle. The two men, George Simmons and Mason Vandevender, hired some local scrappers to burn down Looney's store.

Not long after the fire, a moonshiner out of jail on bail was murdered. Working as a farmhand twenty miles southwest of Looneyville, the moonshiner, Thomas Deskins, had been grubbing a field when the crack of a rifle broke the silence. In a split second, a lead slug passed right through him. Spouting blood, he stumbled toward a fence for cover, but his assailants caught him and beat him to death. When Cunningham snooped around the crime scene in June, he discovered gory evidence—stones stained with blood and matted hair. Still, he later recalled, "everything seemed shrouded in darkness." On Henry's Fork, thirty miles away, he questioned a man in whose face he detected signs of guilt, but he could not draw out a confession. Cunningham kept talking to people until he discovered that the day before the murder, the man, Eli Hambrick, and three others had been seen carrying rifles near the farm where Deskins was working, a place they had never been known to visit before. When a Kanawha County deputy sheriff stopped them, they claimed to be hunting for stray cattle and asked him for directions.

Cunningham had the four men arrested, but at the hearing, no one could prove that they had committed the crime. Then Hambrick's son, Lee, was arrested for setting fire to Looney's store. Curiously enough, though he was from a poor family, the boy was defended by the town's most influential and expensive attorneys. During the trial, Thomas Deskins's widow admitted that the Hambricks had met at their home to plot the arson. On orders from his father, young Lee had torched the store while the other Hambricks made sure to have alibis. The boy, able at his job, earned $2.50, a can of oil, and a pair of boots. It turned out that George Simmons had paid for his attorneys.

Soon, Cunningham got the break he needed to close the case. One of Hambrick's men was arrested for forgery. Sentenced to two years in prison, he broke down and confessed to Deskins's murder and named his accomplices. Indicted in the federal court at Charleston for bootlegging, Deskins had decided to use his knowledge of the Looney-store plot to get money out of Simmons and Vandevender. From jail, he wrote to the two merchants demanding the money. Simmons posted his bail but then hired Hambrick and the other three to kill him. For the murder, each man earned fifty dollars and some flour and bacon.

While Cunningham was successful in Roane County, he also became profoundly aware of how deeply malice ran in some families, how marital ties extended the web of outlawry, and how easily the legal system could be co-opted, not to mention just how paltry was the value of a man's life.

He had seen with his own eyes that pockets of Rebels continued to commit violence and crime, and he attributed quasi-military status to these outlaw clans that surrounded him. But he had also seen how persistence in detective work paid off and how weak a criminal was once he was isolated from his gang and confronted with a prison term. You tore a gang down one man at a time. These were lessons he would carry with him into the Hatfield-McCoy feud.[12]

Chapter 11

~

A Double Whipping

1886

By 1885, so much valuable timber was flowing down the Big Sandy to the sawmills at Catlettsburg and so much related trade was being conducted there that the stockholders of its bank—the Catlettsburg National Bank—decided on a massive expansion. Even the great floods of 1883 and 1884, which laid waste to the city and required three months of cleanup and rebuilding each—the latter having wiped out three-quarters of the town—had not dampened the spirit of enterprise in the Gate City, as it was known. The town of three thousand people was well acquainted with devastation, which is perhaps why it now boasted seven churches, with another in the works. There had been other floods, in 1847 and 1875, and the business district had burned to the ground in 1878, requiring six months to rebuild it in Cincinnati brick. Another fire, in 1884, had burned a grocery store and several dry-goods wholesalers, killing four men. But construction materials flowed freely down the Ohio and the Big Sandy to the town, and its citizens put them to good use.

By 1886, the town's timber business was worth more than a million dollars. Catlettsburg mills sawed and planed the logs into lumber, or timber traders dispatched the whole logs downstream to other markets. To keep up with the volume, steam-powered towboats were employed to drag the logs downriver.

Indeed, Catlettsburg was one of the busiest timber centers in the world, and its prospering bank duly erected a new building with stone and brick walls, stained-glass windows, and an ornate roof of the finest Pennsylvania slate, complete with dormers, chimneys, minarets, and spires. The entrance's stone staircase was flanked by large bronze dragons. Inside, behind a carved wooden counter, a massive vault was partly visible, and a slew of bank officers and clerks busily worked at desks and money tables, counting stacks of greenbacks on their way in or out of the bank. The hallway could fit a hundred people. In addition to a boardroom, there were private chambers for discreet transactions. The bank — "equal to the finest buildings for similar purposes in the great cities of the country," according to one local critic — was the pride of not only the town but the entire valley.

Another source of pride for Catlettsburg was its investment of twelve thousand dollars of its ample tax income in a fire engine and hose that were as good as any in the state, complete with a well-drilled team of firemen ready to extinguish any incendiary threat to the Gate City.[1]

Upriver in the Tug Valley, however, the pretensions remained considerably humbler.

SOMETIME IN THE SUMMER OF 1886, twenty-seven-year-old Jeff McCoy, an older brother of Johnse Hatfield's wife, Nancy, shot a man. Not that it surprised anyone. A son of the murdered Harmon, Jeff, like his three brothers, had a quarrelsome streak. Dirt poor, they wore the shame of their undeserved misfortune like a horsehair coat.

Certain families, as Dan Cunningham had divined, were predisposed to violence. The McCoy temper was legendary. Outwardly proud and sensitive to a fault, Jeff seemed to be in a fistfight every few months. (He and all of his siblings, three brothers and two sisters, would play some role in the feud.) A century later, modern science would discover that the family suffers from a rare hereditary condition now known as von Hippel–Lindau disease (or VHL). Those afflicted with it often have tumors on their adrenal glands that cause the excessive production of adrenaline and catecholamines, substances that trigger warrior, or fight-or-flight, reactions. Friends and adversaries alike are subjected to a hair-trigger temper. At times angry at the world, McCoy family members have described their inability to stand any kind of insult, experiencing rage that turns them red in the face and compels them to fight. Other symptoms include a racing heart, splitting headaches, and hand tremors. In the extreme, an individual with VHL can pass out from an overdose of wrath.[2]

This perhaps partly accounts for Randall's coldheartedness to Roseanna, his inability to forget a slight, and his grating habit of harping on any perceived wrong. Tolbert, the instigator of the Election Day brawl, was considered tough and mean. Harmon's son Lark got so angry that his mouth twitched wildly. Once, as his daughter Vicey was leaving the house after an argument, he was in such a state of fury that he shot her with his rifle, knocking her to the ground. When his wife ran off the porch hysterically shouting that he had killed her, he calmly replied that she was not dead. He had purposely shot her in the fat of the thigh.[3]

Proclivities for anger aside, Randall, who turned sixty in the fall of 1885, had plenty of real grief and concerns to keep him crotchety. Half a generation older than Devil Anse — his first child, Josephine, was born in 1848, whereas Devil Anse's Johnse was born fourteen years later — he had, as tradition demanded, parceled out his property to his children as they wed. Jim and Floyd had both been married for more than two decades, and Randall eked out a living timbering and farming on less land than his rival. Tolbert, who had been prospering, was now gone from the picture. His business partner had managed to wrest away the lion's share of their assets. While Sally had slowly recovered from the shocking loss of her sons, eventually Mary refused to leave her bed; she grew weak and died, most said of a broken heart. So now Randall and Sally had Mel and Cora to raise.

There was also a hidden casualty of the Election Day fight: young Bill McCoy. It was now clear to most people that Joe Davis's positive identification of Bud had been wrong. In fact, Bud had fallen on his sword for his younger brother and best friend. The result was that Bill was essentially lost as well. He could not go out in public; if he did, he risked being killed by a Hatfield or arrested for his part in the murder of Ellison. Rumors circulated that Bill had grown increasingly distraught until he had gone mad, that he wandered in the woods, frequently visiting Bud's grave to brood over his death and sleeping outside for days at a time. Finally, it was said, he fell ill, took to his bed, and died without much of a fight. This story, however, might have been a carefully orchestrated fabrication: Decades later, Squirrel Huntin' Sam would reveal a twist in the narrative. "Bill McCoy," he said, was living "now in Mossy Rock, Washington."[4]

If the fate of his children were not enough to make Randall McCoy a little edgy, then the fact that the Hatfields had placed a target on his back should have been. Still, despite being urged by his family and friends to leave Blackberry Creek and move farther from the West Virginia border to create a buffer between him and the Hatfields, he and Sally refused to go. This was the land of their ancestors, and no one was going to drive them out.

At this point, Cap was increasingly guiding the Hatfields regarding the McCoys. Whether this was planned or due to Devil Anse being too preoccupied with conducting his business to think about the McCoys is unclear. Devil Anse, who owned several thousand acres of timberland, was busy becoming one of the richest men on the West Virginia line. His brother Elias, who owned 650 acres of land, was also prospering and taking special care to educate his sons. A few years later, a reporter would call him "for a man of his class . . . very well-to-do" and "devoted to his children." Elias could only shake his head when it came to Anse's sons. "Anse he's got some boys thet's mighty mean," he declared, saying that "Anse can't do nothin' with 'em," but especially singling out Cap, who had been "trouble" from the start.[5]

Threats went back and forth through the grapevine, and even Squirrel Huntin' Sam admitted that the McCoys exacerbated the situation. "McCoys were awful wicked in those days but in after years joined the church and were very modest," he wrote. Still, "McCoys would talk and threaten. Then the news would be carried to the Hatfields. They would talk but not so much."

"News bees . . . can cause a whole lot of trouble," Sam added.[6]

But if the Hatfields talked less, others spoke for them. Rumors persisted that the Hatfields — believing that if they could get rid of Randall, no one would be able to pursue the charges against them — were planning to ambush him again. Since this was in fact their intention, the Hatfields suspected that there was a snitch in the family.

ON A HOT SUMMER NIGHT, at a dance in Pike County, a mail carrier named Fred Wolford called Jeff McCoy a liar. No one now knows what prompted the insult. But Wolford had made the last mistake of his short life. Jeff pulled out a pistol and shot him dead.

The next day, Jeff fled across the Tug into West Virginia. The modest river had continued to serve as a legal iron curtain, stopping law enforcement officers cold on its banks. Decades later, police officers on the Kentucky–Virginia–West Virginia borders would avoid the formalities of legal extradition by surreptitiously shoving fugitives across state lines to waiting counterparts late at night, but at the time, with war bitterness still lingering, cooperation between the states' law officers was virtually nonexistent. Jeff made his way to the house that Nancy, his youngest sister, shared with Johnse Hatfield and asked if he could hide out there. After his

Nancy McCoy. *(Courtesy of Boyd Phillips)*

marriage, Johnse had sworn off involvement in the feud; now he reluctantly consented to take in his wife's fugitive brother.[7]

Others were even less eager than Johnse to have the hot-tempered Jeff McCoy in their midst. The worst trouble would come, not surprisingly, from Cap. Now twenty-two, cocksure, and brash, Cap lived near Johnse and Nancy. He frequently visited their place, and his cynicism and bestial look—long black hair framing his watery eye; a bulldog nose; and dark stubble covering his beefy neck, befitting the pugnacious brute that he was—made Nancy, whose first cousins had been killed at the pawpaw trees, uncomfortable, especially with Jeff in the house. Cap's constant prodding turned her prickly and then angry. Eventually, Johnse had to tell his brother to stay away. He was no longer welcome in their home.[8]

Cap had hired a man named Tom Wallace, who timbered for Devil Anse, to work on his farm and live there too. The two got on well, and Wallace became a lieutenant to Cap in his duties as a Hatfield deputy. Wallace, a dark-haired twenty-five-year-old child of the war with a distinctive shock of white hair, had had a brief and rocky marriage with seventeen-year-old Victoria Daniels, who went by the nickname Victory. It did not take long for the union to go awry. It was said that Wallace was so mean to his wife that she picked up and went home to her parents.[9]

While this splintered marriage was a personal matter, when the Hatfields planned a raid on the McCoys and word of their scheming inexplicably leaked out, all the interfamily ties came under scrutiny. Victory was the daughter of Bill and Mary McCoy Daniels, the latter Harmon's oldest child, the former one of the witnesses to the Hatfields' crossing of the Tug with the three McCoys in tow. For his part, Wallace had been among those present at their execution. At first, some of the family suspected Johnse's wife, Nancy, but circumstances ruled her out. Then suspicion fell on Victory and her mother. According to some, Mary Daniels gossiped too much for her own good, and Victory took after her mother.[10]

Cap and Tom were told to deal with the situation. One night, they led a group of about a dozen men across the Tug. With masks over their faces, they pushed on the door to the Danielses' cabin, knowing that it was not likely to be locked. Not even latched, it silently opened. The whole family lived in a single room, and they were all in bed. The fireplace's evening embers barely lit the room. The surprise was absolute. Bill Daniels opened his eyes and found the muzzle of Wallace's Winchester in his face. Wallace told him to lie still and keep quiet. Cap ordered Mary — at thirty-five already the mother of ten, the youngest of whom was just an infant — and Victory out of bed. The women, wearing only their nightshirts, obeyed, crying and begging for mercy. According to a later report, "Cap laughed in glee."[11]

Cap now brandished a cow tail that he had cut for the raid. Wrapping the tuft around his hand and flourishing it whip-like about his head, he grabbed Mary by the hair, forced her to her knees in front of the fireplace, and began to strike her across the back. She screamed in pain. With the first two blows, the heavy bone end of the tail cracked two of her ribs. Victory and several children added to the din, wailing in fear. Bill Daniels, a gun still on him, groaned and turned his head away from his suffering wife, but Wallace ordered him to turn his head back and watch. Presumably the beating was also meant to be a warning to Daniels to keep his mouth shut about what he had seen at the Tug.[12]

Finished with Mary, Cap turned to Victory. But then he took the gun from Wallace and handed him the whip. Wallace proceeded to ferociously beat his former wife. On the mantel, an old clock ticked away the excruciating minutes. The beatings lasted more than forty of them. When they finally ended, both women lay on the floor unconscious — dead, the helpless Daniels believed.

The duo and their henchmen recrossed the river, satisfied that they had sent the intended message: mind your own business. Afterward, Bill Daniels was so humiliated and nervous that he fled and sent word back that he would not return. But Mary's younger brother Jeff, eight years her junior, was steelier. When he heard of the beatings — despite the masks, the identity of the perpetrators was no secret — while hiding out at Johnse and Nancy's, he was outraged by this cowardly act against his sister and niece. In a precarious situation himself and needing the immediate goodwill of Johnse and Devil Anse, Jeff plotted, but waited, to avenge the assault.[13]

~

MEANWHILE DEVIL ANSE was busy solidifying his political alliances. As an ally, he was worth his weight in shooting irons and then some. There was the .32-caliber pistol lodged in his front pocket, the always handy .38 Colt—the gun that settled the West was quite unsettling in the East—as well as the Winchester on his saddle and the dozens more in the hands of his kin and associates that he could command on short notice.[14]

In 1886, a tense election for the state senate divided the Seventh District—which included Logan Courthouse, the nexus of the Logan County Hatfields—into two relatively equal camps. This gave a persuasive leader like Devil Anse considerable clout, since he could decisively affect the outcome of the vote. The contest pitted twenty-seven-year-old Democrat John B. Floyd against Republican Simon B. Altizer.

With deep ties to the Floyd family, especially the candidate's uncle and namesake, General John B. Floyd, under whom he, his brothers, and his father had served in the war, Devil Anse was a staunch supporter of the young John B. Floyd. Floyd, who had studied literature and law at the University of Virginia and represented the county in the house of delegates from 1881 to 1882, would rise to even higher stations. The association would serve Devil Anse well as the feud progressed and took political turns far beyond the hollows of the Tug River: Floyd would defend the Hatfields tooth and nail. Devil Anse, for his part, gave the highborn Floyd grass roots and muscle.[15]

Logan Courthouse, a dusty town of frame houses and small stores around a boxy redbrick courthouse attached to the jail, sat on the banks of the Guyandotte River, which with the spring freshets was effectively a log flume, carrying timber to the mills on the Ohio River. On Election Day, the courthouse square teemed with the partisan citizens of the Seventh District, drinking, socializing, and doing their last-minute lobbying.[16] On this particular Election Day, each side felt confident that it had an ace in the hole. Voting practices were primitive, public, and perfectly transparent. There were no secret ballots: men supporting one candidate would line up on one side of the courthouse steps, and men voting for the other candidate on the other.

Dave Stratton, the oldest son of Major William Stratton, a Confederate cavalry veteran from a prominent Irish family in Logan Courthouse, supported John Floyd's opponent, Simon Altizer. Stratton was known to have a supply of gunmen whenever he needed them. Having heard that Stratton planned to influence the vote by preventing Floyd's side from being called over, Floyd paid a visit to Devil Anse to see if he could rely on him to counteract Stratton's tactics.

On the morning of the election, Stratton showed up at the courthouse with twenty well-armed men and strolled about the streets genially addressing those gathered. Just after noon, he ordered his men to herd the electorate in front of the courthouse steps. While it was early to poll the voters, he was eager to take care of the dirty business at hand. Mounting the steps, he held up his hands, quieting the crowd. He announced that he had a few words to say on behalf of Simon Altizer. He had just gotten started when the drum of hooves shook the ground. From around a bend, a hundred mounted men rode into town behind Devil Anse, all carrying Winchesters and Colts prominently displayed. At the courthouse, they fanned out, circling the crowd of voters.

Floyd could not suppress a smile but quickly smothered it. Stratton scanned the scene of this debacle impassively, then resumed his speech. Concluding, he glared defiantly at Devil Anse and commanded all those voting for Simon Altizer to step forward. Before they could, Devil Anse spurred his horse through the assemblage of men, dismounted onto the steps, and strode up to the Irishman. Words passed between the two. Stratton, cursing, reluctantly stepped aside. In a commanding voice, Devil Anse asked all those in favor of John Floyd to step toward him.

For a moment the body of voters, mesmerized by the tense scene, stared at the two ringmasters and did not move. Much more was at stake than simply electing an official to send to Charleston. These people had to live with one another the next day.

John B. Floyd, West Virginia state senator
and assistant secretary of state.

Devil Anse scanned the crowd. Gently, he repeated: "All those in favor of John B. Floyd come to this side."[17]

The saddle leather of a small army crackled under the weight of ominously shifting men. A voter stepped toward Floyd, breaking the ice. A collective shout of *Floyd!* went up as a clear majority moved to Floyd's side. Devil Anse's lined face broke out in a triumphant grin. Floyd was elected.

That day Dave Stratton became an enemy of the Hatfields for life — though that life would soon be cut short by a head-on collision with progress.

~

ON NOVEMBER 17, hearing that Cap Hatfield was away from home, Jeff McCoy and a friend named Josiah Hurley went to pay a visit on Tom Wallace. They found him at work in the yard. Caught off guard, Wallace looked up from his task into the barrels of two guns. Jeff told Wallace they were taking him to Pikeville to be tried on indictments returned against the assailants of the Daniels women. Wallace, however, suspected that his chances of making it to a jail were slim. For one thing, Jeff himself was wanted for murder in Kentucky. What were the odds that he would go riding up to the jailhouse in Pikeville?[18]

Expecting no mercy at the hands of the man whose sister and niece he had nearly beaten to death, Wallace looked for an opportunity to make a break for it. When his captors momentarily relaxed their guard, he dashed into the woods. Jeff and Hurley promptly opened fire on his backside, but Wallace was moving fast and was only grazed by a bullet in the hip. He made it to Cap's house. Cap's wife, Nan, who was seriously ill, was lying in bed, where she had been for almost a month. Her indisposition was a lucky break for Jeff and Hurley, because Nan was not only more educated than Cap — she was teaching him how to read, something that would later transform his life — but also a better rider and, more to the point in this instance, a better shot, able to knock a bird out of the sky with a rifle. But she was too weak at the present moment to do anything except hide under the covers.

Wallace barricaded the door. From the window, he opened fire on his pursuers, and they shot back at him. Though they were unable to hit Wallace, who was protected by the cabin's thick walls, they seemed to take pleasure in shooting up the place and heavily peppered the doors and windows with lead.[19]

When Cap returned and saw the damage to his cabin, he was furious. He immediately went with Wallace to a justice of the peace to swear out warrants against Jeff McCoy and Josiah Hurley. Cap secured himself an appointment as special constable, took the papers, and, despite the fact that Jeff and Hurley were certainly heavily armed and on the alert for a reprisal, went alone in search of the pair. He soon found them together and trained his rifle on them before they could react. He disarmed them both and, directing them with his weapon, set out for Logan Courthouse.

On the way, Wallace fell in with them. After arriving in

Thacker, a small village where Thacker Creek spills into a bend in the Tug, they stopped for Cap to get a drink at Shanghai Will Ferrell's house. While Cap talked to Shang, Jeff slipped free from the rope that bound his hands to the horn of Wallace's saddle. He leaped over a low fence and dove from the eight-foot bank into the Tug.[20]

As he pulled himself across the forty feet of current, lead piffed the river surface, sometimes penetrating next to him, other times ricocheting off the water. Just as he approached the safety of the Kentucky shore, he was hit by a bullet in the left arm. He emerged from the reeds beside the river and rolled behind the only available cover, a sorry bush. The steep, naked bank presented a challenge: he would be fully exposed as he climbed it. But he had no time to come up with another plan.

Cap and Wallace kept up their fire, gauging the fall of the lead across the water and homing in on him. Plunging back into the water and scrambling downriver to a nearby stand of beech trees would have been a better decision, but Jeff, a man of the mountains, clung to the earth. Timing the shots, he suddenly sprang, clawing his way up the bank.

Cap nailed him halfway up the slope.[21]

WORD SPREAD THROUGH THE VALLEY that Cap and Wallace had intentionally allowed Jeff to escape so that they could gun him down. Cap denied it, and no one could prove it either way. In any case, another McCoy had been killed by another Hatfield, the son of a Union soldier murdered by the son of a Confederate. Like father, like son.

Later, Randall prevailed upon Perry Cline, who was both Jeff's uncle and a relative by marriage of the Danielses—his sister was married to Bill's brother—to try to contact Devil Anse. Cline sent more than one letter to his old nemesis. Responding was not easy for Devil Anse, as he could neither read nor write. What Cline said in his letters is now lost to history, but Anse's response is not. On December 26, perhaps caught up in the holiday spirit or taking advantage of a family gathering, Devil Anse dictated his reply to Nan: "We are all very sorry that the Troubles occored but under Somewhat aggravated circumstances it happened," he said. "But I Know And solemly affirm that if such could have been prevented by me I would have stoped the Troubles." He went on to explain the circumstances and claimed that it was Wallace, not Cap, who shot Jeff. He included a statement from Shang Ferrell, who said that when Jeff bolted, "Cap was off conversing with me some 40 or 50 yds and I never seen Cap Hatfield fire a single shot."

Concluding the letter, Devil Anse said that none of the Hatfields bore any "animosity" toward any of Jeff McCoy's relatives, and he trusted they would let the matter drop. Yet he could not help but shift the blame back on the McCoys: "Perry, the very Bottom of this crime is nothing more nor less than Mary Daniels and Her girls: now Bill is gone. And says he wont come back. No person is going to Trouble him. Let him come back." He signed off twice: "Your friend" the first time — though certainly that was something of a stretch — and "Very Respectfully" the second.[22]

Though the embittered Randall had proved to be ineffectual in countering the more powerful Hatfields, he had made at least one right play. Cline, who moved in higher circles of power and politics than he and did not mind getting his hands dirty, now became the McCoy spokesman and began to direct their efforts in the feud. He was about to demonstrate to Devil Anse just how little he valued both his respect and his friendship.

Chapter 12

~

The Enforcers

Spring, Summer, and Fall 1887

Tall and stoop-shouldered, a country lawyer with pale skin and a thick, dark beard who sported a high hat and a frock coat, a Union man for law and order, Perry Cline bore an obvious resemblance to the greatest man of his day—Honest Abe. Having served briefly as a Union soldier, he was now a well-respected deputy sheriff, deputy jailer, member of the Pikeville courthouse committee and board of supervisors, and a former county school commissioner and building commissioner. The *Louisville Courier-Journal* would describe him as having a "very intelligent, gentlemanly bearing... and an appearance of firmness." The reporter concluded, "He probably knows what he is about." A later Hatfield would accuse Cline of trying to cultivate a Lincolnian image "in dress, speech, and mannerisms" for his own benefit and of trying to capitalize on the feud. "Cline understood that if he took up the cudgels for Randall McCoy, his name would be on everybody's lips," historian G. Elliott Hatfield reasoned. "So, with a couple of razorback pigs as a retainer fee, he bent to the task."[1]

The thirty-eight-year-old Cline was indeed a clever man. Unlike Lincoln, he was a Democrat—a proactive Democrat in a Democratic state—and he would use his affiliation to his advantage. At times, his broad involvement in the prosecution of the feudists

Pikeville attorney Perry Cline. *(Big Sandy Heritage Center)*

would call into question his methods and motives. However, he did not work for either razorbacks or sawbucks alone. He had a number of deep-seated and valid reasons for involving himself in the Hatfield-McCoy feud.

Cline had been born into a wealthy family in Logan County in 1849. However, the silver spoon had been yanked from his mouth at an early age. Cline's father, Jacob, sometimes called Rich Jake, had died when Perry was a boy. With his brother Jake Jr., he had inherited five thousand acres of prime West Virginia timberland, property that had been passed down through the generations from Cecil Cline, an early settler in the area.

It was Cline's misfortune that at the beginning of the war, Devil Anse had become his immediate neighbor and possibly, though records are unclear, a renter on Cline's land. Cline lost three brothers-in-law, including Harmon McCoy, and many other relatives and friends fighting for the Union; Devil Anse's war depredations were a wedge between them that would grow as the years passed and the violence between their families increased. After the war, Cline, who had grown up along Grapevine Creek in what was then Virginia, faced an uphill battle to keep the land that was his birthright. In 1868, he had become a ward of Colonel John Dils, the staunch Unionist and regiment organizer who was a bitter enemy of Devil Anse and other West Virginia border fighters.

And then in 1872 came Devil Anse's notorious claim that Cline had cleared timber off his land with the result that Cline was forced to sign over to Devil Anse his property, including his family's Old Home Place. In 1887, with the imminent arrival of the railroads, the value of that tract of land was mounting. It is small wonder that Cline welcomed an opportunity to make Devil Anse regret his actions.

Cline was the lawyer whose assistance Randall had sought when his three sons were being held by the Hatfields. So far, the law officers of Pike and Logan counties had demonstrated that they were not up to the task of curbing the Hatfields' aggression. Cap's merciless beating of Cline's niece and her daughter and murder of his nephew within the past year were confirmation of that fact.[2]

The failure of the legal system in Kentucky was not just a Pike County problem. Kentucky's lone state prison, a cramped 780-cell facility in Frankfort dating back to 1798, was so insufficient that prison sentences were regularly truncated. Nearly all of the inmates suffered from scurvy, pneumonia, or some other disease. Appalled by these miserable conditions, the previous governor, Democrat Luke Blackburn, a doctor who had served as a yellow fever expert during the war, had overhauled the prison system and orchestrated the building of a new facility in Eddyville, but it would not open until 1889. In the meantime, he had pardoned more than a thousand inmates, earning himself the nickname "Lenient Luke" and jeers at the 1883 Democratic nominating convention. Through the 1890s, convicted murderers would serve an average of fewer than eight years of their sentences.[3]

In the final year of his term, the current governor, Proctor Knott, Blackburn's successor and also a Democrat, had also taken full advantage of his power to pardon, both to alleviate the strain on the Frankfort prison and to curry favor with certain voters. None-theless, Perry Cline set about trying to procure rewards for the arrests of the men indicted for the murders of the three McCoy brothers. Knott, whose four-year term had been plagued by law-lessness and feuds in eastern Kentucky and particularly by a violent two-year feud in Rowan County, came through, though with a somewhat tepid hundred dollars per head.[4]

It was not much, but Cline had thrown his first punch.

He immediately set to work on his next, and it would be accom-panied by a flurry that would change the complexion of the fight. The politically deft Cline began campaigning for Simon Bolivar Buckner — never mind that he was a Confederate veteran — to be the next governor of Kentucky. He was well aware that if he could help deliver Pike County to Buckner, he would have political capi-tal to spend, and he knew just what he would spend it on.

IN THE NEAR TERM, the sons of Harmon McCoy were not willing to allow the beatings of their sister and niece and the murder of their brother to go unavenged. Venturing into Cap's realm was too risky, but that spring, they heard that Tom Wallace was working on the railroad extension along the Big Sandy, and they recognized an opportunity. Bud and Jake managed to get the drop on Wallace on their first foray and delivered him to the county jail in Pikeville.

Wallace was placed in a cell with a friend named Charlie Mitch-ell. One morning, Perry Cline's son John Sinclair, better known as Sink, an eighteen-year-old deputy sheriff who had graduated from a military school and was studying to be an attorney, brought in breakfast. One of the two cellmates grabbed the coffeepot and hit him on the head. Sink sank. The pair opened the other cells and let out all of the prisoners, including one John C. McCoy, who was accused of a stabbing unrelated to the feud. Wallace, who had been in jail less than a month, and Mitchell fled toward the West Virginia line and eventually managed to wade across the Tug.[5]

Wallace went straight to Cap for help. Cap gave him a horse and enough cash to get out of the valley. Wallace rode east into Virginia, where he disappeared into the Blue Ridge Mountains. Though it seemed unlikely that they would find Wallace again now that he knew they were after him, Jake, Lark, and Bud McCoy offered a reward for his recapture.

A drifter who needed to earn his keep, Wallace could not simply lie low. Authorities in Virginia soon arrested him for selling moonshine. While this was a minor offense and a nuisance that Devil Anse and Johnse dealt with on a regular basis, for the fugitive Wallace, it would have serious repercussions. His punishment was a fine, but the fine was reported in newspapers, and interested parties in Kentucky took notice.

It was not long before two bounty hunters came riding into Pike County to claim the reward on Wallace's head. They did not have Wallace with them, but they had evidence of his capture: a bloody scalp with that telltale shock of white hair. This evidence was deemed sufficient.

One of those two bounty hunters, as the story goes, was Dan Cunningham.[6]

~

ON A WARM DAY IN JUNE ten years after Nathan Cunningham was gunned down by the Consolidated Band, a man rode into the fledgling town of Kentuck, West Virginia, about eight miles north of Charleston, the state capital. He wore a plain black suit, a linen shirt, and a black tie. He looked to be an itinerant preacher. By necessity the people of the remotest parts of the southern Appalachians had a tradition of "funeralizin'" their dead well after the fact. Since a parlor or porch usually served as the mortuary, families buried their deceased as soon as possible, but, with men of the cloth few and far between, they often had to await the arrival of just such an itinerant or circuit preacher for a proper service to be held. The wait also allowed for the consideration of weather and crops and for word to be passed to friends and relatives. It was not unusual for a funeral to take place on the anniversary of the death, but a decade later was stretching it a bit.[7]

A local greeted the black-suited stranger with deference and then studied the strapping six-footer with his powerful build, no-nonsense look, and bit of a slouch. His manner changed abruptly. This was no preacher. "Lookin' fer a school, Dan?" he sneered. "Old trouble all fergot, eh?"

Back in the heart of what had regrettably become Skean, Counts, and Kiser country for the first time in a long time, Cunningham sat impassively on his mount. An observer would never have known from his demeanor that the local's clan had ruined his father, killed his brother, and run him off his ancestral land, or that he had returned after a decade of preparation to give his brother a proper funeral. He would have no way of knowing that Cunningham's life was now dedicated to exacting justice, or vengeance if that was what you wanted to call it.

But this was not a man worthy of Cunningham's ire. "I haven't forgotten," he replied. Cunningham was no longer simply a teacher either. Lawlessness was all around. Gangs of outlaws were a plague. Nearby, the Kelly Gang—a dozen men from West Virginia, Kentucky, and Ohio—had started a crime spree in the summer of 1886, crossing all three states' borders to rob, murder, and steal and to avoid capture. Cunningham, who now worked for Charleston-based private detective Alpheus Wick "Alf" Burnett's agency, Eureka Detectives, was determined to fight such public enemies. "Nathan is still dead," he said calmly but ominously. "Tell your gang that."[8]

Teaming up with Burnett, one of the leading private detectives of his day, had been pivotal for Cunningham. Burnett, the son of an Irish immigrant from County Tyrone and his New Jersey–born wife, was then thirty-seven, the same age as Cunningham. Slight of

stature, he had learned to fight by necessity. He was college educated, quick of body and mind, and he feared no one. A peace-
loving man, who opposed quarreling, he had nearly entered the
ministry in the Methodist Episcopal Church in Pennsylvania but
instead began an itinerant career as a schoolteacher, bookkeeper,
merchant, editor, and publisher. In 1876, he moved to Charleston
and left the newspaper business to work for the U.S. Revenue Service before going into private practice, attracting such men as Cunningham to his successful law-enforcement operation.[9]

A FEW DAYS AFTER HIS return to Jackson County, on a Sunday evening, Cunningham found what he was looking for — trouble.

As he was riding home through the woods, he heard voices coming from a deep ravine. Smelling smoke too, he dismounted and
crept up to the site. Through the trees, he saw a large still and a
scene of gross debauchery. Working the still was Winfield Scott
Kiser, an albino, distinctive even at a distance. Recently released
from prison for bootlegging, Kiser was already at it again. Around
him, a number of men and women engaged in a drunken orgy. In
his diary, Cunningham would later observe: "Hell's headquarters is
sure in Jackson County." He backed away, climbed up on his horse,
and departed.[10]

Armed with a warrant for Kiser's arrest and a mandate to perform special work for the federal prosecutor, Cunningham and his
twenty-six-year-old nephew Robert Duff later returned to the still.
They arrested Kiser, impounded the distilling equipment, and held
them both until the deputy marshal arrived.[11]

Duff had already enraged the Consolidated Band by taking part
in Kiser's previous arrest, through the deputy U.S. marshal in Parkersburg. Now he was a doubly marked man. So was his uncle. But
Cunningham knew it would be this way because he meant to bring
the gang, whose members had been "against the Flag in time of war"
and "violators of the law since," to its knees.[12]

With Kiser in a Charleston jail cell awaiting trial, about thirty men of the Band met in secrecy at a schoolhouse and argued over how best to derail his return to prison. Wade Counts proposed that they kill the men pressing charges against Kiser. All the Skeans and Countses voted in favor of the idea, but the proposal fell short by two votes. Instead, they decided to try intimidation first. Cunningham, whose family still had allies in the area, had an inside source who slipped through the woods the next day to tell him of his narrow reprieve.

Then came the Band's threat, delivered anonymously: Cunningham and the brothers Robert and George Duff must leave the county within one week, or they would be killed.

~

ON AUGUST 30, 1887, the state of Kentucky inaugurated as governor the former Confederate general Simon Bolivar Buckner, a man whose most notorious act during the war was becoming the first Confederate general to surrender an army. Afterward, he sat in a Union prison cell writing poetry until he was exchanged and promoted, at which point he took part in the failed Confederate invasion of Kentucky.

Following the war, however, Buckner, a West Point graduate with a flamboyant handlebar mustache, became a business and political force. As governor, he would be known for wielding his veto power against special interests and for combating lawlessness and feuding in eastern Kentucky, where, in addition to the Hatfield-McCoy conflict, power struggles raged in Harlan, Letcher, Perry, Knott, and Breathitt counties.[13]

After Cline delivered his corner of the state to the governor, he moved swiftly to reap his reward. It soon became clear to the Hatfields that Cline meant to cause them serious trouble. In response, the day before Buckner's inauguration, Cline received a threatening letter. The writer identified himself as Nat Hatfield and gave his location as the Logan County Courthouse. "We have been told by men from your county that you and your men are fixing to invade this county for the purpose of taking the Hatfield boys," wrote the fictional family member, "and now, sir, we, forty-nine in number at present, do notify you that if you come into this county to take or bother any of the Hatfields, we will follow you to hell or take your hide."

The writer warned Cline that the Hatfields were "the men who regulated matters at this place a short time ago" (a reference to the war), and they could get as many more men as they needed in six hours. "If you don't keep your hands off our men, there is not one of you will be left in six months," he wrote. "Our hangman tied a knot for you and laid it quietly away until we see what you do."[14]

Like Dan Cunningham, Cline was not inclined to be cowed by threats. On September 6, at his request, the Pike County Court clerk made copies of the murder indictments against the Hatfields and their allies. With those in hand, Cline set out for Frankfort, 150 miles away, in the company of county attorney Lee Ferguson and Deputy Sheriff Bad Frank Phillips, a friend of Cline's, to ask Governor Buckner to increase the reward for the wanted men to a level where it would be taken seriously and to formally requisition them from the governor of West Virginia. Cline's efforts had immediate and tangible results.

On September 10, Buckner officially requested that West Virginia governor Willis Wilson extradite the indicted Anse Hatfield and his followers to Kentucky for the murder of the three McCoy brothers. Furthermore, by the time Cline left Frankfort, not only Devil Anse, but also Johnse, Cap, and Guerilla Mitchell had substantial rewards on their heads.[15] All a man had to do was catch one of them and deliver him to the Pike County jail to find himself five hundred dollars the richer.

At Cline's request, Buckner appointed Frank Phillips to receive the prisoners. This was perhaps Cline's most clever move. Burned before by the legal system and now entrenched in it himself as an attorney, jailer, and police officer, Cline well knew the vagaries of the legal process and the influence that sheriffs, politicians, and

Bad Frank Phillips. *(Courtesy of Boyd Phillips)*

other interested parties held over it in these parts. As crooked poker was the norm, he knew better than to put all his cards on the table. He also knew that leverage could be brought to bear in a number of ways. Despite some obvious flaws, Bad Frank was driven, single-minded, and fearless. He possessed the heedless and quick-witted nature so crucial to a bounty hunter. Best of all, he was loyal to Cline.

Perry Cline had introduced a forceful new catalyst to the feud, the counterpunch to Devil Anse's haymaker that Randall had lacked.

~

In October 1887, Dan Cunningham was lynched after robbing and murdering a preacher. Or at least, that's what the October 19 *New York Times* reported. It was an act of vigilante justice, the newspaper said. The mention was brief — and spurious.

True, Cunningham had refused to heed the Band's warnings to leave the county, and a hit team had ambushed him. When their bullets inexplicably did not strike him, he came to believe that he was being watched over by God. And while his opponents did not articulate their feelings, their response spoke more profoundly than words: In the face of this one determined vigilante, the usually mule-stubborn ring of outlaws decided to hightail it. They retracted their operations out of his county—Jackson—and moved east into even more remote Roane County. But this would not rid them of him any more than a false report of his lynching would.

That same month he went into Kentuck on business pertaining to Nathan's funeral, which was to be preached the following Sunday. Before he left, he put feed in the stable for the horse of an expected visitor. He then rode west two miles to Kentuck and stayed there until after nine thirty. The distance from Kentuck to Countsville was twelve miles. These were important facts, because he would be accused of murder in Countsville.[16]

Cunningham belonged to the Methodist Episcopal Church, and he had engaged the Countsville minister Thomas Perry Ryan—known to all as Father Ryan—to perform the overdue service on October 16. At ten o'clock on the night of October 13, however, Father Ryan, a fifty-three-year-old husband, father, and community stalwart, was shot in his bedroom. Frank Skean, a brother of Joe Skean, had ordered the murder because Ryan—a Republican Unionist—opposed them. The bullet that killed Ryan was fired from the outside and passed through the wall of the house, through the footboard of the bed, through Ryan's bowels, and through the headboard before lodging in the ceiling. As he lay dying, Father Ryan told his family that he had heard a voice outside that sounded like that of a man named Perry Drake.[17]

The rest of the Ryan family did not leave the house to deliver the news of his death until the next morning. There was no message sent, no telegram, no other way for the news to spread, but at dawn that morning, Frank Skean and the Consolidated Band's Kentuck faction set out for Countsville, ready to take action concerning the murder. Other members of the gang coming from Jeffreys, twenty miles from Ryan's house, had set out even earlier. The only way they could have known of Ryan's death was if they were involved in the plot. Skean and the other leaders met at a store on the county line.

That morning, Alf Burnett found a .38 shell under Ryan's window and determined that he had been shot with a Winchester rifle. In the afternoon, the Band started after the Duff brothers, who were both teachers when not serving the law, and Ches Coon, all allies of Cunningham who had helped bust up the Band's stills and make arrests. They found Robert Duff at work in the small cottage he shared with his wife. Those stalking him were illiterate and contemptuous of his learning. They easily overpowered and bound him and then ransacked his home. Next they set out to get his younger

Alf Burnett, founder of the Eureka Detectives in Charleston, West Virginia.

brother at their parents' house near Kentuck. Frank Skean's son Bill and twenty men silently ringed the house. George, twenty-two, was reading with his friend Coon, a Texan, when the gang fired a volley through the windows.[18]

George ran to the door. Bill Skean and another man stood there with their rifles raised. Without warning, they fired again. Hit in the stomach and knocked down, George rose and staggered to get his revolver. He and Coon fought the gang, wounding several, including Skean, but they were badly outnumbered and outgunned. Spilling blood from his wound, George soon passed out, fell to the floor, and writhed in death. Coon surrendered, and the gang bound him and took him to Peter Skean's, where they had also taken Robert. More members of the Band arrived, one conveying ropes, and they told the two they intended to hang them for the murder of Father Ryan.

The next morning, the county coroner was summoned to the scene of Ryan's murder. A jury of six men held an inquest over the body. Mrs. Ryan and her son Tom said they did not see anyone and that Ryan told them he heard a voice that sounded like Perry Drake's. The names of Robert and George Duff and Ches Coon never came up. Tom swore out a warrant for Perry Drake, accusing him of the crime under oath, based on his father's last words. But the Ryans would soon about-face.

That day, after the inquest, the Band, including the Skean and Counts boys, arrived at the Ryans' with Duff and Coon. Roane County prosecutor John Vandale, who had marital ties to the Band, saw the prisoners but made no effort to protect them. Arrested on the warrant sworn out by Tom Ryan, Perry Drake and a man named Frank Shamblin were soon ushered into the house. The gang took the four prisoners west to a fork of the Poca River. There, they separated. A fugitive from the state of Virginia named Zack Hubbard and half the men took Duff to one safe house. The constable Squire Gibson and the rest of the men led the other three to another half a mile away. The Lynn Camp schoolhouse stood in between the two. At dusk, using the password *blackboard,* the gang reassembled at the schoolhouse. However, a number of citizens unaffiliated with the Band had learned the password and used it to get in. There, they heard the gang deliberate the fate of the prisoners. Cain Counts, who had set fire to Nathan Cunningham's stables and provided an alibi for his brother Wade when he was arrested for Nathan's murder, argued that they should execute Duff and Coon. In the end, they voted to free Shamblin and Drake, who was married to a Kiser, and to hang Duff and Coon. Ches Coon's own uncle Ben Coon, a scofflaw who had been in and out of jail most of his life and who was so belligerent that he had been left by four wives, agreed to lead the killing.

A mob went and got Coon and dragged him down the creek to the schoolhouse. Drunk and eager for sport, they hanged him from an ironwood tree so that his toes just touched the ground. While he struggled at a losing cause, they hooted encouragement, wagered on his longevity, and guffawed.

Another group of men tramped off to the other house. Duff's wife had showed up, and he was consoling her. Ben Coon and Wade Counts tore him from her grasp, and the pack, which included Cain Counts, many Skeans — among them Dick, Peter, Pop, and Bill, the last having recovered from his bullet wound — and several Kisers, dragged him to the schoolhouse. On the way, one of the Kisers stabbed Duff in the stomach. Outside the schoolhouse, Duff coughed up his last words: "You're killing an innocent man." Wade and Cain Counts pulled his head back and slit his throat. Duff's blood spewed so horrifically in their brother Si's face that he passed out.

The next morning, Sunday, October 16, John Vandale inspected Lynn Camp and saw Coon still hanging from the tree and Duff lying in the road in a pool of blood. Several of the killers met Vandale and impaneled their own jury for a sham inquest, which determined that a mob of "unknown persons" had killed Duff and Coon.

The gang claimed that Coon had confessed before dying and had implicated Drake as a principal in Ryan's murder and Cunningham as the mastermind behind it.

That day, Nathan's funeral sermon was supposed to have been preached over his grave. Instead, Cunningham grieved for his brave nephews, the Texan, and the minister for whose murder he was being framed. The Band, meanwhile, attended their church and gloated that Nathan Cunningham's funeral would never be preached by Father Ryan.

With the help of Si Counts's testimony, the county prosecutor obtained an indictment against Dan Cunningham and Perry Drake. As the Band mobilized to hunt them down, Cunningham got wind of it and fled to Charleston, where he could be protected by the Eureka agency. But that was hardly the end of it. An escaped convict from Ohio, a horse thief posing as a detective named Wells, convinced Tom Ryan to swear out warrants for Alf Burnett and his partner William Baldwin (later the famous railroad detective) as accessories to the murder of his father. Ryan, whom Dan now deemed a "willing tool in the hands of the murderers," also swore out a warrant for him.

KEEPING UP THE PRESSURE ON Cunningham, the Band ransacked the home of his wealthy cousin Isaiah Cunningham; harassed Sam Tolley, who was married to a Cunningham; and threatened to exterminate the Cunningham family altogether. But even after Band members secured the warrants for Dan's arrest, they never dared to cross the Kanawha County line to track him down. "Nor," he said, "did they try to serve the warrant when Alf Burnett was with me in Jackson County or even when I was alone."

In fact, these warrants had no merit, but the Band hoped to use them as a bargaining chip. Vandale offered up a face-saving deal, informing Cunningham that if he would stay out of Roane County, the case would be "nolled," or dropped. Cunningham responded that when it was time for the trial, he would be there. He would come with plenty of protection, too, to keep from being ambushed.

The savvy Burnett knew how to solve one problem: he advised Ohio officials of the whereabouts of Wells, who was recaptured and returned to prison in Ohio. Eureka detectives also learned that there was only one Winchester in the area, and it belonged to Si Counts. The gun quickly disappeared, though; Vandale sent it to John Hammons, a party to Nathan's murder, to be hidden. Burnett and Cunningham knew that ultimately they were fighting a no-win battle in Jackson and Roane counties. They decided that for the time being, they would leave the Band to stew in its own juices.[9]

Chapter 13

~

Diplomacy Failed

Fall and Winter 1887

Like the other men in this true story, Bad Frank Phillips was complex, a fact that might not need to be stated if it were not for history's tendency to simplify and turn flesh-and-blood men into "good guys" and "bad guys." So was his mentor Colonel Dils, who, despite a shocking fall from grace during the war, showed great benevolence to war orphans and freed slaves after it. Even Cap Hatfield, the most universally demonized of the feudists, a pathological killer by some accounts, eventually spurned violence to study law and then start a legal practice.[1]

The Pike County election following Bad Frank's appointment as a deputy sheriff happened to be one of particular interest to the Hatfields, and they sent word to him to stay away or, failing that, to come unarmed and without warrants. Otherwise, they warned, they would kill him. This proved to be a gross underestimation of Bad Frank's character.

His looks were deceiving: "Instead of being the rough, bearded fellow, whose picture imaginative newspapers have printed," James Creelman later wrote in the *New York Herald,* "I found a graceful youth whose face was more like that of an Indian girl than that of a Kentucky border fighter. His eyes are large, soft and expressive, and he blushed when talking about himself. There is no hair on his face, save a faint or dark down on his upper lip."[2]

Appearances aside, Bad Frank was a rat terrier of a man. Though small, he was known to be tough and extremely courageous. He would become one of the Hatfields' worst enemies, so ruthless that he was feared by even the McCoys, whose side he was on. Although he came from an old and respected Pike County family, he had been born in the upheaval of war, in July 1861, and his temperament forever bore the scars. His father, Billy, had been pressed into service as a mountain guide for Rebel Bill Smith, but as soon as he could, he fled from the Confederates and joined his brothers John and Frank in Company H of Colonel Dils's Thirty-Ninth Kentucky Mounted Infantry. Within two months, he was captured. After being marched to Richmond in early 1864, he contracted smallpox in the infamous Belle Isle prison and died. Frank's mother never recovered from her grief and passed away shortly after the war. Frank—like Perry Cline—became a ward of Colonel Dils.[3]

Dils, however, was an imperfect mentor, still shaking off his stunning and public disgrace during the war. Within fifteen months of having formed the Thirty-Ninth Kentucky Mounted Infantry regiment, he had apparently cracked under the stress of military life. A married man, civic leader, and business paragon, Dils, whose wife had spent several months working to gain his release from a Richmond prison at the beginning of the war, openly and lasciviously consorted with a prostitute in camp, even in the company of his officers' wives. His administration of the regiment had been equally unruly. He flouted the regulations for handling confiscated war matériel and was accused of pocketing the proceeds from the sale of nine hundred horses taken from the farms of Southern sympathizers. Widely denounced by his men, he was dishonorably discharged from service by U.S. secretary of war Edwin Stanton.[4]

Dils apparently had his influence on Phillips, who became a drinker and a womanizer. Like Dils, Phillips had two sides. Some called him "cautious, circumspect and shrewd." He was a friend of the unfailingly respectable Cline. Others swore he was a bully who had no qualms about stopping innocent men on the road and making them dance by shooting his pistol at their feet, a stunt that set him howling with laughter.

In 1878, at the age of seventeen, he had married a first cousin, Matilda Phillips, but the marriage was quickly annulled. In 1883, he wed Mary Rowe, with whom he had a number of children, though fidelity, like sobriety, was not his strong suit.

Phillips was not "your ordinary deputy," Kentucky adjutant general Sam Hill allowed. According to Hill, he was a "handsome little fellow, with piercing black eyes, ruddy cheeks and a pleasant expression," but he was a "mighty unpleasant man to project with."[5]

As for the 1887 Pike County election, Phillips let the Hatfields know that his official business demanded that he be there and that he would certainly bring along those bench warrants. If the Hatfields came, he boldly warned, he would either catch or kill them.

During the election, some of the Hatfields approached within gunshot range and fired a volley up through the brush, stampeding the crowd of people gathered around. Uninjured and undeterred, Phillips stayed at the polls until late in the evening but did not feel that circumstances were ideal to try to arrest the Hatfield men. He would wait.

ON SEPTEMBER 10, spurred on by Cline, Governor Buckner officially requisitioned West Virginia governor Willis Wilson to arrest and surrender Anse Hatfield and his followers to Kentucky to be tried for the murder of the McCoy brothers. Three weeks later, Wilson's response reached Buckner. The requisition was denied pending an affidavit, which, the letter explained, was required by state statutes.[6]

On October 13, Buckner sent the requisition again, this time accompanied by the required affidavit. However, by now the Hat-

PROCLAMATION BY THE GOVERNOR.

$500 — REWARD.

COMMONWEALTH OF KENTUCKY,

EXECUTIVE DEPARTMENT.

Whereas, It has been made known to me that by *Tobias Wagner County Judge of Pike County that Anderson Hatfield stands charged in said County with the Crime of murder*

and is now a fugitive from justice going at large; and the said Judge having recommended that a reward be offered for the apprehension of said fugitive;

Now, therefore, I, S. B. BUCKNER, Governor of the Commonwealth aforesaid, do hereby offer a reward of Five Hundred Dollars *for the apprehension of* Said *Anderson Hatfield*

and his *delivery to the Jailer of* Pike *county*

IN TESTIMONY WHEREOF, I have hereunto set my hand, and caused the Seal of the Commonwealth to be affixed. Done at Frankfort, the 10 *day of* September *in the year of our Lord one thousand eight hundred and eighty-* Seven *and in the ninety-* Sixth *year of the Commonwealth.*

S. B. Buckner.

BY THE GOVERNOR

Geo. M. Adams

Secretary of State.

By _____

Assistant Secretary of State.

DESCRIPTION.

An 1887 bounty for Devil Anse, signed by Kentucky governor Simon B. Buckner. *(West Virginia and Regional History Collection, West Virginia University Libraries)*

fields and their supporters had deluged Wilson with letters urging him to reject Kentucky's demands. The governor realized that sending the Hatfields to trial in Kentucky had little political upside for him in his home state and could potentially be disastrous for him as well as his political party.

The Hatfields had a significant political ally of their own. John B. Floyd, a former state senator (thanks in part to Devil Anse) and now the acting assistant secretary of state, intended to run for governor. Floyd's roots were in Logan County, and he would need to carry the district to gain his party's nomination. When he heard of the application to Governor Wilson, he sent word to the Hatfields urging them to produce a petition declaring that they were peaceful mountain farmers who had been oppressed and abused by the relatives of a Kentucky villain, Randolph McCoy, and begging the governor not to capitulate to Kentucky.

Devil Anse heeded Floyd's advice. "The Hatfield Regulators rode up and down the creeks and branches of half of Logan County, carrying their repeating rifles and the petition," reported John Spears in the *New York Sun*. "Every man met signed the petition."

The stage was now set for a stalemate of epic proportions, with Kentucky demanding justice, West Virginia demanding protection from outside authorities, and lawyers and politicians working the middle, often for their own self-interest. The bluff and irritable Buckner, warmly called "the old warhorse" by his officers during the war for his authoritarian streak, responded irritably, ratcheting up the tension as an increasingly vitriolic correspondence careened back and forth between the state capitals.[7] Days and then weeks passed, and West Virginia authorities made no effort to arrest the wanted men and deliver them to Kentucky authorities.

By early November, Perry Cline could contain himself no longer. On the fifth, he drafted a letter to Governor Wilson — an act that later, in court, would be cast as impertinent and inappropriate, a breach of protocol and a usurpation of power. "Several days ago I had the required affidavid made out and sent with the requision for the Hatfields," Cline wrote, with deference. "Will your excellency be so kind as to inform as to the status of the case?" Having heard about the petition and that the Hatfields had hired lawyers to lobby against warrants being issued, he went on to plead his case. The petition was meaningless, he explained, because the Hatfields could "make the people sign any kind of petition they want." He grew up near them and knew them personally: "They are the worst band of meroders ever existed in the mountains, and have been in arms since the war; they will not live as citizens ought to; they stand indicted in the county in 4 bad cases of murder."

Cline complained that Pike County could not hold elections without the Hatfields showing up to sell moonshine and running voters away from the polling grounds. He concluded with a statement about the motives of Pike County. "We want peace and want the laws executed, & do not want our citizens butchered up like dogs, as these men is doing. This county . . . wont do any harm to the Hatfields, except to see they get the law."[8]

Wilson did not respond to Cline's letter. Instead, Cline received a reply from West Virginia secretary of state Henry Walker, dated November 21. The requisition had been honored, Walker told Cline, for all of the indicted men except Elias Hatfield and Andy Varney, who had shown evidence that they were not in the area when the killings took place. But there was a catch: Walker informed Cline that warrants for the other eighteen would be issued upon receipt of a fee required by the state, which amounted to fifty-four dollars.[9]

TIRED OF THE DELAYS, Perry Cline encouraged Frank Phillips to apply pressure. Bad Frank traversed the Tug River a week later. The record of the events that followed, including several arrests of the indicted men, is confounding. The actions and missives from multiple parties crossed and tangled with a Shakespearean flourish. No two accounts are exactly alike, and some vary widely.

Bad Frank was a man of action, to the point of being rash. On the night of December 9, he went after Tom Chambers, one of the indicted men. Bad Frank and Randall McCoy's sons Big Jim and

Sam reached Chambers's house at eleven o'clock. The unsuspecting target was in bed. Inside, a coal fire hissed on the hearth. Outside, a bulldog stood guard. Before it could rouse the sleeping inhabitants, the three men quickly dismounted. Sam rushed to the front door. Bad Frank and Big Jim ran around to the back. Big Jim rammed the rear door with his shoulder, knocking it down. Unrestrained, the massive dog ripped into Bad Frank's thigh as an alarmed Chambers came running. With one revolver, Bad Frank shot the dog. With the other, he took aim at Chambers's forehead, stopping him in his tracks.[10]

Bad Frank had gotten his first man — unfortunately, an innocent one: the Tom Chambers that he had arrested was the stepfather of the wanted Tom Chambers. The younger man, born Tom Mitchell, was an illegitimate child, and after Tom Chambers married his mother, he was called variously Chambers or Mitchell but was best known by the nicknames "Guerilla" and "X."

On December 12, Preacher Anse's brother Sheriff Basil Hatfield and Perry Cline, acting as deputy sheriff, locked the innocent Tom Chambers in the Pike County jail. The next day, using Perry Cline's stationery and claiming to be an agent of the governor of Kentucky, which in a general sense he was, Bad Frank wrote to Governor Wilson, enclosing the required fee, fifteen dollars, for warrants for Devil Anse, Johnse, Cap, Dan Whitt, and Albert McCoy (whom he identified as Selkirk's son). "As to Elias Hatfield and Andy Varney," he said, "we do not care for. Did not intend to intercept them." And regarding some of the rest, he noted, "Some . . . is dead and some gon and left the contery."[11]

On December 17, Wilson's office deflected Bad Frank, replying that fees should be sent to the secretary of state. This would prove to be doubly fortuitous for the Hatfields. It not only delayed the process but brought into play their staunch ally John B. Floyd. Bad Frank was out of what little patience he possessed.

Without waiting for the papers that he sought and that he

A mountain still, purported to belong to the McCoys.

A winter portrait of
the Hatfield family.
(*Dr. Coleman
C. Hatfield Collection,
courtesy of Dr. Arabel
E. Hatfield*)

A late-nineteenth-
century flatboat,
or push boat, used
for traveling and
hauling logs on the
Guyandotte River.
(*Courtesy of F. Keith
Davis*)

Doc and Plyant Mahon in later years. (*Courtesy of Wilma Steele*)

Sam Mahon. (*Courtesy of Wilma Steele*)

Devil Anse and Vicey with their daughter Rose (in dark dress) and her children (and two unnamed women, thought to be domestics), circa 1915. (*Dr. Coleman C. Hatfield Collection, courtesy of Dr. Arabel E. Hatfield*)

Devil Anse and Jim Vance hunting with Auk Damron (left) and Bill Borden (right). (*West Virginia State Archives*)

Devil Anse on his favorite horse, Fred. (*Dr. Coleman C. Hatfield Collection, courtesy of Dr. Arabel E. Hatfield*)

Cap Hatfield and stepson Joe Glenn. (*Dr. Coleman C. Hatfield Collection, courtesy of Dr. Arabel E. Hatfield*)

Locals await the results of a 1929 election in which J. D. Hatfield ran for sheriff of Logan County. (*Courtesy of F. Keith Davis*)

The Hatfield clan, 1897. On the ground: Tennis, Vicey (Johnse's daughter), Willis, Yellow Watch. Seated: Mary Hatfield Simpkins with daughter Vici; Devil Anse; Vicey; Nan (Cap's wife) with son Robert and daughter Louise; Cap. Standing: Rosada; Troy; Betty; Elias; Tom Chafin (nephew); Joe; Auk Damron (hired hand); Shephard, Coleman, and LeVicey (Cap's children); Bill Borden (store clerk). (*T. F. Hunt*)

The Hatfield clan, 1897. Seated: Tennis, Devil Anse, Willis. Standing: Auk Damron (hired hand); Elias, Troy, and Joe Hatfield; Tom Chafin; Bill Borden (store clerk). Background: Vicey and daughter Rose. There are no known photos of the McCoy family; it is said that Randall McCoy burned them in order to avoid dark memories of the feud. (*T. F. Hunt*)

Devil Anse with his pet bears. (*West Virginia State Archives*)

Joe, Troy, and Elias Hatfield, circa 1915. (*Dr. Coleman C. Hatfield Collection, courtesy of Dr. Arabel E. Hatfield*)

A Matewan watering hole. (*Courtesy of F. Keith Davis*)

Willis Hatfield (*Dr. Coleman C. Hatfield Collection, courtesy of Dr. Arabel E. Hatfield*)

Cap's son Coleman A. Hatfield.
(*Dr. Coleman C. Hatfield Collection, courtesy of Dr. Arabel E. Hatfield*)

despaired of ever receiving, on December 20, Bad Frank again crossed the Tug to resume his own extralegal and ad hoc extradition process, this time with Big Jim and his cousin Bud, the murdered Jeff McCoy's brother. They rode up to Perryville in McDowell County, where they had heard they might find Selkirk McCoy working on the railroad. In a little crossroads store near Perryville, they did find him, along with a bonus, Mose Christian, and, catching them by surprise, they arrested both without incident. Bad Frank had thus caught two more men. Ironically, neither of them was a Hatfield, and one of them was a McCoy, albeit the McCoy who had sided with Floyd Hatfield in the dispute over the hogs.

Bad Frank and the two McCoys successfully carried their prisoners back to Kentucky and to the Pikeville jail. Now they had the Hatfields' full attention.[12]

At some point, Pike County sheriff Basil Hatfield fired Bad Frank as deputy sheriff for, according to the *Wheeling Intelligencer,* having "made himself so conspicuous in his efforts to capture and suppress the Hatfield gang." Sheriff Hatfield replaced him with his own son. Bad Frank, however, had been appointed an agent of the governor of Kentucky and thus still had authority to continue in his quest.[13]

In his February 1888 report on the feud to Governor Buckner, Adjutant General Sam Hill would claim that Bad Frank entered West Virginia "to receive the prisoners who...he supposed had by that time been arrested under warrants issued by Governor Wilson." In a nifty bit of rationalization (and conflating the two cross-border forays), Hill explained further that Bad Frank, "learning, after he had crossed the State line, that no warrants had been issued, or at least that no arrest had been made," and "meeting with Tom Chambers, who is said to have taken a prominent part in the murder of the three McCoy brothers, and two others . . . included in the indictments . . . could not resist so good an opportunity to arrest them."[14]

*   *   *

WHEN TOM CHAMBERS, the wrong man, was mistakenly arrested, the prestigious Pikeville law firm of Auxier, Ferrell, and Connolly was retained to defend him. The same firm would also take up the rest of the cases as they came in. Anticipating trouble, Wall Hatfield, who had been reelected to serve as a justice of the peace through the end of 1888, had engaged the legal services of Perry Cline even before Jeff McCoy was killed. "Cline felt bound in honor to stand by Wall, even after Jeff was killed," wrote Spears at the time. "So those now in prison have the best mountain talent to defend them."

Then came a bizarre twist. On December 22, Pike County attorney A. J. Auxier signed an affidavit claiming that as counsel for three of the men being held for the murder of the McCoy brothers, he had received $225 from the accused Hatfields to be paid to Perry Cline in exchange for his efforts to get Governor Buckner to repeal the rewards offered for their capture. Auxier was a former district attorney and U.S. marshal for the District of Kentucky, and his claim carried great weight. Word went around that Cline had in fact persuaded Governor Buckner to offer larger rewards for the Hatfields' capture just so that he could extort money from them, agreeing for a price to use his influence to have the rewards reduced or rescinded. (By one account, the Hatfields had promised Cline to stay out of Kentucky as part of the deal.) Cline claimed the $225 was only reimbursement for some effort on the Hatfields' behalf. Johnse countered with a sworn statement before a notary public that "Cline had not spent any such sum of money in the manner stated by him, but that it was only an excuse for him to take shelter behind."[15]

Presented with this evidence, Governor Wilson had further reason for inaction. Was Cline attempting to extort money from the Hatfields? Or was this an elaborate ruse concocted by the Hatfields and their paid minions? Although we may never know the answer, it would be Auxier's name and reputation that were later sullied in a salacious public scandal, not Cline's.

IN HIS YEAR-END ADDRESS TO the legislature, Governor Buckner condemned the lawlessness and violence in Kentucky's eastern mountains, which, he declared, were tainting the state's reputation. Referring to the murder of the McCoy brothers, he declared, "If, from neglect or inefficiency, we fail to repress this lawlessness, or to bring the offenders to justice, we have no right to complain of the false estimation in which we are held by the people of other states." It was a veritable call to arms.[16]

Devil Anse was marshaling his forces. Fiercely concerned about Frank Phillips, he called a meeting of his clan. Even the Hatfield family was not monolithic. The various members differed in ambition, temper, and willpower, and given the rising level of violence and increasing threat of seizure, some no longer had a taste for the fighting. Because of a bitter dispute with Elias over a parcel of timberland, Crazy Jim had withdrawn from family matters for a time and had not participated in the retaliation against the McCoy brothers. Though at fifty-six he was seven years Devil Anse's senior, the whiskered and muscular six-foot Witcher roughrider was still a formidable figure. Since the war, he had occupied himself with cutting timber and hauling it to Catlettsburg and running a store on Thacker Creek.

But now he was back in the fold and feeling obliged to cooperate, thanks to a good turn Devil Anse had done him. In the summer, Crazy Jim had brought back a mistress from Pike County to his cabin on Thacker Creek. His wife, Mary, objected but was unable to prevent Jim from moving her in. Somehow he managed to make the situation — living with Mary, the mistress, and the children in a one-room cabin — tenable. However, when he was away, Mary and the couple's oldest son, Jim Jr., made sure that the new woman did not live at ease. Eventually, she refused to stay.

Crazy Jim tried to move her in with his son John, who also lived on Thacker Creek, but he and his wife rejected the idea. Finally, Devil Anse agreed to take the woman in. She was still there, and Crazy Jim felt inclined to participate in family matters because of it.[17]

Devil Anse, Elias, Crazy Jim, and a number of others met at Crazy Jim's on an unseasonably warm and sunny Christmas Day. They sat outside on stumps to discuss their options. When it came to clan decisions, Elias's opinions ranked up with Devil Anse's. And while responsibility for the Hatfields' actions has almost always been heaped on Devil Anse's shoulders, here at this critical juncture, it was Elias, who had been indicted for the murder of the McCoy brothers even though he had not taken part in them, who saw no solution other than a preemptive strike on Old Randall. Elias had previously worried that the McCoys were plotting to kidnap him or his son Henry. Now he declared that they were watching his property, looking for an opportunity to shoot him. He claimed that on the hillside above his house there was a brushed sniper's perch with a forked sapling to steady a rifle. He also pointed out that Cal McCoy had a new .38-caliber Winchester, a deadly weapon perfect for the crime.[18]

Devil Anse was against the idea of an attack, according to his grandson Coleman. He doubted Elias's contention that it was a sniper and not a hunter who had set up a stand above his house, and he wanted to let things ride, to continue to hold out and hope that time and the expanding economy would soon make all well again. Others agreed that five years after the murders of Ellison and the brothers, they should continue to bide their time in the hopes that eventually everyone would decide to simply move on.

For Cotton Top Mounts, who would be a key player in what was about to unfold, it was a time of secrecy and confusion. He was on the go for days at a time. He had been at his mother's house on Sand Lick Fork of the Guyandotte River when Johnse and Guerilla Mitchell came looking for him. They told him that Cap had sent for him and that "the Kentucky authorities had rewarded me $500," as

Cotton Top later recounted, meaning that they had put a price on his head, "and that I must stand in or I would get captured and killed." He obediently left with them. They rode over to Island Creek and met up with Devil Anse, his sons Cap and Bob, and Charley Gillespie at the home of a neighbor, where they spent the night. They set out the next day and stayed the night with a Vance relative, going to Henderson and Matilda Varney's at the head of Mate Creek the following day for their noon meal. Then they moved to Floyd Hatfield's place and from there went to stay with Wall's son Eph. On Friday, December 30, they met with Crazy Jim, who, Cotton Top said, had a hushed conversation with Devil Anse, Cap, and Johnse and then rode off. On Saturday, they went to the property of another Hatfield relative and stayed in a shack. Wall and the three Mahon brothers showed up, and more secretive discussions ensued. Next, they went to Crazy Jim's. After further meetings, Cotton Top said, they "called me to them and said some of the parties on the Kentucky side had me rewarded and some of them on the Kentucky side must be killed in order to stop the prosecution of us on that side." They told him he was going to help.[19]

"Anse Hatfield started with us to the McCoy house, but backed down," said Cotton Top later in one of his several confessions. "He said it was absolutely unnecessary to kill old Randall McCoy and his family." Nonetheless, according to Cotton Top, Devil Anse offered him his "big gun," but Cotton Top told him he did not want it and that if he went, he'd take his own gun. "After we left," said Cotton Top, "Anse went to Evans Ferrell on Thacker's Creek and insisted that Ferrell go coon hunting with him so that he could prove an alibi if necessary."[20]

If Devil Anse objected to the attack, he was countered by an unlikely ally of Elias. When it came to slinging a Colt, Crazy Jim was among the fastest around. Eager to put an end to the feud once and for all, he declared that he would lead the raid.

Despite what Cotton Top said in his confession, Cap's son Coleman later claimed that Devil Anse came around and helped draw up a plan: "Anse believed that action later called a 'peremptory strike' was needed, just as it was when he and Randall McCoy killed General Bill France [*sic*] during the War Between the States," Coleman wrote. "This meant that secrecy was needed, which limited the number of men who were sent."[21]

Those involved chose the cusp of the new year on which to strike. Somehow, Dave Stratton, who now associated with Harmon McCoy's sons Lark and Bud, got wind of the plot. There was still time for the McCoys to assemble a force strong enough to repel the Hatfields, and Stratton told Bud and Big Jim that they should go to Randall's house and stay there, that the Hatfields were planning a raid. Several days before it actually happened, Squirrel Huntin' Sam, who had also heard of the plot, further warned family members. But the McCoys reacted without urgency.[22]

The McCoys had let their guard down at the wrong time. Of all the acts of egregious violence in Appalachia in the last two decades of the nineteenth century, what was to come next would prove to be the most notorious.

PART III

~

THE JANUARY RAIDS AND THEIR AFTERMATH

1887–1888

Casualties, 1864–1887

Hatfields

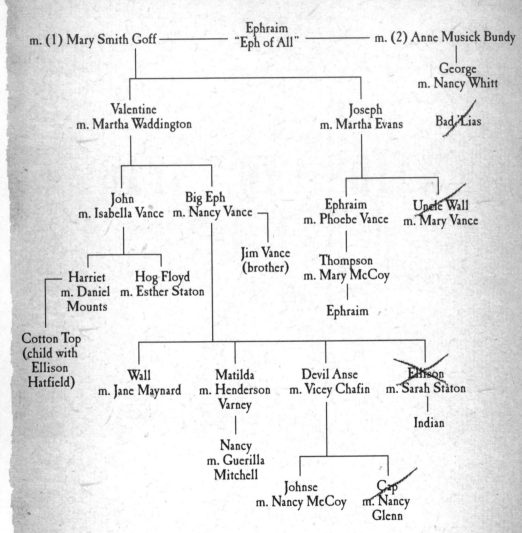

McCoys

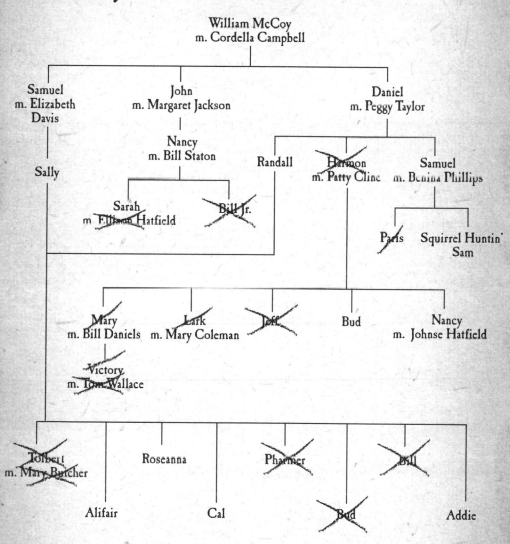

William McCoy
m. Cordella Campbell

Samuel
m. Elizabeth
Davis

John
m. Margaret Jackson

Daniel
m. Peggy Taylor

Sally

Nancy
m. Bill Staton

Randall

Harmon
m. Patty Cline

Samuel
m. Benina Phillips

Sarah
m. Ellison Hatfield

Bill Jr.

Paris

Squirrel Huntin'
Sam

Mary
m. Bill Daniels

Lark
m. Mary Coleman

Jeff

Bud

Nancy
m. Johnse Hatfield

Victory
m. Tom Wallace

Tolbert
m. Mary Butcher

Roseanna

Pharmer

Bill

Alifair

Cal

Bud

Addie

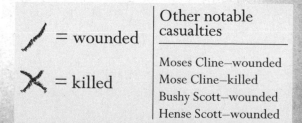

/ = wounded

✗ = killed

Other notable casualties

Moses Cline—wounded
Mose Cline—killed
Bushy Scott—wounded
Hense Scott—wounded

Chapter 14

~

A House Burning

December 31, 1887–January 2, 1888

On New Year's Eve, a winter storm blanketed much of the mid-Appalachian region and surrounding areas in snow. In Washington, DC, the change in weather at first meant a glorious opportunity: society ladies and gentlemen parading in their high boots and sealskin coats, sleighs and cutters decked with jingling bells plying the avenue between the Treasury and the Capitol grounds, the sounds of revelry floating across the city, an impromptu outdoor celebration of the end of one year and the beginning of the next. Then, at around four thirty in the afternoon, the snow gave way to a bitter hailstorm. Suddenly the fun and frolicking turned to danger and panic. Horse-drawn carriages and omnibuses skidded out of control. Streetcars ground to a halt, stranding passengers and blocking traffic from the White House to Capitol Hill. Pedestrians and horses fell painfully on the glassy pavement. "For full three hours there was a surging, shivering, freezing mass of people, practically snow and ice bound," reported one journalist. Four hours after the hailstorm started, the sky cleared and a bright full moon illuminated a town frozen in place.[1]

It was also a bright and bitterly cold evening on the banks of the Tug River, not an ideal night for an operation requiring stealth. But Crazy Jim and Cap, who were leading the raid, were the most volatile and violent of the Hatfields and men of action; adverse conditions were simply things to overcome, not things to derail a mission. The raiding party trekked on foot from Mate Creek to Blackberry Fork. Devil Anse was not with them; some said that he was ill, others that he was hunting. Crazy Jim led the way.[2]

A resourceful, hardworking breed, the Vances—who were avid singers of religious songs, skillful storytellers, and eager quaffers of moonshine—had long been quick to defend themselves with weapons of all makes. "The Vance family had a good side and a bad side to them," wrote Helen Vance Anderson in her memoir, "and believe me, I'd rather be on the good side." She acknowledged that the feud made the Vances and Hatfields look altogether bad. However, she argued, "this wasn't true, because both sides of the families were very friendly and very kind to anyone who treated them with respect." But the man or woman who did not had better beware. "My dad," said Vance, "taught us that we should do no harm to anyone but if they did a wrong to you, don't turn the other cheek but fight for all you're worth."[3]

Vance's raiding party snuck up the hillside outside Randall and Sally's house. A rail fence marked the uphill side of the property. One of the men stumbled against it, and the whole fence avalanched down the slope, rail upon rail. Figuring that the racket had alerted the McCoys, the Hatfields melted back into the forest before they could be discovered.[4]

The next day, Sunday, January 1, 1888, it was clear and cold again. Crazy Jim insisted that they return that night. Cap rode over to find Charley Gillespie, a dark-haired teenager from Tazewell County, Virginia. "Charley, we're going over into Kentucky tonight to have some fun," he told him. "Get a horse and meet us and go along." Gillespie, who worked on one of Devil Anse's timber crews, replied that he would be there and went out and "after a little trouble," as he put it, managed to borrow a horse.[5]

When Gillespie reached the rendezvous point, he saw eight others. In addition to Crazy Jim, Devil Anse's three oldest sons—

Johnse, Cap, and Bob — were there, as well as four of his nephews: Ellison's oldest son, twenty-year-old Indian; Ellison's illegitimate son, Cotton Top; Guerilla Mitchell, the son-in-law of Devil Anse's sister Matilda; and French Ellis. At thirty, Ellis was one of the more senior men along and, like Gillespie, one of Anse's timber hands; his twenty-two-year-old wife, Eska, was a sister of Cap's wife, Nan, both being daughters of Devil Anse's sister Emma. "As unprepossessing, unhung a villain as I have ever had the misfortune to see," was how the journalist T. C. Crawford later described Ellis, with "a small bull head, frosty complexion, washed-out eyes, little pug nose, and great sandy mustache lining the cruel, tightly-nipped mouth."[6]

According to Gillespie, "It was agreed at the start, before the real object of the trip was disclosed, that all should yield to everything [Jim Vance] said and do all he might order us to do." Some claim that Crazy Jim vowed, "May hell be my heaven, I will kill the man that goes back on me tonight, if powder will burn."[7]

Once they were across the Tug, Gillespie later reported, Crazy Jim told them that "if old Randall McCoy and his son 'Cal' were out of the road, every material witness against the men who had taken part in the murder of the three McCoy boys would be removed, and there could be no conviction of any of them."[8] The men were tired of having to be on guard all the time. They wanted to sleep at ease at home, not in the woods with their Winchesters. With logic hard for us to reconcile, they believed that more murders would bring them the peace they sought.

According to Cotton Top, some of the raiders were on foot, at least at first, and took off their boots before they crossed the Tug. On their mounts, they traveled up Pound Mill Branch, over to Peter Fork of Blackberry Creek, and then up Blackberry Creek, which they followed to Jerry Hatfield's. Cotton Top said that Crazy Jim and Cap and Johnse put on a disguise, which he called "fake faces."[9]

*   *   *

IT WAS AROUND TEN THIRTY on New Year's night when the men arrived at the McCoys'. The family had already turned in for the night. Their cabin was actually two buildings connected by a covered passage, all under a single roof. The Hatfields called the main building the big house, and the smaller building the kitchen. Snow clung to the trees and covered the roof of the cabin. Crazy Jim directed Mitchell, Gillespie, and Ellis to the lower door of the big house. According to Cotton Top, he told them not to let any men come out in women's clothing.

Crazy Jim told Indian and Bob to cover the lower door of the kitchen, and Cap and Cotton Top the upper door. He and Johnse would take the main door of the big house.[10]

The McCoys' watchdog started barking. Sensing something awry, Randall and his tall, handsome son Cal, who was twenty-five but still living at home, rose and hastily prepared to defend the family. The previous week, Cal had made a speech in school on the topic of good government, which his schoolmaster, Ambros Goosling, gave high praise. The school only went up to eighth grade, but Cal still attended when he could and often borrowed books from Goosling, who called him one of the most promising young men in the county, "a faithful Bible student and the essence of energy and purity."[11]

Randall, Sally, Cal, and Tolbert's orphaned son, Mel, were all bedded down in the big house. Alifair, now twenty-nine years old; Addie, seventeen; and Fanny, fourteen, along with Tolbert's five-year-old daughter, Cora, were sleeping in the kitchen.

Crazy Jim yelled, "Come out, you McCoys, an' surrender as prisoners of war!"

"Are they coming?" Cap called to Crazy Jim, after a few moments.

"No," Crazy Jim answered.

"God damnit, fire the house," Cap ordered Mitchell, who did not respond. "Where are you, X?" shouted Cap. Then they all began shooting through the doors of the big house. The McCoys shot back.

Meanwhile, some of the attackers rammed the door to the kitchen, which was flimsier than the main door. It buckled. Worried about being shot from inside, they took cover.

Alifair came to the doorway. "Stir a light," growled Crazy Jim. She went to the fireplace and tried to build a fire, but the coals were nearly dead, and she could not get them going again. She returned to the doorway and told them she could not do it. Cap swore he would shoot her if she did not light the fire. Recognizing his voice, she burst into tears: "Cap, I can't; I would, indeed I would, if I could. You wouldn't shoot a woman who never did you any harm, would you?"[12]

"What are you parleying with her for?" Crazy Jim yelled. "God damn her, make no more account of her than you would of a man. Shoot her."[13]

Crazy Jim found a bag of cotton between the two houses, struck a match, and lit a handful of it. He jammed it into a gap where a joist came out of the wall. He flung more of the blazing cotton beneath the shutter of the big house's main door, hoping to ignite the barrier. Sally had churned butter that evening and had four gallons of buttermilk sitting in the churn; crouching by the door with his revolver in one hand, Randall used a tin cup to toss milk on the flames.

Cal climbed into the loft, where several years before they had cut foot square loopholes into the roof for just such an occasion. They had spaced them every six feet so that they could defend the whole perimeter. From his perch, Cal homed in on some of the raiders and started shooting. They scurried behind a log pigpen for protection.[14]

Cal shouted for his sisters to fetch water to put out the flames. As Fanny watched from the kitchen doorway, too scared to move, her older sister Alifair dashed toward the well.

"A girl came to the door dressed in dark clothes," as Cotton Top told it. "Cap and Johnse Hatfield said, 'You, Big Man, goddamn, kill her.'"

Cap had his rifle raised to his shoulder. So did Cotton Top, who squeezed the trigger of his .32-caliber Winchester. A ball pierced Alifair's nightgown just over the left breast. Fanny, still standing in the kitchen doorway, heard her sister call out Cap's name and saw her fall but could not see who had fired because the shooter was hidden behind the well box. Addie crept out to her and asked, "Was it Cap Hatfield?"

"Yes, it was Cap Hatfield," Alifair gasped, "and nobody else."[15]

With a burning torch in one hand, Mitchell climbed up the logs to the roof and held the flame to the roof shingles. Randall squeezed the trigger of his revolver several times, blowing off three of Mitchell's fingers to the knuckle. Mitchell dropped the torch and fell.[16]

Through a rooftop loophole, Cal shot his .32-caliber Winchester, hitting Cotton Top. The relatively light shot of the .32 did not drop the burly albino, but it drilled his forearm, entering at his wrist and exiting just below his elbow. Cal's shooting drove the other Hatfields around the far end of the main house to the covered passageway between the two buildings, where they kept up a steady fire on the front door and at the attic above them while renewing their efforts to ignite the roof with torches. Finally they succeeded. Smoke filled the attic around Cal. He headed downstairs.[17]

With lead flying and blood flowing on both sides, Sally, who had heard the girls scream that Alifair was shot, slipped out of the main door. As she went through it, Johnse fired inside the house at a form on the bed, and the bullet sliced through the quilt. The Hatfields, especially Cap, would later joke that he was shooting at his own son. John Spears would propagate this idea in the *New York Sun,* writing that the boy, supposedly the seven-year-old son of Johnse and Roseanna, "escaped death at the hands of his father by the thickness of a piece of muslin." Since it is generally agreed that Roseanna and Johnse's child was Little Sally, a girl who never survived infancy, the boy was probably Tolbert's seven-year-old son, Melvin.

As Sally passed between the buildings, Crazy Jim swore at her and ordered her to go back inside. Either out of ammunition or hesitant to shoot an unarmed woman (despite his command to Cap), he raised his gun by the barrel end. "I saw it was wrong-end," Sally later told Spears, "and kept on." Crazy Jim swung the gun butt at her, breaking two of her ribs and knocking her flat. Sally rose to her hands and knees and crawled toward Alifair until Johnse waved his pistol in her face.

"For the Lord's sake, let me go to my girl," she pleaded.

"Go back, you, or I'll kill you," Johnse warned.

Sally reached a hand out toward her daughter, who lay in a pool of blood. "Oh!" she wailed, "she's dead. For the love of the Lord, let me go to her. Oh, my God!" she howled. "My God!" Johnse struck her so hard with the backside of his pistol that the hammer penetrated her skull. She was knocked out cold.[18]

The battle lasted an hour and a half, according to Cotton Top. Firing and reloading rifles, shotguns, and pistols, Randall and Cal kept the raiders at bay and at one point drove some of them back behind the pigpen. But it was only a matter of time before they would have to abandon the burning house. Cal told Randall that he was going to try to reach the corncrib, about a hundred yards away. From there, he would provide cover for his father, and then both might be able to cross the creek and make it to the woods.[19]

With a box of cartridges in one hand and his rifle in the other, Cal burst through the door and dashed across the yard. As he cleared the corner of the house, the attackers opened fire. On the cue of the guns' roar, Randall, clad only in a nightshirt and long johns, eyes red and bugging from the smoke, emerged. Looking like a madman, he leveled his double-barreled shotgun at Johnse, pulled the trigger, and blasted him in the right shoulder, though his thick coat absorbed most of the pellets. He wheeled and fired the other barrel at Mitchell, peppering his gut, but his cartridge belt saved him from worse.

Having bought Cal some precious strides, Randall now turned and ran with everything he had left, exiting the glaring light of the fire into the ghastly glow of the full moon. Cal was well away—

seventy-five yards by one estimate — in the shadow of some trees when he was hit in the head by a bullet. At that distance, in that light, it was a fluke shot. No one even saw him drop to the ground, instantly dead. Both Cap and Johnse later claimed to have shot Cal, "in a bragadocia manner," according to Cotton Top, who believed that from the way they were positioned, Cap had done it.[20]

Randall now attracted their attention, but he had gotten a jump on them. With Mitchell and Cotton Top down, the others blazed away in the direction Randall was running. Reaching the corncrib, he paused to gulp the frigid mountain air, then set off again, crossing the creek and fleeing up the mountain on the other side. Once he was in the dark of the woods — woods he knew better than anyone — he was gone. Wet and shivering, he reached a neighbor's farm. Instead of waking the residents, the shocked old man went into their barn, routed their hogs, and burrowed into the hay that had been warmed by their bodies, saving himself from death by exposure.

With the house burning to the ground, the Hatfield gang — injured and otherwise — fetched their horses and secured their wounded. Then they rode off, leaving behind the carnage.[21]

Chapter 15

~

The Death of a Soldier

January 1888

In 1947, Willis Staton, a retired circuit court judge of Pikeville, would finish writing a book about the Hatfield-McCoy feud, a subject that had fascinated him since his youth. In his book, which he called *Hatfields and McCoys. True Romance and Tragedies,* Judge Staton combined his recollections of events and people with dramatic re-creations of the scenes of the feud. He wrote in prose and verse, and he transcribed court records, which, as a judge, he greatly valued, into his own pages. Although he had published several other works, he never found a publisher for this one. The manuscript ended up in the bottom of a chest stashed in a barn.

Four decades later, a farmer who had taken over the property discovered the chest and notified Staton's granddaughters. They published the work in a very limited edition for the family; thus, in 1993, Staton's preserved court records and enigmatic history came back to light, as did the account of the one aspect of the feud that he had experienced himself.[1]

Staton was twelve years old when he attended what he would call "the saddest and most horrifying funeral of all ages." It occurred on the afternoon following the Hatfields' attack on the McCoy home place. Still crackling and hissing, the embers of the cabin's massive beams glowed an evil ruby, and the incinerated articles of daily life emitted a powerful stench. Although the victims had not been dead for even twenty-four hours, there was an urgency to bury them — they were young, and to see or be near their corpses was excruciating. A number of McCoys and their friends and neighbors, mostly women, prepared the bodies for burial and discussed in hushed voices the likelihood that the Hatfields were still in the surrounding woods, as if they might actually be close enough to hear. They feared that the Hatfields, knowing that the McCoys would assemble for the burial, would attack and do them in for good. Young Staton watched Roseanna. So demoralized that she could barely stand, she did not utter a word.

Staton could feel the fear and the sense of vulnerability that lurked in the burned-out and bloody clearing. He listened to the women talking about what had happened. After the shooting ended, Addie and Fanny escaped from the burning house. Melvin, who had been clutching Randall's leg when he ran out, fell at the door, crawled around a corner of the house, and hid. Suddenly he realized that little Cora, who was a cripple, was still inside, and he dashed into the smoke-filled annex. He found his sister and pulled her out by the hand just before the roof collapsed. Addie and Fanny had placed Alifair on some old bedding and dragged her away from the burning house. They returned and got Sally, who had fallen beside Alifair, and drew her, still unconscious, to safety. The two sisters built a fire, and the five of them huddled by it until morning, when Big Jim and some neighbors arrived and found them. Sally, whose ribs had been broken near the spinal column, was unable to walk, and her bloody hair was frozen to the ground. Addie's feet were badly frostbitten.

On the day of the funeral, there were so few McCoy men available that the women had to send for men from other families to come help. Staton's father, Joe, was one of the few to answer the call. He did not believe that the Hatfields would attack, but just in case, he warned his son: "If shooting should start, you fall to the ground and lie there until it is over."

The men dug one large hole in the winter-hard earth next to the graves of the four McCoy brothers, the three who had been shot and the fourth, Bill, who should have been with them but instead was said to have died—of guilt and grief—because he was not. They carried the two coffins up the hill to the grave site, which sat beneath an old peach tree and was protected by a split-rail fence. Staton nervously crept up to Alifair's crude coffin and gazed on a sight he would never forget. He thought she was beautiful and later described his feelings in verse:

> T'would be better she hadn't been born,
> Or that she had died when she was young.
> But a new life God can give and adorn,
> Where hate, strife, and killing is now known.

As for the Hatfields, Staton was not so sanguine:

> Where is the joy for those who kill?
> Can they who bathe in hell know heaven?
> Oh, if they shed man's blood for revenge,
> What shall the answer be in heaven?

In mountain fashion, lacking a preacher, they buried the dead without a service. By the time the bodies were in the ground, a contingent of McCoys, including Randall, Big Jim, and Sam, was well on its way to Pikeville. There, the distraught family members would take refuge and plot their revenge.[2]

EVEN IN THIS TOUGH REGION, the bald-faced brutality of the New Year's Day raid was shocking, particularly the murder of helpless Alifair, which, according to John Spears, "roused Pike County as it had not been roused since the Civil War."[3] "A Murderous Gang" ran the headline in the *Louisville Courier-Journal* on January 8, "Mother and Son Murdered, While Father and Daughters Escape a Fiery Grave." This brief (and not completely accurate) report linked the raid to the killing of the three McCoy brothers and the recent arrest of one of the gang (which could have been the wrong Tom Chambers, Selkirk McCoy, or Mose Christian, who had all been arrested shortly before). The *Courier-Journal* wrongly reported that Sally, not Alifair, had been killed, but with a reasonable foreboding concluded that although the Pikeville jail was well defended, "fears were entertained at the hour of writing that an attempt would be made to release the member of the gang confined there."[4]

The following day, the *Wheeling Intelligencer* called the attack "one of the most wanton and diabolical cases of arson and murder ever committed in the State of Kentucky" and announced that a total of $2,700 in rewards was being offered for the capture of the guilty men. These and other early newspaper accounts of the raid were received with some skepticism. As the story spread across the country and more details became known, however, the skepticism gave way to revulsion. This was not just another inflated tale of bloody retaliation from the backwoods but the true story of a premeditated midnight raid against an entire family, including women and children. It involved the intentional burning of their home, the savage clubbing of an innocent woman—a grandmother—and the gunning down of two of her children, one an unarmed girl. The Hatfields were called a murderous gang. The editorials assailed the authorities of Kentucky and West Virginia for allowing the conditions that had led to such needless violence.[5]

Locally, constable Matt Hatfield's wife, Maw, now barred her cellar door. Devil Anse and his brothers and sons were blood relatives, but they were no longer welcome. "I don't want anything to do with anyone that had a part in killing a woman or a child," she said adamantly. And Squirrel Huntin' Sam, who had tried to remain apart from the feud—he had considered Big Ellison a dear friend but was also close to Randall—now took up arms against the killers.[6]

The governors of Kentucky and West Virginia were now on red alert, and state guard units in both states were ordered to be prepared to intervene along the Tug Fork if violence flared up again. Governor Buckner was outraged. Governor Wilson, finding himself in an increasingly precarious position, braced himself for the next epistolary blow or—diplomacy having been stretched to its limits—legal maneuver.

In Pikeville, Bad Frank Phillips, having already sidestepped legality, figured he now had the moral authority to track down the Hatfields no matter where, no matter how. "If the governor of West Virginia is determined to continue the protection of his murderous pets," he declared, "I will protect the citizens of Kentucky, or die in the attempt." Fueled by the local outrage, he raised a posse. Despite claims to the contrary, Squirrel Huntin' Sam reported that Randall joined it. "I were for peace and tried to keep things down and let the law work it out," wrote Sam. "Randolph nothing would do but he must go. I done my best to keep him back and I could not, so I went along. I knew I could keep Randolph from killing some of them."[7]

Bad Frank knew just where he would start tracking, too. Someone in the raiding party was badly wounded and had left behind a blood trail. Early on the morning of January 6, before reports of the tragedy hit the Louisville papers and only four days after Alifair and Cal were laid to rest, Bad Frank and twenty-three riders, including Big Jim and his brother Sam and a Pinkerton detective named John Yates, left Pikeville headed toward West Virginia. With them was Pikeville lawman and politico Bud Rutherford, whose grandfather and uncle (Asbury and Flem Hurley) were killed at the hands of Devil Anse during the war and whose father, Doc, who had tended to Big Ellison on his deathbed, had since had a bitter falling-out with the Hatfields.[8]

After riding all day from Pikeville and picking up the blood trail at the McCoy place, where nothing was left of the cabin except charred timbers and two stone chimneys, Bad Frank and his posse headed for the Tug. On the way, he showed his remorseless side, arresting two locals—John Gooslin and Stonewall Cline—who had done nothing but who he feared would try to warn the Hatfields of the coming posse. The first seeds of dissension within his own ranks had been sown. Squirrel Huntin' Sam, for one, objected. "You ain't going to take those boys with us, are you? If that be the case, I'll go back home," he drawled through his walrus mustache. "I will not go with any such crowd. I believe in making friends at home in place of enemies. Suppose you take them over there and get into a fight, which you expect to, and they get killed. What about it?"

"I wouldn't say anything," Big Jim responded flatly.

"Let them go," Squirrel Huntin' Sam said. "Jim, you can uphold for such if you want to, but I don't tolerate no such." It was settled by Jake Mounts, one of the posse and a justice of the peace, who made Gooslin and Cline swear not to alert the Hatfields.[9]

The posse crossed the Tug, then remarkably was able to pick up the blood trail on the West Virginia side of the river. Night was coming on, however. Most of the posse made camp at Larkin and Emma Smith's place at the mouth of Grapevine Creek. Emma was a younger sister of Devil Anse. Nerves were on edge, and Jake Mounts and another man decided not to stay. They headed back to Kentucky in the dark.

A contingent led by Big Jim continued on to Devil Anse's place on the banks of the Tug. They pounded on his door late that night. Not surprisingly, only Vicey and the children were at home. Big Jim and five others decided they would stay and bivouacked on the property that night, waiting for Devil Anse to return. He never did.

Early the next morning, after Big Jim and his men rejoined them, Bad Frank's posse—Spears called it "the mob"—set out for Thacker Creek. A letter later sent to John B. Floyd from a lawyer living in the area reported that Phillips ordered his men to sweep up anyone who might inform the wanted men of their presence, including women and children. The writer said that they drove

Larkin and Emma Smith and their family, including their daughter Nan, who was Cap's wife, and her children, "like beasts before them" four or five miles down the river to Shang Ferrell's.

Over several days, the posse traveled swiftly, striking strategically at odd hours. When they showed up at Ferrell's cabin, Bad Frank sent Squirrel Huntin' Sam in to search it. He found three guns in the bedroom, but he hid them between the feather bed and the mattress; he had come to hunt the guilty, not to harass the innocent, many of whom — Ferrell included — were his friends. Bad Frank did not care whether Ferrell was innocent or not, and he seized the Hatfield associate to prevent him, too, from spreading the alarm. The lawyer reported to Floyd that Bad Frank ordered the women and children to be left here, threatening them with trouble if they sent warnings to the men they were after. With Ferrell in tow, the posse proceeded up a creek from Thacker to Jim Vance's place. No one was there.[10]

AFTER THE RAID ON THE McCoys, the Hatfield gang had returned home by the same route they had come. Johnse was more stunned than hurt, but Cotton Top's shattered left arm was a mess. On the way back, he passed out from the loss of blood. When he came to, Ellis, Gillespie, and Indian took turns leading him down the trail. Slowly, in the dark, they made their way to Cap's place, where most stayed overnight. Crazy Jim and Johnse continued on to Crazy Jim's house, up Thacker Hollow, where the others joined them the following night. Once they were reassembled, they made their way on remote paths to the head of Horse Road Fork of Mate Creek and from there to Slick Rock Fork of Pigeon Creek, where they hid in the woods for almost a week.

Operating in country only they and their kin knew, they visited allies on the Guyandotte River who provided them with food and provisions. At some point, Cotton Top was taken back to his home on Sand Lick Creek, a tributary of the Guyandotte, where a Dr.

Brown dressed his wounds. In his confession, Cotton Top said, "I told him how I got shot."[11]

On Friday, January 6, Crazy Jim's wife, Mary, who had joined them in camp, roasted two raccoons that Crazy Jim and Cap had shot for their supper. Weary of being in the woods, the three of them set out for Cap's place the next day, climbing Thacker Mountain with Mary out front as a scout. After crossing a ridge not far from the Vances' cabin, Mary looked down on the sight they had dreaded: a posse was coming up the other side of the mountain on horses.

She turned and shouted: "Here they come!"[12]

"How many?" Crazy Jim called back.

"About forty, I reckon."

Bad Frank and his men spurred their horses up the steep slope. Bad Frank led the way; behind him was Yates, and then the ever-observant Squirrel Huntin' Sam. "Frank, I see two men," he warned. "One has a gun."[13]

In the strange interval as the horses scrambled up the hillside — an eternity and no time at all — Crazy Jim, who was ill from eating too much rich raccoon meat, told Cap that he was not going to run. He would stand and fight it out, but he said Cap should get away as soon as he could.

As the riders rushed past Mary on her way down, Crazy Jim waved his hand and shouted: "Halt!" And then, "Rally around the point, boys!" He hid behind some brush with Cap, and they began to shoot at the posse. Crazy Jim's orders were a bluff, of course; there were no boys to rally, but the posse took cover. Yates dove behind a fallen oak and, according to Squirrel Huntin' Sam, did not come out until the fight was over. (Sam would later return to the oak and joke to his comrades, "This here's a Pinkerton wall. If you wanna be safe, get behind this.") As the rest of the posse began to fan out, Cap had his gun shot out of his hand. Realizing that to stay would be useless, he picked up his rifle and made a break for it, taking a flesh wound in the back on the way. Bullets winged through the woods as he ran, dodging from one tree to the next, making his way up a ridge between Grapevine and Pigeon creeks.[14]

Except for a sixteen-shot repeating rifle, .45- and .38-caliber revolvers, and a haversack full of loaded cartridges, Crazy Jim was alone on the narrow ridge. He squatted behind a locust stump and in front of a boulder that marked the center of the Hatfields' backwoods haven. From there, a man who still had sap in his legs could peel off down any of half a dozen hollows and disappear into the dense wilderness. In each of these hollows, Crazy Jim could find a friend who would not hesitate to pick up his gun and use it against an intruder if for no other reason than he knew the one and not the other. But Crazy Jim was feeling old, cramped in the stomach, and unwilling to run.[15] Instead, he raised his gun to his shoulder and took aim at the man leading the charge — Bad Frank. If he could hit his mark, the others might lose their gumption, too.

Just as Crazy Jim squeezed the trigger, Bad Frank dropped to the ground, dodging a bullet that might have reshaped local history. Squirrel Huntin' Sam thought he had been hit and killed, but Bad Frank leaped to his feet again, fired his gun, and dashed to an oak tree for cover. Before he could get there, Crazy Jim fired again but missed.[16]

Bad Frank took a breath, peered around the tree to return fire, and realized that the barrel of Crazy Jim's gun was already trained on him. He pulled his head back just in time to keep it from being drilled by a West Virginia bullet, which instead spat bark in his face. He fired his gun at Crazy Jim's stump. The shot pierced the rotting wood and hit Crazy Jim's cartridge belt, knocking him off his feet. Now he was exposed. Before he could recover, Bad Frank pumped in a fresh cartridge and shot him through the body. Crazy Jim crawled behind a log, and Bad Frank ran forward.

Crazy Jim might also have been hit by some of the other men, who had moved to the left and the right.[17] In any case, he was mortally wounded, but not yet dead. With both his hands, Crazy Jim — the best pistol shot in Logan County — aimed at Bad Frank. While dying was bad, it could be a bit less so.

But then his eyes jittered and rolled as his body briefly convulsed. In that moment, Bad Frank hit the earth with his rifle out front. Crazy Jim regained control, lifted his head, and took aim. The barrel of Bad Frank's Winchester, a Model 1886 .45-90 lever-action used for felling big game, twitched up and locked on. Both men squeezed their triggers. Crazy Jim's hat flew ten feet above his head, like a cap tossed in victory. Some of his brains were inside it.[18]

Shang Ferrell looked at the dead man and said, "He'll burn no more houses." The men all stared at Ferrell. None of them had any idea that Jim Vance was even involved in the house burning (let alone that he had led it). They had really wanted Cap. If Crazy Jim had not shot at them, they would have left him alone.[19]

CAP SURFACED AT HOG FLOYD's place. He borrowed a horse and did not even saddle it before racing off to warn his father of the danger. After he rode into camp and told his story, Devil Anse immediately assembled his men. They sketched out plans to lure the posse into an ambush and kill Bad Frank. Then they hurried off to see if Crazy Jim was still holding out. They found only his semi-headless corpse, Phillips and his men gone.

The death of Crazy Jim — one of the flintiest and most feared of the Hatfields — was a hard blow to the clan. Family members did not want the public to attend the funeral, and they did not want his grave to be vandalized, so they buried him in a secret place in Thacker Hollow.[20]

Now emboldened, Bad Frank and his men crossed back into Kentucky, but only to regroup. The next night, they returned for more. This time they stormed up Beech Creek in midday to Wall's place. They leaped the fence on their horses and charged the house. Hearing what he thought was a ruckus among the cows, Wall ran to the door to see what was the matter and found a lot more than he had bargained for.

Looking up the length of a Winchester barrel, he saw a grimacing Big Jim McCoy Wall raised his hands. Bad Frank's posse entered the house and found Doc Mahon, who was married to Wall's daughter Sarah, and his brother Sam, both also wanted for the murder of the McCoy brothers.[21]

Part of the posse, led by Squirrel Huntin' Sam, Randall, and two other McCoys, went after Andy Varney, who lived on the West Virginia side of the Tug just above the mouth of Knox Creek. Varney saw them first and ran for it. Leaving Randall behind at the cabin, Sam and his two cousins tracked Varney up a hill. When Sam, overheated, paused to take off his overcoat, he heard a voice coming from the bushes. It was Varney. "I'll surrender. I've got nothing but a pipe," he said. "You can have it if you want it."

Sam — the most level-headed and fair-minded of the lot, at least according to his autobiography — shook hands with Varney and said, "I ain't over here to kill people and burn houses. The Hatfields never harmed me nor me them. I am sorry this has all happened. You listen to me and do as I say and you be safe."

They went back to Varney's cabin. When Randall saw Varney, the rage within him rose, and he leveled his rifle on him. But Sam caught the gun in his hand and looked Randall in the eye. "Is this the way you are going to carry on?" he asked. "You promised you would listen to me." Randall held his gun tight. "Now tell me, are you going to do as promised?" Sam asked. "If not say so, and I'll get on my mare and ride for home."

"Well, by goddamn, I reckon you'll have your own way," Randall muttered, lowering his gun.[22]

The two groups reconvened at Wall's and wrapped up the raid by apprehending Plyant Mahon and L. D. McCoy. Their success must have put them in high spirits because at one point, Varney tried to escape and instead of shooting him, they simply ran him down and dragged him back.

Bad Frank and his posse managed to hustle their six prisoners to Pikeville on January 12. The Pike County sheriff served them with warrants of arrest and delivered them to the jailer, Abner Justice.

Now nine of the twenty-three wanted men had been captured, even if by illegal means, and were in the Pike County jail awaiting trial for the murder of the McCoy brothers.[23]

By the time the men reached Pikeville, Bad Frank's exploits were already being spun into legend. No sooner had "the last sad rites of the late butchery" taken place, said a Catlettsburg newspaper, than the McCoys' posse set out "for the purpose of annihilating the gang." The newspaper also reported that Jim Vance, who had "killed several men in the McCoy neighborhood," had been shot seven times and that Johnse Hatfield and Tom Mitchell had been killed along with him, which would have made interesting reading for the latter two—had they been able to read—since they were alive and hiding out in the woods. In fact, Johnse was preparing to set off for Colorado, leaving Nancy and the family behind to await his return. Nancy, however, would turn out to have other ideas.[24]

ON THE SAME DAY THAT Bad Frank landed his prisoners in the Pikeville jail, the Schoolhouse Blizzard struck Nebraska and Minnesota and the Dakota, Montana, Wyoming, and Idaho territories. Like the Hatfields' New Year's Day attack, the storm came furtively and did its damage ruthlessly. In strong winds and powdery snow, but only moderate temperatures, locals set about their chores, rode to town, or walked to school. When the total whiteout came, it took them by surprise. Five hundred people, many of them schoolchildren on their way home, froze to death.

However, in the Big Sandy Valley there had been little snowfall that year, and the usual winter rise of the Ohio had not occurred. Four of the previous six years had seen early winter precipitation, a sudden thaw, and heavy spring rain, but this year there was little hope of a spring freshet, which disgruntled the lumbermen. They would have to work their timber down to the riverside using flumes and sleds, muscles and sweat, and hope for a modest rise of the water level, a foot or two, in April to float their rafts down to the mills.[25]

During these raw winter months, the chill between the West Virginia and Kentucky capitals deepened. Having sent the requested affidavits to Governor Wilson in October, Governor Buckner believed that he had complied with all the necessary legalities to have the fugitives sent to Kentucky to stand trial. Not only had that not happened, but these same men had committed new atrocities. Frustrated, Buckner wrote Wilson again, asking if "there was then anything which prevented the rendition of the criminals?"[26]

Wilson now believed there was. His state had been invaded, and one of its citizens murdered. In all, nine men had been illegally arrested, kidnapped, and forcefully removed from the state. His fellow West Virginians were not going to let him forget these facts. On January 16, John B. Floyd told the *Wheeling Register* that the Hatfields "knew nothing of the burning of McCoy's house and the killing of his son and daughter." Like Squirrel Huntin' Sam, he claimed that Randall McCoy was riding with Frank Phillips, a point that Governor Buckner would dispute with Governor Wilson in a January 30 letter, saying, "Old Randolph McCoy was not with this raiding party . . . but was at that time in Pikeville, Kentucky, as the citizens of that place will all testify." Floyd reported that Shang Ferrell and other men whom they forced to guide them said that Randall "intended to kill Cap, cut a slice of meat from his body and eat it."

"The people of Logan County," Floyd declared, "are alarmed and indignant."[27]

Chapter 16

~

Bad Frank and the Battle of Grapevine Creek

January 18, 1888

In the days following Bad Frank's West Virginia raids, newspaper accounts said that the Hatfields had sent word that they planned to burn Pikeville and rescue their comrades locked up there. Perry Cline was ready. His jail was built of solid brick and held its fourteen prisoners—nine of them of the accused Hatfield faction—in iron cages. Its three guards, armed with Winchesters and revolvers, made sure the inmates remained secure. At night, pickets posted in all directions guarded the town.[1]

Meanwhile, Bad Frank, who weighed no more than 135 pounds but whose stature was growing by the day, finalized his plans for a third raid into West Virginia. He was not, as the *Courier-Journal* would erroneously report, "related by blood to the Hatfields," but a little more of their blood on his hands would have suited him just fine. This time, on January 16, thirty-three riders rumbled out of Pikeville. They again included a number of McCoys—namely, Big Jim, his brother Sam, and their cousins Bud and Lark. The latter, at age thirty-one, now had a temper that matched his rage over the murder of his father, Harmon. Two days after setting out, they roared across the Tug River into West Virginia, opposite Peter

Creek, and rode down along the riverbank toward the mouth of Grapevine Creek, where Cap lived.[2]

This time, Bad Frank would not surprise anyone. A patrol that Wall, who was in jail, would call "lawfully formed by the West Virginians to keep the Pike County people out" waited in front of Cap's house. It was composed of Devil Anse, Cap, and nine others, a group one contemporary journalist referred to as the Logan Regulators, a holdover from Civil War times. One of the nine was Charlie Harrison, a twenty-two-year-old distant cousin of Devil Anse's from Tazewell County, Virginia. Wiry, strong, woods-smart, with piercing blue eyes later described as "heady," he was not the youngest of the bunch. That honor belonged to Charley Gillespie, the dark-haired teenager who had participated in the New Year's Day raid and who was also originally from Tazewell County. French Ellis, who was a neighbor of Cap's, was there, as were two lawmen, the constable John Thompson and a special deputy, Bill Dempsey. Thompson had arrest warrants for Bad Frank and his men for the killing of Jim Vance. There was also an emissary sent by Governor Wilson to ascertain the truth behind the feud, William Floyd, brother of John B. A dusting of snow covered the frozen ground, and the wind cut like a scythe. Though the men longed to be inside by the fireplace, they could not keep watch from a windowless cabin. For warmth, corn liquor would have to suffice.[3]

Harrison sat on his horse among cousins and friends. Someone produced a jar of moonshine and passed it around. "It's the best you ever laid your lips to," one of them said. "It's a dad burn good thing to have on a day like this."

"Warms your blood a little so's you won't freeze stiff as a polecat on your horse," joked another. Then the conversation came to a dead halt.[4]

The Kentucky band would also be cast in Civil War terms. The *Wheeling Intelligencer* reported: "The Peter Creek Guards, twenty strong, have joined the capturing party, which now numbers over forty, and are in hot pursuit of the Hatfields."[5] Pacing a single-file line of riders on a narrow road as they neared Grapevine Creek was Big Jim McCoy. Carrying the rifle that Cal had used the night he was killed, he let his testy brown-and-white mare run, and she pulled ahead by about a quarter of a mile. When he rounded a spur of the mountain, Big Jim found himself riding straight at a dozen squinting, moonshine-furnaced West Virginians.

Squirrel Huntin' Sam said that the Hatfields, having been warned of the posse's approach, had started up Grapevine Creek and were in the process of crossing it when Big Jim came around the bend. Big Jim saw them and jerked the reins back, but he was already in gunshot range. As the Hatfields began to shoot, Big Jim's mare reared, whinnying and scissoring her legs in the air. Her frantic gyrations sent Big Jim into involuntary evasive maneuvers and may well have saved his life.

The Hatfields knew that he was not alone. As they fired, they ran for cover behind a fence. Amid the barrage of bullets, Big Jim leaped off his mount. He laid Cal's rifle on the ground, flung his overcoat onto his saddle, and let the horse go. He grabbed the rifle and found cover at the corner of a stone wall. Cal's weapon, which he always carried now, was a visceral reminder of why he was here, but more than anything, he sought vengeance for his sister Alifair. A man of deep religious faith, he was sure that the Hatfields would pay for their sins, and he had no qualms about being a messenger of the Lord.

Aiming over the wall, Big Jim hit a man with his first shot. The special deputy, Dempsey, fell next to Harrison as the cold air became luminous with gun smoke. Harmon McCoy's son Bud was the next Kentuckian to round the bend, and he took a bullet in his shoulder. The rest of Bad Frank's contingent dismounted, hastily secured their horses to pawpaw trees, and, almost in one motion, scurried for cover behind the stone wall. Some of the horses were shot; others were spooked, broke free, and galloped off, away from the crackling gunfire. Seeing the stampede, Devil Anse decided to maneuver his men lower down Grapevine Creek in

Harmon McCoy's son Bud. *(West Virginia State Archives)*

order to cut off and trap the McCoys. However, before the Hatfields could get there, Bad Frank's men ran down their horses.[6]

The two sides fired on each other for, by one estimate, more than two hours. When they started, Joe Glenn, Cap's five-year-old stepson, who was staying with his grandparents Larkin and Emma Smith, ran outside to see the shooting. The Smiths knew who the attackers were because they had bivouacked on their property the night before they killed Jim Vance. Joe's granny, a Hatfield, quickly retrieved the boy and barred the door.[7]

After the initial strikes, the outnumbered Hatfields took the worst of it. Already missing fingers, Mitchell was shot in the side. Indian was drilled in the thigh. A man named Lee White was hit three times.

Just who had the better arms in the battle is a matter of dispute as each side subsequently tried to downplay their weaponry. "The Hatfields fought with the best rifles that money could procure, heavy caliber Colts and Winchester rifles," wrote journalist Charles Mutzenberg. "The Kentuckians were armed less perfectly, about half of them using rifles and shotguns of the old pattern." According to him, only Bad Frank and two others had repeating rifles, which accounted for the Kentuckians' "heavy losses in horses and wounded men."[8]

Cap's son Coleman disagreed, saying: "Anse, Cap, and a few other of the Hatfields were armed with .45 caliber one-shot cartridge Spencer rifles. The remainder of the Hatfield side had only cap-lock squirrel rifles and such other muzzle-loading weapons as had been handed down from the Civil War." He claimed that the McCoys used Winchester repeating rifles bought from the riverboats that plied the Levisa Fork to Pikeville.[9]

In either case, the relative lack of sophisticated weaponry was indicative of just how slow "progress" was in coming to the region, despite its increased economic well-being. It was certainly a factor in the number of casualties suffered in the feud. Had they had better and more accurate guns, more people would have died.

Firearms had evolved rapidly since the war. The original Winchester — the Model 1866 lever-action repeating rifle (like others, named for its introductory year), which fired multiple shots without requiring reloading — had changed gunfighting forever. The highly portable 1873 carbine with its short, twenty-inch barrel was so widely disseminated (to the tune of 720,000) that it has been called the gun that won the West. Colt adapted its Peacemaker revolver to fire the same ammunition, allowing those armed with both to carry only one type of cartridge. And everyone from buffalo hunters, Texas Rangers, and Canadian Mounted Police to Geronimo carried the '76 Winchester, which celebrated America's centennial with more potent firepower.

But it was not so much rifle type as the fact that the Kentuckians outnumbered the Hatfields — by, depending on the account, up to three to one — that determined the outcome of this fight. Though four men had been shot, only Bill Dempsey, whose leg had been shattered, was immobile. Leaving him behind, the Hatfields retreated into the forest, making a run for the gap of Thacker Mountain. "We fled," Harrison would relate pensively at the age of ninety one, "leaving Bill Dempsey, a cousin of the father of Jack Dempsey, lying bleeding to death. . . . I couldn't help him."[10]

But Dempsey was still alive. He dragged himself to a shuck pen and hid inside. French Ellis's wife, Eska, heard him cry out deliriously for water and went to try to help him. But when she ran into the yard, the McCoys fired at her. She was forced to take cover behind a heavy wooden puncheon, though not heavy enough: the minié ball of a muzzle-loading rifle ripped right through it, barely missing her head.

The Kentuckians entered Cap's yard. Blankets, overcoats, and other discarded Hatfield possessions were strewn around the grounds. Big Jim called out that he had shot a man who was almost certainly too hurt to go far. The men found a trail of blood that led to the shuck pen. Inside, Bill Dempsey lay dying.

"What's your name?" asked Bad Frank.

"Bill Dempsey," he replied, holding up his hands. "I'm not armed, gentlemen, and am dying. Please don't shoot me any more." Bad Frank drew his pistol.

"Don't . . . don't . . . ," Dempsey pleaded.

Bad Frank abruptly put the barrel up to Dempsey's neck. When his men saw what he was about to do, several jumped to stop him, but before they could, Bad Frank discharged the gun; the blast severed Dempsey's head from his neck.[11]

Another person — another innocent — had died in the Hatfield-McCoy feud. With the sharp smell of powder and new death in the air, Big Jim stared at Bad Frank. "The McCoys don't want no cold-blooded murders laid at their door," he said. The others looked on tensely as the two men squared off, hands on pistols. Finally, Big Jim's brother Sam talked him down while Lark did his best to calm Bad Frank.[12]

Dempsey was a law officer who had come there with arrest warrants for the Kentucky raiders and to prevent the type of violence that took his life. After this second murder that Bad Frank committed during his unsanctioned January raids in West Virginia, the pendulum of moral authority that had swung sharply the McCoys' way after the rapacious New Year's attack now reversed course.[13]

On Wednesday, January 25, 1888, the *Louisville Courier-Journal* picked up a news story out of Cincinnati, noting that it was a "special from Catlettsburg" with reports fresh off the steamer *Frank Preston* from Pikeville. Entitled "Bloody War in Pike County," it announced that "the war of extermination between the Hatfields and the McCoys is still going on in the wilds of West Virginia" and reported that the governor would be "asked to send troops to the mountain wilds to force a truce." One subhead read: "Shot His Head Off."

The *Courier-Journal* reported Bad Frank's inhumane and criminal dispatching of Dempsey, which, it noted, angered one of the posse so much that he returned home. What is perhaps most telling about the story, though, is how much it harked back to the Civil War enmity between the Confederate Hatfields of Logan County and the Unionist McCoys of Peter Creek: "The Hatfields were organizing for a raid over on Peter Creek...to murder people, burn property and kill stock," the daily claimed, while "the Peter Creek guards, twenty strong, have now joined the capturing party, which now numbers forty odd, and are in hot pursuit of the Hatfields." Twenty-three years after the close of the war, it was the same old story.

In Kentucky, the report continued, the fear had spread well beyond Peter Creek. Pike County was feverish, "as the Hatfields have warned the people that they propose to kill them and burn their property. They have sent word that they intend to burn Pikeville, and extricate their...comrades, now in jail there." The jail was currently heavily guarded around the clock, and the evening pickets continued. Moreover, Pike County judge Tobias Wagoner and county attorney Lee Ferguson were heading to Frankfort on board the steamer *Frank Preston* to ask the governor for protection and guns.

Regardless of which side had the better weapons at Grapevine Creek, the battle set off an arms race. With the support of a council of Hatfields, Devil Anse instructed Cap to have Nan draft a letter to the makers of the Winchester in Springfield, Massachusetts, requesting the purchase of a number of guns and ten thousand rounds of ammunition, and on January 24, officials from Pike County traveled to Catlettsburg and bought sixteen more .38-caliber and .44-caliber Winchesters.[14]

IT MIGHT HAVE COME AS a surprise to readers of the local papers, but Devil Anse was not spoiling for a fight. The raids had deeply affected him. Crazy Jim was dead; Wall and others were in jail; and the entire family now felt threatened at all times, even in their own neighborhoods. Devil Anse was making plans not to attack Pikeville but to protect his family. He even went to Logan Courthouse to ask for help, but providing a standing border patrol to guard the Tug River, which could be crossed in many places, for months on end was not feasible.

Randall also seemed stunned and confused by what fate had wrought. Just days after the killing of Crazy Jim, he told a reporter from Pittsburgh: "I used to be on very friendly terms with the Hatfields before and after the war. We never had any trouble till six years ago. I hope no more of us will have to die. I'll be glad when it's all over." According to the reporter, Randall exhibited no signs of resentment. Instead, "he spoke like a man who had been bent and almost broken by the weight of his afflictions and grief."

Devil Anse discussed the situation with Major James A. Nighbert, a Logan Wildcats veteran, wealthy landowner, and leading citizen, as well as a friend. Nighbert offered to let him ride out the tide on his land on Dingess Run near Blair Mountain, where he could keep his family safe and where plenty of raccoon, turkey, and bear awaited hunting.[15]

So worried was Devil Anse that he promptly began dumping his property at Grapevine Creek, the very lands that had once belonged to Perry Cline, whose actions had turned the course of the feud. Devil Anse was relieved to sell to a group of Philadelphia coal investors, though the next month Lee Ferguson would gloat to the

Courier-Journal that he had received only seven thousand dollars for what was worth more than twice that (and would be worth five times more when the railroad arrived in a few years). But Devil Anse was in a hurry. Not only did he no longer feel safe along the Tug, but after the violence at Grapevine Creek, his creditors had suddenly come calling.[16]

Cap also sold off his property—the property given to him by his father—took the eight hundred dollars he made from the sale, and headed off through the woods, careful to avoid anyone who could identify him. After walking for five days, he jumped a train in a place far enough away that he knew no one would be looking for him. He was headed for Texas.[17]

Based on a complaint and information on oath from Constable Thompson, who had been present at the battle, and two others, on January 24, a Logan County justice of the peace issued a warrant for the arrest of the Kentuckians who on January 19 did "felinously, willfully, maliciously, deliberately, and unlawfully slay, kill and murder one William D. Dempsey." The warrant named twenty-eight men: Frank Phillips; nine McCoys—including Randall, Big Jim, Sam, Squirrel Huntin' Sam, Bud, Lark, and Paris—Perry Cline's son Sink; and Jacob and Bud Hurley, among others. Thompson returned the warrant the next day, notifying Judge James Monroe Jackson: "Not found within my County nor State."[18]

"There were 28 of the McCoys and others all together indicted at Logan Courthouse," wrote Squirrel Huntin' Sam, who could not resist adding, "A hundred dollars apiece for each one. I did not know the boys were such cowards as they were until the detectives got to stirring around." But they had good reason to be fearful.[19]

~

ON JANUARY 25, Judge Wagoner and Lee Ferguson arrived in Frankfort to ask Governor Buckner for weapons and state troops to end the fighting in their county. Buckner refused, saying that a local military company led by responsible men should be enough to handle the situation. The *Courier-Journal* found his thinking "highly satisfactory." A bill was proposed to allow him to immediately form six new state guard companies, one to be based in Pike County. But those opposing the idea insisted that the state should bear no expense beyond providing arms and ammunition for the troops.[20]

Buckner was feeling pressure from both sides. On January 26, Governor Wilson sent him a telegram about the Dempsey murder and asked him to help stop the warfare. Buckner telegrammed back that he had heard a different account of the skirmish. Jockeying for the high ground, the two leaders busily drafted letters with an eye toward their future use in court.[21]

The sensationalist press, in both state capitals and across the nation, only fueled the fire. The *New York World* proclaimed a "war of extermination," predicting the Hatfields "will be wiped out." The *Wheeling Intelligencer* cried foul at the *World*'s coverage: "When will our eastern contemporaries learn that Pike County is situated in Kentucky, and that the blood-thirsty 'West Virginia Vendetta' they prate about so much are Kentucky outlaws? Such publications . . . are doing this State much damage in more ways than one." And the *Louisville Courier-Journal* lauded the Pike County posse, which "will not give up the chase till the last bird is bagged," declaring that the locals were "greatly in need of a real, genuine, first-class hanging."[22]

West Virginia state guard units in several counties offered up their services by telegraph to Governor Wilson. On January 30, at Wilson's request, the Goff Guard, with thirty-five men, and the Auburn Guard, with forty, set out from Ritchie County for Parkersburg, with plans to carry on to Charleston and leave from there the following morning for Logan County. Wilson also dispatched the Confederate veteran Colonel W. L. Mahon to investigate the hostilities.[23]

After arriving at Logan Courthouse, Mahon paid a visit to several of the Hatfields and, echoing John B. Floyd's opinion, found them to be "good, law-abiding citizens." The colonel also talked to their neighbors and found that the Hatfields held their "respect and confidence." Mahon rushed back to Charleston, reaching the capital on the afternoon of January 30, with good news: while he described a "tumult bordering on a genuine young war," he noted that "peace has again been restored, and the belligerent parties on both sides have disbanded, and no further trouble is anticipated."

To Mahon, the "strangest part of the whole affair" was the "fact that the Hatfields and McCoys are related." What caused the hostility, however, was no surprise to the Confederate veteran, who had surrendered at Appomattox and well knew how long the bitter feelings could last: The troubles, he reported, "began in the war."

Wilson, buoyed by the news, countermanded the order calling out the military and sent the Goff and Auburn guards back to their respective towns. The likelihood of a clash between the states over the feud dramatically decreased.[24]

The same day that Mahon returned to Charleston, Judge John M. Rice, a pugnacious fifty-eight-year-old former two-term Democratic U.S. congressman, called upon Governor Buckner in Frankfort to dispel rumors that he refused to hold the upcoming session of court in Pikeville without the presence of the state guard. He assured the governor that he would personally convene the criminal court in Pikeville on February 27 and that "he would proceed to the discharge of his duty without fear."[25]

Buckner received another communication from Wilson that, in contrast to the blunt actions of the feud, was an obfuscatory masterwork of bureaucratic haze, the centerpiece being Wilson's assertion that the application for the requisition "does not appear to be made or supported by any official authority of Pike County." Buckner — the state's chief executive — was dumbfounded. He immediately drafted a letter to refute this sophism, pointing out that the "Executive making the demand, must be the sole Judge of the circumstances under which it would be proper." Furthermore, Wilson's facts were plain wrong. The application for the requisition had indeed been made "by the County Judge of Pike County, indorsed [sic] by the Judge of the District Court, and urged by the Commonwealth's Attorney of the district."[26]

Even as Buckner shaped his extensive response to Wilson, he dispatched Sam E. Hill, the state's adjutant general, to Pike County to investigate the border war (and thus engendered, some say, the expression "What in the Sam Hill is going on?"). That morning, January 29, Hill had telegraphed the Lexington Guards to mobilize and prepare to deploy but then rescinded the order. He set out from Frankfort that night. After traveling some forty miles across the mountains, he caught up with Judge Wagoner and Lee Ferguson in Catlettsburg on the morning of January 30. Though rebuffed in their request for troops, they were returning to Pikeville with ten new Winchester rifles and a thousand rounds of ammunition.

The tension on the border was palpable. At the train depot, a West Virginian harangued the Pikeville men, shouting that Kentucky had invaded his state and murdered his fellow citizens. Ferguson, small but fearless, retorted that this was a "God damn lie" and that it was the West Virginians who had invaded Kentucky, torched its property, and committed cold-blooded murder. An angry crowd gathered, and it looked as though the two men would come to blows. But the West Virginian, seeing just how bad the odds were, made a hasty escape.[27]

So raw were nerves in Pikeville that Hill authorized the formation of a state guard company there. Knowing the bellicose nature of his fellow Kentuckians, he cautioned them to use force only when ordered to by the civil authority to maintain "the peace and dignity of our Commonwealth." Over four days, he sought out the most reliable sources and questioned them, he later told Buckner, to better understand the true details and origination of the hostilities. He did not have to travel to do so because the raids had caused many families to leave their homes near the Tug and take refuge in Pikeville. Hill also visited the county jail to confront Wall Hatfield. To his surprise, he found him affable and noted that he "deprecates with apparent sincerity what has been done."

Hill interviewed Sally McCoy, who was still recovering from her injuries, and her daughter Addie, whose frostbitten feet continued to cause her pain. They told him about the house raid. He was so moved that he "could not avoid weeping freely as the old lady detailed . . . the horrors of that terrible night."[28]

Buckner did not wait for the results of Hill's investigation to dispatch a voluminous—two-thousand-word—response to Wilson. In addition to rebutting Wilson's objections, he recapped the feud events and the correspondence between the two and urged his counterpart to issue the requested requisitions and turn over the wanted men. And so it went, letters back and forth, a diplomatic feud of its own, ink and rhetoric in place of gunpowder and lead.

Among the new issues Wilson raised was the character of Perry Cline, who seemed to have extorted or been bribed by the Hatfields, an issue that Buckner tried to head off by noting that he already knew about Cline's "efforts . . . to secure a withdrawal of the requisition and rewards" in exchange for the wanted men's promise not to enter Kentucky again, and that he had declined the "cool proposition." The idea that Cline could be bribed by the Hatfields with several hundred dollars was unlikely. Perhaps it was a plot by agents of the Hatfields to muddy the waters. But even if they had managed to bribe Cline, Buckner argued, that was no reason to delay the issue of the requisition to the proper authorities, whose conduct was not in question.[29]

Regarding the battle of Grapevine Creek, Buckner gave no ground, arguing that Phillips and his posse had been ambushed and had killed Dempsey in self-defense and that "Phillips, the agent appointed by me to receive the fugitives . . . is not the murderous outlaw your Excellency seems to suppose." He acknowledged, however, that Phillips had arrested men in West Virginia without a warrant and agreed to designate another agent to receive the prisoners.[30]

In the meantime, William Floyd, Governor Wilson's emissary at the battle of Grapevine Creek, petitioned Wilson to release the West Virginia prisoners in Kentucky, maintaining that they had been "taken from the state without any legal process whatever, and in violation of the laws of the state."[31]

On February 2, Governor Wilson boldly turned the tables on

his counterpart and dispatched Colonel W. L. Mahon, who had investigated the feud in person the previous week, to Frankfort to deliver requisition papers to Governor Buckner for the return of the illegally obtained prisoners. Three days later, Buckner gave his answer: No. It was a matter for the courts to decide, in this case, Judge Rice of the Pike County Circuit Court.[32]

After a brief but intense stay in Pikeville, Sam Hill returned to Frankfort and wrote up his report, which he submitted to Buckner on February 7. The night before, he told a *Courier-Journal* reporter, "It is all a mistake about the feud having had its origin in war times. The Hatfields and the McCoys, so far as political faith goes, are members of the same party, and have always been such." He blamed the fighting on Devil Anse, whom he called "a bold, bad man."[33] This discounting of the Civil War as the root cause of the feud was a misinterpretation that would be perpetuated. Hill did not seem to realize that a number of the posse hunting down Devil Anse, Crazy Jim Vance, and the other Hatfield combatants were the sons, nephews, and brother of Harmon McCoy and the sons of Asbury Hurley, men killed by Crazy Jim and Devil Anse in the war.

Not surprisingly, Hill gave the story a Kentucky slant: "The assertion that Anderson Hatfield and his sons Johnson and Cap are reputable, law-abiding people is not sustained, for the stories of their lawlessness and brutality, vouched for by credible persons, would fill a volume." As for the other side, Hill (who interviewed denizens of Pike County only) could find no fault: "old man McCoy and his boys are represented as law-abiding, honest people by reputable men."

Hill advised his fellow Kentuckians to refrain from entering West Virginia and especially to avoid doing anything that would provide West Virginia officials any "just cause of complaint." He, like so many others, was well aware of the threat of a war breaking out along the border, a border that had not so long ago been engulfed in the most vicious of fighting.[34]

Chapter 17

~

Disorder in the Courts

February–May 1888

I n 1888, Louisville, Kentucky, was a growing and ambitious city. Having added to its population by more than 10,000 people the previous year, surpassing the 175,000 mark, it was starting to feel its powers. The year 1887 had been a robust one for the local economy, with trade up in excess of $50 million over the previous year. More than seventy manufacturing businesses had launched in 1887, bringing in capital and fifteen hundred new working-class jobs. A tobacco town, Louisville had constructed additional warehouses to handle the rising tide of hogsheads that passed through its limits (that year, more than 110,000 of them, each weighing 1,000 pounds). Whiskey, jeans, leather, and cement had also boosted the city's bottom line. But the biggest impact of all on Louisville's prosperity was the opening up of eastern Kentucky, where, according to an annual report on the city's economy, new capital had promoted the development of "phenomenally rich" iron, coal, and lumber resources. Railroads were laying tracks in the area, and prospects for the city, the report concluded, were "brighter now than at any time in its history."

By 1888, another industry, steadily expanding since 1880, had surpassed even tobacco in value: the lumber trade. Some 125 million board feet, valued at more than $25 million, had flowed into Louisville that year from eastern Kentucky, making lumber the city's leading business.[1]

But it was another import from eastern Kentucky that held the minds of the Louisville populace on the evening of February 16. The 7:15 Chesapeake and Ohio train pulled into the city's Eighth and Water Street depot, a bit tardy, greeted by a crowd who packed the platform in the hopes of seeing the so-called Hatfield Gang—the nine bearded, tattered, fanatical mountain feudists they had read so much about in the news—who were being delivered on writs of habeas corpus for a hearing in the United States District Court.[2]

Inside the train, the prisoners sat in a second-class coach, two to each cushioned seat. They were Selkirk McCoy; Andy Varney; Wall Hatfield; the habitual scofflaw Mose Christian, who also happened to be Perry Cline's cousin; L. D. McCoy; Guerilla Mitchell, who was also under indictment for two murders in Virginia; and the brothers Doc, Sam, and Plyant Mahon.[3]

Opposite them rode the guards. These included deputy jailers Perry Cline and his son-in-law Charlie Yost, as well as two of Cline's sons, sixteen-year-old Allen and nineteen-year-old Sink. Allen and Sink, along with another guard, Jim Sowards, were officers in Buckner's Rifles, the fifty-four-man Pikeville militia company that had been organized to prevent more feud trouble. Each guard wore a cartridge belt and a heavy revolver in a leather holster. Winchester barrels glinted over their heads. They had left behind a jittery citizenry in Pike County, despite the fact that they had cleared out the Pikeville jail.[4]

Wall and the others, who knew little of the legal wrangling that surrounded their capture and incarceration, had learned only two days earlier that West Virginia was attempting to free them. As word of their departure from Pikeville spread, Wall worried about violence. Indeed, ever since arriving in Pikeville, he had been expecting a lynch mob to show up. According to him, Randall had declared that "he could not desire us in a better place than the jail," because there he could blow the prisoners "all to pieces with dynamite." But when Perry Cline assured him that that would happen over his dead body, Wall said he "was not much disturbed after that," and he confessed that he was treated well in jail, where he was rarely locked in a cell.

When the West Virginia prisoners were taken from the jail down to the docks on the Levisa Fork to board a steamboat, a crowd hooted, but no one attacked them. They paddle-wheeled down to Catlettsburg, where they stayed overnight in the local jail. En route to Louisville, the West Virginians coolly and confidently professed their innocence to a *Courier-Journal* reporter who interviewed them in their coach. "I know nothing about the crimes which have been committed in the quarrel between the McCoys and Hatfields," Wall lied, "and I don't think any of the men with me know or had anything more to do with the killing and fighting than I do." Wall, who the reporter observed appeared to be a "quiet non-offensive citizen" and whom he deemed the smartest of the group, told how they had been ousted from their homes by the posse. "As it seemed safer to submit than to resist and risk being murdered," he said, "we went with the men who came after us." Wall claimed that those who, "from all I have been told, committed the crimes were not taken," while "those of us who did not expect any trouble and who remained quietly at home were."

Lee Ferguson, Randall McCoy, and his attorney Jim York also rode with the group. Ferguson snorted when he heard Wall's claims. While the worst of the Hatfield crowd had not been captured, he admitted, these prisoners were undoubtedly part of the gang.

With a morose stare, Randall described to the reporter the deaths of his children at the hands of the Hatfields. He talked of riding to hunt down the Hatfields with Big Jim and of his desire to return to his farm.⁵ Ferguson attested to the fact that Randall and his sons were, in general, "orderly and quiet" and that, unlike with the Hatfields, their names did not fill the court records with their crimes and misdemeanors.

After the other passengers disembarked and the station platform cleared, Cline directed the exit of his party in quasi-military fashion. The prisoners formed up in twos, arms locked. Guards with rifles flanked each pair. Others took up positions fore and aft, cocooning the prisoners. The guards then set out swiftly, clearing a path through the rowdy crowd curious to see the barbaric mountain men.

The phalanx marched up Seventh Street to Main, along Main to Sixth, and then up Sixth and around Jefferson to the county jail. As barbarians, the prisoners were something of a disappointment. "Their appearance was very unlike that of the mountaineers who are frequently guests of the United States while attending court here for making moonshine whiskey," observed the *Courier-Journal* reporter wryly. "Soft felt hats covered all of their heads and there were nine mustaches among the nine prisoners. Each maintained an air of indifference and there was no exhibition of bravado or ruffianism."

Still, the escort of small boys clinging to the outlaw parade grew steadily as they proceeded the short distance to the jail. After the jail door swung shut behind them, Perry Cline officially surrendered his prisoners to the U.S. marshal.

The next morning, Friday, a lengthy front-page article in the *Courier-Journal* announced the arrival of Louisville's country cousins to hash out what it called "one of the bloodiest feuds on record in the country." One of the key issues, the paper noted, was going to be the legality of the arrests and detainment of the prisoners. "They say that after we were over the boundary line of West Virginia, we were legally arrested," the cagey Wall told the *Courier-Journal,* "but I've never been aware of any legal steps to confine us being made." The media-savvy Lee Ferguson, who in addition to being the county prosecutor also published a Pikeville Republican newspaper called the *Times,* countered with the Kentucky point of view; namely, that the prisoners had been legally arrested after they crossed the border into Kentucky. Since West Virginia refused to arrest the wanted men, Kentucky was thus justified in taking the matter into its own hands to protect itself from the violent outlaws "who had only to cross a narrow stream to commit the most atrocious crimes and then cross back again to safety from the law."

Ferguson also defended Frank Phillips, who, he stated, was far from the desperado he was portrayed to be by the West Virginia counsel Eustace Gibson. Indeed, Ferguson said, he was "mild-mannered but courageous," a man who had been chosen to lead the McCoy posse because of his "shrewdness and excellent personal qualities." While they were in West Virginia, he falsely asserted, "all the fighting the Kentuckians had done was in self-defense."[6]

IT WOULD BE A WEEK before the West Virginians appeared in court. Making themselves at home with the other prisoners, they became the center of attention. Wall, who was respectfully dubbed Judge by the others, conversed freely with all manner of inmates. While the locals tended to idle about until after midnight, the mountain men went to sleep immediately upon being locked in their cells at dark. Up in the morning by five o'clock, the musical mountaineers would serenade their fellow inmates back to life with a fiddle, bones, a horn, and a triangle. During the day, they often sat around as a group and listened to one of the locals read aloud. Hair-raising adventure stories were a favorite, and George Peck's wry stories about a boy whose chief aim in life was playing pranks on his pa elicited great guffaws all around.

The West Virginians piously engaged in the jail's prayer service on Sunday, singing heartily when called upon. Wall, towering over

Simon Bolivar Buckner, governor of Kentucky
(1887–1891), in Confederate uniform.

the swindler and the forger on either side of him who shared his
hymnal, wailed out "One More River to Cross."[7]

THE HABEAS CORPUS CASE WAS heard on Saturday morning, February 25. Judge John W. Barr presided. Just how significant the feud
had become was indicated by the high caliber of men representing
the two states: Kentucky attorney general P. Watt Hardin was
accompanied by former Kentucky governor Proctor Knott. The
Honorable Eustace Gibson, a former Confederate officer, Speaker
of the West Virginia House of Delegates, and a U.S. congressman,
represented West Virginia with the assistance of Kentucky colonel
John Willis St. Clair and Governor Wilson himself. Notably absent,
however, was the West Virginia attorney general, Alfred Caldwell,

who had officially advised the governor that he did not believe that there was a legal justification for habeas corpus proceedings.[8]

In a preliminary hearing two weeks earlier, Judge Barr had stated that the Kentucky attorneys failed to show that the prisoners had been placed in the Pike County jail through due process of law. Thus, he was inclined to grant the writs of habeas corpus. It was an initial victory for West Virginia.[9]

Now, while the nine defendants sat impassively in two rows of carved wooden chairs before a packed courtroom, their legal representatives sparred with those of Kentucky over the scope of the case and the admission of evidence. After several hours, Judge Barr adjourned the court until Monday morning. On Sunday afternoon, the Hatfield contingent again took part in the jailhouse religious service. Although the organ recently installed in the jail for such occasions was silent due to the fact that the organist was out of town, they prayed, sang hymns, and then listened to a sermon delivered by a preacher who had been assaulted by two of the inmates prior to their incarceration and then invited by them to lead services. The preacher told how he had once been on his own "rapid course to destruction" and how he had found God's light and been delivered. A reporter observing the service noted that the story of his life "seemed a revelation" to the Hatfields, and he was sure that they had been "charmed" by the tale and that it would have great effect on them.[10]

By Monday, Governor Wilson had arrived, accompanied by his trusted assistant secretary of state, John B. Floyd, and a pile of books and documents. The case was clearly quite important to Wilson, and he was well versed in the facts and legal arguments. A small, slim man of exceptional ability, Wilson sat just behind Gibson and St. Clair in the packed courtroom.

At ten o'clock the bailiff called the court to order, and the lawyers for each side began a series of procedural moves that would determine the accepted facts of the case, the evidence that needed to be examined, and what had to be proved. The court ordered that

Portraits from the February 17, 1888, *Louisville Courier-Journal,* of (in order from the top) Randall McCoy and the defendants Wall Hatfield, L. D. McCoy, Selkirk McCoy; Doc, Sam, and Plyant Mahon; Tom Chambers, Mose Christian, and Andy Varney.

the proceedings be advanced in the name of Andrew Varney, whose petition rose first.

The Kentucky counselors began by admitting that the papers had not been served on the captured men until they reached the Pike County jail. They also admitted that the arrest by Frank Phillips was illegal but asked why the State of Kentucky should be held accountable for Phillips's individual acts, for which he alone was responsible. Phillips had been appointed as an agent to execute a special purpose, and that was all he had the right to do. He had no authority to negotiate with Governor Wilson.

St. Clair opened for West Virginia. He said that he would show that this was not a case of kidnapping but one in which, as required by the Constitution, a treaty for the extradition of men from their homes to a foreign state was in progress and that Phillips's correspondence proved that he was acting as an agent of the state. Thus, St. Clair pointed out, an agent designated by the governor of Kentucky had, without proper authority and by fraud, arrested the

Willis "Windy" Wilson, governor of West Virginia (1885–1890).

fugitives in West Virginia. Since the arrest and present holding were not legal, he argued, the prisoner was entitled to his liberty.

A master tactician, Governor Wilson bit at his bushy red mustache as he focused on the proceedings, often advising the attorneys sitting in front of him. An issue of debate was his reluctance to honor Governor Buckner's requisition. St. Clair wanted the court record to show that any delay was due only to the governor's care in so grave a matter. Then, while Wilson was arranging to convey the fugitives to Kentucky, St. Clair stated, Buckner's agent had murdered one of the fugitives, a citizen of West Virginia.[11]

This was the first time in the nation's history that its courts were called on to quell warfare on the borders of two of its states. At the close of arguments, Judge Barr declared that the case was too important for him to render a judgment just yet. He needed additional consultation and reflection.

FIVE DAYS LATER, on the morning of March 3, a crowd again filled the courtroom, eager to see the prisoners and the men who had argued their cases, Gibson on one side and Knott and Hardin on the other. Judge Barr delivered his decision orally, warming up by restating the facts of the case over the course of about thirty minutes. "The case which is here presented perhaps has never arisen before," he declared, "at least no case has been called to my atten tion, and I have seen none on the subject, and, so far as I know, the question has never been adjudicated by any state court or federal tribunal." And here he got to the meat of the matter. "But, whatever may be the law on this subject: to this proceeding this court cannot consider it because it is beyond its jurisdiction." By the time he reached his culmination, all eyes and ears were on him. "In matters of contest where there is a controversy between states, by the express provision of the federal constitution the jurisdiction is exclusively the United States Supreme Court."[12]

In effect, Kentucky had won the first round. The court denied the motion for the discharge of the prisoners. Then there was a discussion about who should keep them. Andy Varney, for one, had had enough, announcing that he wanted to be sent back to Pike County. The county's court was in session for only one week, and he wanted to be there to prove that he was innocent and then go home. This was an embarrassment to the West Virginia counsel, as they were arguing that the prisoners feared for their lives in Pikeville. Varney, who showed that he was no backwoods simpleton or an unwilling pawn of his own state, replied that he did not think it was fair to make him and others with him suffer so that West Virginia could fight its legal battle. "This put the laugh on the representative of West Virginia," noted the *Wheeling Intelligencer.* A somewhat annoyed Barr ordered the marshal to return the men to the Pike County jailer.[13]

Two days later, on Monday, March 5, Eustace Gibson and Proctor Knott presented short arguments before Judge Barr regarding whether an appeal might be sent directly to the U.S. Supreme Court. The West Virginia representatives contended that the indicted men could not get a fair trial in Pike County and that they were in real danger of being assassinated there. An appeal was granted, but only to the U.S. circuit court in Kentucky, also in Louisville. There, Judge Howell E. Jackson heard the same arguments. On the stand, Phillips again took responsibility for his acts, attempting to bolster the claim that Governor Buckner had nothing to do with any illegalities that might have occurred in his arrests. The case was argued at length for days, and then Judge Jackson granted an appeal to the Supreme Court.

ON MARCH 11, the Great Blizzard of '88 struck at around midnight and continued a full day, dumping four and a half feet of snow in some places, wreaking havoc on the East Coast from Maine to Virginia. Winds of up to eighty miles per hour knocked out the telegraph system and piled snowdrifts fifty feet high. With daytime temperatures in the single digits, more than four hundred people perished from the storm and the bitter cold. In the Atlantic, two hundred ships grounded or wrecked, killing a hundred seamen. With fire stations snowed in, $25 million worth of property burned up.

Devil Anse was still living in the woods, where he felt at home—no matter how bad the weather—and where he always managed to thrive. He had a knack for acquiring large tracts of land through atypical means, and he soon put that skill to use again. This time the source was Lewis "Old Hawk" Steele, a bearded and long-haired rover with a divot in his upper lip that spoke of his wild ways, and the tract in question was on Main Island Creek, not far from Logan Courthouse and safely back from the Kentucky line. Steele now bartered away his hereditary five thousand acres, loaded with valuable hardwoods, for a percentage of the return on Devil Anse's timbering of the property.[14]

Across the Tug, as the interstate legal wrangling grew more heated, the Hatfield prisoners became a political and financial hot potato, their status a media obsession. On March 16, Perry Cline returned to Louisville to take custody of the jailed men. He had been in Frankfort asking Governor Buckner to help him secure funds to pay the bill for their transportation to Louisville for the trial as well as to cover the costs of their imminent return trip and their upkeep. The tab already exceeded nine hundred dollars. Buckner assured Cline of his support.

Cline planned to set out with the accused on the 450-mile journey at six in the morning on March 17. The first leg, by rail, would take them back to Catlettsburg. After that, the party would board a boat up the Big Sandy to Pikeville, a distance of about sixty miles. With expenses accruing, Cline hired only three guards for the nine inmates, but he was unworried. "I do not anticipate the least trouble," he told the *Courier-Journal,* "but if we should have any we will be prepared."[15]

"We are sure we will be released on bond, and we have overwhelming evidence to prove our innocence," Wall told the same reporter. "The men who really did the deeds have not been arrested at all." When asked who murdered the three McCoys, Wall blithely answered, "Well, my brother Anderson and his three sons, Robert, Johnson and 'Cap' Hatfields [sic] and four or five others. They are all bad men." Wall, being a justice of the peace, had decided to trust not in his clan but in the justice system. Indeed, he had broadcast his independence of the clan by offering to turn himself in, and now he had taken another step in naming his brother and his nephews. He wanted only to clear his name and return to life as the respectable, law-abiding citizen that he considered himself.[16]

Wall also tried to clear up his reputation in another regard: "I wish you would contradict the statement that I have seven wives. I have never had but one," he deadpanned, "and . . . I don't want any more." [17]

On February 10, Devil Anse and Vicey had added another Hatfield to the hollows. They named their new son Emanuel Willis Wilson, in honor of the governor, who was proving to be a faithful friend. Like a lot of kids in the Tug Valley, Willis was born with ready-made playmates—a plethora of his own nephews and nieces.

Around the beginning of April, after the last frost, Devil Anse and Vicey set up their new household on Main Island Creek, deeper in the hills, where detectives and the McCoys would have a hard time disturbing them. That summer, New York Sun reporter John Spears would poke his head inside Devil Anse's old house on the Tug, which sat abandoned but still intact. Over the fireplace, he noted, hung "a gaudy lithograph motto, which read: 'There is no place like our home.'" But Spears apparently was not the first visitor to the dwelling; another had taken a lead pencil and scrawled beneath the carefully colored letters: "Leastwise, not this side of hell."[18]

At his new abode, Devil Anse prepared as if the devil proper might choose to pay him a visit. He began building an endgame log bunker, using twenty-three-foot logs that were almost two feet in diameter. It would be a massive, windowless structure, a sturdy, squat fortress that he and his brothers and their sons and friends could defend against a small army. The door was made of solid oak.[19]

Meanwhile, Randall and Sally reluctantly came to the conclusion that they could not move back to their farm, the home that Sally had inherited from her father before the war and where they had planned to be buried, alongside their children who had died in the feud. Sally was too feeble to move back. Randall was depleted mentally and physically. And with the Hatfields angrier than ever, the threat of violence there was undiminished. The McCoys would sell their farm the next month.

~

By Wednesday, April 18, Eustace Gibson was in Washington, DC, seeing to the printing of the legal brief he planned to present before the Supreme Court the following Monday. In it, he maintained that the men who had captured and kidnapped the West Virginians in question were Kentucky officials and that the state had thus violated their constitutional right to liberty.

On April 23 and April 24, *Mahon v. Justice* was argued, *Justice* being Abner Justice, the Pike County jailer. Opening for West Virginia, Gibson took ninety minutes, out of an allotted two hours, to make his case; speaking for Kentucky, Proctor Knott took up only twenty minutes of the court's time.[20]

Despite the brevity of the argumentation, its result would stand the test of time. *Mahon v. Justice* would be cited in no fewer than a dozen cases over the next century, helping to maintain order and civility in interstate jurisdictional disagreements and to establish the right of a court to jurisdiction regardless of how a defendant arrived in its midst.

On May 14, Justice Stephen Field, an 1863 Lincoln appointee from California, delivered the opinion of the court, declaring that since the states' sovereignty was limited by the federal Constitution, they could not authorize reprisals on other states. If law violators escaped from the state, their surrender could be secured only by a proper demand on the executive of the state to which they had fled. But, said Field:

> No mode is provided by which a person unlawfully abducted from one state to another can be restored to the state from which he was taken, if held upon any process of law for offense against the state to which he has been carried. If not thus held, he can, like any other person wrongfully deprived of his liberty, obtain his release on habeas corpus. Whether Congress might not provide for the compulsory restoration to the state of parties wrongfully abducted from its territory upon application of the parties or of the state . . . are not matters for present consideration. . . . No means for such redress through the courts of the United States have as yet been provided.[21]

The arrest and abduction of Mahon were illegal acts, he continued, for which Phillips could be punished under the laws of West Virginia. However, the process emanating from the Kentucky governor gave no reason for charging complicity in the wrong done to West Virginia. For the case at hand, then, the only question for the court to decide was whether a person indicted for a felony in one state and abducted from another by parties acting without the proper authority was entitled to be released because of the illegal abduction.

West Virginia had contended, he noted, that the appellant had been held in violation of the constitutional provisions for extraditing fugitives from one state to another but also of the Fourteenth Amendment, which says that "no state shall make or enforce any law which shall abridge the privileges or immunities of citizens of the United States, nor shall any state deprive any person of life, liberty, or property, without due process of law." As to the latter, the court argued, it was difficult to see how it bore upon the subject, since Kentucky had passed no law infringing on these rights or authorizing the abduction of the prisoner. The law enforced by that state was for murder.

As to acquiring the fugitive in an extra-constitutional manner, it was unclear how that pertained to his being held by the state in which the crime was allegedly committed; the jurisdiction of the court was not impaired by the manner in which the accused was brought before it. Among the many precedents to support this, Justice Field noted, English courts had customarily focused on a defendant's presence before the court and showed little concern for the method of his apprehension.[22]

Precedent had established that no extradition treaty entitled a fugitive of the United States to asylum in another country. Field now extrapolated that because under the law a fugitive from another state could, upon proper proceedings, be surrendered to the state where the crime was committed, he had the right of asylum in the state to which he had fled unless removed appropriately. Thus, even with the illegal mode in which the defendant was brought from another state, no constitutional right was violated by his arrest and imprisonment in Kentucky.

Two of the justices dissented. Joseph P. Bradley, a Grant appointee from New Jersey, wrote the dissent, and John Marshall Harlan, a Hayes appointee from Kentucky, no less, concurred. In Bradley's opinion, "the writ of habeas corpus was properly issued," and Mahon, having been kidnapped and carried into Kentucky in a clear violation of the Constitution, should have been returned to West Virginia.

Bradley and Harlan's variance notwithstanding, the Supreme Court upheld the decision of the lower court. Kentucky had won. West Virginia had lost. Both states, however, would feel the repercussions.

Chapter 18

~

The Lawmen

1888

In the South and the West in the late nineteenth century, if a man was not carrying a firearm, he was likely carrying a knife. And if he ever did find himself in need of a gun, it could easily be procured in just about any house, office, or store. The *Louisville Courier-Journal* ran a regular front-page crime column detailing homicides ranging from Mexican bandits shooting ranchers in Texas to a gang of Kentucky men from respectable families gunning down a young woman in her doorway for no apparent reason. Though there are plenty of crimes committed by psychopaths or outlaws, what draws one's attention in this record is the remarkable number of murders of honor — some of which were retaliations in long-standing feuds.

To be sure, there was abject depravity. In early March came news from Springfield, Ohio, of a man named Anderson Merrit who had murdered his wife with a club. Having long ago sired a baby by her sister, who was now married to his brother, Merrit took up residence with this daughter and her husband, drove off the husband, and "eloped" with his own daughter. But for every jaw-dropper like that, there was a slaying where personal or family honor was at stake.

Even a quarter century after the Civil War, reprisals from that era were not unheard of. Also in early March, at Logan Courthouse —

back in the heart of Hatfield-McCoy territory—Uriah Buskirk was sitting with several other men in the drawing room of the Dejarnette Hotel when John Thompson, the constable who had been with the Hatfields at Grapevine Creek, stepped up on the hotel porch, took aim through the window, and shot Buskirk in the left side of the chest, mortally wounding him. Twenty-six years after Buskirk had killed Thompson's father in the same hotel during the war, Thompson avenged the death.[1]

GIVEN THE ONGOING LACK OF local legal authority and the inadequacies of the sheriff-constable system, private detectives had to fill the law enforcement void. Many were ruffians, scarcely more scrupulous than the men they were pursuing. Some few, however, like Alf Burnett, whom Dan Cunningham had joined forces with in Jackson County, had made a reputation for being competent, respectful of the law, and fearless and were often retained by local and state officials to tackle high-profile cases.

Burnett's services were in such demand that in 1878 he and several partners had formed Eureka Detectives in Charleston, West Virginia, the "first agency of the kind South of Mason and Dixon's line," for the purpose of "detecting, arresting and bringing to justice" anyone charged with or suspected of committing a crime. Burnett took the title of superintendent, while twenty-eight-year-old William Baldwin, one of Burnett's most trusted and capable agents (who would later go on to form the famous Baldwin-Felts agency), became secretary. Eureka quickly grew to be one of the most formidable private law enforcement agencies anywhere. By 1890, it would amass 1,200 arrests, including 334 for felonies.[2]

It was dangerous work, to be sure. Burnett's wife, Fanny, had no misconceptions about that, and while encouraging her husband to do the work he was clearly meant to do—pursuing the most nefarious men in the land—she held on to a hefty life insurance policy that if need be would see her through her days. As a reminder of the risks, Burnett had a purple groove tattooed across his scalp from a close call on an early job, one that had cemented his reputation for tenacity. He had been pursuing a clever gang of store robbers in a county northwest of Charleston and had tracked down seven of the outlaws but lacked the evidence to make a conviction stick. Rebuffed in court three times, he finally discovered their hideout and loot stash, giving him the proof he needed, but by then, the gang had taken to the deep hills. Undaunted, Burnett tracked the ringleader, Perry Wetzel, and a henchman to a remote forest hut. The pair emerged occasionally to be fed at the nearby cabin of one of the gang members. Burnett lay low, learning their rhythms and signals. Silver wood smoke rising from the chimney meant "come in, no danger"; inky coal smoke, the contrary. One morning, just after dawn, silver smoke drew the two robbers to the cabin. As Burnett and a partner crept across a bald patch to the hut, a woman fetching water saw them and yelled out a warning to the men inside.

Wetzel sprang from the front door, firing at Burnett; it was this shot that seared his scalp. Burnett dodged more slugs from Wetzel's revolver and squeezed the trigger of his double-barreled shotgun. The first barrel fired; the second failed. Burnett coolly extracted the charge, loaded it in the other barrel, and fired. The shot pierced Wetzel's nose and peppered his body, but he managed to flee. The relentless Burnett tailed him all the way to Kentucky. Finally, Wetzel surrendered, and Burnett brought him back in handcuffs to serve nine years in prison. He would ultimately send the other six thieves to prison too.[3]

THE UNINTENDED RESULT OF THE Supreme Court decision in *Mahon v. Justice* was to create an open season in West Virginia on any man wanted by the State of Kentucky, and in Kentucky on any man wanted by West Virginia. Private detectives and bounty hunters could now depend on a payday if they could bag a wanted man, get him across the state line, and turn him over to the sheriff of the appropriate county.

In West Virginia, twenty-eight Pike County men were wanted for the kidnapping of the nine West Virginians as well as for the murders of Jim Vance and Bill Dempsey. The state offered a $100 reward for the arrest of each of the Kentucky kidnappers except Frank Phillips. He commanded $500, and the Hatfields promised to match that with another $500. That put the price on his head midway between Kentucky's offer of $700 for Devil Anse and $1,250 for Cap. Johnse, at $700, and Elias, at $500, also had valuable heads. Most of the other indicted West Virginians carried a $100 reward, and Governor Buckner promised an additional $500 for each man proven to have taken part in the attack on Randall McCoy's homestead.[4]

Combined, the two states were offering some twelve thousand dollars' worth of rewards. "Detectives" from around the region arrived to hunt down men on both sides of the Tug River. For some time after the New Year's Day raid, the Hatfields had kept a low profile, and no one else had been arrested. Slowly they emerged again from the deepest recesses of southern West Virginia, appearing in public with guarded freedom. Seeing Devil Anse and Cap back in their homes unharassed, Bill Tom Hatfield came out of hiding, but unlike his cousins, he grew careless. Officers lured him to the Tug by having a man pretend to befriend him and invite him to come along on an adventure on the river. At a prearranged spot, the men surrounded and disarmed Bill Tom, but before they could carry him across the river into Kentucky, news of his capture spread. Twenty-eight-year-old Newton "Doc" Keadle, the sheriff of nearby Williamson, summoned a posse and started in pursuit. A stocky, commanding six-footer with pale hair and blue eyes, Keadle was known to be a decent man. He rarely carried a gun, and in this case he prevented a bloody encounter by prevailing upon the Kentuckians to release Bill Tom. It was only a temporary reprieve for the captive, however, who lacked a measure of discretion. He was caught again later that year and would eventually be convicted for his role in the murder of the McCoy brothers.[5]

Nevertheless, from the start, West Virginia seemed to have the advantage, in large part because the Eureka Detectives, with their potent combination of doggedness, guile, and brute force, happened to be located on that side of the river. As citizens of the state, the Eureka agents naturally had their designs on Bad Frank. After Johnse fled to Colorado to ride out this treacherous time, they asked Nancy, who conveniently knew how to read and write, to help them ensnare Bad Frank. With the approval of the Hatfields, she moved back across the Tug to her mother's house on Peter Creek. It did not take her long to seduce the lawman.[6]

Though Bad Frank had been unable to lay hands on Johnse, he undoubtedly took perverse pleasure in laying hands on Johnse's wife. While he was enjoying Nancy's company, living with her along with her mother in their one-room cabin, she was secretly dispatching weekly letters to Alf Burnett, informing him of Bad Frank's whereabouts and activities as well as passing on any information she could glean about other indicted Kentuckians.

Somewhere along the line, however, Bad Frank discovered that Nancy was informing on him—and he turned the tables. Now, instead of ratting on Bad Frank, Nancy became his mistress. The following year she had a baby by him, a girl, Elsie. Bad Frank was still married to his wife of eight years, Mary, the mother of his first two children, but both Mary and Nancy would give birth to several more of his children in coming years.[7]

ON FRIDAY, JUNE 1, 1888, Alf Burnett and his partner Tom Campbell rode out of Charleston, heading southwest. Their intended prey was Dave Stratton, a thirty-five-year-old Logan County native and the political adversary of the Hatfields who had the showdown with Devil Anse over the Altizer-Floyd election. He now lived on the Kentucky shore and was one of Bad Frank's posse. Otherwise, there was a sudden dearth of targets: many of the Kentucky posse at Grapevine Creek, including Frank Phillips and John Yates, had been locked up in the Pike County jail for the illegal shooting of some outlaws from Letcher County. Because of the uproar created by the jailing of these community guardians, who were considered heroes by many, the Pikeville sheriff was in a state of high alert, with sixty armed men on patrol. It was the vigilantes' good luck to be in jail, however, on the day the Eureka detectives hit the area.

Burnett and Campbell started with a predawn visit to Stratton's house, at the mouth of Knox Creek. They woke his wife, who told them that Stratton was not there, but she inadvertently revealed that he was out flatboating on the river.

The detectives combed the riverbanks. At daybreak they discovered half a dozen men still asleep under blankets on a sandbar on the West Virginia embankment. Though they were outnumbered three to one, they had surprise on their side. Silently, they crossed the Tug, picked out Stratton, and pounced on him. He lurched awake with a pistol barrel at his throat, unable to reach for either the Winchester or the Colt concealed beneath his blanket. His cohorts wanted nothing to do with the businesslike detectives with their weapons drawn and did not move. Stratton raised his hands above his head as he was commanded, and they handcuffed him and led him away.[8]

In short order, the Eureka detectives managed to seize four other Kentucky posse men — none of them McCoys — and ferry them across the river to face charges of kidnapping and murder. If Kentucky could do it, West Virginia could too.[9]

~

WHILE BURNETT AND HIS MEN were stalking the banks of the Tug, the brawny redheaded Dan Cunningham looked to take care of unfinished business in Jackson and Roane counties with the gang that had run his family into the ground. But it was an uphill battle. The Jackson County prosecutor told law enforcement officers that it would cost the state too much to pursue and prosecute the Consolidated Band and that it would "destroy his town." Cunningham, not surprisingly, considered him "a miser and a coward."[10]

In the summer of 1888, a list of those who had witnessed the gang's deliberations and murders at Lynn Camp was introduced at court in the town of Spencer. The judge was ready to act on it, but the foreman of the grand jury (a minister, no less) was under the influence of the Consolidated Band and sandbagged the proceedings. At a second grand jury, matters only grew worse — malign, in fact. Two jurymen bore grudges against Cunningham. He had exposed one's brother as an accessory to murder, and the other had been a political foe of his pro-Union father. This dynamic still governed allegiances: you were either a Union man and a Republican or a Secessionist and a Democrat. Overwhelmed by anti-Union sentiment, the jury, incredibly, indicted Cunningham as an accessory to the murder of Father Ryan. It was an attempt to run him out of the county. Bristling, Cunningham informed the county prosecutor, John A. A. Vandale, that he would most certainly be on hand for the trial at the next term of court. In the meantime, the Band set about finding false witnesses. When the trial came, however, Cunningham did not even testify, and the jury did not leave the courtroom to deliberate before pronouncing him innocent. Vandale, who had assembled eighty bogus witnesses, was humiliated. The Band, noted Cunningham, "slunk out of the courthouse."

But then the winds changed. Bob Skean was arrested and indicted for the murder of George Duff. The circuit court judge refused to try the case, so Huntington-based judge Thomas A. Harvey was called in. Eleven of twelve jurors voted to find Skean guilty of first-degree murder, the holdout being a son of a leader of the Band. The case was carried over to the next court term. The state again presented ample evidence to convict, and it seemed inevitable that Skean would be hanged or imprisoned for life. However, another twist was in the works. Out of the blue, Judge Harvey ordered the clerk to enter a nolle prosequi, vacating the charges and closing the case forever.

The legal system had once again been subverted by what Cunningham called "Secessionism." Harvey, a Confederate veteran wounded at Fort Donelson and educated at Washington College (now Washington and Lee University), where Robert E. Lee had signed his legal diploma, had exonerated a blatantly guilty man because of his ties to the Confederacy. The deaths of Robert and George Duff, who had striven to bring law and order to the region, were for naught.[11]

In the end, Cunningham would not get Wade Counts, the man who had murdered his brother, either. But perhaps, as he had come to believe, divine assistance was on his side. One day, Counts was passing near the murder site of Coon and Robert Duff when, as Cunningham described it, a "bolt of avenging lightning broke forth from a cloudless sky . . . and smote him dead." With evident satisfaction, Cunningham related that Counts's body sat for four days in the August heat before it was found and "hauled in a wagon past the place where he helped murder my brother, a swarm of green flies following him."

The injustice of these cases (celestial wrath notwithstanding) stuck with Cunningham for the rest of his life. In his memoir decades later, he inked an open letter to Tom Ryan, prodding: "If you have one jot of evidence . . . [concerning] that Kentuck Band of Rebels with what few dirty followers they enlisted to commit the crimes they did . . . go with me and we will . . . ask for a prosecution. . . . There are some few of the murderers living."

It seems somewhat inevitable that at this point Cunningham (who would remain unattached until 1893, when, at forty-three, he wed Beulah Greenleaf, half his age) would pull up stakes and head south to apply his obsessive pursuit of justice to the nation's most notorious feud.

~

ONE OF CUNNINGHAM's first visits was to the Hatfields, a dangerous family to drop in on unannounced, especially if Cap, who did not mess around with small talk, was on guard duty. Cunningham's account of what transpired with Cap on this August day was cryptic: "All was gone except Cap Hatfield, who was setting on a sled in the yard with a Winchester across his lap and two large revolvers hanging to his side." Cunningham introduced himself. "Cap said he had been sick and he had come to the conclusion that in less than two days another strange face would appear in hell."[12]

Whatever transpired between the two after that is unknown. A tireless investigator, Cunningham was no doubt doing his due diligence on his quarry, Bad Frank and the McCoy posse. Afterward, he headed to Pikeville for some reconnaissance and to work on a map of the McCoys' locations. He did not have to use it, however, since they came to him.

On August 22, he was eating dinner at the Williamson Hotel in Pikeville when he was interrupted by a group of men he called the McCoy faction. They arrested him, charged him with kidnapping, and held him prisoner for two days, trying to scare him into a confession. Finally, realizing that the stone-faced lawman was not going to break, they let him go and sent him unescorted back to West Virginia. That was a mistake. Cunningham headed for the Tug, yes, but on his way he detoured to follow one of his leads and arrested "one of the McCoy gang." He hustled the man across the Tug and took him to Logan Courthouse, where he was put in jail. One more wanted man down.

Then on a late August or early September night, Cunningham returned to Kentucky with two Eureka men, Kentucky Bill Napier and Treve Gibson, to search for Peter Smith, a member of Bad Frank's posse. In the moonlight, they walked along the road beside

Deputy U.S. Marshal Dan
Cunningham as depicted in
McClure's Magazine in June 1904.

Peter Creek, and when they were about two miles from Smith's farm, Cunningham heard a voice behind him. He swiveled and saw men crossing the road into the creek. Two more groups of men appeared, one ahead in the road and one even with them across the creek. The Kentuckians—more than forty of them—were determined to put an end to the bounty hunting on their turf.

Cunningham may have felt somewhat invincible at this point. Back in Jackson County, word had spread that he was "'witched' against bullet and poison." The Band would try both. "The bullet, fired with a close and steady aim from ambush, cut through the breast of his coat, barely burning the skin," one journalist later wrote, "the arsenic, skillfully prepared in an apple by the 'yarbwitch' of the Band, he tried on a hen." The hen would die.[13]

On Cunningham's command, the three detectives bolted from the road toward a beech tree. They leaped over a low fence into a cornfield and sprinted toward the foot of a mountain thirty yards away that might offer them shelter. The patrolmen unleashed their full fusillade, blasting the cornfield and ripping the clothes of the three detectives. Unharmed, they stopped, returned fire, and moved forward again. As they did so, a haversack with biscuits in it was shot off Kentucky Bill's back. Again they stopped and returned the fire, repeating this pattern until at last they managed to climb into the waiting arms of the dark woods on the mountainside.[14]

As quickly and quietly as they could, the detectives made their way to the top of the beehive-shaped mountain. The Kentuckians positioned themselves strategically in the passes that separated it from the peaks on either side and at the base to block the trio's access to the Tug River, which they would have to cross to reach safety.

At the first light of dawn, Cunningham, Kentucky Bill, and Gibson, who had fortified themselves during the long hours on the mountain with pork jerky and raw onions, made their move down the mountain. Ready for action, a patrolman saw them and began to shoot. The detectives returned the fire and bobbed and weaved down the slope, heading for a hollow that would lead them to the river. They had about four hundred yards to travel. Calculating their trajectory, the patrolman moved in that direction to cut them off.

Cunningham looked at Kentucky Bill, a tall, gangly ruffian with long hair à la Buffalo Bill — his hero — and whiplike mustaches that flew out several feet from his chin. "What're we gonna do now?" he shouted.[15]

"We gonna give 'em a helluva fight!" Kentucky Bill called back.

There was only one problem with that plan: the detectives each had only three rounds left. Nevertheless, Cunningham agreed. "We best play Lewis Wetzel on 'em," he responded, referring to the famous Ohio Valley Indian fighter whom the Indians had dubbed Deathwind for his skill in shooting and reloading at a dead run.

Cunningham, Kentucky Bill, and Gibson descended on a dry creek bed to the south and east. The guard crossed through woods to cut them off again. About a quarter mile down, the trio suddenly stopped in their tracks, doubled back, and went up and over another mountain, losing their pursuers. When they appeared again at the river's edge, they were out of firing range. They dove into the water and swam for it. On the other side, Cunningham counted nine bullet holes in his coat.

Back in Logan County, he made for the home of Jim Vance's widow, Mary. Apparently he was a known quantity there and was welcomed in. But on this visit something profound happened: Mary Vance and her children told him what they considered to be the truth about the feud. Cunningham was shocked. As he listened intently, he recorded on six pages of foolscap paper a stunning indictment of Crazy Jim and the Hatfields, including the details of the burning of Randall McCoy's house. Mary blamed her husband and even considered Bad Frank's killing of him justified.

Cunningham suddenly saw that he had taken up with the wrong faction in this fight. He now understood the lay of the land, and this land looked a lot like the one he had just come from. The Hatfields were unreconstructed Rebels — the Skeans, Kisers, and Countses of their realm. He could even link the Hatfields to his archenemies Zeke and Cain Counts, whom he called "pals of the Hatfields all

through the war." The parallels were clear. They were Secessionists, scofflaws, bootleggers, extensively intermarried. They were
bent on dominating their region by any means. Some Hatfields came
from the Clinch River Valley, and there were even loose family
connections between them and the Consolidated Band.

Disregarding the danger, Cunningham got on his horse and rode
back into Kentucky to find Lee Ferguson. After he related what he
had learned, the two agreed to bury the hatchet. Dan Cunningham
was now allied with the McCoys.[16] This was a little-recognized
watershed moment in the late stages of the feud.

Cunningham, who well knew the vicissitudes of detective work —
how innocent questions might lead to solving a crime and how a
solid case might be derailed by corrupt officials — was by luck and
diligence set on a course to wreak havoc on the Hatfield clan, inso
far as that could be accomplished.

CHARLEY GILLESPIE, THE TEENAGER who had participated in the
New Year's Day raid, had had a falling-out with Devil Anse. The
Hatfield patriarch had taken a liking to Gillespie's mother, quar-
reled with his father, and then run his father out of the county. As
Devil Anse now split his time between his home on Main Island
Creek and the Gillespie house, the youth, who had taken his father's
side in the dispute, felt like he was constantly in jeopardy. He fled
to a cousin's house in Knapp's Valley, in southern Virginia along the
West Virginia border, an area where the Gillespies held sway.
Cunningham happened to be in the area and caught wind of a new-
comer who had ties to Devil Anse. When he discovered that it was
Charley Gillespie, he devised a plan to catch him.

Clean-cut and handsome, Cunningham still had the appearance of
a circuit rider. When he arrived at the cousin's house, he introduced
himself as a friend of Gillespie's with important news for him. He had
forged a letter addressed to Gillespie saying that his two sisters were
dying from the flux (as dysentery was then known), which at the time

was the scourge of the region. Gillespie was not there, but the cousin's wife read the letter and was fooled into thinking that Cunningham was simply a good-hearted messenger and a family friend. She was more than happy to welcome such a fine specimen of a man into her house. She talked easily with him and told him that Charley spent his days out in the woods, returning only at night to bed down.[17]

Not wishing to arouse suspicion, Cunningham took his leave and went into the countryside and sniffed out the trails. That evening, September 15, he spied Gillespie, a tall, erect eighteen-year-old, rifle in hand, walking toward him along a remote path in a clearing. Cunningham adopted a nonchalant air and began whistling a tune as he strolled toward Gillespie. The ploy worked. The teen was not alarmed by the cheerful hunter coming his way. As they came face-to-face, Cunningham moved with a whippet's speed, catching the fugitive by the wrists. Gillespie struggled, but Cunningham had viselike strength in his hands and closed steel cuffs around the youth's wrists with a couple of deft moves.[18]

He handcuffed Gillespie to himself, and the two set off. By dawn the next morning, they had already traveled twenty miles from the cousin's house.

The detective did not make a beeline for Pikeville, where he would eventually go to pick up his reward for the capture of the young fugitive. Instead, he transported him across West Virginia to Charleston. How he did this covertly and under whose orders are now unknown. In Charleston, the Eureka Detectives secretly held Gillespie at the home of Alf Burnett, and he confessed to Burnett's wife, Fanny. Then, for reasons that remain obscure but perhaps to avoid thorny jurisdictional issues, they transported him across the state line to Ohio, to the home of Eureka Detectives partner P. A. Campbell in the small town of Wellston. Gillespie made a second confession, which Campbell's wife recorded and Gillespie signed in the presence of Wellston's mayor. Finally, the detectives took him to jail, half a day's ride away in the town of Ironton, Ohio. There, Gillespie became, as the *Louisville Courier-Journal* later put it, a "mysterious inmate of the Ironton jail." The identity of the handsome dark-haired, dark-eyed young man was carefully concealed by those who were aware of it, and news of the arrest would not be made public for nearly a month.[19]

During the day, Gillespie, whom the *Cincinnati Enquirer* would describe as "very gentlemanly in appearance," was allowed to move around the town under Campbell's watchful eye. No one bothered him. At night, he returned to his cell. Although Gillespie was committed to jail for only fifteen days, the *Courier-Journal* would report, he had voluntarily recommitted for another term to stay in a place where he was well treated and safe from any reprisals.

On Thursday, October 11, Lee Ferguson and Alf Burnett arrived with requisition papers from Kentucky, and Gillespie was offered a deal: if he testified against the others, he could secure his own release. He had admitted that he participated in the house burning, but he claimed that he and Indian Hatfield were stationed on the road as guards and did not take part in the shooting. (Perhaps that was the understanding he came to with his confessors to spare him the gallows, but the claim also defied logic: if he was on the road, how could he describe the raid in such detail?) News of his statement broke in the October 13 *Louisville Courier-Journal* and the October 14 *Cincinnati Enquirer.* By then, Gillespie had already been transported to the Catlettsburg jail and from there delivered by Big Jim McCoy to the Pike County jail.[20]

WHILE CUNNINGHAM WAS DEALING WITH Gillespie, Kentucky Bill was getting acquainted with Bad Frank Phillips. When a West Virginia fugitive named Jim Hurley, who had a hundred-dollar bounty on his head, came to the Peter Creek area, Bad Frank arrested him and promptly escorted him back to his home county in cuffs to claim the reward. It was a brash and foolhardy move; Bad Frank was riding into the Hurley stronghold, and he himself was wanted in West Virginia, with a price on his head of one thousand dollars — ten times that of Hurley. The Hurley clan chased Bad Frank all the way back to the Kentucky line. They did not intend to stop there either. They engaged the well-known bounty hunter Kentucky Bill as their guide, and together they all went on a hunt for Bad Frank.

On Friday night, September 21, they found him, along with some of his allies, and they fought like trapped badgers. In the clash, one Hurley was hit by a life-threatening bullet that passed all the way through his body, and Kentucky Bill was shot through the heel. Bad Frank got away, and the Hurleys suddenly lost the taste for pursuing their grievance with him.[21]

THE SEPTEMBER 12, 1888, *Wheeling Register* led with the simple truth: "They Were Not Tried." The report out of Catlettsburg revealed that despite the sound and the fury, including a hearing in the U.S. Supreme Court, none of the Hatfield gang indicted on murder charges had been tried. On top of that, some of the captured men had been let go. False—and, to many, troubling—reports of the acquittal of several of them came out, according to the *Register,* after Andy Varney, Selkirk McCoy, and L. D. McCoy were freed because they had turned state's evidence. Guerilla Mitchell, Mose Christian, and Plyant Mahon had been released on bail. Bail was denied only to Wall Hatfield, considered the leader of the gang, and Doc Mahon, said to be his lieutenant. Their cases would not be heard for five more months, however, meaning they would spend more than a year in jail before going to trial.[22]

With legal matters still in disarray in Kentucky and West Virginia, and the political leaders, media, and local citizens in a state of agitation, two New York City heavies were dispatched to the scene. They were both experts at their work: adroit pugilists, trained to detect lies and traps, and masters of assassination—character assassination, that is. They were reporters.

~

Chapter 19

Yellow Journalists on the Bloody Border

February–October 1888

While the term *yellow journalism* would not be coined until 1895, after the sensationalist *New York World* ran a colorized cartoon featuring the Yellow Kid (a boy in a yellow nightdress), the appeal of lurid stories with graphic descriptions and exaggerated headlines was already recognized by the industry. With the shocking explosion of violence in the exotic Appalachian Mountains resulting from a feud that threatened to draw two Civil War border states back to arms, the race was on to capture the most riveting news story in America—and in late September two of the most legendary yellow journalists of the day were given the assignment.

The two had been beaten to the punch in January, however, by the *New York Herald*'s ace reporter Jim Creelman, who had recently interviewed Sitting Bull after the defeat of Custer and who during his career would converse with such luminaries as Leo Tolstoy and Pope Leo XIII. As Creelman rode the train on the Kentucky side of the Tug from Catlettsburg (which he described as "full of unkempt, frowsy idlers, who slouch about like human buzzards") to Peach Orchard, along what he called "the bloody border," he heard one inflamed passenger swear that if the Hatfields attacked Pikeville,

New York Herald correspondent James Creelman.

the people of Kentucky would "invade Virginia, and wipe the whole State out of existence."

Creelman planned to ride right into Devil Anse Hatfield's stronghold and confront the feudist face-to-face. After crossing the Tug, he was repeatedly urged to abandon this ill-advised scheme. A *Pittsburgh Times* reporter, he was told, had thrown in the towel just three days earlier. Despite the fact that no one he asked would guide him, the bulldoggish reporter continued on, begging directions as he went. Finally, he was accosted by a stout, furtive, malign-looking horseman who warned him to turn back or be shot. Creelman told the man that he had nothing to fear and would carry on. With a shrug, the man rode off.

It was not until the roar of a Winchester reverberated deafeningly off the close mountain walls and a bullet sped in his direction that Creelman changed his mind. If he survived the next few seconds, he promised himself, he would do an about-face.

Creelman was in luck. No lead hit home. It was perhaps a warning shot, for he had been a sitting duck. He tugged on the reins of his mount and spurred it on in the opposite direction. Deciding hastily to go see Randall McCoy instead, he rode for two days to get to Pikeville. He found the town in a state of high alert. Frank Phillips, sporting his war trophy — Jim Vance's pistol — in his holster took him to visit Randall and Sally, who were being guarded around the clock by armed men. Deputy sheriffs, edgy and bearing rifles, prowled around the county jail while the young enlistees of Adjutant General Sam Hill's new National Guard company traversed the town eagerly transforming themselves into soldiers. Creelman settled in and harvested the facts of the feud from the McCoys.

The notion that a new civil war might ignite on this old fault line was certainly not far-fetched, he discovered. To a certain extent, it already had.[1]

ALTHOUGH CREELMAN HAD GOTTEN the scoop, returning to Gotham with the first comprehensive description of the nation's most infamous family feud and marking another notch in his quill with a colorful account in which he branded West Virginia governor Windy Wilson "a poltroon and a coward," he had, in poker parlance, left the game with money still on the table. To capture its share of the spoils, the *New York World* dispatched Theron "T.C." Crawford, a flamboyant egoist with a rapierlike pen, while the more staid *New York Sun* sent the relatively moderate and congenial John R. Spears. Both knew that Creelman had tried and failed to reach Devil Anse's lair.

The lanky thirty-eight-year-old Spears set out, like Creelman, from Catlettsburg, but he proceeded directly to Pikeville. An alumnus of the U.S. Naval Academy, Spears had recently covered the international yacht races between the *Mayflower* and the *Galatea* (1886) and the *Volunteer* and the *Thistle* (1887), stories that were a far cry from the dispute that had begun, as he would write, over "two long-nosed, razorback, elm-peeler hogs." The trip did, however, begin with a water view on the train ride up the Big Sandy River fifty-seven miles to the last town on the line, where he caught a hack — in this case, a three-bench, platform-spring wagon hitched to a brace of mules.

On the way into Pikeville, the hack driver recalled his last visit there, as a cook for a floating sawmill. A leading citizen, angry because the mill's saw could not cut his four-foot-wide sycamore log, had pulled out his Winchester and threatened to blast them all. "There's [a] right smart of shooting done thereaway," he said, "but nobody'll never harm you unless they take you for a detective, nor nobody as attends to his own business."

They stopped at a tavern in Prestonsburg, where a Winchester-toting sheriff with a box of cartridges in his coat pocket nonchalantly kept a lookout for the family of a man he had shot and killed for resisting arrest after murdering a deputy. They were coming to shoot him at any time, a matter that did not seem particularly alarming to anyone but Spears. Several miles beyond Prestonsburg, the hack stopped again, and a new passenger, a man with an assiduously trimmed mustache and a stern countenance, climbed on board. It was Dan Cunningham. The square-jawed and stoutly built lawman was on his way to Pikeville to claim his reward for arresting Charley Gillespie, one of the Hatfield gang. The drive gave Spears ample time to learn about the role of the lawmen in the feud from a bona fide source, and Cunningham was persuasive: "The only hope of clearing out the criminals and ending the feud," Spears would write in the *Sun,* "is in the efforts of detectives working for the rewards."

After the hack forded the river marking its arrival in Pikeville, Cunningham leaped off, darted up an alleyway, and disappeared. Despite his effort at stealth, a number of people on the street saw him and immediately went to warn Randall and Big Jim that Cunningham had just arrived in town. Not only that, but he had brought a well dressed stranger—clearly a detective—with him, a mistake that would make Spears's first hours in Pikeville rather tense.

The McCoy cohorts tracked down Cunningham and told him to leave town and take the new bounty hunter with him. They would not allow a gathering of detectives, who had a checkered reputation, at best, in Pikeville. Cunningham tried to convince them that the new man was just a reporter, an argument they scoffed at on principle. That night Big Jim, his brother Sam, and their comrades loaded up their Winchesters while they figured out what to do with the stranger.

In the meantime, Spears checked into a hotel owned by the prominent attorney W. M. Connolly. Spears convinced Connolly of his profession and purpose for being there and earned his stamp of approval, which not only opened up access to the parties he wanted to talk to around town but, even more importantly, ended discussions over what to do with him. Over the next two days, Sunday and Monday, Spears interviewed a variety of people, including Randall and Sally, the prosecutor Lee Ferguson, and the Hatfields being held in jail. He found the McCoys straightforward, even regarding Bad Frank's cold-blooded dispatching of the wounded Bill Dempsey. "They admitted that this was an awful crime," he would report. Nevertheless, they told Spears that they had to "stand by Phillips for the sake of the good things he had done."

His impression of the Hatfields was not so positive. The flickering light of a chimney-less kerosene lamp painted Wall's cell in chiaroscuro as Spears interviewed him through the jail bars. Head tilted down, Wall looked at him haughtily through spectacles and claimed that he was being unjustly held for the crimes of Johnse and Cap. Spears was not convinced.

On Tuesday morning, Spears set out in the direction of Logan Courthouse, eighty miles to the east, in a hired one-horse buckboard driven by Big Jim. They rumbled over a narrow, bone-jarring road that traveled in the streambeds when possible and up over passes between mountains when necessary. Most of the houses along the route were windowless cabins, ventilated through the chinks between the logs. All had piles of soft coal in the yard, dug from ready seams, for heating and cooking. (Many of the locals would soon sell their mineral rights for nothing more than a personal lifetime supply of this same coal.) After traveling twenty-three miles, Spears and Big Jim spent the night with a man named Mont Runyan, who had a frame house and a cast-iron stove and charged a dollar for room and board for the two men and the horse. Big Jim slept with his Winchester by the bed.

On Wednesday morning, he took Spears as far as the old McCoy place on Blackberry Fork. All that was left was the two massive sandstone chimneys standing among the ashes. Although they were still nine miles from West Virginia—over the divide to Blackberry Fork, past the election grounds where Big Ellison had been fatally stabbed six years earlier, and then across the Tug—Big Jim would venture no farther. He was not willing to risk meeting up with a West Virginia posse that might nab him and take him to jail or shoot him. Beyond this point, the road narrowed to two feet, where it was not washed away entirely, and the buckboard could go no farther. Before he turned back, Big Jim passed Spears off to a seventeen-year-old boy, who he promised could lead him to the pawpaw patch where Big Jim's brothers had been killed. The boy would take Spears there and then across the Tug to Shang Ferrell's place, where he could engage another guide. The Hunts had only one horse, so Spears walked.

As they got closer to the pawpaw patch, the boy suddenly denied knowing the way. They asked for directions at a schoolhouse, but when they approached the site, Spears could tell the boy was scared and was not surprised when he claimed he could go no farther, making an excuse about having to return his borrowed horse.

Spears paid the boy the dollar he was promised and then crossed the Tug on a raft of logs that had been lodged on a sandbar, ready to be floated down the river on the spring current. On the West Virginia side, he went to the house and store of a Bill McCoy, who fed him lunch but refused to go with him to Ferrell's. So Spears set off again on his own, not without trepidation. "I was getting anxious to have a guide," he later wrote, "for I thought that in case I met the Logan Regulators, they would be more likely to welcome me if I were accompanied by a friend of theirs."

He was told that Ferrell's was the third house he would come to following the river, about three miles on. Partway there, he ran into three men. Much to his relief, they were not Hatfields but surveyors working for the Norfolk and Western railroad, laying out the line that was about to be built along the Tug. The three wore heavy leather leggings. They explained to him that the riverbank was snake-ridden and that as they hiked along their route, they sometimes stepped into nests of rattlers. The snakes struck their leggings with such ferocity that their fangs stuck, and their heads remained attached even after the men hacked off their bodies.[2]

"You'll find this the devil's own country, but they won't disturb *you*," one of the surveyors told Spears, with reassurance that was less than convincing. "You're all right if they don't mistake you for a detective. They are suspicious of strangers though."

"After you've learned all about these mountain bushwhackers you'll feel like shaking hands with the next rattler you meet," said another. "The rattler never strikes without first warning his victim."

Spears found Shang Ferrell, a large and hardy man, working in his fields. Ferrell secured Spears a new guide, George Duty, and two horses. He told Duty to tell anyone who asked "that I said the gentleman is from New York, and he is all right." And they needed little more than to see him ride to authenticate the claim. It was Spears's first time on a horse. The two men rode back down the Tug and then headed up Mate Creek, where Duty showed Spears what remained of the schoolhouse in which the McCoy brothers had been detained before they were killed. The wooden structure had been burned to the ground. Though Duty would not directly accuse anyone of torching the place, he mentioned that rumor had it that Pike County raiders had done it.

After roughly twelve miles of riding horseback and another dozen walking on a bridle path, they stayed the night at the house of Steve Atkins. The valleys were so narrow here and the fields pitched at such steep angles that even a mule was useless, and the earth had to be tilled with a hoe. Streams and brooks defined the fields on the lower side, and on the upper, virgin timber stretched to the ridgeline.

Atkins, like Shang Ferrell, was a large and outgoing man who had met with success in life. His roomy house had a separate building for cooking and a coal fire around which the family gathered to smoke stoneware pipes with fish-pole stems or chew snuff. The mountain women, who wore plain dresses of calico or homespun cotton or wool and who kept their hair pulled back although bangs were then fashionable, joined in the pipe smoking. One daughter, however, a shapely seventeen-year-old, refrained and was, they said, being groomed for city life. Spears was smitten and reported that she was so pretty, she would have made a scene even in New York City.

That night, after the guests had gone to bed, a band of riders galloped up to the house, frightening everyone. It was immediately assumed that Spears was not a reporter but a detective and that the riders were Hatfields or McCoys coming to get him. Spears noted that Atkins was ready to hand him over before he discovered that the riders were not, in fact, regulators but an eloping couple with an escort of half a dozen young men.

On Thursday, Spears and Duty had traveled another nine miles when Duty stopped to ask an old couple for directions to Logan Courthouse. This surprised and disturbed Spears. Shang Ferrell had said that the direct route was straight up Mate Creek and over the pass to the Mud Fork of Island Creek. "We aren't going that way, are we?" he asked Duty.

"No, seh," Duty responded. "We'll shortly git thar this way."

Spears determined that because Devil Anse and Cap lived on the Mud Fork of Island Creek, Duty had taken it upon himself to bypass the area, even though it would take an extra five miles of traveling, through country he did not know.

After riding twenty-seven miles, they at last reached Logan

Courthouse on the banks of the Guyandotte River. Spears checked into Buskirk's Hotel, owned by J. B. Buskirk, who was also the town's postmaster and jailer, and soon arranged to meet a Hatfield — in this case, Elias. Like Wall, Elias placed the blame for the feud on Johnse and Cap. "Cap is a fool," he said, explaining that twice Cap had tried to shoot one of Elias's sons for refusing to join the New Year's Day raid on the McCoys. The only reason he had not gone after Cap himself, Elias claimed, was that then he would be at war with his own brother Devil Anse.

Several of Frank Phillips's posse, captured by the Eureka detectives, were incarcerated in the Logan County jail attached to the boxy redbrick courthouse, which had replaced the frame courthouse burned to the ground in 1864 by Union troops. That fall, a mother bear had chosen to come down the mountainside daily to frolic with her cubs in the cornfields across the river in full view of the courthouse. Each day a portion of the town's population of two hundred, plus visitors, gathered outside the shops and hotels and blazed away at them. Fortunately for the bears, the locals generally

Logan Courthouse, circa 1890. *(Courtesy of F. Keith Davis)*

carried three-foot-long muzzle-loading rifles, whose light shot cost about half a cent, compared to six cents for a Winchester's brass cartridge. The muzzle-loaders were useful for knocking squirrels out of trees but were no match for bears.

Spears reported that the trials of Bad Frank's posse men Dave Stratton, John Norman, John B. Dotson, and Joseph Franklin Smith for aiding and abetting in the murder of special sheriff Bill Dempsey at Grapevine Creek would be heard in town on October 2. These high-profile prisoners were under heavy guard for their own safety in Hatfield country. The firm of McComas and Kelly, Smith and Stratton, fronted by Major William Stratton, a Logan County circuit clerk, Confederate cavalry veteran, and the father of Dave Stratton, represented the defendants while the Confederate veteran Judge Thomas Harvey, who had had the charges dropped against Bob Skean in the murder of George Duff, was presiding. A similar result would occur in this case. But Spears, eager to file his story and perhaps compelled to leave town in a hurry for other reasons that he did not care to admit, did not stick around to hear it.[3]

While Spears, like Creelman, had gathered an admirable amount of information about the feud, he too abandoned his efforts to meet Devil Anse. Logan Courthouse had only two horses for hire, and both were already spoken for. Instead of waiting for the horses to return, Spears took to his boots, setting out for Brownstown, on the Kanawha River fifty-two miles away over a mountainous wagon trail. There he would be able to catch a train on the Chesapeake and Ohio line. Spears walked a grueling twenty-seven miles on the first day. After six miles the following day, he was able to hire a horse.

~

A COUPLE OF DAYS behind Spears, rival reporter T. C. Crawford, a man of admirable pluck and amusing bombast, arrived in Charleston declaring that he wished to seek out Devil Anse Hatfield because he was eager to help settle the feud. Somehow he managed to persuade John B. Floyd and Clarence Moore, a clerk at the federal courthouse, to take part in the mission and accompany him on the eighty-six-mile journey south to Logan Courthouse.

Having recently returned from a sojourn in England, whose gentility he had found suitable to his tastes, Crawford was little prepared for the three-day ride on a West Virginia buckboard wagon. "After the first fifteen miles leaving Charleston there is not a single rod of good road," he would write. "The rider, whether in a wagon or on horseback, is in constant pain from jolting, bumping, and sliding over the rocks and down steep inclines." Crawford's jaundiced eye did not stop there. In the roadside hamlet of Racine, he found the accommodations "primitive" and the fare "coarse, harsh, and . . . repulsive," including pork "floating in a perfect pond of melted fat"—and Racine, he noted, was the best place on the route. The closer he got to Logan Courthouse, the worse the going. "The roads are only a mere name," he opined. "When the waters are up, the route is absolutely impassable. Days and weeks will pass without any more word coming from Logan Court-House to the outer world than could be gotten out from Central Africa." After five days, the constant pounding and his inability to eat the food had put him in a "benumbed state," heedless of the fact that "there is a danger in Murderland, and that investigation of the murderous ways of this barbarous country might lead one to find nothing more interesting than a bullet from the bush."[4]

Crawford and company reached Logan Courthouse just days after Spears departed. They lodged at the Bunce Hotel, where Crawford declined to bed down with a stranger in a communal room and finally persuaded the owner to give him a private room to share with Moore. Being from far away, Crawford fascinated the locals, who strolled into his ground-floor room without knocking or bothering to make excuses for being there. His visitors all drank whiskey together from pint flasks, and some, including a deaf and blind man (Crawford described him as looking like a "ghoul"), even climbed in through the windows. "Locking the door," Crawford lamented, "simply produced coldness in the community and a

Logan County Courthouse (1875–1905). *(Dr. Coleman C. Hatfield Collection, courtesy of Dr. Arabel E. Hatfield)*

suspicion that we were detectives hatching plans to carry off some of their leading citizens."

It was not every year that two visitors from New York City strolled through the town's business district, which consisted of, in addition to the courthouse, a post office, five stores, and two hotels. In fact, it was not every decade. Initially laid out in 1824 as Lawnsville, Logan Courthouse, though small, boasted a newspaper — the *Logan Democrat* — thanks in large part to the fact that its advertising page was a favorite of one particular industry: it featured ads from every major firearms maker in the United States.

Indeed, every night that Crawford was in town, he heard gunfire and witnessed an "absolute orgy." With the coming of darkness, the unruly crowd routinely overwhelmed the local sheriffs and stormed the locked courthouse. Once inside its halls, they bought, sold, and quaffed moonshine, gambled, fought, and fornicated, swore, smoked long-stemmed pipes, and spat tobacco juice on the floor. Painted women, whom Crawford dubbed "she-devils," wearing scandalous dresses not much below their knees, coarse wool socks, and men's boots, brazenly plied the world's oldest profession and joined the men in the wrestling and fistfights. One old man sporting a black hat with dozens of colored rags attached to it claimed to be Grover Cleveland. By any measure, the Logan County seat was a colorful backwater, and Crawford was up to the task of describing it. The morning after his arrival, he found out that Spears had beaten him there. Court was in session, and the town was teeming with mountain men who had come to drink and carouse. Crawford learned from the crowd form- ing around him that Spears had not even stayed in town for twenty- four hours. "He was in such a hurry that he would not wait until noon, when he could have obtained a horse," wrote Crawford, mock- ing his competitor. "Such was his haste to get out of Murderland before any committee could call upon him that he left on foot."

Crawford relished the fact that Spears, like Creelman, had failed to penetrate the Hatfield defenses and meet Devil Anse. Still, he felt the clock ticking. Spears was now on his way back to New York City with his dispatches. Crawford needed to bag his quarry and get out swiftly.

The first Hatfield he encountered   Elias — made a surprising impression on him: he liked him. Wearing a butternut-brown suit with his pants tucked into his boots, a blue-jean shirt, and a straw hat, Elias sported under his waistband a leather girdle with a pistol in a holster.[5] He described the murder of his brother Ellison and admitted to the reporter that he had tried to kill one of the McCoys on that day but said that that was the only time he took part in the hostilities. He had moved to Logan Courthouse to get away from the fighting and was focused on raising his family on a two-hundred- acre farm. Nervous and ill at ease, reticent, Elias told Crawford that several attempts had been made on the lives of his three sons. "All that I want is to be let alone," he said, "but if people will persist in bothering and wronging those who are dear to me — why, let them look out."

John B. Floyd offered Crawford some sage advice on his quest to meet Devil Anse: "the best way to see Hatfield was to go right to him and not to ask any permission." Elias, trusting Crawford, sent one of his sons on Tuesday night to tell Devil Anse that Crawford, Floyd, and Moore were coming to see him the next day.

Crawford and his two companions hired horses and a guide the following morning and set out on the fifteen-mile journey to Devil Anse's Main Island Creek farm. This route, to Crawford's dismay, lay across even harsher terrain. They traveled over boulders and through deep gorges and, worn out from the previous days of travel and suffering from what he called a "malarial fever," Crawford soon had them turn around. But back in Logan Courthouse, instead of giving up, he ditched their recalcitrant guide, whom they neither liked nor trusted, turned in their three poor mounts, retrieved the wagon they had ridden in from Charleston, and hired a better team of horses. They then set out again.

As their route snaked through the wilderness from clearing to clearing, Crawford saw how easy it would be for a lone messenger to streak through the woods to warn others of an approaching party. Furthermore, he became acutely aware that each farmer was also a guard. Whistles, hoots, and other "strange cries, signals passing from one neighborhood to another," preceded them, echoing off the hills.

The first sentry they came to was Elias himself, who was walking with a bag of cornmeal on his left shoulder and a long-barreled Winchester rifle in his right hand. A young girl walked behind him, also carrying a bag. The rifle barrel ascended to hip level as they approached him, and it eased down again after they identified themselves as the friends of the day before. They next encountered the thuggish French Ellis tending to a water mill on a thrashing stream. A Winchester sat across his lap.

Likewise, Devil Anse, who was out in a field near his house, was carrying a Winchester in addition to a Colt pistol in a holster under his brown coat. He wore a blue shirt and blue jeans tucked into his boots, and a faded black hat on his head. His thick brown hair, mustache, and beard showed no signs of gray. His smile endeared him to Crawford. He greeted them, the reporter recalled, with "ardor and enthusiasm."

Devil Anse had spent the fall in bucolic pursuits. Despite the continuing paucity of deer in the county, he managed to track down and shoot three of them among the forks of Island Creek. He also shot a bear. As a bonus, he sniffed out ten bee trees, the honey and honeycomb from which netted him just shy of fifty dollars in store goods.[6]

The house at Main Island Creek had two rooms connected by a hallway, the back room being a smaller cooking and dining area and the front used for almost everything else. Washing up was done outside in the creek, conveniently just twenty feet away. Men, women, and children, as well as guests, all slept in the same room. The women and children retired early, climbing onto their pallets in nightclothes while the men sat together in the room and talked as if nothing else were going on. But when it came to sexual relations later at night, there was, as Crawford put it, "as much modesty and decency observed as if each person had a separate room," though how exactly he knew this is questionable, since he refused an offer to stay the night.

As Crawford sat in front of the fireplace and interviewed the fifty-year-old legend before and after dinner, he came to understand just how authentic a creature of the mountains and how original and entertaining he was. Devil Anse's gray eyes gazed out from underneath bushy eyebrows, and Crawford could sense the magnetism that attracted both grown men and grandchildren to his side. When Crawford cheekily asked him why it was that so many shots were fired in the feud but so few people were actually hit, Devil Anse responded without pause: "I'll tell you. The human varmint is the most coorious an' cunningist varmint thar is. When he goes into a fight, he turns his body sidewise, so that there is presented for the bullet only four inches of life space, and even that he doesn't hold up fa'r and squar'. He jest keeps a-dodgin' and friskin' about, and so when the bullets come along they don't find him."

But it was the fact that Devil Anse knew nothing of the New York newspapers that so dominated Crawford's life — that he seemed to have little concept of where or what New York City even was — that struck a chord with the reporter. Devil Anse had heard about the visitor from New York City who departed rather abruptly and asked Crawford if he knew him. "I was obliged to answer in the negative," Crawford later wrote. "That was enough for Ance Hatfield. The man had said he was from New York, and here was another man from New York who did not know him. No greater proof was necessary to show that the first comer was a detective."[7]

Vicey worked through dinner, pulling hot dishes from the blaze as needed. She served fried pork, beans, sweet potatoes, corn pone, and sliced tomatoes. Afterward, Devil Anse insisted the visitors stay the night, but Crawford, noting that there were twelve family members, including three young women, as well as nine guards to occupy the two rooms, declined the offer. Outside by the stream, Devil Anse and his men showed off for the visitors with an impressive round of target practice.

It was Crawford who first planted the seed of celebrity with Devil Anse, telling him that after his story came out in the *World,* Devil Anse and Cap could come to New York, dressed just as they were and carrying their Winchesters (Crawford had counted fourteen sitting around the great room of the cabin) and Colts, and make five hundred dollars a week by being on display.

"When this here Hatfield-McCoy feud is settled," offered Devil Anse, not missing a beat, "I want to come down to New York, and if you will get me that thar engagement, why, I'll give you half I get out of it."

Before Crawford and his companions departed, Devil Anse volunteered to show them Rock Fort, which lay on the stream about a quarter mile from the cabin. Crawford was impressed by the stout, windowless, six-log-high structure topped by a steeply pitched heavy-shingled roof. Defenders could shoot from all angles through the gaps between the logs. The nine men then on patrol around the house conducted themselves in military fashion, as if they were engaged in a war. Inside, the fort was furnished with nothing but a pallet with a feather bed, where, it was pointed out, Kentucky Bill had recuperated after he was shot in the heel.

It was outside the fort that the most dramatic moment of the visit occurred. Floyd, who was a friend of the Hatfields but had also boasted to Crawford that he could bring the whole lot in if he felt so inclined, ambled up to Cap and in an instant whipped a pistol from his holster and pointed it at him.

Cap was dumbstruck. He rushed forward and grabbed Floyd's wrist, but Floyd, who was a powerful man, shook him off. Cap forced a smile. It was a joke but not one he liked. "No man ever did that before," he said, "and bet your life no man will ever ketch me again that way."

THE FOLLOWING MORNING Crawford and Moore set out for Brownstown, where Crawford would catch the train back to New York. Their wagon gave him little confidence as it jolted over gullies, boulders, and tree trunks at less than four miles an hour. It finally crashed on an impediment that would not be glossed over. Crawford's hopes of scooping his rival looked to be dashed, but Moore quickly unharnessed the horse and told Crawford he was going after the drummer (as traveling salesmen were then known) who had recently passed them. Before long, they had the wagon fixed, much to the relief of Crawford, who was at least as worried about his health as he was about his story and later confessed that "not having swallowed a morsel of wholesome food for nearly ten days, and having had nearly six days' continuous riding over the road to this region, I had reached the limit of my ability to live the life of a mountaineer."[8]

ON SUNDAY, OCTOBER 7, the crosstown rival newspapers the *New York Sun* and the *New York World* published major feature stories on the feud. The *Sun* billed John Spears's whopping (ten-thousand-word) blow-by-blow account as "a remarkable story of murder and outrage."

Notably, it included a portrait of "Rose Ann's boy," who appeared to be about age five or six but who did not in fact exist. Still, Spears was a top reporter, and his colorful account would prove to be one of the feud's most enduring.

On three consecutive Sundays in October, T. C. Crawford's story on the feud ran in the *World*. On October 7, the editors launched it with ample hyperbole: "Mr. T. C. Crawford has travelled through the blood-stained wilderness along the mountainous boundary of Kentucky and West Virginia, and he gives the *World* a truthful picture of lawlessness and moral depravity unparalleled in our history."

With Jack the Ripper on an appalling crime spree, murdering and mutilating prostitutes in London — and stealing the front-page headlines — Crawford, a consummate raconteur, wasted no time in striking the most memorable lines written about the feud: "I have been away in Murderland for nearly ten days" came his opening salvo. "No one unless he has had the actual experience of a visit to the region made notorious by the Hatfield-McCoy feud would believe that there is in this country such a barbarous, uncivilized and wholly savage region."

He painted a detailed portrait of what he had observed, often in stark and unflattering terms, as when he described Vicey, "one of the strongest and most muscular-looking women" he had ever seen, as having "no more idea of right or wrong than a mastiff dog." Written in haste, Crawford's voluminous account is sometimes contradictory. "It would take but little energy on the part of the authorities of either State to bring this disgraceful vendetta to a sudden end," he wrote with one stroke, and with another: "The road is so wild and rough going from Logan Court-House to Devil Anse's fort that it would be impossible to march any body of men through there so as to reach the outlaw." Furthermore, his traveling companion, Clarence Moore, a federal court clerk, had told him that it was almost impossible to serve the Hatfields with any process of the court. He had more than once dispatched an officer to serve writs on them. "This officer would ride straight . . . to the mountain country, where the person desired was living, only to find in the majority of cases that he had already received notice of the officer's coming and had disappeared."

Crawford achieved his goal. Devil Anse gained equal billing with the day's "JACK THE RIPPER" headline in the *Cincinnati Enquirer,* which ran his story on the front page concurrently with the *World,* under the headline "DEVIL ANCE: The Outlaw King of Kentucky," essentially taking the piece national (although failing in accuracy, since Devil *Anse* hailed from West Virginia).

On October 14, Crawford's headline read "American Barbarians: The Heroes of the Bloody Hatfield-McCoy Vendetta." Devil Anse's two oldest daughters were depicted in an illustration barefoot, in long, plain dresses, one modestly buxom and the other quite so, both with short-cropped hair. In another, the men, in boots, waistcoats, and jackets, some holding rifles, were gathered around the kitchen table, apparently holding a war council. A week later, the paper wrapped up the series with "The Land of the Vendetta," which included an illustration of Crawford's horseback expedition. The reporter concluded with a begrudging tip of the hat to the Hatfields, with whom his time had not been entirely unpleasant: "The Phillips crowd who now control the Peter Creek region are even more desperate than the Hatfields," he noted. "I do not think the Hatfields would shoot down strangers on general suspicion unless the stranger made some direct move against them. But over in the Peter's Creek region the fact that a man is a stranger is quite enough to invite shots from the numerous ambuscades which are occupied along the line of this most wretched locality."[9]

On the third Sunday, Spears jumped back in with another full page (one that until now has been lost to history), this time depicting his journey to Logan Courthouse and giving the only written description of Devil Anse's distilling operation, the details of which had been furnished by Big Jim from his days of working with Devil Anse before the feud heated up. Spears made a point of highlighting the delicious food he ate in the region, including a "sumptuous meal of string beans cooked with bacon, ham, sweet potatoes, fried apples, hot corn bread (a specialty of the region), biscuits, plum preserves, and apple butter, followed by apple pie and coffee." While this was not news, it was excellent for tweaking the nose of his puffed-up rival at the *World,* who had whined that the food was inedible and that he had lost fifteen pounds while in West Virginia for fewer than ten days.

The locals would weigh in later. The following May, the *Logan Banner* reprinted a few pithy lines from the nearby *Journal,* which captured the broad consensus: "A Kentucky newspaper correspondent who left home two weeks ago to write up the Hatfields and McCoys is missing and is supposed to have been murdered in the wilds of the Kentucky mountains. If he was one of the sensational, unreliable correspondents that have been operating in that territory, the Hatfields and McCoys did the work of their lives when they fed him to the vultures."

~

GUERILLA MITCHELL did not keep his nose clean for long. At the end of October, he, Cotton Top, and Indian decided to get in on the bounty hunting. For these men of few prospects, catching Bad Frank would be akin to winning the lottery. Just as they were hatching their plan, however, the Tug rose to impassable heights. While they waited for it to recede, they stayed in the house of a man named Jeff Skean, who lived on Mate Creek and was a first cousin of the Hatfields and also of the Skeans, who murdered Nathan Cunningham.[10]

By the time the three novice bounty hunters were finally able to set out on their stab at glory, Dan Cunningham, Kentucky Bill Napier, and Treve Gibson were waiting for them. The trio had perhaps been sold out by Johnse's wife, Nancy, who, according to a later Hatfield, "carefully studied the movements of Mounts and furnished expert information on his activities." Indeed, if Nancy was sending information about Frank Phillips to Alf Burnett, it is possible she was playing the other side of the fence as well and providing him with news of the Hatfields.[11]

It is also possible that the intelligence came straight out of Devil Anse's cabin. Charlie Harrison, who rode with the Hatfields and would marry Anna Hatfield, a cousin of Devil Anse, later explained it this way: Kentucky Bill had been shot in the foot, and the Hatfields found him. The wounded bounty hunter had reached behind his back to a sheath hidden between his shoulder blades and whipped out a bowie knife. Wildness lit his eyes, framed by greasy bangs. It was a desperate move. Devil Anse, who was known to admire a man who stood up for himself in a bad situation, was impressed. Instead of shooting Kentucky Bill, he applied his devilish charm and talked him down from a grim precipice. Kentucky Bill put his knife away. The Hatfields took him home. "Devil Anse was compassionate to the suffering of humanity," Harrison said, and "touched by the humility of Kentucky Bill . . . nursed him back to health until he was able to travel." Yet it was while Kentucky Bill was recuperating at the Hatfields' that he learned about Cotton Top's plans to capture Bad Frank. When Kentucky Bill finally cut and ran, he took this information with him.[12]

By sunup on Monday, October 29, Cunningham, Kentucky Bill, and Gibson were waiting behind trees by a creek near the head of Mate Creek, where they knew the three West Virginians would pass. Just after dawn, the three came along as expected, traveling down the creek bank. Cotton Top, the most powerful, was in the lead. He was Cunningham's designated target while Kentucky Bill planned to take Indian and Gibson to handle Mitchell. Cunningham had a heavy stone in one hand and his rifle in the other. With Cotton Top nearing him, he maneuvered around the tree to get the best jump on him. As he did, he stepped on a stick, and it snapped loudly. Alerted, Cotton Top whipped his rifle to his shoulder. Before he could level it, Cunningham swung his arm, cracking him across the chin with the stone and stunning him long enough to pounce on him.

Shots rang out down the trail as Kentucky Bill and Gibson leaped out at their adversaries at the same time. Cunningham wrestled the gun away from Cotton Top, and the two tumbled over the six-foot-high creek bank. Cotton Top was as big and nearly as strong as Cunningham, but the detective was fighting-fit, and his fists slugged Cotton Top's face like hammers. Cotton Top tore at Cunningham, too, doing damage, but Cunningham pounded Cotton Top again and again until the force of the blows had carried them to the far side of the creek. Finally the lawman handcuffed his battered quarry to a buckeye tree.

By the time Gibson and Kentucky Bill returned, Cunningham was washing his bruised and cut face in the creek. The two had traded pistol shots with Indian and Mitchell, but their targets had escaped. Gibson had been shot in the leg.

The three lawmen took Cotton Top across the Tug to a place called Edgar. The river was closely watched now, and it was not long before word spread and Bud McCoy and a dozen men showed up. The Kentuckians demanded that the lawmen hand their prisoner over to them. Buying time to think, Cunningham, who was not keen on anyone taking the law into his own hands, asked Bud what he would do with Cotton Top.

"Kill him," Bud drawled, "and cut him up in inch pieces."

This reply did not sit well with Cunningham. "Then you'll kill me first," he said, raising his rifle barrel.

Bud consulted with his party. They came back and promised, in such a way that Cunningham believed he could trust them, to deliver Cotton Top to Pikeville. He handed over the prisoner.

Though not as flamboyant as Kentucky Bill, Cunningham, with this capture, was now the principal hunter of the Hatfields. Wrote one reporter of the broad-shouldered six-footer who rivaled Alf Burnett and William Baldwin in fitness, power, quickness of mind, and moral conviction, "He does it as he would hunt rattlesnakes, and as his warrants for 'moonshine' whisky distillers often take him to the Hatfield country, he is likely to get more of them.

"Cunningham," the reporter concluded, "is not the sort of man that one would care to have on his trail."[13]

PART IV

~

THE HUNTERS
AND THE HUNTED

1888–1898

Casualties, 1864–1888

Hatfields

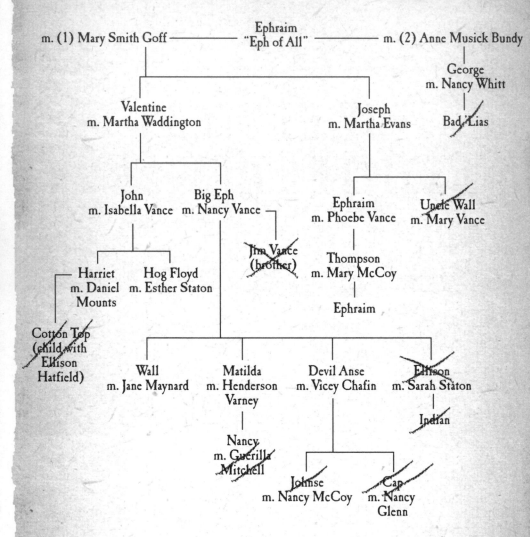

Ephraim
"Eph of All"

m. (1) Mary Smith Goff — — — m. (2) Anne Musick Bundy

George
m. Nancy Whitt

Valentine
m. Martha Waddington

Joseph
m. Martha Evans

Bad Lias

John
m. Isabella Vance

Big Eph
m. Nancy Vance

Ephraim
m. Phoebe Vance

Uncle Wall
m. Mary Vance

Jim Vance
(brother)

Thompson
m. Mary McCoy

Harriet
m. Daniel
Mounts

Hog Floyd
m. Esther Staton

Ephraim

Cotton Top
(child with
Ellison
Hatfield)

Wall
m. Jane Maynard

Matilda
m. Henderson
Varney

Devil Anse
m. Vicey Chafin

Ellison
m. Sarah Staton

Indian

Nancy
m. Guerilla
Mitchell

Johnse
m. Nancy McCoy

Cap
m. Nancy
Glenn

McCoys

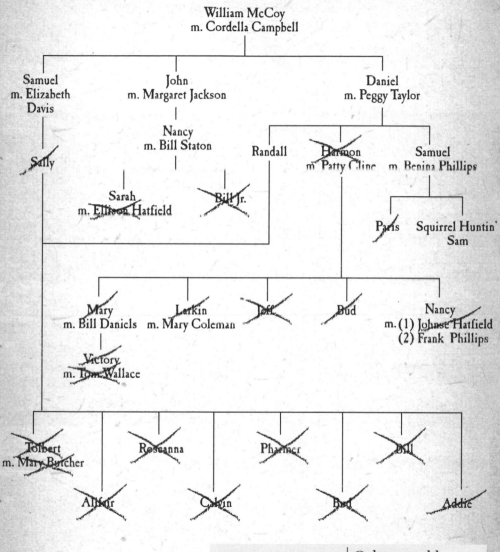

William McCoy
m. Cordella Campbell

Samuel
m. Elizabeth
Davis

John
m. Margaret Jackson

Daniel
m. Peggy Taylor

Nancy
m. Bill Staton

Randall

Harmon
m. Patty Cline

Samuel
m. Benina Phillips

Sally

Sarah
m. Ellison Hatfield

Bill Jr.

Paris

Squirrel Huntin'
Sam

Mary
m. Bill Daniels

Larkin
m. Mary Coleman

Jeff

Bud

Nancy
m. (1) Johnse Hatfield
(2) Frank Phillips

Victory
m. Tom Wallace

Tolbert
m. Mary Butcher

Roseanna

Pharmer

Bill

Alifair

Calvin

Bud

Addie

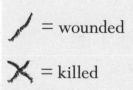

/ = wounded

✗ = killed

Other notable casualties

Moses Cline—wounded
Mose Cline—killed
Bushy Scott—wounded
Hense Scott—wounded
Lee White—wounded
Bill Dempsey—killed

Chapter 20

~

The Trial

1888–1889

After his capture, Cotton Top Mounts confessed on at least three occasions. In the first known—and, until now, largely forgotten—confession, at Edgar, on October 29, 1888, just after he was apprehended, he naively said, "I was led into this scrape by the older Hatfields and have seen no peace since I killed the McCoy girl." It was a major score for Dan Cunningham, who also walked off with the rifle Cotton Top would no longer need, since he would never be free again. At the end of this confession, Cotton Top said, "The Winchester with which I killed Alifair McCoy, I gave to Dan Cunningham for his kindness to me since my arrest." Cotton Top signed the confession ("Ellison Hatfield"), as did the witnesses Dan Cunningham, Treve Gibson, Mary Daniels (the woman whipped with a cow tail by Cap), and Jane and Margaret Blackburn.

Removed from the woods, Cotton Top seemed to have no instinct for self-preservation at all.[1]

He reached the Pikeville County jail by Friday, November 2, 1888, and on the following Monday, was induced by the powers in Pike County to confess again, this time in a more formal setting. In this second confession, he described the circuitous route he and some of the others took and the furtive meetings to which he was not wholly privy in the days leading up to the raid on the McCoys.

In addition, he confessed to the murder of the three McCoy brothers, also implicating Devil Anse, Johnse, Cap, and Bill Tom Hatfield, along with Charlie Carpenter, Guerilla Mitchell, Alex Messer, and others.

Cotton Top did not stop there. Cap had told him about the killing of Jeff McCoy, and he detailed that, naming another supposed accomplice, a man named Boney Nickels. He also told what he knew about the whipping of Mary Daniels. This confession was signed by Cunningham, Gibson, Perry Cline, Lee Ferguson, and Colonel Dils.[2]

AT THE END OF OCTOBER, Devil Anse's shipment of Winchester repeating rifles arrived at Brownstown. Nan had left a zero off the order for ten thousand cartridges, so they received only a thousand, but the twenty-five octagonal-barreled rifles gave them state-of-the-art firepower. Devil Anse sent Cap and a hand named Elias Simpkins in a buckboard to get them; it would take the duo a week to accomplish their mission on the craggy bridle paths that passed for roads. Like the McCoys, the Hatfields were not going to sit idly by as a U.S. deputy marshal slowly picked them off.[3]

Preparing for another foray against the now heavily armed clan, Dan Cunningham stayed at the Kentucky home of Ralph Steel, near the Tug. The water was high, and the local men had seized the opportunity to head downriver on rafts of logs to be turned into timber at the mills below. That absence gave the Hatfields enough breathing room to pay a timely visit to Steel's place. About ten of them crossed the swollen river. They beat Steel's door in with the butt of a fence rail and captured Cunningham.

The detective was ushered across the river to the Hatfields' stronghold. He later admitted that he thought this might be it for him, but he was a man of deep faith, and he began praying. Cap removed Cunningham's hat, put it on a pole, and ordered him to bow down and kiss the earth. "Shoot and die," Cunningham said, refusing to bow.

"No, we've a better fate in store for ya than this," roared Cap. "We're gonna kill ya slowly and show ya how to suffer."[4]

Instead of following through on the threat then, they left him tied up while they drank moonshine, saving the deed for the morning. But they passed out, to a man, and Cunningham managed to free himself. "God answered my prayers again," he later said, "and I made one of the most miraculous escapes of my career."

IN THIS GAME OF CAT AND MOUSE, Cunningham and Treve Gibson next set their sights on Alex Messer, the man most often blamed for dispatching young Bud McCoy with a shotgun blast at the pawpaw patch. Now in his early fifties, Messer was one of the older — and also considered one of the more desperate and dangerous — members of the Hatfield contingent. On November 16, 1888, Cunningham and Gibson found the dark-eyed former Union soldier shopping in a store on Big Ugly Creek, a tributary of the Guyandotte River. The detectives struck up a conversation with the unsuspecting fugitive, who was happy to have some company for a change and invited them to his house for a drink. Their host was putting away his groceries when Cunningham slipped between him and his gun and slapped the handcuffs on him. Messer, like Gillespie and the others who had been taken so skillfully, gave up without a struggle. Later, he repeatedly lamented the fact that he had made the cardinal mistake of letting anyone come between him and his firearm.[5]

With the capture of Messer, the feudists were down one more man, and it was beginning to feel like the swarming lawmen were feasting. And then the Hatfields asserted themselves in a surprising way. Cunningham, an agent named Dick Evans, and another detective had perhaps brazenly and certainly ill-advisedly entered Logan County and made their presence widely known. According to the rumor making its way about, Cunningham and his accomplices intended to shoot Devil Anse, Cap, and French Ellis, whom they considered the three most dangerous West Virginia feudists. It was said that the lawmen felt confident they could mop up the rest with little trouble.[6]

Word of the detectives' braggadocio soon spread to the Hatfields, and although Devil Anse had resolved to distance himself from any further violence, this was more than he could tolerate: If outside lawmen and bounty hunters could come into his own county and brashly declare that they were going to hunt him and his family down, then there would be hell to pay. He was not going to sit back and let detectives ambush his boys or storm his home. He had all the advantages. He knew that surprise was his best ally, and he set about preparing a trap.

When word came that the lawmen were on their way to Main Island Creek, Devil Anse and his men got ready. After Cunningham, Evans, and their colleague had ridden deep into the woods, the Hatfields waylaid them from a strategic position. Cunningham would prove to be one of the era's most prolific bounty-hunting lawmen — and still live to be ninety-two years old. He and his accomplices were heavily armed and knew how to fight. This time, however, the Hatfields had the drop on them — and also a surprise, one that disarmed them in a way that Winchesters never could have.

There was no gunfight. Instead, the Hatfield contingent produced legal papers and presented them to the lawmen. They were arrest warrants for the three detectives, sworn out on January 12 before a justice of the peace. The Hatfields had turned the tables.

It was a simple yet brilliant stroke on Devil Anse's part. In January 1889, at the height of the feud, when bounty hunters had invaded his home turf, when violence would have been easy and definitive, Devil Anse did not resort to gunfire and murder. He turned to the law to fight the lawmen.

And then, true to his roguish personality, he humiliated them with flamboyance and a distinctly Devil Anse sense of humor. As they left the deep woods, they had to cross mountain streams. At each, Devil Anse and two of his men climbed on the backs of the gunslingers and made them carry them piggyback across the water.

"Laughter was long and loud the day the feudists marched the three hawkshaws into town and turned them over to the jailer," the historian Virgil Carrington Jones later reported.[7]

IN DECEMBER 1888, the *Big Sandy News* of Louisa, Kentucky, reported to the Hatfields' shock that Johnse had been killed nearby. Cap, who had thought it advisable to take a holiday in Texas after the battle of Grapevine Creek, had returned to West Virginia. Shaken by the news of the death of his brother, he now wished to bring the whole feud affair to a reasonable conclusion. He was weary of being on the run.

In a letter written on January 21, 1889, and sent from the Cow Creek post office in Logan County, Cap addressed Governor Buckner of Kentucky: "I this morning appeal to you for mercy concerning my past life." He told Buckner that he intended to surrender, "as I am greatly moved at my Brother's death as my life is no satisfaction," but only in Frankfort and never to the detectives that were now plaguing his family. Cap had a number of other conditions, including "that non of the McCoys men or woman shall not come as testimony against me," and also, "no man of the Hatfield gang nor any one of the woman sex of the Hatfield faction."

"No one on earth knows any thing of my intention at this times," Cap wrote. If he received the assurances he sought, he planned to take the train to Frankfort and would call on the governor as soon as he arrived.[8]

He never heard back from Buckner. Then it turned out that Johnse was not dead after all. The Hatfields were learning not to trust the press.

THE HATFIELD CLAN CONTINUED TO withdraw from the border. At the end of March and the beginning of April, Devil Anse sold 1,385 acres on the Tug and 749 acres on Mate Creek, and Johnse

580 acres on Grapevine Creek. Jim Vance Jr. sold parcels of 730 acres and 1,338 acres, also on Grapevine Creek, and Elias plots of 1,354 acres and 322 acres on Mate Creek. Their hub was now Logan Courthouse, where Elias served on the town council, a Chafin was the sheriff, and Devil Anse's Civil War pal the Reverend Dyke Garrett could be found preaching on the courthouse steps one Sunday each month.

Still, the area was none too secure. On the night of March 26, 1889, Devil Anse's barn, corncrib, and stables caught fire and burned down. Jerry Hatfield was visiting and managed to get his horse out, but Devil Anse was not so lucky. His loss was estimated at $500, including a prime riding horse worth $150 and 150 bushels of corn. A letter sent to the paper stated that "some one, thought to be D. W. Cunningham" was the perpetrator of this "outrage and disgrace to the public at large." The letter, which was signed only *J.H.*, a Hatfield presumably, perhaps Jerry, since he was there, concluded, "Now we ask the detectives to not interfere with our business and we will not interfere with them. We meant to have peace, we do not want any trouble."[9]

But peace would not come so easily. That same month, Cotton Top, jailed in Pikeville since early November, was grilled by county prosecutor Lee Ferguson and signed another lengthy confession, which Ferguson publicized, increasing pressure on the Hatfield clan.

In late August, the trials of the men being held for the murders of the three McCoy brothers began with the stalwart Judge Rice presiding in Pikeville. The indictment charged a conspiracy on the part of the accused men to commit willful murder, and Ferguson felt he had compelling evidence against seven of the nine indicted: Cotton Top, Wall, Messer, Gillespie, and the three Mahon brothers. Wall was tried first. He maintained that he and his sons-in-law Doc and Plyant had not taken part in the killings; certain that they would be acquitted, they had surrendered to face the charges and put an end to their ordeal.[10]

Twenty-two witnesses testified against Wall, including Dan and Jeff Whitt, who had turned state's witnesses. Randall led off the testimony, followed by Sally. Although the deaths had occurred seven years previously, her grief was still raw, and her matter-of-factness damning: "I am the mother of Pharmer, Tolbert and young Randolph McCoy," she stated. "They are dead." She described seeing her sons at the schoolhouse near Mate Creek:

> When I got there, Val Hatfield was sitting by them with a shotgun across his lap. I was talking, praying and crying for my boys. While over at the mouth of Mate Creek I heard Val Hatfield say that if Ellison Hatfield died, he would shoot the boys full of holes.... The boys were lying on something on the floor, tied together with a rope. I fell on my knees and began praying and begging and crying for my children. Some one said there was no use of that, to shut up.[11]

When asked to tell who was present at the execution of the brothers, Jeff Whitt listed twelve names and Dan Whitt fourteen. Neither mentioned Wall. Both brothers maintained that they were in the process of leaving, along with Mose Christian and one of the Mahons (one said Plyant and the other Sam), when the shooting started.[12]

Wall testified in convincing detail about his efforts on behalf of the three McCoys and his whereabouts when the shots were fired: "Just after we had passed the mouth of Sulphur, my brother, Elias, stopped to meet a call of nature, and while he was down the firing on the opposite side of the river began, about three hundred yards below us."[13]

To the prosecutors, however, Wall was still a participant in the murders. They maintained that though he "remained with his gun on the opposite side of the river, some two or three hundred yards distant," he did so in order to be "ready and near enough to give aid and assistance should an attempt be made to rescue the prisoners." Wall, the leader of the group, the prosecution insinuated, both stood guard and swore his gang to secrecy or death. Those not guilty of pulling the trigger but who actively aided and abetted the commission of a crime were, under Kentucky law, just as accountable for the results.[14]

Since the evidence in Wall's case was mixed, a plea arrangement on reduced charges, such as accessory to murder or kidnapping, might have been expected, but no negotiation of that sort was attempted. Furthermore, Judge Rice, who had begun his legal career in Pikeville in 1853 but later moved to Louisa, where he practiced law and served as a judge on the county criminal court, gave the jury men no leeway in their decision. They were told to return with a verdict of guilty or not guilty. If they found a defendant guilty, they could choose his sentence: life in prison or capital punishment.

When the jurors returned, they pronounced Wall guilty as charged. They sentenced him to life in prison. His attorneys argued for a retrial, but this was denied. They were, however, granted an appeal, and Rice suspended the judgment for sixty days.

With this precedent, most of the other defendants fell like dominoes. Alex Messer and Doc and Plyant Mahon were tried together. Messer confessed to the killing of Bud. They were convicted, sentenced to hard labor for life, and remanded to the state penitentiary at Frankfort.

At this point, Messer asked to address the bench: "Hit's mighty little work I can do, Jedge. Hain't bin able to work none o' any 'count for several years."

The judge had to pound his gavel to bring the court to order as the assembly guffawed at Messer's concerns. Like Wall, the Mahons were granted an appeal. For his part, Bill Tom Hatfield was sentenced to life in prison. After serving six years, however, he would be pardoned. The cases of Sam Mahon, who had become very ill during his six months in jail, and Charley Gillespie were continued, to be resolved at a later date. Unlike his brothers Doc and Plyant, Sam was, in fact, innocent.

The September 6 *Wheeling Register* announced the convictions and life sentences of Wall and Messer, noting that there was no way of knowing "just how many lives have been sacrificed in this famous vendetta" that had caused "so much terror" on the Kentucky border. The belief that more lives were lost in the feud than ever would be known was a contemporary one — not just an exaggerated notion that developed over time.

THE TRIALS CONTINUED. Cotton Top, represented by attorney W. M. Connolly, was now tried for the murder of Alifair during the New Year's Day raid. From an old and tony local family, Connolly, owner of the Pikeville hotel where John Spears had stayed and a co-owner of the newspapers there and in Lawrence, Kentucky, did little for his client. Having already confessed with no negotiation for leniency, Cotton Top was taken by surprise when the prosecution called Sally McCoy to the stand. She was the only witness, and his unease grew as she told what had happened that night, describing the brutal way her daughter had been slain and she herself had been beaten. Her testimony made a deep impact on the jurors, who deliberated for a mere forty-one minutes before pronouncing Cotton Top guilty. Then they sentenced him to death.[15]

Cotton Top could have withdrawn the guilty plea at any time before the verdict, but afterward it was too late. Connolly was grossly incompetent or willing to sacrifice Cotton Top to bring the violence to a halt, and Cotton Top had been double-crossed by the county attorney, who had milked the slow-witted and cooperative Hatfield son for all the information he could get and then thrown him to the wolves. The next day, Connolly fruitlessly moved to withdraw the original plea and enter a plea of not guilty. He also filed a statement explaining that Cotton Top had been induced to enter the guilty plea believing the jury would be merciful to him and spare his life. While Cotton Top was not allowed a retrial, he was, like Wall and the Mahons, granted an appeal.[16]

On October 20, Cotton Top gave an interview to a reporter from the *Wheeling Intelligencer*. He refused to leave his cell but invited the reporter in and lit the lamp that hung there, illuminating a dingy and stifling space. The two sat on his cot. "I don't blame the McCoys," Cotton Top told him. "The Hatfields brought me to this. Twice they came after me with guns, telling me to come on and take the lives of those who had killed my father." He said that he did not expect a commutation of his sentence. "Nobody seems to be doing anything for me. My lawyers come here and talk to me; then go away and forget that I am alive."

Cotton Top was a "tool in the hands" of others, the reporter concluded. His hanging would not satisfy the need for justice. Still, he predicted it would be "one of the biggest events in the history of Pikeville."[17]

ON NOVEMBER 9, the appeals for Cotton Top, Wall, and the Mahons were heard in the Kentucky Court of Appeals. The Mahons' and Wall's cases were heard together, and they were represented by a battery of Pikeville attorneys, including A. J. Auxier, W. M. Connolly, and, most remarkably, Perry Cline, who had been retained by Wall much earlier and had chosen to stand by him despite his own feelings of enmity for Devil Anse and his disgust for the feud. The lawyers did the defendants little good. The Mahons were written off virtually in a breath: Their case, the decision said, "depends solely upon the testimony establishing their guilt. We forbear to discuss it further." Since it involved interstate issues, Wall's situation demanded a little more attention, but not much. The gist of his appeal lay in the fact that he was in West Virginia when the murders occurred and not in the jurisdiction of Kentucky and thus he should be tried, if anywhere, in West Virginia. The court disagreed, saying: "It is not pretended that the courts of one state can enforce its laws beyond the state boundary, but it is well settled that, where one puts into operation the force or power that causes the injury, he is responsible where the wrong is perpetrated, although he may not actually be present. If either of the appellants had stood on the Virginia [sic] shore, and shot the deceased on the Kentucky side, the offense would have been against the laws of Kentucky."[18]

The court seemed particularly inimical to Wall. "From the inception of this reckless violation of the law to its conclusion," the "presiding judge of this murderous clan," as the court poetically described Wall, "could at any time have stayed the hand of the murderers and saved the lives of these young men."

To this day, the Hatfields maintain that Wall was innocent. Wall's grandson Estil Hatfield claimed that it was his grandfather's infamous philandering that got him in trouble. "My grandfather loved women. And these two boys on Beech Creek wanted to be with one of his women," he told a reporter. "So they said after the killings of the McCoy boys that they heard the hoot of an owl. My grandfather was known for that birdcall, and so he was arrested in the murders. But he wasn't involved. . . . Those boys wanted him out of the picture."[19]

In the end, the court was swift and unequivocal in its opinion, affirming the lower court's decisions and melodramatically declaring, "To find a more cruel and inhuman murder we must leave our own civilization and resort to the annals of savage life." As far as this tribunal was concerned, the sentence of life in prison was merciful.

Cotton Top's appeal was no more successful. The higher court maintained that unless the defendant had an agreement from the state to reduce the punishment, which was not the case, the state had the right, even with a guilty plea, to introduce testimony showing the severity of the crime. Furthermore, since no motion was made to withdraw the plea of guilty at that time, the lower court was not in error in overruling Cotton Top's later motion to with-draw it.[20]

~

ON TUESDAY NIGHT, November 19, 1889, the citizens of Charleston received a shock: Devil Anse Hatfield and an entourage of armed men came riding into town. While Wall, Cotton Top, and the others were facing the wrath of the law in Kentucky, Devil Anse had his own legal challenge to confront—an indictment for selling whiskey based on the testimony of Hatfield adversary Dave Stratton.[21] Dating back to the spring of the previous year, it was a lesser charge to be sure, but it was a federal one and could include a prison sentence. Devil Anse had a seemingly unlimited supply of influential friends, however, and federal judge John Jay Jackson, a Lincoln appointee known as the Iron Judge, agreed that if he would appear in his Charleston courtroom voluntarily, then the court would guarantee him protection from arrest or assassination on his journey to Charleston and back home again. Thus, even after the U.S. Supreme Court upheld a case in which Governor Wilson's refusal to honor the governor of Kentucky's requisitions was an issue, the federal court promised Devil Anse protection against state authorities (as well as detectives and bounty hunters of all sorts). Even if Wilson wanted to, he could not arrest Devil Anse for the murders of the McCoy brothers while he was under the custody of federal marshals.[21]

In conjunction with Judge Jackson, U.S. marshal Henry S. White, a Union veteran and staunch Republican who had just been appointed in April, dispatched chief deputy William J. White (no relation) to bring in Devil Anse. The chief deputy, a big, rawboned, genial man, had stormed Devil Anse's stronghold—and sweet-talked him into submission. Based on White's promises, Devil Anse agreed to go with him. Before they set out, however, Anse summoned five of his men, all armed with Winchesters, who he said would be coming along too. Fearing an ambush from the McCoys or bounty hunters, White hired a number of additional guards for the eighty-six-mile journey, among them Devil Anse's cousin Jerry Hatfield, the former Pike County sheriff (who would be shot and killed four months later during an argument in a brothel).

When the group reached Charleston, Henry White, a small and indomitable man who in addition to being a U.S. marshal was a successful merchant, railroad representative, timberman, and state legislator, took Devil Anse into custody and assigned twenty-five special deputies to keep the peace while the Hatfields were in Charleston.

Now fifty-two, Devil Anse appeared remarkably youthful, his bushy beard still dark brown, not gray. A reporter described him as "a medium sized man, very stoop shouldered, with a quick eye that seems to look in all directions at once," adding "no one would judge from his appearance that he is the blood thirsty villain that imaginative newspaper men have pictured him to be." He wore a navy-blue suit with his pant legs stuffed into his rough boots, and Major Alderson, whom the *Wheeling Intelligencer* identified as "a good friend of Anse," hired a hotel porter to give the boots a patent-leather sheen — a formidable task that took more than twenty minutes of intensive polishing.

The dapper Devil Anse was well represented by attorneys George W. Atkinson — a future governor of West Virginia and the former U.S. marshal who had hired Dan Cunningham as a deputy marshal — of Wheeling and C. C. Watts of Charleston. Spectators packed the courtroom, some wanting just to catch a glimpse of the famous defendant and others hoping to figure out a way to seize him and collect the reward for his head.

Judge Jackson, a stern hawk-nosed tyrant on the bench, treated Devil Anse like a visiting dignitary. The proceedings lasted most of a day, with the defense arguing that the charges were trumped up and that the whole thing was merely a conspiracy by Dave Stratton and various detectives to get Devil Anse out of his stronghold so they could capture him and take him to Kentucky to claim the

George W. Atkinson, U.S. marshal (1881–1885) and governor of West Virginia (1896–1900).

bounty on his head. (The requisition from Kentucky was introduced at the trial to impugn Devil Anse, but it "had no effect.") After listening to the evidence and the testimony, the jury acquitted him. Judge Jackson instructed Henry White to ensure that Devil Anse was amply protected on his way home. As the courtroom cleared, Jackson commented to general laughter, "When Hatfield gets back to his house, I certainly have no objection to any of you arresting him that may want to try."[22]

The next day, November 21, Devil Anse granted a two-hour interview to a reporter from the *Wheeling Intelligencer,* which remains one of the chief sources for feud histories. Devil Anse claimed, among other things, that Marion, Tom, and Johnse McCoy, who had served in his company of irregular soldiers during the war, were "now trying to kill me." He denied that he or his sons Johnse and Cap had anything to do with the slaying of the three McCoy brothers, saying, "As a matter of fact we knew nothing of the murders until several days after they had been committed."[23]

Devil Anse's satisfaction at being treated with respect by some of the best men in the state was tempered, however. He had another predicament in the family, one that he was trying to gain some purchase on. "Mounts has been tried and sentenced to be hung," he told the *Intelligencer*.

The hanging had originally been set for December 3, 1889, but after Cotton Top lost his appeal, Governor Buckner set a new execution date of Tuesday, February 18, 1890. Still, there was not much time for Devil Anse to save his nephew.

∽

Chapter 21

The Bitter End

November 1889–February 1890

That same month, November 1889, the *Detroit Free Press* picked up reports out of Milton, West Virginia, of "another bloody battle" between the Hatfields and the McCoys, although this particular battle began between the McCoys and a family named the Blumfields. In the account, the McCoys "crawled up through the dense underbrush and poured in a volley on their sleeping foes," wounding a dozen men and killing two, including John Blumfield, one of the clan's leaders. Somehow, as in a dream, the Blumfields became the Hatfields, who returned the gunfire and, "although taken by surprise, were so much better armed than the McCoys, having repeating rifles, that they soon put them to flight."

The *Free Press* reported that four McCoys were taken by the Hatfields; one was left to die, and the other three — Charles Lambkins, John Cain, and Peter McCoy — were herded off to the Hatfield camp, where a "court-martial" was held. "The prisoners were not allowed to speak in their defense, and after a short deliberation a vote on their life or death was taken by the entire Hatfield party." The result, not surprisingly, "was unanimous and the three men will be tied to trees and shot to-day. Nothing can save them unless the McCoys can defeat the entire Hatfield party and effect a rescue." For good measure, the story noted that "the courier who brought this news was shot at twice from ambush while riding through Lincoln County."[1]

The November 23 *Wheeling Intelligencer,* however, reported that news of the alleged Blumfield-McCoy vendetta in Lincoln County, "blood-curdling accounts of whole communities being arrayed against each other and factions thirsting for the blood of their enemies on account of certain grievances," were false tales from "penny-a-liners who find for them a ready sale to the newspapers for the outside world."

There had in fact been a crime that set off the reports. Two men, Haley and McCoy—their first names lost to history—had waylaid a man named Al Brumfield and his wife and shot them. A mob seized Haley and McCoy and riddled them with bullets. That ended the matter. No vendetta existed. A businessman who had just returned from the region told the *Intelligencer,* "There is not a word of truth in the sensational reports recently imposed upon the newspapers, and through them on the reading public."[2]

THREE MONTHS AFTER DEVIL ANSE'S journey to Charleston, Cotton Top Mounts prepared to die on the scaffold. A large crowd showed up, but Perry Cline would not attend the execution, nor would he permit any of his family to be present at the spectacle. Randall McCoy, who now lived in a modest house on the Pikeville riverbank and ran a ferry, watched but derived little pleasure from it. The loss of his sons, the burning of his home, the near-fatal beating of his wife, and the death of his daughter had ruined him, and he was known to roam the streets muttering about his woes.

Cotton Top rode to the execution site, at the base of a low hill—now on the campus of Pikeville College, founded in 1888 by Presbyterians—atop his own coffin. He was given a last opportunity to speak. He coolly announced that he would make no speech

Scene of Cotton Top Mounts's hanging, February 20, 1890. (*Big Sandy Heritage Center*)

and that "he was ready to die, and he hoped that all of his friends would be good men and women, and meet him in heaven." Standing on the gallows, in the last seconds of his life, Cotton Top, all alone, strove for justice in the only way he could. He hollered the anguished, accusatory plaint that would be long remembered by those involved in the feud: "The Hatfields made me do it!"

At six minutes to one o'clock, the black hood was adjusted, and the trap was sprung. As Cotton Top writhed between heaven and earth, a gasp rang through the crowd. After hanging ten minutes, he was pronounced dead by the attending physician, and his body was cut down and subsequently viewed by hundreds of curious spectators. They were looking at the fresh corpse of the only man who would be legally sentenced to death and executed as a result of the feud.

A photographer snapped a picture of the gallows, which has been widely circulated and republished, so much so that it has become one of the feud's most enduring images. It appears to have been taken just before the hanging. The figure crouching against a fence post to the left and rear of the scaffold is possibly Cotton Top. Eight men are on the scaffold. Five of them are on their knees.

One — perhaps the Reverend J. W. Pastor of the Methodist Episcopal Church, South, in Pikeville, who was also the jail physician — is
looking to heaven and leading them in prayer. A guard in the left
foreground holds his rifle extended horizontally in one hand and his
hat in the other. His eyes are lowered to the ground.[3]

Just as there had been little assistance at his trial and no rescue
from his relatives, there would be minimal effort made for Cotton
Top's burial by those who received his body. He was laid to rest
across the Levisa Fork in Dils Cemetery — among McCoys, no
less — in graves marked and unmarked. No one bothered to place a
stone by his head. "His dust is lost in the earth," Truda McCoy
would write.

His reputation, however, endured for others to excoriate. The
yellow journalist Charles Mutzenberg would call Cotton Top a
"criminal by nature" but in the same breath say "he was easily influenced to obey the command of those who used him as a tool."
Indeed, Cotton Top was not a "criminal by nature," if there is such a
thing, but a simpleton led astray. Mutzenberg, however, spun a
melodramatic epitaph for the dead man: "Ellison Mounts had ceased
to be a dread to humanity," he wrote. "Ignorant as the savage of
interior Africa, he had no conception of the magnitude of his
crimes. . . . Shedding human blood was a pastime with him."[4]

From the minute it happened, the hanging of Cotton Top
Mounts was widely construed as the lancing needed to end the
Hatfield-McCoy feud. "A vast crowd gathers to see the last act in a
famous tragedy," the Thursday morning, February 20, *Louisville
Courier-Journal* announced.

That year, even the geography was changing; the town of Matewan was being laid out at the mouth of Mate Creek by a Norfolk
and Western Railway civil engineer. It was named in honor of both
Richard Ferrell's lost hunting dog, Mate, and the engineer's home-
town, Matteawan, in upstate New York.[5]

However, despite everyone's hopes, it was premature to designate the hanging as the feud's last act. The struggles between the

families and the greater forces they had set in motion did not come to a sudden halt on that fateful day. Devil Anse, Cap, and Johnse, still wanted for the murders of the McCoy brothers and the latter two for the New Year's Day raid as well, remained at large. And no one had forgotten about them, least of all the McCoys. Bud boasted that he could put together on short notice a posse of a hundred men to hunt Hatfields. Feeling heady, the Pikeville authorities decided to leave the scaffold standing for the time being, in case they needed it again soon.

A few days after the hanging, a package from Randall's supporters arrived at Devil Anse's house. Inside was a length of the rope used to string up Cotton Top.[6]

Chapter 22

~

After the Hanging

1890–1895

Among the crowd of thousands gathered in Pikeville to see Cotton Top Mounts swing were some who possessed more than just a passing interest in the proceedings: they were bounty hunters hoping that the Hatfields would actually turn up, or at least that they might be able to sniff out some clues to help them find the chinks in the family's armor.

For many of the feudists and lawmen, Cotton Top's hanging did provide closure of sorts. Some of the feudists set about turning around their lives in remarkable ways. Wall, who was now locked up for life, was not one of them. He would never again hear his son Smith, a professional musician, play the fiddle and never again see his daughter Nancy, who was known for the cloth she made on her old spinning wheel. Nancy and Smith were but two of many, and the free-spirited Wall, who it is said left behind fifty-five children and certainly a slew of broken hearts, did not have the will to last behind bars. He died in prison after only two years. His family had no contact with him and never even found out where he was buried. His sons-in-law Doc and Plyant would serve fourteen years before being pardoned and released.[1]

In March of 1890, one of the guns that had been sent to Logan Courthouse to help the militia bring peace was used in the murder of Jerry Hatfield. Jerry, who had been a Pike County deputy sheriff and then a prosperous merchant in Logan County, was shot in a brothel by a man named Mike Lee wielding the rifle.

The following month, Bad Frank Phillips was back in the news when it was reported that he was killed by Rebel Bill Smith, who had once terrorized the Kentucky Unionists and brazenly attacked Colonel Garfield's forces as they traveled up the Big Sandy River by push boat. Rebel Bill had led Devil Anse during the war; his son Larkin was married to Devil Anse's sister; and their daughters — Eska and Nan — were married to French Ellis and Cap. Though flawed, Bad Frank was still a hero to many in Kentucky, the one man who had dared to marshal troops and plunge into the lions' den. He certainly hated Rebel Bill, who had captured his father during the war and sent him to his eventual death in a Richmond prison. As the story went, Rebel Bill had been sawing ties for the Norfolk and Western railroad in the Peter Creek area when he and Bad Frank ran across each other. Bad Frank threatened to kill Rebel Bill and the next night broke into his room while he was sleeping and shot him. But the shot caused only a scalp wound. Rebel Bill swore out an arrest warrant for Bad Frank and was said to have killed him on April 19 or 20 while trying to serve it.

In fact, although it was not clear exactly where Bad Frank was, he was not dead. And several prominent men were called upon to vouch for the fact that Rebel Bill had neither arrested nor killed him. It was yet another case of reported fiction getting well ahead of verifiable fact. The volatile Bad Frank lived on, to be shot to death another day.

One of Bad Frank's chief deputies was not so lucky. On May 14, Dave Stratton was expected home but did not arrive. The next morning his wife went out to look for him and found him lying unconscious on the ground not far from the house. His skull was split and bloody, and there was a massive hematoma on his chest from a terrible blow. He never regained consciousness. Word went around that he had been beaten to death by Devil Anse, Cap,

Johnse, and Indian. Kentucky Bill rushed from Charleston to Brownstown, swore out warrants for the arrest of these men and three others suspected of being involved, then headed off into the mountains to find them. In the meantime, it was determined that Stratton had in fact gotten drunk, passed out on the train tracks, and been hurled aside by the cowcatcher of a Chesapeake and Ohio locomotive.

Kentucky Bill was incommunicado for some time. Then in July, it was heard that his body had been found in Hatfield country with a bullet through the heart. It was not true, but the rumor went undenied for two weeks, until he was found testifying in a moonshining case in the town of Oceana, West Virginia. When Kentucky Bill was shown his own death notice, he allowed that he was "the liveliest corpse to be found in those back woods."[2]

While Bad Frank, Dave Stratton, and Kentucky Bill were dominating the news, Charley Gillespie finally and mysteriously escaped from the Pike County jail. The jailers considered the exits so secure that at first they believed he was still somewhere inside, hiding. But their search failed to produce him or any evidence of his escape. Some believed that he eventually managed to make it back to West Virginia, but he never returned home, so it was impossible to know.

ALTHOUGH MEN WERE STILL WANTED by the law on both sides of the Tug, West Virginia governor Aretus Fleming, who took office in February 1890 (the fourth of five consecutive Democratic governors), decided it would be best for the state to put the feud behind it. The railroads had at last brought modernization to West Virginia. Timber, minerals, and especially coal were now being exploited on a larger scale, and the money at stake was much greater. Law and order were vital to this progress. Recognizing that one of the catalysts for the feud was the bounties placed on the heads of the wanted men, Fleming withdrew the rewards for the Kentuckians.

In Pikeville, in the fall term of the criminal court, the cases involving the Hatfields stayed on the docket but were given little attention and little hope of being resolved. At the moment, the residents were more concerned with a pair of scandals rocking the small town's legal fraternity. Two Civil War veterans had accused Lee Ferguson of stealing their pensions after helping set them up, and a woman had accused the prominent attorney A. J. Auxier, a member of one of the Big Sandy Valley's oldest and most exalted families, of having fathered a child by another man's wife. A salacious slander suit followed, with Auxier being lambasted in the media.

Meanwhile, the McCoys' tribulations continued to mount. The most prominent feudist to actually die during this period was Harmon's son Bud (not to be confused with Randall's son Bud, killed at the pawpaw patch), who had ridden with Bad Frank on his expeditions in West Virginia. Bud was riddled with bullets outside a Peter Creek timber camp. The brutal slaying — eighteen slugs were counted in his body — was initially blamed on the Hatfields but was actually carried out by a McCoy. Ples McCoy, a teenager, with the help of a friend, murdered Bud over an unresolved grudge.

With Pikeville's attention captured by the scandals and an apparent lack of interest in pursuing the rest of the wanted men in West Virginia, Johnse, who had turned twenty-eight the month before Cotton Top's death, seemed none too worried and nothing like a fugitive now. He married again, on October 28, 1890, putting Nancy, from whom he was divorced, behind him and settling down. He and his new wife, Rebecca Browning (also twenty-eight and, like him, a descendant of Abner Vance) would have two children, Moss and Vickie. But no matter how domestic Johnse's life appeared to be, he was not out of the woods.

That December, Elias and his son Greenway made the journey to Charleston to face federal moonshining charges. Like Devil Anse, they were acquitted — and it was back to business as usual.[3]

On the other hand, Devil Anse's fourth son, Elliott, who had trained as a doctor, came back home to make good. One day, Lark

McCoy, who had lost his father and a brother in the feud, was saddling up a horse to ride over the mountain to Pikeville for medical help for one of his granddaughters when Elliott happened by. "Pa was troubled plumb fantastic, for ma had done all she could with home yarbs and sich, but nothing seemed to holp the child," Lark's son Bud later recounted. "Old Doc Slusher, the yarb doctor, was past goin', and his eyesight played out." When Lark saw Elliott, he summoned him.

"Lark," said Elliott, according to Bud, "you don't aim to serve me like they served Jeff, do you?"

"Ell't," his pa responded, "I wouldn't harm a harr of your head. I've got nothin' in this world agin you. You never harmed me nor mine and you can't holp what your folks has done to mine. Come in and see what you can do to holp my pore little sick girl." Dr. Hatfield dismounted, went inside the cabin, and tended to the sick girl. "She was soon well," Bud recalled, "and the father never forgot the doctor's kindness and help in his hour of need."[4]

ON FEBRUARY 24, 1891, Cap Hatfield, perhaps finding hope in the impending death of Perry Cline and necessity in the upcoming nuptials of a cousin, Aaron Hatfield, to Sophia McCoy, announced in a letter to the editor of the *Wayne County News* that an amnesty had been declared and that "the war spirit in me has abated." He proclaimed an end to the fighting in language that once again evoked the Civil War: "I sincerely rejoice at the prospect of peace. I have devoted my life to arms. We have undergone a fearful loss of noble lives and valuable property in the struggle." Even while trying to turn the other cheek, he could not escape a dig at the other side — and a biblical one, at that — adding, "we being, like Adam, not the first transgressors." He concluded, "Now I propose to rest in a spirit of peace."

Perry Cline died of tuberculosis on March 19, 1891. The enigmatic man who essentially inherited the feud, escalated it, was accused of trying to profit from it, and both jailed the Hatfields and defended them in court was gone. The accusations of extortion against Cline, who was Lincolnian in appearance, profession, and passion and who was a pillar of the community, seem to have been spurious and tactical. As one of his legacies, the Pikeville attorney, county official, and state legislator had helped pass the 1886 bill that established free schools for black children in Kentucky. With his death, the political pressure to sweep the feud into the past would steadily rise. Only the bounty hunters—empowered by the Supreme Court decision and the rewards that remained in place in Kentucky—and the press, including the *New York Tribune,* the *Wheeling Intelligencer,* and the *Louisville Courier-Journal,* the last of which made hay with Cap's letter, maintained a passion for the feud.[5]

For Johnse, who had hoped for escape from past entanglements, the heat of this passion proved to be too much. He consulted with Devil Anse and decided to disappear again. Devil Anse recommended he head out to the new state of Washington, to Spokane specifically, where a friend named Sam Vinson, who was accused of killing Lon McCoy, had moved and where an experienced lumberjack could find a job. Johnse would be gone for more than two years. In Spokane, he was attracted to a bar advertising Kentucky whiskey, and there he found his man. Vinson, who owned the bar, helped him find work as a timber hand. Johnse was content to bide his time. But the tireless Dan Cunningham had a wide network of informers, and he too would soon take a jaunt out west.[6]

∼

ANDY CHAFIN was just four years old at the time of Cotton Top's death, which occurred about the same time that his father, Holbert Chafin, Vicey Hatfield's cousin, uprooted his family from their cabin. A blacksmith and miller, Holbert could make or fix just about anything a farm or timber operation needed, and he also operated a water mill, grinding corn for the local farmers. He shoed horses and sharpened plows, and he manufactured ox yokes, grabs, and chains for the Yellow Poplar Timber Company. The Chafins moved to a place on a creek fork down the mountainside about a mile from Vicey and Devil Anse's farm and uphill from Cap's. "Aunt Vicey just thought never a man lived like my dad," Chafin later recalled. "She could always depend on him when Uncle Anse or Cap was in trouble and them was the same way."[7]

Trouble could come in the form of U.S. deputy marshals or Internal Revenue agents or an array of bounty hunters. "Cap's wife, she bootlegged," Chafin related. "They lived in a log house and they had to core a hole through the logs. And a fellow come up and tap on a piece of metal they had, to make a noise, and she'd scoop that chute out to him and he'd put in, a dollar, or whatever he put in, and she'd pull it back in, put the liquor in and put something back in the box. She had to do it or starve, that's all there was to it; there was no other way. A little farm there, but then you couldn't raise enough on the farm with all the kids." And while Devil Anse raised cattle and hogs and owned three thousand acres of timberland, according to Chafin, he also ran a saloon and store in Kentucky where he sold corn liquor in half-gallon and gallon jugs.

Devil Anse had gathered his family in a tight protective web. Chafin's family lived on the farm rent-free. His uncles John, Moses, and Tom Chafin owned land nearby and worked on Anse's timber crew or partnered with him in one of his other businesses. Devil Anse and Vicey lived well, in a large cabin with eight children at home, including Willis, who was two years younger than Chafin, and a toddler, Tennis, born in August 1890. Their grandson Ken came around often, and so did a neighbor named Lonnie Lee, who was a year younger than Chafin. Vicey, whom the reporter T. C. Crawford described as "hard as iron," had a soft spot for the children and served up foot-long loaves of hot corn pone with bacon cracklin' to keep them full. Lee liked this and also admired the Hatfields for their wealth, noting that they "went hunting in better clothes than I could wear on Sundays."

Devil Anse had developed a siege mentality and remained constantly on the lookout for bounty hunters. Chafin recalled gunslingers working their way into the woods on Devil Anse's property and shooting at him. "They just couldn't get him out, that's all," he said. "They got in there, but they didn't get him out."[8]

DEVIL ANSE HAD TAKEN CHAFIN under his wing. One morning when the boy was walking to school, he passed by Devil Anse. Pretty soon he passed by again, heading home. Devil Anse asked him what he was doing. He replied that the schoolmaster had sent him away. Devil Anse, who had built the schoolhouse, told the boy to come back later and then went to see the schoolmaster. When Chafin returned, Devil Anse told him to go on to school, and he did, whereupon he found the old schoolmaster gone and a new one in his place.

"Anse Hatfield was one of the finest men that ever lived," Chafin would later say about his mentor. "If you was sick, he'd send help to you right quick. If you needed, he'd see that you got help. . . . But he wouldn't accept no foolishness. He didn't take no foolishness."

Devil Anse soon discovered that Chafin had an innate ability to sense when trouble was approaching, and so he invited the boy to live with him. Chafin bunked with his cousins: Mary (age seventeen), Elizabeth (fifteen), Elias (twelve), Troy (nine), Joe (seven), Rose (five), Willis, and Tennis. The older girls looked after the little ones, and Chafin was a favorite. Devil Anse, who liked playing pranks on his boys and telling far-fetched stories, joked that he had a sixth son in the house, Chafin, and that his sixth son had a sixth sense.

Devil Anse taught the boys how to hunt and shoot. Chafin could shoot a squirrel out of a tall tree by the time he was seven. Troy in particular inherited his father's gift for marksmanship and was a deadeye with a revolver (though he and his brother Elias would be gunned down by a rival whiskey seller in 1911). Troy dazzled crowds by shooting half-dollar coins tossed into the air. "Many donated their coins not fearing they would be hit, but in all such cases these 'Doubting Thomases' came up short fifty cents," wrote a reporter.[9]

When Lonnie Lee, whom Devil Anse also taught to shoot, went to work as a logger in 1904, at age eighteen, he packed a pistol on each hip as a matter of survival, since logging camps attracted outcasts and criminals. "They'd murder somebody and go to a logging camp to hide out. . . . They didn't care if they killed you." When he finally had to shoot a man, a drifter from Pennsylvania, in self-defense, Lee put a bullet in the stranger's leg to knock him down without killing him, then hauled the wounded man to a doctor. "Well that's a damn poor way to introduce yourself," the doctor told the newcomer. "You shot at the best marksman around here."

Devil Anse and the boys often hunted the afternoon away and then, after an early-evening nap, went back out after dark. One such night, they shot three raccoons. Chafin strapped one across his shoulder and another across his body. He carried an ax and a lantern as well. As they descended through a culvert on their way home that morning, they suddenly heard singing. They had forgotten what day it was. "Ah, hell," said Devil Anse, "it's Sunday and they're holding meetin' right by the house." They set down their weapons and the carcasses by a massive beech tree and joined in.[10]

Cap was still roving in the woods for safety, staying in various cabins and hideouts. Chafin delivered messages and food and guided visitors through the woods. When he was out, he kept his ear to the ground, and if he heard anything that pertained to the safety of the Hatfields, he rushed home and reported it.

To signal one another, they used animal calls that Devil Anse had taught them, like the barking of a squirrel or the hooting of an owl. One afternoon, Chafin was walking home from school with a dozen other kids when he heard a squirrel bark. He stopped and told his brother Oliver to go on home. "Where you going?" Oliver asked.

"I'm going to see that squirrel," he responded.

"What's that?" he asked. "You got no gun."

Chafin said, "You go on and do what I tell ya. I heard a squirrel barking, going to see what it is."

The "squirrel" was Cap, and he was with a fellow named Radford and four others. They were hungry. "Tell you what you do," Cap said to Chafin. "You up and tell your mother to fix a good mess of chicken and dumplings." And so he did.

For a night rendezvous, Chafin carried a miner's lantern. When he needed it to go dark fast, instead of blowing out the lantern, which was slow and inconvenient, he pulled it up under his long shirt. During whispered conversations in the woods, he kept it that way, ignoring the heat of the lantern, which he had learned to tolerate.[11]

Devil Anse's brother Smith, one of a set of twins who were fifteen years his junior, also pitched in whenever necessary. Before Big Ellison was killed, Smith, who operated a gristmill at the mouth of Mark's Creek, had had a bitter relationship with him, as Ellison was careless with logs he sent downstream and had damaged

Cap Hatfield (third from right) at a cave near Main Island Creek that served as a hideout during the feud. *(West Virginia State Archives)*

Smith's mill. Indeed, Smith, who was closer in both age and relationship to his nephew Johnse, detested Ellison, his own brother,
more than he hated any McCoy and was never directly involved in
the feud. However, he would defend his kin, and he helped his
brothers dig out a rock house under a ledge and then barricade it
with split rails. A consummate woodsman, Smith could tell by
smell if a groundhog was in its den or if a copperhead, with its scent
of hot cucumber, was nearby. Like Chafin, he often slipped through
the woods without a trace to deliver food or intelligence to those
hiding out.[12]

However, the family's defenses were not foolproof. One bounty
hunter managed to infiltrate Devil Anse's farm as a handyman. He
had been there for nearly six months when he accompanied Anse
and Chafin on a hunt. After Chafin shot a raccoon, Devil Anse
hoisted it up on his shoulder. The handyman raised his gun and
pointed it at Devil Anse. "Just drop the coon," he said. "I've been
looking for this opportunity a long time. I'm a detective."

Devil Anse dropped the animal and stood with his hands hanging
at his sides. The detective began to read him his rights. In a flash,
Devil Anse pulled a pistol from his pants. "The gun cracked and
he was gone, and that was all there was to it," Chafin later said. "Just
like a piece of lightning." They buried the man on the spot and never
spoke about him again.[13]

ON INFORMATION FROM NANCY PHILLIPS and possibly with expense
money from Randall (though he could ill afford it), Dan Cunningham and a posse of detectives, including Alf Burnett, Kentucky Bill
Napier, and Treve Gibson, traveled out west to bring in Johnse.
They had one thing going for them: even in his thirties, the handsome Johnse still stood out in a crowd. At a timber camp on the
Snoqualmie River, they spread the word that they were looking for
a West Virginian with dirty blond hair and blue eyes who went by
the name of Jim Jacobs.[14]

But Johnse, who had never stopped being a ladies' man, had a helpful friend, a young woman named Midgie McCarthy. She dispatched a messenger with a note to the foreman of Johnse's logging crew, telling him to warn Jim that trouble was on the way. At dawn the next day, Johnse looked down the valley to see riders approaching. He had just enough time to drop his ax and run into the woods. Seven detectives swept up through the valley combing the area. The messenger, half Siwash Indian, guided Johnse to a hiding place near a river.

"I never spent such terrible hours as I did watching them hunt for me," Johnse would later say. A flock of Canada geese surrounded the thicket he was in and made a racket that he thought was a dead giveaway. But the detectives looked everywhere except where the geese had landed.[15]

After they left, Johnse swam the river, made his way to Seattle, caught a steamer for British Columbia, and disappeared for the next two years. Meanwhile, in an effort to give Johnse a fresh start, Sam Vinson, the bar owner, sent Devil Anse and Vicey a lock of Johnse's hair along with a note telling them that he was dead.

Chapter 23

~

The Last Murders and Manhunt

1896

Sometime in the spring of 1896, a good-looking man in a sharp suit showed up unannounced at Devil Anse and Vicey's cabin door. The dearly departed walked again: Johnse had returned from the Pacific Northwest. After so many years on the lam—though not, as reported, in a better place—he gave Vicey a big hug.

Johnse, now thirty-four, promptly set about establishing a new life, getting involved in the business he knew, timbering, and, to be safe, staying away from the Tug River and Kentucky. He launched an operation on the Guyandotte, which flowed through Logan Courthouse on its way to Huntington. Being Johnse, he also soon found a new wife, his third of four. On July 28, 1896, he married twenty-one-year-old Roxie Browning. Their firstborn child was a girl, and they named her Midgie—after the woman who had saved his life, or at least his liberty, out west.[1]

Although Cap, like Johnse, was still wanted for murder in Kentucky, he had no qualms about leaving his mountain farm and taking his fourteen-year-old stepson, Little Joe Glenn, to Matewan on Election Day, which fell on Tuesday, November 3, that year. Cap had moved from Main Island Creek over to Mate Creek, about five miles from town, the year before. With the coming of the railroads and the sudden growth of the coal industry, life and landscape were changing rapidly. However, a lingering depression had descended on the country three years earlier, and Cap announced that he planned to buck the family trend and vote Republican in the hope of making things better.

Cap and Little Joe—"my boy," as his stepfather called him—were both armed: Cap carried a Model 1873 Winchester rifle, and Little Joe a double-barreled shotgun that he used for hunting squirrels. Each also had a Colt pistol stuffed under his shirt.

They had been at the polls only briefly when they encountered John and Elliott Rutherford, locals who had sided with the McCoys in the feud. They were the sons of Doc Rutherford, a Hatfield friend until he was involved in a shootout with Vicey's brother John Chafin. Chafin was hit in the spine, leaving him barely able to walk, and the families had been bitter enemies ever since. Just months before, the Rutherfords had accused Cap of shooting up John Rutherford's house.[2]

At a Pike County saloon just across the river from Matewan, John—who was a fearless roughneck with an explosive temper—told a group of Democratic campaign workers that Cap was voting Republican and being noisy about it. John and his buddies had reason to worry about their candidate's chances. Elias's son Henry, a twenty-one-year-old doctor who had gotten his medical degree from the University of Louisville, would walk twelve miles to Matewan that day to vote for the pro-business Ohio Republican William McKinley over Nebraska Democrat William Jennings Bryan, and a majority of West Virginians would be of like mind. The state would also elect a Republican governor, former U.S. marshal George W. Atkinson—who had made his name as a revenuer busting moonshiners—ending a streak of six Democratic governors and beginning a Republican run of five. The last of these would be Henry himself.

But Henry Hatfield was not their concern on this day. Cap was. "If he comes down here and votes the Republican ticket," John told his drinking pals, "let's put him over in Kentucky." They all knew what that meant regarding certain Hatfields; they would be arrested, and the old murder charges pressed.[3]

Overhearing this, Cap's double cousin Greenway looked at John and said, "You'd better kill him if you're gonna do anything, 'cause if you start something, he'll hurt some of you."

As Cap and Little Joe walked onto the polling grounds, where the vanity fair of drinking, arguing, laughing, gossiping, and courting was under way, they passed a store owned by Doc Rutherford. Inside and outside, more of Doc's sons and their friends were throwing back whiskey and carrying on. Among them was his son Lewis, whom Cap had quarreled with over a woman several years earlier. Lewis had been "jealous," according to Cap, and had demanded an apology for a grievance. Now he saw Cap and tried to bait him into an argument. Cap tried to ignore him, at least that is how he would tell it.

Others, however, say that as the day progressed, Cap continually glowered at the Rutherfords, and after a while, they felt it would be wise to leave. Before that could happen, according to unnamed witnesses cited by journalist Charles Mutzenberg in 1917, Cap turned on them, whipped his Winchester to his shoulder, and began shooting.

Cap's son Coleman would later claim that it was the other way around: "John Rutherford walked up behind Dad and shouted, 'Look here, Cap Hatfield. Look here!' and fired his shotgun twice." One shot singed the skin of Cap's ear. The other blistered his neck. As John pulled a pistol from a holster and fired again, Coleman explained, Cap shot him in the side.[4]

Cap snatched the double-barreled shotgun from Little Joe. A bullet struck the barrels, shattered, and spit lead fragments into Cap's knuckles. (Cap would later point to the dent on the underside of the gun barrel as proof that Rutherford had shot at him first.) Cap fired his rifle twice with his good hand and then his Colt with his bloody hand. Amid a spattering of buckshot and bullets, Rutherford fell in the dust.

A son-in-law of Doc Rutherford, Henderson Chambers, who was a merchant and a prominent citizen, rushed from his store to intervene in the fight. Chambers was the brother of Tom Chambers, Guerilla Mitchell's stepfather. Little Joe mistook him for another assailant and squeezed the trigger of his pistol. Chambers, a father of five, dropped to the ground, dead.[5]

Cap and Little Joe now ran down an alley in the direction of the railroad tracks and the road out of town. They passed a policeman, and Little Joe shouted at him, shocking even Cap with his audacity,

E. B. Chambers's general store in Matewan, circa 1915. *(Courtesy of F. Keith Davis)*

"Now you tell those goddamned men we're the stuff!" As Ed Rutherford, Reece Halsey, and Doc's sixteen-year-old grandson, Elliott, gave chase, Cap and Little Joe crossed the county road and dashed up along the Tug to the mouth of Mate Creek. From a railroad trestle that was built above the road, Elliott blazed away with two pistols while Little Joe ran up the creek and Cap crouched behind an abutment. When Elliott had emptied both barrels, Cap dashed again, aiming the Colt with his bloody hand, hitting Halsey in the foot and deleting several toes. As Cap caught up with Joe, Elliott finished reloading and fired two shots that hit between Joe's feet. Joe pivoted and returned the favor with the Winchester but shot high.

Cap grabbed the Winchester from Joe, wheeled, and aimed at Elliott, who was crouched and preparing to shoot. Cap squeezed the trigger and blasted Elliott in the chest. Doc Rutherford had now lost a son, a son-in-law, and a grandson.

Cap and Joe crossed the dry bed of Mate Creek and climbed up a steep slope into the hills. They rested when they got to the top of the ridge, where they had a clear view all around through the trees that hid them and could hear the activity in the shaken town below: men shouting, women crying, dogs barking.[6]

WORD OF THE SHOOTOUT REACHED Sheriff Doc Keadle in Williamson, a town experiencing unprecedented growth, enjoying its stature as the new Mingo County seat, and feeling eager to distance itself from the lawlessness and feuding going on around it. (In fact, Mingo County had been carved out of Logan County after a jurisdictional dispute in a moonshining case showed that Logan was too large to police properly.) Keadle organized a posse to track down Cap, and they set off on Wednesday morning, November 4. Keadle dispatched men to outposts along the only nearby railroad line with orders to search all trains and sent others to stake out the likely routes into Kentucky (and surely at least some appreciated the irony of the idea that Cap Hatfield would seek refuge in the bosom of Kentucky).

At three o'clock on Thursday afternoon, the intense effort, which had gone on uninterrupted all night, paid off. A messenger reached Keadle outside Williamson, where he had returned to raise another posse, and told him that Cap and twenty men had been spied at Rock Fort. While this was good news, it was also ominous. On a tributary of the Guyandotte River, twenty miles from Williamson, the fort was tucked into a rock canyon, and approachable from only one side. It was, noted a *Cincinnati Enquirer* correspondent, "impervious to anything less than a 24-pounder." Keadle soon set out for the fort with fifty more men. They would arrive there by ten o'clock that night.

He knew that outside detectives were undoubtedly on their way to come try to capture Cap and claim the reward on his head. "The whole country is aroused," reported the *Enquirer,* "and the interest manifested in the outcome of the bloody encounter which is almost sure to ensue within the next few hours is intense."[7]

Many wheels were already in motion to suppress any such bloody encounter. Newspaper publisher Henry Clay Ragland, who had always held a begrudging respect for Devil Anse, denounced Cap in the *Logan County Banner,* the paper he had founded in 1888. A vocal Democrat and booster of a coal-mining and railroad economy, Ragland argued that a failure to stop the violence would retard the region's growth. Meanwhile, detectives arrested Devil Anse and two of his sons—one of whom, eighteen-year-old Elias, was wanted for murder—and handed them over to Logan County authorities to prevent them from interfering with the effort to take Cap. They were briefly placed in jail, but no sooner had the detectives ridden off than the Logan County authorities, who were not looking for trouble with the Hatfields, saw fit to let them go. When the news of their release got out, Mingo County was in an uproar again.[8]

By the time Sheriff Keadle reached Rock Fort, deputy sheriff

J. H. Clark had learned from a mountaineer that the fugitives had left the fort headed for Kentucky. Clark and his men immediately set out after them. They did not have to go far, however. As they passed near a house belonging to some Hatfields, they made out two figures on a ridge above Grapevine Creek. Little Joe and Cap were bivouacked not far from the house, where they had gone to eat. After they settled in, Cap was supposed to stand guard, but he had dozed off. The lawmen stealthily worked their way up to the perch. November 5 was the darkest night of the month, and there was no moon to give them away. After they surrounded the duo, Clark yelled at them to wake up. Little Joe reached for his gun. Cap, realizing the jig was up, knocked it out of his hand to prevent him from getting himself killed.

Clark and his men hustled the two captives to a railroad stop and escorted them aboard a train to Huntington. They arrived early the next morning. Later in the day, Cap and Little Joe, looking exceptionally well-groomed for two recently captured fugitives, sat for an illustrated portrait, which appeared in the next day's *Cincinnati Enquirer*. Both wore jackets, buttoned vests, neckties, and felt hats. Little Joe, in homespun jeans, was clean shaven, while Cap sported a thick dapper mustache. In the accompanying article, the reporter noted that they "seemed to enjoy the notoriety which they were getting."

He was right about that, but, like so many journalists before him, he brought his coverage to a naive conclusion: "The probabilities are now that he has killed his last victim, for the officials of West Virginia will likely see that justice is meted out for the many murders which have been committed in that wild and mountainous region."[9]

On Saturday morning, November 7, Sheriff Keadle set out for Huntington to retrieve Cap and Joe, an effort that found little appreciation among his constituents, who had breathed a collective sigh of relief at the news of the captives' imprisonment in another town. They feared that if the sheriff brought them to Williamson, trouble would soon follow with the Hatfield clan, who, they knew, could muster a small battalion of well-armed men.[10]

IT TOOK SEVERAL MONTHS FOR Cap to come to trial. The way he would tell it later, the jury members were convinced that he was innocent, that he had fought only in self-defense, except for one old man, who felt that with three corpses to show for the shootout, someone had to pay. While the others argued to acquit Cap on all charges, the old man dug in. Finally, he offered to settle for a conviction of manslaughter. No one wanted to report a hung jury in this much-watched trial, so they compromised with a conviction of involuntary manslaughter, which carried a sentence of only one year in jail and a fine of five hundred dollars. Little Joe was sent to the state reform school at Pruntytown.

The shootout of November 3 had finally put the most notorious Hatfield behind bars. But it did not keep him there long. In the diminutive county jail at Williamson, Cap was an outsize inmate with few restrictions. Once when his infant daughter, Louise, was sick and Sheriff Keadle and his deputy were out of town, Keadle's wife, Lucie, allowed Cap to go home for a visit. He did and soon returned, as promised. At other times, Nan and various family members and friends visited him freely, often drinking moonshine and growing rowdy. But after three months, according to his son Coleman, Cap, who was a suspicious man, heard rumors that he might be sent to Kentucky on the old feud charges. So he decided to escape.[11]

To do so, he needed funds, and he directed Nan to sell their land on Mate Creek to the Red Jacket Coal Company, which had recently formed, for five hundred dollars. On the night of Friday, July 30, 1897, Cap threw a party in his cell that was even rowdier than usual and kept the joint hopping until midnight. Nan smuggled in a hand drill, and while all the revelry was going on, Cap and his helpers used it to cut away at the jail's sixteen-inch-thick brick wall. Mean-

while, Devil Anse sent Andy Chafin, who was now ten, to Williamson with two horses and two pistols. Chafin went where he was
told and, as planned, sat on a particular bench. Soon he looked up
and saw Cap coming. He had not broken out of jail, not exactly.
They had cut a hole big enough for him to escape through, but in
the end it had been easier for him to go out through the unlocked
door. A jug of moonshine was better than a chisel. The Keadles,
who lived in quarters at the jail, failed to notice that anything was
amiss.

Cap and Chafin went to the farm of one of Chafin's uncles, Melvin Browning, on Cow Creek, arriving around dawn. They put the
horses up in the barn and slept all day. That night, Chafin took the
horses back home and then returned with his father a couple of days
later. Cap got on Chafin's horse, the boy riding behind him. The
two said good-bye to Chafin's father and rode across the creek to
hide out.[12]

CAP'S JAILBREAK WAS, not surprisingly, big news. Some — like the
Cincinnati Enquirer — claimed he had slain eighteen men. He was so
notorious that the newly elected governor of West Virginia, George
Atkinson, who had defended Devil Anse in federal court in Charleston, declared that he was prepared to send the militia to aid in the
manhunt. Finally, regional had found something they could cooperate on. Kentucky's first Republican governor, William O'Connell
Bradley, who had ousted Buckner partly by criticizing his excesses,
including the building of a much-needed new state prison, offered
assistance. So did Governor Trip O'Ferrall of Virginia, the former
commander of all the Confederate cavalry in the Shenandoah Valley, who vowed that Cap Hatfield would find no asylum in his state.
Likewise, Ohio governor Asa Bushnell lined the banks of the Ohio
River with armed men to prevent the fugitive from entering his
territory.[13]

Rumors swirled regarding Cap's getaway, but no one seemed to know that he had walked straight out the door, finding the hole he had cut in the wall ultimately unnecessary. Whether or not the fix was in — the amount of money that Cap raised indicates that it probably was — Williamson and the surrounding region on both sides of the Tug were in an uproar over the "escape." News also spread of the excesses that he had enjoyed while in jail, embarrassing Mingo County. Angry citizens, feeling Mingo's reputation was on the line, called for Doc Keadle's badge. Within a day of the jailbreak, word went out that Cap was wanted dead or alive. Keadle formed another posse, with private citizens kicking in money to defray its expenses.[14]

On Wednesday, he and his men searched the hills again, spreading out to cover as wide a swath as possible and advancing in unison across the rugged terrain, to no avail. That night, they camped on lower Beech Creek, an old, deep groove winding through Hatfield territory to the Tug. The bright moon revealed a column of smoke up the creek. Rock Fort sat on higher ground about four miles off in that direction. Keadle's camp spent the rest of the night abuzz and sleepless. At daybreak, the posse set off toward the fort. Fearing a trap, the men grew increasingly cautious as they approached it. Then, about a quarter of a mile before reaching it, they spotted Cap and some other men in the woods. But Cap was not in the mood for a gun battle, and he and his men bolted deeper into the forest. Ever mindful of an ambush, the posse cautiously pursued them.

Keadle decided that they must be heading for the Devil's Backbone, a rocky pinnacle that Devil Anse had once single-handedly defended against a large Union force. (Some say this was where he actually earned the moniker Devil Anse.) The only approach was on a precipitous hemmed-in footpath wide enough for just one man at a time, which was the reason Devil Anse had been able to defeat his Union pursuers. A man with good aim could keep a small army from getting close, and there would be no way of taking Cap if he and his friends reached the point. Keadle hurried to cut them off. When the posse made it to the foot of the rise, he sent half a dozen men up the narrow path and led the rest on a longer flanking trail at a higher elevation.[15]

It was late in the afternoon before the first shots rang out. Keadle's contingent reached a bald that had a view of Devil's Backbone yet was still too far away for accurate aim, but the others got a bead on Cap and his gang as they raced to the top. Rifles cracked as both sides fired at each other. Finally, the reports ceased briefly. Through field glasses, Keadle could see that Cap was stopped below the crag and that two of the gang appeared to be wounded. The gunfire started again, and Keadle and his group maneuvered into firing range, leaves raining down on them as lead shot whizzed past. Slowly, Keadle's other half dozen men advanced, tree to boulder to tree. They now had Cap pinned down, though it was a near thing and came with a heavy price—two deputies went down, fatally shot.

Darkness brought the battle to a halt. The reunited posse made camp and discussed its options. Some wanted to advance up the spine that night. With two already dead, others voted for a siege. Instead, Keadle bided his time. Early the next morning, the two sides exchanged fire, and another member of the posse was hit. The stalemate lasted until noon, when reinforcements led by J. H. Baldwin, a hard-nosed, commanding leader, not to mention a deadly shot, arrived on the scene. Baldwin assessed the situation and then called for two of his men to go back to Williamson to fetch what he hoped would provide the decisive edge: dynamite.

While they waited, Baldwin aimed his rifle at the enemy line. Cap and his comrades were taking every precaution not to provide a target, but that evening, when one of the gang rose a little too carelessly to get water, Baldwin had his chance; he squeezed the trigger and hit his mark.

The Baldwin men returned with the dynamite in the morning. Two hours later, they had planted the charge without being detected and were ready to light the powder train. Baldwin gave the command. The quite visible sizzling trail of powder brought matters into sharp focus. Shouting, Cap and his men chaotically leaped to get clear of their hideout, attracting rifle fire as they did so. The posse quickly downed three of them. The others jumped back into their nest as the powder hissed on. Realizing that their only chance was to stop the burning fuse, they heaved rocks at it and rolled boulders down the slope in the hopes that they could smother the flame or sever the train.[16]

Baldwin had not stinted on his payload. The explosion reverberated off the granite with a windblast of smoke, dust, and debris. Jagged shards of rock and splintered trees erupted in every direction. Chunks of Devil's Backbone rained down the steep pitch as the pinnacle was mostly destroyed. Focused on the shootout, three of the posse were knocked down by the blast and injured. Some of Cap's men, still armed and still dangerous, clung to what remained of the Devil's Backbone; in the smoke and confusion, no one could tell if Cap was among them. Baldwin ordered his men to place another charge of dynamite beneath the crag. This time, all in the posse took cover and at a greater distance.

When the smoke cleared after the second detonation, Cap's gang managed a convincing volley, but the explosion had destroyed what remained of the pinnacle. Baldwin had no more dynamite, but it did not matter. Cap had already vanished under the cover of smoke and dust.[17]

So it was told, a great story, selling newspapers and aggrandizing the feud. However, when several present-day Hatfields took me to see what they say is the Devil's backbone, which today sits on the property of a coal-mining interest, I found it intact, looming over Ellison Hatfield Cemetery and the old Hatfield home place on Mate Creek. A subterranean coal fire, burning since the 1950s, sends smoke seeping up through fissures in the ground, making it more devilish than ever, but clearly the yellow-journalist version of the confrontation was more explosive than the factual.

Cap, however, did indeed get away on that fateful day. According to Coleman, he and his brothers Elias and Troy fled to Webster

County, where Cap hid out in the Yew Pine Mountains, which were so remote that "in some places it was forty miles from one house to another."

Once again, Cap had been blessed by fortune. His getaway was not only a success but the beginning of a new phase for him. Above all, he had managed to avoid the fate that was about to befall his brother Johnse.

Chapter 24

~

The Last Dance:
Cunningham Gets His Hatfield

1898

Bad Frank made his name fighting Hatfields, but he had never gotten the true prize. He had failed to catch Devil Anse or Cap. Johnse would soon be captured, but not by his doing. He yearned to put the other two behind bars, yet he had often crossed legal boundaries, and for the respectable people of eastern Kentucky, such transgressions were no longer an acceptable means to an end, even one so desirable.[1]

A few years earlier, Bad Frank had tried to dupe the Hatfields into believing that he had given up the fight. In the summer of 1895, he crossed the Tug to spend a day in the new town of Matewan, visiting various members of the Hatfield family and trying to convince them that he was a changed man and wished to end the hostilities. Although he was heavily armed and accompanied by two fellow fighters, he appeared to be sincere. He would, after all, soon marry Nancy Hatfield, with whom he had already sired three children — Elsie in 1889, Jesse James (called J.J.) in 1892, and Flora in 1893.

As much as they wanted to believe him, in the end they did not dare.[2]

So Bad Frank had given up the ruse and inevitably veered back to the conflict that had consumed him for a decade. On July 1, 1898, having recently returned from a foray in search of Hatfields, he was carousing with his friend Ransom Bray and Bray's girlfriend near Knox Creek in Pike County. The more Bad Frank drank, the more petulant he grew, and he soon picked a fight with his friend. Bray and his girlfriend left and went to the home of an elderly widow named Ruth Hurley. But Bad Frank was not finished: he followed the pair to Hurley's house, where he stood outside and shouted for Bray to come out. Bray had little hope of ending the affair if he did not. The arguing picked up where it had left off, with Bray trying to calm Frank down. He was not successful: Bad Frank pulled a knife and lunged at him. Bray dodged him, ran behind the house, pulled out a pistol, spun around, and shot Bad Frank in the thigh, felling him. Their fury spent, Bray carried Frank into the house and put him to bed. He had a nasty wound, and after several days, gangrene set in.[3]

Frank was moved to his own house, and at his request, his ex-wife Mary Rowe, the mother of five of his children, was sent for. Though Mary had no love for Bad Frank anymore, when she heard that he was dying, she reluctantly consented to go and traveled quite a distance to see him.

With a mixture of emotions, she stood over the dying man she had once promised to love and to cherish and asked, "Did you want to see me?"

"Yes," he said. For a long time, he told her, he had believed that one of their sons was not his. He asked her now for the truth.

Mary broke down in angry tears. "Good God, Frank Phillips," she snarled, "of course you were his father!" Then she stomped out of the room.[4]

Bad Frank died on July 12 and was buried at the mouth of Phillips Branch of Knox Creek on a ledge jutting out from the forest. Nancy McCoy Hatfield Phillips was left on her own to raise the three older children plus a ten-month-old baby girl, Goldie (though Nancy would be gone too before Goldie turned six).

More than four years later, the January 7, 1903, issue of *National*

Police Gazette led off with a bulletin about Phillips: "The report of the killing of Frank Phillips, the notorious desperado, in Lawrence County, Ky., has been denied. It appears, however, that Phillips was seriously wounded in a recent fight and is now in hiding. He will probably be heard of again before long." Although ignorant of the fact that Bad Frank was no longer in a position to be killed, the *Gazette* placed a fitting epitaph on his figurative tombstone: "Since 1888 Phillips has led a life possible nowhere else in the United States. Even in the wilds of the Rocky Mountains he would have been arrested or killed long since. His adventures have been innumerable, and almost always thrilling."

Bad Frank was dead, but his reputation lived on.

～

It was around this time that Dan Cunningham showed up again. The man who had captured Cotton Top had kept a low profile since then, at least as far as the feud was concerned. He was still a deputy U.S. marshal and had served his country in that capacity for two decades now. Thanks to him, as well as Bad Frank and other lawmen, Doc and Plyant Mahon and Alex Messer were in the Kentucky State Penitentiary in Eddyville. Ironically—and, to Cunningham, tragically—nobody had put away a Hatfield, other than Cotton Top, for the crimes the family had committed. But with Cunningham still on the prowl, the Hatfields were like a man with a leaky roof: sooner or later the rain was going to get in.

Cap was safely out of sight, bootlegging on the Williams River, in the Yew Pine Mountains of central West Virginia. Nan gave birth to another child, a boy, five months after the gunfight. With three sons from her first marriage and four other children under the age of ten to look after in addition to the newborn, she retreated to Main Island Creek to be closer to Devil Anse and Vicey.[5]

Johnse was making his living harvesting timber along the Guyandotte River, far away from the McCoys, but soon he would find himself in Cunningham's crosshairs. Based at Leatherwood Shoals,

Cap Hatfield and his wife, Nan, with their children Coleman, LeVicey, and Shep. *(Dr. Coleman C. Hatfield Collection, courtesy of Dr. Arabel E. Hatfield)*

about nine miles southeast of Logan Courthouse as the crow flies, Johnse happened to be in a bitter dispute with Humphrey E. "Doc" Ellis, a first cousin of French Ellis and a rival logger. Doc Ellis lived in the nearby town of Gilbert and worked the same section of the Guyandotte River as Johnse did.

No one now knows what started the dispute, but Johnse had sworn he would kill Ellis on sight. The threat did not stop Ellis from doing whatever he was doing that made Johnse mad, nor did it dissipate Johnse's anger. In late spring, Johnse decided to go on the offensive. Ellis must have guessed what was on his mind because he hired a gunslinger named Hopkins to act as his bodyguard.

In mid-June, Cunningham ran across Doc Ellis in Gilbert and heard of Johnse's threat against him. "I've got a little business with Johnse myself," he mentioned. "Reckon I'll hang around for a few days."[6]

Two days later, at dusk, Hopkins rushed into Ellis's house to warn him and Cunningham that two men with Winchesters were hidden in a ragweed patch outside. He thought one of them was Johnse Hatfield.

"We'll go out and get them," Cunningham said. Ellis and another visitor, a timberman, insisted on joining Cunningham and Hopkins. They left the house by a back door and crept along a gully that led to the ragweed patch. With Cunningham in the lead and Ellis right behind him, they worked their way up behind Johnse and his accomplice. In the fading light they could see that Johnse had his Winchester pointed at a window in Ellis's house.[7]

"Don't reckon we'll get him tonight," Johnse murmured to his friend.

"Shall I shoot the damn murderer?" Ellis whispered to Cunningham.

"No," he responded. "I want him alive," and as the words were leaving his mouth, the deputy marshal sprang from his hiding place. Johnse wheeled around with his weapon, but in a flash Cunningham had his Winchester pointed between Johnse's eyes, inches away. The other sniper turned on all fours and scurried off into the darkness. "Reach for the stars, quick," Cunningham growled. Johnse dropped his rifle and put his hands up. The detective briskly relieved him of a .44-caliber revolver and an impressive English dagger. He then left him with Ellis's gun trained on him and dashed after the other man, whom he soon collared.

The man was Auk Damron, a convicted murderer and fugitive of the gallows mixed up with the Skean family. Following a dispute between Rich Skean and a rival named Joe Freeman, both owners of large tracts of land in Wise County, Virginia, Skean's boys had raided Freeman's house and shot him. Freeman survived, but later, one of the Skean boys and Damron murdered his son. They were tried and sentenced to be hanged but had broken out of jail. Nothing would have surprised Cunningham less than to learn that the Hatfields and Skeans were one link removed in crime, but he was unaware of Damron's past and let him go.

Cunningham was more interested in securing Johnse's arrest anyway. He spirited him out of West Virginia and to the Pikeville jail, where he collected a five-hundred-dollar reward. Johnse was eventually tried in Prestonsburg, Kentucky, for complicity in the murder of the three McCoy brothers. He confessed to his role and offered no resistance to the prosecution, telling Cunningham that he would rather be in the penitentiary serving a life sentence than outside dodging every bounty hunter who came down the pike. He added that he looked forward to the time in prison, when he could ask for forgiveness from his Maker.[8]

∼

IN OCTOBER 1898, Elias, age twenty, and Troy, seventeen, both scrappers and crack shots who had briefly been on the lam with Cap, got into an argument with a roughneck named Dave Kenney, whom they worked with in a timbering operation. Kenney was killed shortly afterward. At first Cap was indicted for the murder, but then the charge against him was dropped, and Elias and Troy were accused of the crime. Cap felt responsible for his younger brothers and agreed to go with them out to the Oklahoma Territory. Once he got there, he decided it was not far enough for him, so he kept going to Colorado, where he got in touch with some of Nan's relatives in Gunnison and worked nearby as a farmhand. After a few months he headed back to his family, a changed man. He had seen a bit more of the world and now wished to reform his ways.[9]

Still, the feud and violence clung to the Hatfields like dark to a coal mine. In 1899, young Andy Chafin was working as a callboy in the Gray Yards railroad station, about twenty-five miles east of Williamson, for the N&W; his cousin Elias also had a job there, as a railroad security officer. Elias, whose quick smile won him many friends, was like an older brother to Chafin and had taken him under his wing.

At around eleven o'clock on the morning of July 3, Chafin had taken a seat to rest when train number eleven pulled into the station. Onto the platform stepped Doc Ellis, who had, according to Coleman, "boasted triumphantly to his friends" about his role in the capture of Johnse, telling them that he "had enough greenbacks to burn a blackjack log five feet in diameter" and that he "felt no fear . . . his money would see him through."

Ellis was on his way to Williamson to be one of the masters of ceremonies for the July 4th celebrations — a parade of bands and troops and speeches by dignitaries — and when he saw Johnse's younger brother standing on the platform, he called out, "Hello, Elias."

Elias replied, "Hello, Doc. Do you think you can take me to Kentucky as easy as you did my brother, Johnse?" Elias, who had not been involved in either of the two feud events for which indictments were still outstanding and who, in fact, sometimes worked in Kentucky, was merely taunting Ellis. According to some, he called Ellis a "son of a bitch" for good measure before turning around and striking up a conversation with a passenger who was walking by. Ellis is said to have responded, "I'll show you who's a son of a bitch!" He went back on the train and returned with a loaded gun.

Chafin saw Ellis rush onto the platform and raise a pistol, and he shouted, "Look out, 'Lias!" The passenger with whom Elias was talking saw what was happening too and shoved Elias aside. Elias, dropping out of the way, pulled out his pistol and fired. Some witnesses would say that only one gun fired, but Chafin saw two flashes. Elias's shot, taken in haste, was off the mark but not by much: the bullet struck Ellis's wrist, broke it, ricocheted into his neck, severed his jugular vein, and exited through the top of his head. The wealthy timberman fell to the platform, dead before he hit.

Elias turned to Chafin. "You go home and tell dad I killed Doc Ellis and run up the railroad," he told the boy. When Devil Anse heard what had happened, he saddled up a horse and sent Chafin to Island Creek to tell Cap. Once again, the family was called to arms. They knew where to meet Elias.[10]

Eventually Elias was convinced to surrender and was tried in the Mingo Circuit Court in Williamson. He pleaded self-defense.[11]

Rumors that Devil Anse was going to storm the town and reclaim his son circulated, but Devil Anse was no longer in charge of such operations in the family. Instead, in August 1899, Cap arranged for a successful prison break. The two brothers, aged thirty-five and twenty-one, fled the state together but parted ways to avoid attracting attention. Cap hunkered down in the Oklahoma Territory for a time. Elias hid out in parts unknown but soon tired of being away and returned to West Virginia. He was arrested, convicted of murder, and sent to the state prison. Governor Atkinson, the Republican for whom Cap had voted, soon paroled him.

IN 1902, ELIAS AND TROY went to work as special railroad agents for Baldwin's Detectives in Thurmond, a coal boomtown on a bend of the New River. They answered to Albert Felts. (Thus, when Dan Cunningham joined Baldwin's agency, he—the hunter of Hatfields—might well have been sent on an operation with the sons of Devil Anse.)

It was thanks in part to their outlaw father that Troy and Elias had an opportunity to work in law enforcement. The owner of Baldwin's Detectives, William Baldwin, had once enjoyed a night of Devil Anse's hospitality. While hunting a fugitive in the Tug River Valley, he came upon the Hatfields' cabin after dark. Asking for a place to sleep that night, he avoided divulging his name and his business. "Well, stranger, if you can put up with fare," Devil Anse replied, "I guess you can stay all night." After supper, Anse showed him up to a sleeping loft. The uneasy detective slept with his pistol in easy reach. As dawn approached, Hatfield climbed the ladder and poked his head through the trapdoor. "Now, Mr. Baldwin," he said. "I think the old woman's got breakfast ready. If you'll hurry down and eat, I believe I can get you away from here without you getting hurt. You know, I've got some bad boys. If they find you here, they may kill you."[12] After breakfast, Devil Anse showed Baldwin to the top of a nearby ridge and bade him farewell. Baldwin never forgot it.

Elias and Troy guarded trains and coal-mine paymasters for seven years. Then on July 30, 1909, they broke bad, donned masks, and held up the New River Collieries paymaster, nabbing $4,391.16 in broad daylight. It is still considered one of the boldest robberies ever committed in West Virginia. Albert Felts, suspecting them or, at least, dissatisfied with their efforts since it occurred on their watch, fired them. They then joined forces with union organizers in an ill-fated attempt to frame Felts for the robbery. They were laughed out of court. The result was that the brothers were forever out of the detective business, but they had the funds to set themselves up in the whiskey trade, a career move that would soon seal their doom.

~

A LITTLE MORE than five years later, the Hatfields and the Rutherfords would be at the center of another violent episode, a last gasp of the Hatfield-McCoy feud and one that again raised the specter of the old mountain justice. The March 30, 1902, *New York Times* reported a multiple murder under the headline "Hatfield Feud Renewed." Apparently, John Rutherford, a detective, had obtained a warrant for the arrest of Ephraim Hatfield, who was wanted in South Carolina but hiding out in Pike County at his parents' house. (Ephraim's father, Thompson, was a double first cousin of Devil Anse's, and his mother, Mary, was a McCoy.) Thompson, sixty-two and a veteran of Yankee Bill's militia and of the Kentucky Mounted Infantry, was dangerous, and so was his son. Rutherford enlisted the help of Harry Watts. Just why Watts, who was the wealthy and well-liked proprietor of the Palace Hotel in Williamson, a man known throughout southern West Virginia, would want to assist on such a dangerous mission is unclear. The two rode out to the Blackberry Creek home of Ephraim's parents and broke the door down. As they were subduing the thirty-year-old fugitive, Thompson managed to grab his gun and took aim at the intruders. Watts and Rutherford pulled their triggers at virtually the same time that he did. Fire flashed from gun barrels, a hail of deadly metal spewed, and a blast rocked the cabin, which filled with acrid smoke. (One report said that a thirteen-year-old girl in the cabin wielded a gun too.) When the smoke cleared, Ephraim's wife and children found all four men dead or dying.[13]

~

EVEN WITH SUCH VIOLENCE seemingly part of their DNA, something about the fierce, independent ways of the Hatfields, their straight-up manner of bargaining with larger powers, and their collective will to succeed — or, rather, not to be defeated — kept the clan speeding forward.

Johnse had been sentenced to prison for life, but a life sentence was a relative thing — relative to the influence you could bring to bear on the system. Some, like Alex Messer, would serve a life term (he died in the Kentucky State Penitentiary in Eddyville in 1923, at the age of eighty-five), but others, like Johnse, found ways to shorten their stays. When an inmate armed with a fork attacked the prison warden, hurled him to the floor, and stabbed him in the neck, Johnse managed to wrestle him off the warden. The inmate, described as a "burly Negro giant," then turned on Johnse, who slashed his neck with a penknife, cutting his jugular and killing him. Although it was another grisly murder, Johnse's defense of the warden made him a hero, and the warden campaigned for his pardon.

It was Johnse's bad luck, however, to have a temperance advocate in the Kentucky executive office, J.C.W. Beckham, who repeatedly refused to pardon him. Then Johnse, who was suffering from inflamed kidneys caused by Bright's disease, got a break. During a hiatus in Beckham's governorship, while he was traveling out of state, lieutenant governor William Thorne, who had different views on the matter, took over for a brief stretch. Knowing that Johnse's wife, Roxie, had died, leaving their two small children without a parent to look after them, and having Johnse's promise to stay out of Kentucky as well as a petition requesting his pardon signed by the McCoys, who wanted to put the feud behind them once and for all, Thorne pardoned Johnse.[14]

"The McCoy and Hatfield people, parties to the feud, after twenty-six years desire peace," Thorne wrote. "Both sides of the old feud are anxious to cross out all old scores and settle their differences, and every law-abiding man should be only too glad to render whatever assistance he can to bring these results about."

Four years later, the *Louisville Courier-Journal* reported the gruesome demise of Bill Tom Hatfield. He was captured by enemies across the Tug Fork, according to the stories, taken into the Kentucky woods, tied to a tree, and left to freeze to death. Until then, Bill Tom, one of the least known feudists, had enjoyed good luck, having fought the battles but escaped unscathed. Found alive but not before several fingers and toes had frozen solid, he was taken to Louisa, where both legs had to be amputated, killing him. "Members of the clan are vowing vengeance," the *Louisville Courier-Journal* reported.

It was not until after the *New York Times* also ran the story that a letter arrived at the offices of the *Courier-Journal* pointing out that the Tom Hatfield in question was a distant cousin of the feuding Hatfields. This Tom Hatfield, the thirty-year-old deaf-mute son of a Baptist minister, had been robbed of a gold watch, hundreds of dollars, and his coat before being bound and left to freeze to death. Rescued, he had been unable to identify his assailants because he could not speak or write. Bill Tom Hatfield, on the other hand, would go on to live to a ripe old age, dying of natural causes at his home on the Tug more than three decades later.[15]

Coda

~

March 4, 1913

A gusty March wind riffled the Kanawha River as it coursed through the heart of Charleston. Hands secured top hats on the heads of those waiting outside the state capitol to hear the new Republican governor, the youngest governor ever elected in West Virginia, deliver his inaugural address. A thirty-seven-year-old doctor from the southern reaches of the state, he traveled the route of his inaugural parade in an automobile — a first for West Virginia. With him rode the hopes of the Progressive Era, blossoming across the nation, with its promise of social and political reform. On this ceremonial day, however, West Virginia was in crisis. In the Kanawha coalfields, not twenty miles away, a state of war existed, and martial law reigned.[1]

The man chosen by the voters to see the state through the hostilities, which had already lasted a year and crippled the energy industry, had been educated at three institutions of higher learning and had risen through the halls of government to become the president of the state senate before being elected governor. He was Henry D. Hatfield, a son of the feudist Good 'Lias and a nephew of Devil Anse.

Though a New York City–educated medical doctor, Henry Hatfield was solidly a man of the people. The son of a Confederate soldier, he had been born on lowly Mate Creek on the Tug River, at the epicenter of the nation's most notorious feud. The hostilities that his family had been involved in had been broadcast far and wide and were a black eye to his state. But at the same time his tough background seemed to be an asset.

Just a year before his election, twenty miles down the Kanawha from the state capital, in the town of Cannelton, his cousins, Devil Anse's sons Elias and Troy, private detectives turned whiskey dealers and saloon owners, had fought a vicious gun battle in a territorial dispute. An Italian rival, Ottavio Vagliozzo, had fatally wounded the brothers before being riddled with bullets himself. Born into violence, Troy calmly told those who found him dying, "You need not look for the man who did this, he is dead."[2]

Even as Henry Hatfield's campaign for office was kicking off, another cousin, Devil Anse's son Willis, a personnel officer for a mining concern, shot and killed a pharmacist who had berated him and refused to serve him because he was a Hatfield.[3]

Despite the fact that Good 'Lias was a feudist, Henry and his brothers had thrived. The oldest, Greenway, served as the sheriff of Mingo County, having taken over from Doc Keadle. Greenway was elected sheriff twice on the Republican ticket (and again later as a Democrat) and was a formidable political ally of Henry's.[4] But even some of the non-feuding Hatfields seemed destined for extreme violence. In August 1914, Greenway would hunt down the infamous Glen Alum payroll robbers, five men who had waylaid and murdered three payroll guards. In an all-night gunfight, Greenway and his men would kill all of the bandits, blasting them with dynamite and spraying them with bullets.

A GRADUATE OF FRANKLIN COLLEGE at age fifteen and of medical school at the University of Louisville at nineteen, Henry was one of the most visionary and most distinguished West Virginians of his generation. After he received a second medical degree for surgery at New York University in 1904, he worked as a railroad surgeon, a mine physician, and a county health commissioner. Because the southwestern part of the state sorely lacked health facilities, he became an activist, appealing to the legislature and gaining funds for a hospital, Miners Hospital No. 1, in the town of Welch before being elected to the state senate himself.

In 1913, in the coal-rich gorges of Cabin Creek and Paint Creek, thousands of desperate miners and their families, having fought mine guards in a yearlong struggle between organized labor and management, had been driven from company-owned houses and were living in camps. For the miners out on strike, it had meant months of hunger, illness, hardship, and violence. Governor William Glasscock, Henry's predecessor, had imposed martial law three times. Henry estimated that more than 30,000 men were affected by the strike, which had cost the state many lives and in excess of two million dollars.

In his inaugural address, Henry—steeped in the collective wisdom of his family's experience and buttressed by the courage, conviction, and self-reliance of the mountaineer—revealed himself to be an eloquent yet humble statesman with a bold outlook. "In the matter of progress," he said, "we must place our state where she rightfully belongs as a peer of any other state in the Union." A Republican and an advocate of women's suffrage, he wished to extend the "progressive principles" inspired by Lincoln.[5]

The new governor's chief concern was correcting the unfair dynamics of the state economy. West Virginia contained more coal than Ohio, Pennsylvania, and Virginia combined and ranked second among the states in coal production, but it was only thirty-fourth in the value of its manufactured products. The state powered the great iron and steel industries, but its coal operators made too little money because of the long railroad haul to market. The bulk of the coal consumed in West Virginia was used by locomotives carrying the raw material out of state.

Other natural resources included more than 300 million tons of iron ore, seemingly unlimited limestone, glass sands, and clays and shale for making brick and tile. The state's petroleum was first-rate, and it produced vast quantities of natural gas. The problem was that more than 80 percent of the fuel and raw materials was used outside its boundaries.

Henry's vision for the state, which he believed held the most beautiful mountain scenery anywhere, included "good macadam roads . . . filled with admiring tourists." He wanted to protect the common laborer as well as the businessman. He would rein in the government and put an end to corrupt voting practices. He pronounced the state's school system "bunglesome," declaring that boys and girls in poor rural school districts should have the same advantages as those in wealthy areas. Among his accomplishments would be progressive health-care legislation and the nation's first workers' compensation laws.

But first, on the day of his inauguration, Henry announced that he planned to go into the Paint Creek and Cabin Creek areas to investigate conditions. Although his security advisers warned him that his life would be in danger, Henry, who would serve as a chief surgeon in the Army Medical Corps in World War I, packed his black medical bag and at dawn the next day headed alone into the strike zone. When asked later why he went, he replied simply, "They needed a doctor."

Based on this firsthand experience, and ignoring death threats and schemes to kidnap his daughter, Governor Hatfield would impose a contract on the warring factions. Neither labor nor management got everything it wanted, but he achieved a break in the Mine Wars. It was an uneasy truce, but it held. He had created a third side to the dispute — the Hatfield side. And this time, at long last, the family name stood for peace.[6]

Epilogue

~

Mine Is the Vengeance

From the extensive reporting of the *World*'s T. C. Crawford, the *Sun*'s John Spears, the *Herald*'s James Creelman, and many others, the Hatfields became celebrities of sorts, and they were happy to pose for photographs. In one sitting, Devil Anse, Cap, Johnse, and French Ellis each pose wearing Mexican bandito stage props, including a felt sombrero with four large stars embroidered on the underside of the bill. Bearded Anse holds a Winchester across his lap. Cap and Johnse, both with mustaches drooping over their upper lips, Johnse a thinner version of Cap, hold pistols with gun barrels crossed on their chests. Ellis, who would later die from a shotgun blast, holds a rifle with its butt resting on the floor and clenches a large cigar between his teeth.[1]

By all accounts, Devil Anse in many ways lived a charmed life. He hunted his fill, enjoyed more than his fair share of children and business success, and was married to the same woman for half a century. Just a few days before the murder of Elias and Troy, his friend and Civil War compatriot the Hardshell Baptist preacher "Uncle Dyke" Garrett baptized him, at the age of seventy-two.

But Devil Anse and Vicey were terribly shaken by these latest deaths in the family. At the double funeral on Main Island Creek, Vicey, a regular churchgoer, was joined by her seven remaining sons—Johnse, Cap, Bob, Elliott, Joe, Willis, and Tennis—who themselves made a public confession of their faith in God and promised Uncle Dyke that he could baptize them.[2]

The brothers had done remarkably well, all things considered. After serving six years of his life sentence, Johnse went on to become a land agent for the U.S. Coal and Coke Company in and around Logan County. Cap, who should long since have died in a hail of bullets, eventually returned to his native hollows. In 1908 he went to Tennessee and studied law for six months and then moved back to Logan County—where his younger brothers Joe and Tennis served at various times as sheriff and hired him as a deputy sheriff. He later started a law firm with his son Coleman, who was blind, and they were eventually joined by Coleman's daughter Aileen, who became one of the first female practicing attorneys in southern West Virginia. Bob, the third son in the family, became a merchant and wealthy property owner. Elliott, the fourth son,

Tennis Hatfield, sheriff of Logan County. (*Courtesy of William Keith Hatfield*)

studied medicine, graduating in 1898 from City College of Louisville, Kentucky. He practiced in Charleston.[3]

DEVIL ANSE DIED OF PNEUMONIA at the age of eighty-two on January 6, 1921. An expensive Italian marble monument topped by a life-size statue marks his grave in the Hatfield Cemetery on Main Island Creek and identifies him using his de facto rank: Captain. Vicey died eight years later at the age of eighty-seven, also of pneumonia, and is buried beside him. The monument lists the names of their thirteen children.

Cap and Elliott were estranged for years. On his deathbed, Devil Anse requested that they forgive each other. At his funeral, the two brothers shook hands as tears ran down their faces. Beside his father's grave, Cap, the fierce feud lieutenant, told Uncle Dyke that he had made peace with God and wanted to be baptized. "I will baptize you, boy," the old preacher told him, "in the very hole whar I baptized yore pappy." Raising his hands over his head, Cap declared

Vicey Hatfield and family in front of Devil Anse's grave. *(Courtesy of Mark and Arabel E. Hatfield)*

Devil Anse's funeral, January 6, 1921. *(Courtesy of William Keith Hatfield)*

Some five thousand mourners attended Devil Anse's funeral at his home on Main Island Creek. *(Dr. Coleman C. Hatfield Collection, courtesy of Mark and Arabel E. Hatfield)*

to the riveted crowd gathered there to say farewell to Devil Anse that he was finished with hatred and fighting and that if any man wanted his life, he would not resist.[4]

Cap lived until August 1930, when he died at Johns Hopkins Hospital in Baltimore from a brain tumor or, as some contend, a bullet fragment pressing on his brain.

~

BIG JIM McCOY moved his family to Pikeville, where he and his wife, Melissa, raised their nine children and where he served as a police officer. He and Devil Anse's youngest son, Tennis, the sheriff of Logan County, reconciled in 1928 and were photographed together.

Sally died around 1894, though no one knows the exact date or cause. Her funeral was performed about a decade later by William Tyree, the pastor of the Methodist church in Pikeville, at the request of Big Jim. Randall died on March 28, 1914, in the Pikeville home of his grandson Melvin, Tolbert's orphaned son. Randall had been severely burned after stumbling into a fireplace the previous fall. He was still famous enough that his death merited a brief notice in the *New York Times*.[5]

Among the McCoys' successes, Harmon's great-grandsons (via his son Lark) Joe "Mix" McCoy and Leonard "Tab" McCoy started the Cancy Branch Coal Company in the same Kentucky hollow where Harmon was killed during the Civil War. This grew into the McCoy Caney Coal Company, based in Phelps. The two became millionaires and did much to improve the town. They eventually sold the company and relocated to Lexington, Kentucky. In 1976, they erected a granite monument beside the graves of the fallen McCoys at the family homestead on Blackberry Creek.[6]

~

FOLLOWING THE FEUD, Dan Cunningham maintained a busy and diverse career. In 1902, while serving warrants and arresting violators

of the injunctions against union organizing in the New River coalfields, he was involved in several spectacular gun battles with striking miners, including the battle of Stanaford. While six union
sympathizers were killed in that battle, Cunningham remained
impervious to the whizzing bullets. In her autobiography, the labor
organizer Mother Jones derided him as a "big elephant."

After retiring from the U.S. Marshal Service, he served as a
Charleston city detective, as a special police officer for the Kanawha
and Michigan Railroad, and as a deputy game warden for the West
Virginia Game, Fish, and Forestry Commission. He was a member
of the Kanawha County Board of Examiners for teachers for eight
years.

In 1904, *McClure's Magazine,* the national periodical credited
with launching muckraking journalism, ran a feature on his exploits
during the feud. Cunningham penned two memoirs — one in 1928
and a second in 1938. He lived to be ninety-two and died in Charleston in 1942.[7]

~

IN 1998, the time had come, Bo McCoy, a minister from Waycross,
Georgia, told me, to bring the two tribes together. For generations
of Hatfields and McCoys, the feud was viewed as a great familial
shame, the embarrassment of Appalachia, and a topic not to be discussed. McCoy set in motion the first reunion of the Hatfield and
McCoy families. About a thousand descendants of the two famous
fighting clans came to the inaugural event — some from as far away
as South Korea. Now the annual Hatfield and McCoy family
reunion, which features a tug-of-war across the Tug River and a
marathon, takes place each fall in the towns of Matewan and Williamson, West Virginia, and Pikeville, Kentucky.

The Hatfields and McCoys are thriving throughout the United
States and beyond, largely at peace, though when the subject of the
feud comes up, one is likely to see shoulders stiffen just a little bit.

The famous feud was back in the news in 2003, when the two

sides—led by Reo Hatfield and Bo and Ron McCoy—signed an official peace treaty in the wake of the 9/11 attacks. They wanted the world to know that given an assault on American soil by a foreign enemy, even the Hatfields and McCoys would unite. The event drew national and international headlines, proving once again that the story of the feuding families of Appalachia maintains a lasting grip on our hearts and imaginations and a special page in the history of the American experience.

ACKNOWLEDGMENTS

~

First and foremost, I'd like to thank all the Hatfields and McCoys who so kindly shared their stories, documents, photographs, and knowledge of the feud with me and who generously entertained me and showed me around the feud sites on so many occasions. This is their story.

Among the McCoys, the best I-told-you-so came from Betty Phillips Howard, as in "I told you I was related to everyone in the feud but Perry Cline and Jim Vance." She is, and she knows exactly how. An expert genealogist, she is a descendant of the Phillipses, McCoys, Hatfields, and Varneys. Her genealogical guidance and her fierce McCoy partisanship helped immensely and can be felt throughout *The Feud*. Betty and I exchanged several thousand e-mails and many hours of phone calls during the writing of the book. Civil War experts Robert Baker and Randall Osborne and family researcher Lee Crutchfield have worked with Betty on various aspects of the feud and generously shared their research with me.

Others who have studied the Civil War aspect of the feud and who contributed to my efforts include Jim Prichard of Louisville, who answered my questions about his invaluable essay on the subject and shared documents and research material, and Randy Jackson, who is descended from the McCoys, the Hatfields, and the Messers, and contributed research on Alex Messer.

In Pikeville, Martha Ridenour, Perry Cline's granddaughter, provided an invaluable summary of Cline's life, both in writing and on the phone.

Among the McCoys who at various times provided useful guidance were Ron and Jack Blackburn, amateur historians, related to both the Hatfields and McCoys; Mary Holley; Bo McCoy; Ron McCoy; Debbie McCoy Autry and Kathy Dotson, daughters of Leonard "Mix" McCoy; James and Tammy Quick and family; and Jimmy Wolford.

I'd like to thank, in Pikeville, Everett Johnson, curator of the Big Sandy Heritage Center, who provided access to valuable resources and enthusiasm for the project; Tony Tackett and Jay Shepherd of Pike County Tourism; and Edna Fugate at the University of Pikeville's Frank M. Allara Library, which holds the Henry P. Scalf Papers.

Others holding feud materials include the Kentucky Historical Society and the Kentucky State Archives, in Frankfort, and the William T. Young Library at the University of Kentucky, in Lexington, where research coordinator of the Breckinridge Research Room, Matthew Harris, generously gave of his time and expertise.

At the West Virginia Archives and History Library in Charleston, state archivist Joe Geiger, archivist Debra Basham, staff historian Greg Carroll, and library manager Robert Taylor all kindly made their resources available to me. I'd also like to thank Kevin Fredette, coordinator for public services, West Virginia and Regional History Collection, and James Mitchell, curator, West Virginia State Museum. Catherine Rakowski of West Virginia University, in Morgantown, provided scans of photos and documents from the Spivak Papers and film of the *Logan Banner*. Vicki Kolota, the Logan Circuit Court Clerk, helped me access historical county records.

IN THE MATEWAN AREA, I'd especially like to thank Scotty May and Alvin Harmon, descendants of the Chafin family, who first welcomed me into the Mate Creek area on a ride up the ridge above Newtown to see Devil Anse Rock and who spent many hours over a number of years discussing the feud with me and leading a variety of exploratory research excursions. Their neighbors also contributed in a variety of ways and include: former boxing champion, deputy sheriff, and coal miner Tommy Copley, whose life story could fill another book; his son Thomas Copley; Dionne Collins; Barbara and Roby Chafin; Francie May; John T. Davis; Jimmy Simpkins; Wilma Steele; and Yvonne Dehart; also Peggy Kinder, keeper of the Ellison Hatfield Cemetery, and her daughter Carole Busick. Others nearby who met with me and showed me documents include Smith Hatfield descendant Hester Keatly, who provided me with two family journals, and Rhodena Pack of Beech Creek, who showed me a land deed of Wall Hatfield's. Matewan mayor Sheila Kessler kindly allowed me to search through the town's archives and those of the Matewan Depot Museum. Don and Cathy McCoy entertained me on their front porch on several occasions. Sharon Garland and her late husband, Pat, owners of the Historic Matewan House Bed and Breakfast, always provided sage advice, a hearty breakfast, and a helmet for four-wheeling.

In Williamson, West Virginia University Extension associate professor, filmmaker, and feud expert Bill Richardson provided insight and guidance. The late Charlotte Sanders of the *Williamson Daily News,* who was still a beat reporter at the age of ninety-two, when I met her, preserved many feud memories that came from the last generation to hear the stories directly from the feudists themselves and then shared them with me.

John Vance, a descendant of Crazy Jim Vance, owns the property on which lie the graves of the three McCoy brothers and others killed in the feud. He was always willing to discuss the feud with me and gave me a copy of his sister Helen Vance Anderson's memoir, *Tug River Memories,* which held some unique insights into growing up in the area.

Cap Hatfield descendants Mark Hatfield of Charleston and his sister Arabel Hatfield of Logan discussed their memories with me and kindly gave me permission to use the Dr. Coleman C. Hatfield photo collection. Keith Davis, author and owner of Woodland Press in Chapmanville, West Virginia, then provided me with the photos (along with some of his own). Reo Hatfield, of Waynesboro,

Virginia, who negotiated the modern-day Hatfield-McCoy truce with Bo McCoy and Ron McCoy, welcomed me into the Hatfield world early on. Others from the greater Hatfield clan who helped in so many ways include Tennis Hatfield-descendant William Keith "Billy" Hatfield of Tulsa, Oklahoma; Andy Chafin of Memphis; Brad Chafin of Germantown, Tennessee; and Betty Avril of Dallas. Harriett Keadle Pyles provided information on her ancestor Sheriff Doc Keadle.

MY DEEP APPRECIATION GOES TO Craig Kaderavek, director of forest operations for Forestland, and Terry Elkins, forester, who showed me around the feud region and were subject to the shots fired in my direction during my first research trip, and to Hunter Jenkins, who made the trip possible. Others who, like them, contributed their expertise to my research (albeit from a safer reach) include Ken Bailey, retired dean of the College of Business, Humanities, and Sciences and emeritus professor of history and geography at WVU Tech, and author of many books and articles on West Virginia history; Ludwell Johnson III, William and Mary history professor emeritus, whose work on Dan Cunningham was an excellent resource and provided additional background on that previously little known detective; John Velke, author of *The True Story of the Baldwin-Felts Detective Agency,* who advised me on the world of private detectives during feud times; Jim Mylott, author of *A Measure of Prosperity: A History of Roane County; Ripley's Believe It or Not* researcher Luke Stram; U.S. Marshals historian David Turk; firearms historian Thadd McClung; and Phillips family genealogist Harry Sellards Jr. Dave Grabarek, an interlibrary loan specialist at the Library of Virginia, put many rare books and newspaper archives at my fingertips, and the library provided excellent facilities and guidance in accessing them.

MANY PEOPLE HELPED CONTRIBUTE TO every phase of the making of this book. Without Little, Brown editor Geoff Shandler's guidance, enthusiasm, and editing, this book would never have been possible. Thanks to Liese Mayer, Brandon Coward, Jayne Yaffe Kemp, and the rest of the Little, Brown crew, and copyeditor Tracy Roe, who put all the parts and parts of speech in the right places. My agent, Jody Rein, is always supportive and offers sage advice, editorial and otherwise.

I would like to thank John Freeman and Ted Hodgkinson at *Granta* and Jim Meigs and David Dunbar at *Popular Mechanics* for running stories based on my research, and Hong Kong–based photographer Philipp Engelhorn, who accompanied me on one trip while shooting for the latter. David Keane, Arcadia Berjonneau, Aaron Bowden, Gordon Stettinius, and Gordon Wallace went on adventures with me and helped record the research in various ways.

Library sciences expert Caroline Rogers stepped in and took the research and organization of this project to another level. She traveled to Logan, Matewan, and Morgantown, West Virginia; Bowie, Maryland; Washington, DC; and New York City to further our quest for records and accounts. Gordon Valentine assisted with the presentation of photographs.

At home, my wife, Jessica, my personal copy chief, primary critic (in a good way), and life adviser, is the first and last reader. I fix her coffee — well, tea. My daughters Hazel and Grace accompanied me on research trips and helped search archives and record data. Hazel bravely endured an up-close experience with real bullets. Grace was undaunted at the microfiche viewer for hours on end. My nieces Liza Pope, to whom this book is dedicated, and Sarah Pope also helped with the research. A special thanks to lifelong family friend Priscilla Haden, whose home was my home when I was researching in Charleston, West Virginia.

And finally, he who was first, Morgan Entrekin, I thank last, though quite heartily.

NOTES

~

Throughout the book I have regularized the spellings of names for consistency.

Prologue: The Fate of Cotton Top Mounts

1. Horace Kephart, *Our Southern Highlanders,* 290–96. "After close study of mountain speech," wrote Kephart (294), who spent much time in the Smoky Mountains in North Carolina and Tennessee, "I have failed to discern that the word for draft is understood, except in parts of Virginia and Kentucky mountains, where it means a brook."

2. Ibid., 290–91, and James Creelman, "Bloody Border War," *New York Herald,* Feb. 9, 1888.

3. Theron Clark Crawford, *An American Vendetta: A Story of Barbarism in the United States,* 9. Crawford's 1889 publication was based on articles he wrote for and published in the *New York World* in Oct. 1888 (see bibliography for titles).

4. Charles G. Mutzenberg, *Kentucky's Famous Feuds and Tragedies,* 90–91; Charlotte Sanders, "Emma Hatfield Reminisces About 'Uncle Anderson,'" *Williamson Daily News.* That Thursday morning, Feb. 20, 1890, the *Louisville Courier-Journal* ("Mounts on the Scaffold") estimated the crowd at between 4,000 and 8,000.

5. Truda Williams McCoy, *The McCoys,* 228–29, n. 15, and Betty Howard, "Descendants of Harmon McCoy." Money conversions from one era to another are an inexact science, but for a rough conversion of the dollar amounts in this book to today's currency, multiply by a factor of twenty-five.

6. *Louisville Courier-Journal,* "Mounts on the Scaffold"; Truda McCoy, 232, n. 23; Willis David Staton, *Hatfields and McCoys: True Romance and Tragedies,* 176; and Deborah McCoy Autry (phone interview with author, Nov. 3, 2011).

7. *Louisville Courier-Journal,* "Mounts on the Scaffold"; Mutzenberg, 91–92; Staton, 176–78; and Truda McCoy, 232, n. 23. In Staton's account, Bud McCoy is allowed to take Phillips with him and sobers him up. They swear allegiance to Maynard and join the guard taking Mounts to the gallows.

8. Mutzenberg, 92. The *Louisville Courier-Journal* ("Mounts on the Scaffold")

said the gallows were two miles from the courthouse; however, the distance was closer to a quarter mile. Truda McCoy, 215, 232, n. 23.

9. Jeff Todd Titon, "Old Regular Baptists of Southeastern Kentucky: A Community of Sacred Song," *1997 Festival of American Folklife Program Book.* Lyrics from www.blueridgeinstitute.org/ballads/vancesong.html. See also Shirley Donnelly, *The Hatfield-McCoy Feud Reader,* 29–30, and L. D. Hatfield, *The True Story of the Hatfield and McCoy Feud,* 10–16. Details concerning "Vance's Farewell" are sketchy. According to oral history, Vance's daughter had an encounter of a sexual nature with either Lewis Horton or his brother Daniel in 1817. As a result, Vance quarreled with the Hortons and shot Lewis off his horse in the Clinch River. After his conviction and failed appeals, Vance composed the song while awaiting execution in Washington County, in 1819.

10. William Ely, *The Big Sandy Valley,* 203–4.

11. John A. Velke III, *The True Story of the Baldwin-Felts Detective Agency,* 8–9.

12. *Louisville Courier-Journal,* "Death by Law," and Virgil Carrington Jones, *The Hatfields and the McCoys,* 179.

13. According to the 1880 U.S. Census, Elison [*sic*] Mounts was born in 1864. U.S. Census of 1880, Magnolia, Logan, West Virginia, Daniel Mounts household, sheet 299A, family 2.

Chapter 1: War Comes to the Big Sandy

1. Jean Thomas, *Big Sandy,* 73–80, and Jerome Doolittle, *The Southern Appalachians,* 54–59.

2. Charles Darwin took a keen interest in the spike-horn, noting that its sharp single horn, projecting unicorn-like from the brow, allowed it to run more swiftly through forests than the common buck with its cumbersome rack and that the single horn was an even "more effective weapon." This exemplar of natural selection was gaining on its more common relation, propagating the "peculiarity in a constantly increasing ratio" and might one day surpass it in numbers, he theorized. Charles Darwin, *The Descent of Man and Selection in Relation to Sex,* xvii, 5.

3. Doolittle, 148–51. The story of the bear hunt is adapted from Coleman C. Hatfield and Robert Y. Spence, *The Tale of the Devil,* 20–23. Descriptions of Devil Anse are found in Sanders, "Emma Hatfield Reminisces." While there is no Big Pigeon Mountain on contemporary topographical maps, Pigeon Creek passes through the area. Horsepen Mountain, at 2,534 feet the highest peak in southwestern West Virginia, is also nearby.

4. Doolittle, 154; "Logan County History," www.polisci.wvu.edu/wv/Logan /loghistory.html; and "Early History of Logan County, West Virginia," *SHG Resources: State Handbook & Guide,* www.shgresources.com/wv/counties

/logan/. In the 1990s, a group I was with spotted a wildcat in the woods near Helvetia, in eastern West Virginia.

5. Hatfield and Spence, 20–23, and Helen Vance Anderson and John Vance, *Tug River Memories,* 52–55. Hatfield and Spence (18) said Nancy Vance was the illegitimate daughter of the Reverend John Ferrell and Betsy Vance. They said Big Eph was "six-feet-four inches and weighed 260 pounds." While various accounts claim Big Eph was six feet six or more, his service records put him at six feet even.

6. Hatfield and Spence, 18.

7. Ibid., 23–24, and Thomas, 179. The nicknames used for Anse Hatfield — as well as their timing and intent — have been debated. Writing in the *New York Sun* in 1888, John R. Spears called him "Bad" Anse, as did the *Louisville Courier-Journal,* which explained that this was to distinguish him from another Anse Hatfield, presumably "Preacher" Anse. In what is the first verifiable use of the nickname that came to be more popular, T. C. Crawford, also writing in 1888 in the *New York World* (and the only reporter at that time to meet him face-to-face), said he was "commonly known as Devil Ance." Hatfield and Spence gave several anecdotes indicating that the name was a term of endearment.

8. Ely, 203–4.

9. Ibid.; Truda McCoy, 239; Mutzenberg, 49–50; Ron G. Blackburn and Betty Howard, "Ephraim Hatfield Genealogy Chart"; and John Frederick Dorman, "Petitions from Kentuckians to the Virginia Legislature," *The Kentucky Genealogist* 11 (Jan.–Mar. 1969): 27. Four McCoys and nine Hatfields signed the petition to the Kentucky legislature. A partially legible signature transcribed on the petition by Dorman as "Asa Harmon 'Rumby'" is possibly Asa Harmon McCoy, and thus a fifth McCoy to support the effort, which, had it passed, might have saved his life.

10. Truda McCoy, 11, 308; Kephart, 326–27, 342–43; Margaret Hoffman, "Hatfields, McCoys Bury the Hatchett," 9; and Jeffrey Carleton Hause, "Appendix 4: Allied Families: McCoy Family Genealogy," *Sons of Johann Hause Genealogy,* www.hausegenealogy.com/mccoy.html.

11. Jeffrey C. Weaver, *The Civil War in Buchanan and Wise Counties: Bushwhackers' Paradise,* 18; Jones, 16.

12. James M. Prichard, "The Devil at Large: Anse Hatfield's War," in *Virginia at War 1863,* 58; Philip Hatfield, *The Other Feud: William Anderson "Devil Anse" Hatfield in the Civil War,* 65. Harmon McCoy was not unusual in being a slaveholder in Kentucky, where slaves were nearly 20 percent of the population.

13. Prichard, 61; Howard, "Descendants of William 'Yankee Bill' Francis" and "Descendants of Thompson Hatfield." After the war, Thompson Hatfield

would marry a McCoy, Mary, in Pike County. According to Johnse Hatfield's cousin Emma Hatfield (Sanders, "Emma Hatfield Reminisces"), Johnse is pronounced with two syllables, as noted.

14. Prichard, 59. Devil Anse might have previously served in the Confederate 129th Militia, leading to his commission as an officer. Although he would frequently be referred to as Captain Hatfield, lieutenant is the highest recorded rank that he attained.

15. Prichard, 65; Kentucky, Pike County Circuit Court Cases 2177 and 2183; and G. Elliott Hatfield, *The Hatfields,* 188, 192. Also, correspondence between Lee Crutchfield and Betty Howard in her "Descendants of William 'Yankee Bill' Francis." The Dec. 17, 1862, *Richmond Daily Dispatch* called the Peter Creek home guard "a terror along the Kentucky State Line."

16. Dan Cunningham, "The Horrible Butcheries of West Virginia," *West Virginia History,* 40, and Prichard, 62–63. After the war, only the other man, Riley Sanson, would be charged with the murder. Though Devil Anse was implicated, during the trial he was called on only to testify on behalf of Sanson, who he said was a regular soldier following orders.

17. Weaver, *Civil War in Buchanan,* 169.

18. John R. Spears, "A Mountain Feud: A Remarkable Story of Murder and Outrage," *New York Sun;* Prichard, 58, 66, from the *Logan Banner,* Dec. 2, 1938; G. Elliott Hatfield, 211; Cunningham, "Horrible Butcheries," 41; and Howard, "Descendants of William 'Yankee Bill' Francis."

Chapter 2: Un-Civil Warfare

1. Prichard, 60, 69, and Robert Baker and Brian E. Hall, "Organization and History of the 39th Kentucky Mounted Infantry Regiment and Company 'F,'" Blue Gray Historical Group, www.bluegrayhistoricalgroup.org /39thktymtdinfhis.htm.

2. Prichard, 66–68. There is much confusion regarding the Logan Wildcats. For example, G. Elliott Hatfield (197) said that Devil Anse "served as a Lt. and Capt. in Co. A, 45th Va. (Confederate) Infantry, famous 'Logan Wildcats.'" But the Logan Wildcats were actually Company D of the Thirty-Sixth Virginia Infantry, assembled in June 1861. Led by officers Henry Beckley, James Nighbert, Dick Ferrell, and others, the company of eighty-five mustered into the Confederate Army under Colonel John McCausland at Charleston. Reorganized, it served at Fort Donelson under General John B. Floyd and in the Shenandoah Valley from 1864 to 1865. According to West Virginia historian Robert Spence (in *e-WV: The West Virginia Encyclopedia*), a band of armed irregulars active in Logan and Wyo-

ming counties late in the war under Devil Anse also called themselves the Logan Wildcats. There is no known muster of this group of irregulars.

3. Prichard, 68–69. After the war, many of the raiders, including the Hatfields, Johnson McCoy, and Jake Cline, would be sued. In an 1869 deposition, Devil Anse testified for Cline and confirmed that Cline had been forced to go on the raid.

4. Prichard, 70, and Cunningham, "Horrible Butcheries," 40.

5. Cunningham, "Horrible Butcheries," 40. Cunningham, perhaps with excessive zeal, discusses Devil Anse's wartime record and specifically accuses him of these crimes, though the records show that it was often associates of his who pulled the trigger. Prichard, 61–62. Regarding Charlie Mounts's death, while Cunningham might have heard it differently, postwar court records indicate that a Virginia State Line party scouting on Peter Creek shot and killed Mounts in a gunfight. Devil Anse may well have led the party.

6. Prichard, 71, and G. T. Swain, *History of Logan County West Virginia*, 113–14. This was probably tongue-in-cheek, as McClellan was popular with his men but considered a tepid fighter.

7. Truda McCoy, 11, and Prichard, 72. War records show several prisoner-of-war entries for a Randall McCoy from Pike County, but it is impossible to say with certainty which, if any, pertains to the Randall McCoy of the feud. According to tradition as well as historian Leonard Roberts (Truda McCoy, 225), Ellison Hatfield "fought for the Confederacy from the heroic stand at Gettysburg to surrender with Robert E. Lee at Appomattox." However, while he did serve a long stint, he probably did not see service at either of these monumental events.

8. Creelman, "Bloody Border War"; Richard Vance enlisted in the Virginia State Line in Dec. 1862 and died at Wytheville in Jan. 1863.

9. Cunningham, "Horrible Butcheries," 41–42, and Truda McCoy, 6–11. Prichard (58, 62, 73–74) compared Cunningham's account with other accounts and added details. Charlotte Sanders added details from Lark McCoy through his family in the *Williamson Daily News* ("Ollie Jane McCoy Smith Going Strong at 87"). Some say it was one of the slaves, Pete, who went to warn McCoy (Hatfield and Spence, 164–66, and Anderson and Vance, 145). L. D. Hatfield (31) tried to shift the blame to Harmon and exonerate Devil Anse, who he said "was confined in his bed with fever" when "he received a letter from Harmon McCoy stating that he (Harmon) was coming to kill him." According to L.D., Jim Vance was at Devil Anse's when the letter arrived and told him to look out for Harmon that night, "but if he don't get here tonight you need not be afraid." The next morning Harmon McCoy was found dead.

10. Prichard, 73–74; Sanders, "Ollie Jane McCoy Smith"; and Truda McCoy, 11. Waller said that Harmon's killing was "the expression of a consensus which branded him an outcast and a traitor," which, as we have seen, is incorrect. Although Waller relied on Truda McCoy at other times, she ignored her assertion that the murder of Harmon would have been avenged if Randall had been present, arguing instead that "there was no attempt at retaliation, public or private — strong evidence that even Asa Harmon's family was not prepared to defend his behavior."

11. Truda McCoy, 11.

Chapter 3: Timbering the Sublime Forest

1. Governor Henry D. Hatfield in his Mar. 4, 1913, inaugural address.

2. Doolittle, 148–51, and George R. Stewart, *Names on the Land*, 139–40. Yet another possible source is the Cherokee word *tugulu*, which means "the fork of a stream or river."

3. Hatfield and Spence, *Tale of the Devil*, 18, 37–38, 56; Donnelly, 29–30; L. D. Hatfield, 10–16; G. Elliott Hatfield, 71, 188; Sanders, "Emma Hatfield Reminisces"; Helen Blankenship Roesch, "Hatfields of Southwest Virginia, Kentucky," Henry P. Scalf Papers; and Thomas, 11, 20, 95–96, 136–38.

4. Anderson and Vance, 3–4, 52–55; Lee Maynard, *Crum*, 101; and Truda McCoy, 226.

5. Truda McCoy, 4–6; Doolittle, 54–57, 59, 63, 147; Charles R. Bourland Jr., "Biography of Henry Solomon White," 5; and Thomas D. Clark, "Kentucky Logmen," *Journal of Forest History*, 150.

6. Clark, 150–53.

7. *New York Sun*, "Logging on the Big Sandy."

8. West Virginia, "Ellison v. Torpin et al.," 416–17, and Waller, 41–44.

Chapter 4: The Importance of Razorbacks

1. Merle T. Cole, "Soldiers of the New Empire: The Gaujot Brothers of Mingo County," *West Virginia Historical Society Quarterly*.

2. Michael A. Broadstone, *History of Greene County, Ohio*, 421, and L. D. Hatfield, 9.

3. Truda McCoy, 281; Swain, *History of Logan County*, 184; Jones, 18; Donnelly, 1–2; and Matewan.com, "Matewan, West Virginia."

4. Anderson and Vance, 147. "I have often been asked why anyone would be willing to kill someone over a lowly swine," John Vance, who penned one of the chapters in his sister's *Tug River Memories*, told me. "My answer has always been the same — survival."

5. "Mingo County," *West Virginia Cyclopedia,* www.wvexp.com/index.php/Mingo_County (Jan. 10, 2011); John Vance, "The Hatfield and McCoy Feud Connection," in Anderson, 146–47; and United States Department of Agriculture, *Fourth and Fifth Annual Reports of the Bureau of Animal Industry for the Year 1887 and 1888,* 216–17.

6. Anderson, 146–47, and Mutzenberg, 32–34.

7. In his memoir, Sam McCoy (*Squirrel Huntin' Sam McCoy,* 60–61) gave an account of this dispute that, while uncorroborated by others, offered the detail and ring of truth. However, Sam, the only feudist to record his memories in full—in 1931, at the age of seventy-one—presents problems for historians because his memories were often at odds with the known sequence of events. After this point in his account of the razorback dispute, he conflated elements of other feud episodes with this one. Truda McCoy's account of this event (13–19) differed in that she did not mention Thomas Stafford. Instead, Randall McCoy went directly to Floyd Hatfield's farm, where he discovered what he thought were his hogs. Stafford and Floyd Hatfield were married to Staton sisters.

8. Spears, "Mountain Feud"; Sam McCoy, 61; Jones, 18, 19, n. 1, 169–70; Truda McCoy, 222, n. 2; Donnelly, 2; Waller, xiv–xvii; and L. D. Hatfield, 17, 20 (caption). Devil Anse and Floyd were the sons of brothers Eph and John Hatfield (respectively), who were a year apart in age, and Nancy and Isabella Vance (respectively), sisters of the feudist Crazy Jim Vance. Spears incorrectly identified Floyd Hatfield as Devil Anse's brother and Matthew Hatfield as the presiding justice of the peace. Donnelly incorrectly identified Floyd as a son of George Hatfield; he was a son of John Hatfield and a cousin of both Preacher Anse and Devil Anse. Jones and others mistakenly identified Randall McCoy and Floyd Hatfield as brothers-in-law. In Mutzenberg's account (32–34), Floyd Hatfield drove a number of hogs from the forest and confined them in a pen at Stringtown. A few days later, Randall McCoy saw the hogs, claimed they were his, and demanded their return. Floyd refused to hand them over, leading to a hearing before Wall Hatfield.

9. Truda McCoy (16) noted that for this trial "jurymen would be as scarce as hen's teeth" because no one wanted to fall on the wrong side of either family.

10. Jones, 19, 273, and Truda McCoy, 16.

11. Spears, "Mountain Feud," and Sam McCoy, 61.

12. Jones, 19–20.

13. Mutzenberg, 32–34; Spears, "Mountain Feud"; Truda McCoy, 280–81; and Waller, xiv. Most chroniclers of the feud do not differentiate between the

elder Bill Staton and the younger. Mutzenberg and Spears made this distinction, though Spears confused the issue by saying that "old Bill Staton" was a "brother of Floyd Hatfield's wife, Esther" and that "his sister Sarah Ann was married to his brother, Ellison Hatfield." In fact, old Bill Staton was the father of Esther and Sarah Ann, and young Bill Staton was their brother. Most remarkably, while some histories point out that the elder Staton daughter, Sarah Ann, was married to Ellison Hatfield, none point out that Staton's youngest daughter, Esther (born 1849; listed as "Polly Easter" in G. Elliott Hatfield, 198), was actually married to Floyd Hatfield (born 1847).

14. Truda McCoy, 17.

15. Leck Hatfield was probably Lexious Hatfield, Preacher Anse's next older brother, born in 1833 and married to Lydia (Musick) Smith in 1859. G. Elliott Hatfield, 192.

16. Truda McCoy, 17, and Waller, 64, 79; also, Jones, 17–24, and Mutzenberg, 32–34. Jones (20) mistakenly called Selkirk McCoy the "husband of a Hatfield." Otis K. Rice (*The Hatfields and the McCoys,* 55) wrongly suggested that he gave "testimony against the claims of Randolph McCoy."

17. Spears, "Mountain Feud," and Swain, 184–85. This incident is based on Spears, who mistakenly called Ellison Hatfield Floyd's brother. He was a cousin of Floyd's and a brother-in-law. Jones, writing later, mentioned it in one sentence with distinctly different detail: "The only demonstration of violence came when Randolph McCoy called Bill Staton, one of the Hatfield witnesses, a liar and hurled a rock at him" (21).

18. Sam McCoy, 62; Truda McCoy, 249–50, 252–53, 280–81; Waller, 62–65; Mutzenberg, 32; and Jones, 21–22. Lon and Lark McCoy were the sons of Allen McCoy, nephews of Sally, Randall's wife; this Lark is not to be confused with the Lark who was the son of Asa Harmon McCoy.

19. Sam McCoy, 62–63 (regularized name spelling), and Truda McCoy, 226.

20. Spears, "Mountain Feud"; Sam McCoy, 93, 132; Mutzenberg, 34; Waller, 65–66 (trial 1878), 272, n. 31; Truda McCoy, 314; Swain, 184–85; and Charlotte Sanders, "'Squirrel Huntin' Sam' McCoy Played Active Role in Feud," *Williamson Daily News.*

21. Truda McCoy, 280–81, 311, 315–17. Truda McCoy gave the birth dates of 1855 for Squirrel Huntin' Sam and 1860 for Paris. However, Sam McCoy (132) gave Paris's birthday as Nov. 27, 1854, making him a year older than Sam.

22. Mutzenberg, 35; Sam McCoy, 124; and Sanders, "McCoy Played Active Role." Crawford (*American Vendetta,* 19) got this backward, with Paris pulling the trigger as Sam grapples with Staton. In Sam McCoy (93), Sam's son Hobert claimed his father killed 38,000 squirrels with one rifle and 40,000 with another.

23. Swain, 185–87. While Squirrel Huntin' Sam McCoy left out his involvement in the killing of Staton in his memoir, Truda McCoy (316) wrote: "In 1940 'Squirrel Huntin' Sam' told a grandson about the killing of Bill Staton. Sam said that he and his brother, Paris, were farming. Two little girls were playing nearby. Bill Staton rode up and told Sam and the little girls to stand back. With that, he shot Paris. He then began beating Paris with a pistol butt. Paris cried for help and Sam shot and killed Staton."

24. Logan County Courthouse Law Order Book B, 247; Mutzenberg, 35; Jones, 23; G. Elliott Hatfield, 190; Howard, "Descendants of Richard Ferrell"; and Waller, 87, 272, n. 31. For trying Paris and, separately, another man accused of a felony offense, Wall billed Logan County twenty-one dollars. He also billed the county fifty cents for "warming" road workers, probably giving them temporary shelter and possibly feeding them a meal. Donnelly (1–2) incorrectly said it was Ellison Hatfield, as opposed to Elias, and went on to say that he "vigorously prosecuted the two McCoys" and was thus "hated by all the McCoys." Truda McCoy's version (21–24), as told to her by her father, Jim Williams, is a McCoy screed and seems to be less credible than most of her other re creations of events. Some accounts place the shooting of Bill Staton shortly after the hog trial, and the capture and trial of Sam and Paris McCoy within months of Staton's death. Wrote Spears ("Mountain Feud"): "Within six months young Bill Staton was shot dead in the road on one of the Pike County creeks. Parish [sic] and Sam McCoy, Randall's nephews, waylaid him. They were young men who had been persuaded into making trouble for young Bill by their uncle, the Hatfields say." Jones (23) had Paris arrested "in a few days" and Sam "in a few weeks." Waller was inconsistent, writing: "Paris was arrested within a month and was tried . . . in September" (66) and "Paris was arrested the following summer" (272, n. 31). In reality, the shooting happened nearly two years after the hog trial, the arrest of Paris McCoy nearly a year after that, and the arrest of Sam McCoy another year later. A recap of the feud in the Mar. 29, 1902, New York Times (and another on July 11, 1904) showed that many of the distortions had already crept into the record: The article had Paris and Sam killing young Bill from ambush a few months after Randall McCoy called his father a "perjurer" and Bill hit him in the head with a stone. It also said the brothers were acquitted in a Kentucky court, though it was in West Virginia.

Chapter 5: Moonshine and Love

1. Joseph Earl Dabney, Mountain Spirits, 10–11.
2. John R. Spears, "The Moonshiner's Still," New York Sun; and Dabney, 7–8.

In an article that I found in the pages of the *Sun* in the spring of 2012, Spears detailed Devil Anse's moonshining operation. He had been guided through Pike County on his research journey by Big Jim McCoy, who told him about the operation. With no byline and published two weeks after a well-known article by Spears in the *Sun* (that was reprinted as "The Dramatic Story of a Mountain Feud" in *Current Literature: A Magazine of Record and Review*), this article and two others about the feud by Spears that appeared on the same page had been lost to feud historians until now.

3. Logan County Courthouse Law Order Book B, 243. Sam Simpkins, Joe Murphy, and Bill Ferrell were also on the panel.

4. Thomas, 66–68, 71.

5. Truda McCoy, 24–26; Ely, 202; and Charlotte Sanders, "'Hog Trial' Is Part of Feud Legend," *Williamson Daily News*. Jerry Hatfield lived in a two-story house where Hatfield Branch empties into Blackberry Creek. Preacher Anse would later move from Raccoon Hollow to this house.

6. John L. Spivak, "Interview with Cap Hatfield"; Truda McCoy, 25–27; and Spears, "Mountain Feud." The Feb. 17, 1888, *Courier-Journal* ("The Hatfields Arrive") reported that Wall confessed to having "five living wives and thirty-three living children" and noted that he had a "particular idea of polygamy and does not marry his wife according to law but takes them and appropriates his time out between them."

7. Spears, "Mountain Feud"; Jones, 18–19; Rice, 19, 21; and Truda McCoy, 25–31, 222. McCoy described the meeting and courtship of Johnse Hatfield and Roseanna McCoy as told to her by Jesse Gooslin, who was present at the polling grounds, and by Martha McCoy, Roseanna's sister-in-law (married to her brother Sam). Truda McCoy often overstepped the boundaries of historical accuracy when she re-created events (even supplying the interior thoughts of some of the individuals), but here she presented a plausible series of events and convincingly explained how this unlikely courtship came to be.

8. Truda McCoy, 28, 32. McCoy said that Devil Anse allowed Roseanna to stay out of spite for Randall, "enjoying the situation immensely," knowing how much it would gall his adversary to find that his daughter was sleeping with a Hatfield out of wedlock.

9. Truda McCoy, 34–35, 249, and Spears, "Mountain Feud." The only John Hatfield in Truda McCoy's genealogy at the time was just fourteen.

10. Truda McCoy, 36–37.

11. Ibid., 38–39.

12. Logan County Courthouse Law Order Book B, 274, 298, 299.

13. Sam Hill, "Report of the Adjutant General of Kentucky"; Spivak, "Inter-

view with Cap Hatfield"; and Waller, 273, notes 42 and 43, citing *Commonwealth of Kentucky v. Andrew Hatfield, Elias Hatfield, et al.* The romantic Truda McCoy (43, 47) wrote that the McCoys secured a warrant for "seduction."

14. Truda McCoy, 39–40, 223–24, n. 5, and Howard, "Descendants of Reuben Rutherford, Sr." Truda McCoy said that Aunt Betty was the wife of Allen McCoy, a brother to Sally. However, a highway sign identifies Aunt Betty's house as the Uriah McCoy House and says she was Uriah's wife, née Elizabeth Rutherford.

15. In Spears's version of events, Roseanna was still living in her family home, but I have opted to follow Truda McCoy's chronology, which had her already at Aunt Betty's, believing this more likely than the two carrying on an affair under the nose of Randall and his sons, who were in a state of high alert. On the subject of catching the couple in flagrante, Spears noted: "In the eyes of the mountain folks along Tug River, this sight was enough to make the boys 'right mad,' but it was not a case for blood." Some accounts give the lead role in the capture to Randall's oldest son, Big Jim. As Truda McCoy (44) described the capture of Johnse, Randall and Jim were with Tolbert and Pharmer.

16. Spivak, "Interview with Cap Hatfield."

17. Margaret Hatfield interview transcript, 4, and Spivak, "Interview with Cap Hatfield." Spears said she borrowed a mule.

18. Crawford, *American Vendetta*, 50, 74.

19. Margaret Hatfield interview transcript, 4, and Spivak, "Interview with Cap Hatfield." Spears said that Roseanna "ran the mule to Anse Hatfield's house, Johnse's home, and told what had happened [to] Johnse."

20. Hill, "Adjutant General"; Spears, "Mountain Feud"; Sam McCoy, 63; L. D. Hatfield, 36–38; and Waller, 71. In Truda McCoy's romanticized account, she wrote: "Randolph motioned to Johnse with his pistol. *'Ye'll never see her again.'*" Roseanna wailed and thought "they meant to kill him—she was sure of it now" (45). She also maintained that Devil Anse raised forty men within ten minutes (46).

21. Truda McCoy, 48.

22. Margaret Hatfield interview transcript, 3.

23. Andrew Chafin interview transcript, 6–7.

24. Ibid., 26.

25. Some say Devil Anse shouldered his rifle to show just how displeased he was at the current state of affairs and that Cap urged him to kill the McCoys. Crawford (*American Vendetta*, 21) said Elias talked Devil Anse out of it. According to L. D. Hatfield (36–38), the Hatfields ordered the McCoys "to kneel and pray for they were going to be killed." Only Big Jim

refused the order, saying, " 'You can shoot me down, but I won't get down,' whereupon Devil Anse called to his men to hold their fire and said to Big Jim, 'I admire you for the nerve you have shown.' They were then allowed to go on their way." In Truda McCoy's version of events, a starry-eyed victim throughout, struck Devil Anse's shotgun, which was aimed at Randall, after he "pulled back the trigger of his gun" (she must have meant *hammer*). The gun "exploded on the ground at the feet of Ranel's mount" (47). Johnse thus saved Randall's life. Neither account seems accurate, given the modesty of Tolbert's filed complaint.

26. Keith F. Otterbein ("Five Feuds," 232): "In a cross-cultural study of rape, I found that societies with a high frequency of rape also had a high frequency of feuding."

27. Ibid.

Chapter 6: The Wages of Love

1. Lawrence Block, *Gangsters, Swindlers, Killers, and Thieves,* 103. It would not be until after the 1901 assassination of William McKinley that the Secret Service, founded in 1865, would take on the task of protecting the president.

2. Roy C. Woods, "History of the Hatfield-McCoy Feud with Special Attention to the Effects of Education on It," 33, and Spears, "Mountain Feud."

3. G. Elliott Hatfield, 211–12, and Donnelly, 28.

4. Truda McCoy, 311, and Waller, 36, 266, n. 10. Johnson and Sarah McCoy named their only child, a daughter, LeVicey Chafin McCoy, after her aunt.

5. Spears, "Mountain Feud"; Truda McCoy, 52–57, 224, n. 6, which noted that the child's "birth, age, and death are unproved"; and Spivak, "Interview with Cap Hatfield." A historical marker labeled SALLY MCCOY (no. 2176), on Kentucky Highway 272, marks the burial place and reads in part: "Sarah Elizabeth (Sally) McCoy . . . born in 1881 . . . contracted measles and pneumonia, and died a few months after her birth."

6. Truda McCoy, 59, 309–10, and Howard, "Descendants of Perry A. Cline." Martha Jackson McCoy, Roseanna's sister-in-law (married to her brother Sam), told Truda McCoy about the death of Roseanna's baby, Alifair's illness, Roseanna's time at the Clines' in Pikeville, Johnse's visit there, and Roseanna's refusal to marry him. Despite Truda's portrayal of Johnse as a sympathetic, romantic, and tragic figure, historian Leonard Roberts, who edited her book, still concluded that Roseanna was "jilted to death by Johnse" (224, n. 6).

7. Truda McCoy, 61, 224, n. 6, and G. Elliott Hatfield, 211. Truda McCoy is the chief source of information on this period. Her chronology does not

quite square with the fact that Johnse married Roseanna's cousin Nancy McCoy on May 14, 1881. Little Sally could not have been born until at least April, and she lived for several months, making it unlikely that Roseanna could have nursed Alifair, cared for the Cline child, and met and rejected Johnse in Pikeville before he married Nancy.

8. Truda McCoy, 11, 60–68, 224, notes 6 and 7, 226, n. 10, 313–14. Also, Ollie Jane McCoy Smith, Lark's daughter-in-law, and Sadie McCoy in Charlotte Sanders, "Ollie McCoy Converted Larkin McCoy," *Williamson Daily News*, Mar. 29, 1998 (reprint from 1982). Truda McCoy's source was Elsie Phillips Ford, Nancy's daughter by a later husband.

9. Waller, 66, 272, n. 31, and Sam McCoy, 124–25. Waller cited this date based on the Logan County law order books. All other accounts place the trial of Paris and Sam shortly after the murder of Bill Staton.

10. Truda McCoy, 23. Although McCoy provided no dates, she had both the arrest and trial of Squirrel Huntin' Sam occurring before the Aug. 1880 election. Based on the account of her father, Jim Williams, she also said that only Sam and Paris testified at the trial, which contradicts the record. Sam McCoy was entirely mute on this topic in his memoir. Waller (*Feud*, 66) said that Paris was tried in Sept. 1880 while Sam was tried in the spring of 1882, but confused the chronology by relating the 1880 Election Day romance as if it occurred after Sam's acquittal.

11. Truda McCoy, 23–24. It would be a continuing irony of the feud that many incidents pitted McCoy versus McCoy or Hatfield versus Hatfield. Here, McCoy testified against McCoy, and not just one or two brave souls. Eight McCoys from both sides of the Tug—Denas, Elliot, Eva, Jasper, Josephine, Sarilda, Sylvester, and Uriah—testified against the two brothers.

12. *Louisville Courier-Journal*, "Hatfields Arrive"; Jones, 23; G. Elliott Hatfield, 211; Truda McCoy, 316; Waller, 66, 272, n. 31; and Charlotte Sanders, "Beautiful Beech Creek Valley Not Always Peaceful," *Williamson Daily News*. "Sam McCoy walked out of the courtroom a free man," wrote Truda McCoy. "Both the judge and jury were convinced that it was a case of self-defense" (24). Not every account mentioned a jury, while Sam McCoy (124) did but claimed it was an all-Hatfield jury. "The acquittal of the two McCoy boys angered and outraged the Hatfields. They concluded that no West Virginian could get justice in a Kentucky court in a capital case," wrote Spears ("Mountain Feud"), confusing matters, as the trial was held in West Virginia, presided over by a West Virginia justice of the peace.

13. Truda McCoy, 69, and Spears, "Mountain Feud."

14. Truda McCoy, 69.

15. Ibid., 70, 309; Spears, "Mountain Feud"; Rice, 24; and Staton, 83–87.

Tolbert's first child was an out-of-wedlock son named Melvin, now two. Melvin's mother, Adda Maynard, a daughter of Dr. J. B. Maynard, would also have a son, Wayne, by a Hatfield. The two half brothers would frequently fight each other, as one was a Hatfield and the other a McCoy.

16. *Huntington Advertiser,* "The Story of the Hatfields and McCoys According to A.M. (Lonnie) Lee."

17. Mutzenberg, 36. West Virginia did not have a lock on this sort of corruption. In fact, during George Washington's third campaign for the Virginia House of Burgesses, in 1758, after losing elections in 1755 and 1757, he supplied the 310 voters with 169 gallons of beer, cider, wine, and rum. He won this election, unlike the previous ones, when he did not ply voters with alcoholic libations, by a landslide (Dabney, 44–45).

18. Dabney, 27, and L. D. Hatfield, 16.

Chapter 7: Tumult on Election Day

1. John R. Spears, "Mountain News Getting," *New York Sun.*

2. Regarding tobacco use, Thomas (13) quoted a hypothetical Appalachian old-timer: "Hit's all right for the wimmin folks to smoke a pipe, p'tkler old granny wimmin. . . . But for us men folks it's a heap more comfortabler for us to take a chaw of t'backer. We can step around where we're a-mind to, not wearyin' about a hot coal from the foirplace to keep a pipe a-going'."

3. Donnelly, 6–7; Swain, 187; Waller, xi, 74; Spears, "Mountain Feud"; and Cathy Patton, *Welch Daily News,* "Hatfield Heirloom Warms Local Clan." L. D. Hatfield (17–19) suggested that Ellison Hatfield was a marked man but otherwise confused who was involved in the killing of Bill Staton. He wrote: "Sometime prior to this date three of Randolph McCoy's boys . . . had been over in West Virginia and had some trouble with these two Staton boys [Bill and John] and Bill Staton was killed by the McCoys." But it was Paris and Sam McCoy, cousins of Floyd and Tolbert McCoy, who were involved in that incident. While some suggested that Ellison's involvement in the violence this day was almost coincidental, L. D. Hatfield maintained that the McCoy brothers expected Ellison to be present and that they had "sharpened their knives so as to be in readiness."

4. Spears, "A Mountain Feud." Spears put the amount of money in dispute at $1.75; Rice (24) concurred. L. D. Hatfield (18–19) gave the amount as fifty cents. While Sam McCoy gave a graphic and detailed account of the events, he also confused the names and ages of the McCoy brothers, giving Pharmer's age as thirteen and saying he was known as Bud, when that was the nickname of Randolph Jr., whom Sam referred to as Dick. Spears likewise

gave a detailed and descriptive account that, while differing substantially from other standard accounts, had the ring of authenticity. However, he called Tolbert "Talbot" and described Bad 'Lias as a nephew of Ellison and Elias when he was in fact their cousin. While the argument was over a small amount of money, Spears later said Tolbert left his wife, Mary, with quite a substantial inheritance.

5. Regarding the ages of the McCoy brothers, there is considerable confusion. According to Kentucky birth records, Tolbert was born on June 16, 1854, which made him twenty-eight at this time. Truda McCoy (309–11) gave approximate birth years for Pharmer (1863), Bud (1864), and Bill (1866). This means that in Aug. 1882, Pharmer was eighteen or nineteen. "Bill was fifteen and somewhat large for his age," McCoy wrote. "Bud, or Randolph Jr., was seventeen." Mutzenberg (46) took his ages from Pike Circuit Court records for *Commonwealth v. Val Hatfield*, in which Sally McCoy stated that at the time of their deaths, "Tolbert was 31, Pharmer 19 and Bud 15 years old."

6. Donnelly 19–24, and L. D. Hatfield, 19.

7. Spears, "Mountain Feud"; Rice, 24; and Swain, 187.

8. Spears, "Mountain Feud"; G. Elliott Hatfield's genealogy (194) lists only one Matthew Hatfield (born 1848), a great-grandson of Eph of All and later a sheriff of McDowell County, West Virginia.

9. L. D. Hatfield, 19–20; Donnelly, 6–7; Mutzenberg 36–37; Prichard, 66; and Waller, 72. Various versions describe the fight in different ways. According to Sam McCoy (65), "Elison [*sic*] Hatfield...hollered out he were the best g.d. man on earth. Said it over three different times right in the presence of Tolbert McCoy.... Tolbert replied, you look more like a turd on earth than anything else I know of."

10. Mutzenberg, 36–37.

11. Spears, "Mountain Feud"; L. D. Hatfield, 19–20; and Sam McCoy, 65. Spears was the only chronicler to record that Ellison was armed.

12. Sam McCoy, 65; L. D. Hatfield, 21, 22 (caption); Rice, 24; and Spears, "Mountain Feud." The shirt that Ellison Hatfield wore when he was murdered, a faded plaid pullover made by his wife, was preserved and later came to be in the possession of Devil Anse's son Joe, who holds it in a picture appearing in *Life* magazine on May 22, 1944. A shirt depicted in Coleman C. Hatfield and F. Keith Davis (*The Feuding Hatfields and McCoys*, 166, 171), although said to be the same shirt, does not appear to match the one in *Life* magazine, nor is it in the collection of the West Virginia State Archives as reported.

13. Sam McCoy, 65. Also, L. D. Hatfield, 19–20, and G. Elliott Hatfield, 212–13.

14. Spears ("Mountain Feud") and others. Pharmer's name is spelled variously "Pharmer" (Sam McCoy, Truda McCoy, and Rice); "Farmer" (Spears); and "Phamer" (Mutzenberg and Jones). Once again, we have conflicting accounts of what happened at this point: Mutzenberg (38) wrote that Pharmer "dropped the weapon and sought safety in flight. He was pursued by Constable Floyd Hatfield [as opposed to Matthew] and captured." Sam McCoy (66) reported that Elias fired his gun in Pharmer's face three times from point-blank range but missed. "His face were all powder burnt," Sam described, "but the bullets went wild, never touched him." Amazed, Elias declared, "I'll never try it again. If I can't hit a man that close, I'll quit." Rice (24) maintained that Elias "forced the revolver from Pharmer's hand and tried to shoot him" before he "ran and sought cover in the nearby woods." According to L. D. Hatfield (21), Elias "rushed up and grabbed Tolbert McCoy by the shirt collar and emptied his revolver in his face but every shot missed its mark." L.D. was the only one to identify Tolbert as the intended victim.

15. Truda McCoy, 75. Truda McCoy noted that Sam, Jim, George, and Martha McCoy all agreed that it was Bill and not Bud who had stabbed Ellison. She wrote: "They said it was a natural mistake, that the bystanders identified the wrong boy—since they looked so much alike" (225). Spears ("Mountain Feud") added his own wrinkle. "Randolph McCoy, Jr., . . . came running up just as Farmer was brought back to the polling place," he wrote. "He was accused of cutting the Deacon in the legs by a Hatfield who mistook him for the young boy, Budd." But Bud was actually the nickname of Randolph Jr.; Spears meant Bill, a mistake that would be perpetuated by others. "This fact is now admitted on all sides," wrote Spears, "but the McCoys deny that Budd [meaning Bill] did any stabbing, and say that Talbot did it all." Jones did not mention Bill and did not even list a child of Randall and Sarah McCoy named William or Bill in his McCoy genealogy.

    While Truda McCoy added invaluable details to the history, she also made some perplexing errors, among others placing Devil Anse at the scene, to be chastised by Tolbert McCoy's wife, Mary: "If you'd a-kept your durn set in West Virginia where they belong, this wouldn't a-happened" (75). In her account, Anse "with the aide of relatives, raised his bleeding brother to a cot that someone had brought for the purpose" (76). In no other accounts was Devil Anse present.

16. Spears, "Mountain Feud"; Rice, 25; Sam McCoy, 66; and Waller, 73. Warm Hollow now ends at the highway outside Matewan but originally traveled to the Tug Fork, meeting it just below the mouth of Blackberry Creek.

17. "Plaintiffs Bill of Exceptions," 1; L. D. Hatfield, 21–23; Mutzenberg, 38; and Waller, xv.

18. "Plaintiffs Bill of Exceptions," 1; Spears, "Mountain Feud"; Mutzenberg, 38; Sam McCoy, 66; Rice, 25; and Waller, 73. According to Waller (xiv), Doc, Plyant, and Sam Mahon (sometimes spelled "Mayhorn" or "Mahorn") were married to Wall's daughters, Sarah (age twenty-two), Victoria (twenty), and Mary (eighteen), respectively, but this is incorrect regarding Sam, who was married to Mary Mounts; according to G. Elliott Hatfield (211), Mary Hatfield was married to Richard Blankenship. Among the marital intricacies in the region at the time, it was not uncommon for the siblings of one family to marry the siblings of another family and have children who were double first cousins, as was the case when Big Eph and his brother John married sisters Nancy and Isabella Vance.

19. Sam McCoy (66–67) and Waller (73–74) said that Ellison remained in Kentucky that night. Spears ("Mountain Feud") and others said they moved him immediately to West Virginia. L. D. Hatfield (23) wrote that Devil Anse reached the Blackberry Creek polling ground at dusk on the night of the fight and "forcibly taking the prisoners away from the constable, escorted them across the river into West Virginia." A number of works confused the sequence of events, especially the timing of Anse and Wall's arrival and the point at which Ellison was carried across the Tug. As Spears told it, "When morning came, there were over seventy of the Hatfield family from West Virginia about the house of John Hatfield on Blackberry Creek, where the prisoners were kept over night."

20. "Plaintiffs Bill of Exceptions," 1; Staton, 197; Mutzenberg, 38; Rice, 25–26; and Waller, 36. Mutzenberg said they were overtaken by, among others, Wall, whom he called Val, and Bad 'Lias, "brothers of the wounded Ellison." However, it was not Bad 'Lias, Preacher Anse's brother, but Good 'Lias, Devil Anse's and Wall's brother, who helped waylay the Pikeville-bound contingent. Wall mentioned Dr. Rutherford in his testimony at his trial (Staton, 197). Jones (46, 50, 205) later misidentified him as Dr. Jim Rutherford. Based on Jones, Rice made the same mistake. However, it was actually Elliott Rutherford, who went by Doc, a prominent citizen and future first mayor of Matewan. Jones might have been confused by Doc's father, James (born 1792). Howard, "Descendants of Reuben Rutherford, Sr."

21. "Plaintiffs Bill of Exceptions," 1–2.

22. Mutzenberg, 38–39, and Waller, 79. I have largely used Mutzenberg's chronology here. Rice (25–26) maintained that before they could set out again, a large party of heavily armed Hatfields and their partisans, led by Devil Anse, arrived. Waller said that they encountered Devil Anse at Preacher Anse's.

Rice concurred with Spears: "After daylight appeared on Tuesday, the prisoners and their guards ate breakfast and set out for Pikesville [*sic*] jail. They had not traveled over a mile, however, before they met a gang of West Virginia Hatfields headed by old Bad Anse Hatfield." Regarding Alex (Alexander Elac) Messer, he is widely held to have been a sheriff with "twenty-seven notches" on the butt of his gun (Jones, 156), but no supporting documents exist to confirm this. Documents do show that he was a former Union mounted infantryman.

23. "Plaintiffs Bill of Exceptions," 2–3; Spears, "Mountain Feud"; Mutzenberg, 39; Staton, 197–98; and Waller, 74, 79.

24. "Plaintiffs Bill of Exceptions," 2; Spears, "Mountain Feud"; and Rice, 25–26.

25. "Plaintiffs Bill of Exceptions," 3; Staton, 193, 196; Woods, 28; Thomas, 68, 90, 109–10, 248; and Mutzenberg, 46. Thomas talked of rain and swollen creeks at this time, so using a skiff to cross the Tug makes sense. Others talk of fording or walking across the Tug, which is possible in places. Some say Devil Anse was on the skiff, but this contradicts two eyewitnesses, including Bill Daniels, who identified these men (see *Commonwealth of Kentucky vs. Anderson Hatfield and Others*, Staton, 196). In the same trial (Staton 194–95), James M. McCoy named these men, excepting Murphy and adding Ralph Steele. Wall later testified, "When I went to the mouth of Blackberry, the first thing that I saw was that they were standing on the opposite side of the river. I have no recollection of crossing the river with them" (Staton, 198). While Rutherford Branch is a mile up Mate Creek, some say that the schoolhouse where the McCoy brothers were taken was in the hollow directly across from the present-day town of Matewan, about a quarter of a mile from the Tug. A historical marker is placed there.

Chapter 8: Mountain Justice

1. Velke, 3, and Merle T. Cole, *A Comprehensive History of the West Virginia State Police, 1919–1979*, 2, 46. Border patrols, such as the Texas Rangers (organized in 1835), and other state agencies with law enforcement functions, like the Massachusetts State Constables (formed in 1865), were early iterations of state police forces, but it was not until after the turn of the century that such forces really took hold: the Arizona Rangers formed in 1901, the Connecticut Police in 1903, and the Pennsylvania State Constabulary and the New Mexico Mounted Police in 1905. Most state police forces were created between 1919 and 1939.

2. Dabney, 45.

3. Spears, "Mountain Feud"; Rice, 28; and Waller, 37, 267, n. 18. A decade

previously, along with Big Eph, Doc Rutherford had led an effort to bring education to the area.

4. Spears, "Mountain Feud"; Rice, 28; and Woods, 31.

5. Spears, "Mountain Feud," and Mutzenberg, 39.

6. Spears, "Mountain Feud," and Rice, 26–27.

7. Mutzenberg, 40; Spears, "Mountain Feud"; and Truda McCoy, 309.

8. Truda McCoy, 248, 240–60. Truda heard of Sally and Mary's trips to Mate Creek from Martha McCoy, the wife of Randall's son Sam, and "many first-hand" sources (225, n. 9). Selkirk was married to Louisa Williamson, the stepdaughter of his grandfather Samuel McCoy, who, with his first wife, Elizabeth, had seventeen children, including Selkirk's aunt Sally, Randall's wife. Louisa was one of three children of Samuel's second wife, Nancy.

9. Spears, "Mountain Feud"; Mutzenberg, 41, 46; and Rice, 26–27. At least one account maintained that Wall told the women that if Ellison died, he would personally "shoot the boys full of holes."

10. L. D. Hatfield, 23, and Waller, 41–50.

11. Sam McCoy, 67–68. Like others, Squirrel Huntin' Sam, who recorded his version of the feud many decades after it took place, turned Bud into a boy of fifteen, which was Bill's age. I have adjusted the timing of Preacher Anse's appearance, described by Sam, moving it to where it more likely occurred.

12. Mutzenberg, 41, and "Plaintiffs Bill of Exceptions."

13. Spears, "Mountain Feud." Spears reported that the messenger rode out on a mule while Mutzenberg (42) said it was a horse.

14. Sam McCoy, 67; Mutzenberg, 42; and Spears, "Mountain Feud."

15. Mutzenberg, 44, 48–49. Mutzenberg also wrote, "But this good man volunteered to stand guard and prevent any interference or interruption of the butchery." See also Hatfield and Davis, 35–37.

16. Sam McCoy, 67; Staton, 194, 198; Spears, "Mountain Feud"; Mutzenberg, 44; and Swain, 188. I have primarily followed Wall Hatfield's court testimony as recounted in Staton. Reports of the encounter with the moonshiner Joe Davis vary. Some say the whole group ran into him and that he confirmed that Bud had shot Ellison. Others say that Wall was sent to ask Davis if Bud had stabbed Ellison. According to Sam McCoy (67): "They sent Wall Hatfield up to Joe Davis's to see Davis if the little boy had anything to do in cutting Elison, if so he were to hoot like an owl." Davis brought over a pint of whiskey, but Wall told him he did not want any, saying, "I come to see if that little boy had anything to do with cutting brother Elison with a knife." And Davis gave his reply. Sam went on to say that Wall gave the signal to let the others know Bud was guilty. Whether or not he did remains a matter of controversy. Spears went as far as to say that

Wall, standing on the West Virginia side, called out the execution commands, "Take aim. Fire."

17. "*Commonwealth of Kentucky v. Anderson Hatfield and others;* Murder Judgment," per Staton, 195, and Thomas, 70. In the *Louisville Courier-Journal* story "Hatfields Arrive," Wall said, "The killing was done on the bridge between Blackberry and Mate's Creek."

18. Spears, "Mountain Feud"; Rice, 27–28; Anderson, 62; Sam McCoy, 67; Jones, 275, n. 11; and Staton, 194. Mutzenberg (42–44), who tended toward outrage and sermonizing, painted a particularly lurid picture: "Around them stands the throng of bloodthirsty white savages, reared in the midst of a Christian country. . . . Not one voice is raised in pity or favor of the victims, an unfortunate man, a youth and a child. The monsters dance about them in imitation of the Indian. They throw guns suddenly into their faces and howl in derision when the thus threatened prisoner dodges." Spears, however, described a sober scene and one of quasi-military discipline. The depression on the banks of the Tug where it is said that the boys were killed is today marked by a roadside historical plaque, though the accuracy of this site has been questioned. Writing in the 1940s, Jones (275, n. 10) noted that the roadwork done there had severely altered the place.

19. Spears, "Mountain Feud."

20. "Plaintiffs Bill of Exceptions."

21. Spears, "Mountain Feud"; Staton, 193; Rice, 28; and Truda McCoy, 90, 308. Billy Anse McCoy would never forget the roar of the firing squad. He would describe it to his son Sailor, who told his daughter Mattie about it, and she repeated it to Charlotte Sanders, who reported it in "Golden Wedding" (a caption) in the *Williamson Daily News* in 1989, more than a century later.

22. Staton, 198.

23. In Mutzenberg (43), the Hatfields act like a ruthless gang: "Alex Messer now approaches closely to Phamer [*sic*] McCoy and deliberately fires six shots into different parts of his body. This is not an act of mercy, to end the man's suffering. No, he has taken care to avoid the infliction of any instantly fatal wound. Messer steps back, views the flowing blood and pain-distorted face and laughs."

24. *Paducah Sun,* "A Relic of Feudism." Others attribute the line to Devil Anse and Crazy Jim Vance, who was not there.

25. Spears, "Mountain Feud"; Mutzenberg, 44; and *Paducah Sun,* "Relic of Feudism." L. D. Hatfield uniquely maintained that Crazy Jim Vance "placed his gun close to the back of his head and fired, blowing out his brains, saying 'A dead man tells no tales' " (24). No other accounts even place Crazy

Jim at the scene. Messer later told a *Paducah Sun* reporter that his alleged murder of Bud McCoy was "false" and "that 'they were all plague gone lies and he knew it,' for he was 'standing within ten feet of the boy' when shot." Other Messer details come from his "Declaration for Pension" and from a Bureau of Pensions questionnaire stamped Apr. 16, 1915.

26. Spears, "Mountain Feud"; *Southwestern Reporter,* 309–10; and Staton, 199. Although the record of Big Jim McCoy's testimony ("Plaintiffs Bill of Exceptions," 4) is somewhat confusing, it indicates that some form of oath was given. "I saw Wall with a paper," Big Jim said, "but do not know what it contained." Big Jim said he "heard Wall in the presence of Doc and Plyant call for signers" and "saw Plyant walk up to Wall." He did not know whether Plyant signed or not.

27. Spears, "Mountain Feud," and Staton, 196.

28. Truda McCoy, 89–90.

29. "Plaintiffs Bill of Exceptions," 4–5; Rice, 28; and Mutzenberg, 46. Elias died in Anse Ferrell's house.

30. Sam McCoy, 67–68.

31. In the fall of 1888, Elias, in answer to questions from journalist Theron Clark Crawford ("An American Vendetta," *New York World*), claimed that, as Crawford put it, "a strong party came up and took possession of the prisoners and went off with them in the darkness, and the guards were in no way responsible." As recently as 2008, in Hatfield and Spence (118–21), Coleman C. Hatfield, Devil Anse's great-grandson and the son of family historian Coleman A. Hatfield, claimed that the schoolteacher Charlie Carpenter, whom the latter called "a convincing mob leader," carried out the "murderous plot." He said that Carpenter, a tall, red-haired teacher in his early forties, captured the imagination of his students by telling them stories about the world beyond their ridgetops (and managed to teach them how to read and write in the process). He exuded guilt, his "large tiger-like" eyes always nervously scanning the distance, shifting rapidly "as if he sensed danger." He kept a .38 tucked under a loose shirt and could "shoot the walnuts out of a tree." Soon afterward, Carpenter crossed the hills toward the south and never returned.

32. Mutzenberg, 46–47; Spears, "Mountain Feud"; "Plaintiffs Bill of Exceptions," 3–4; and Hatfield and Davis, 35–37. Though a number of men would pay a price for the events of this day, no one can now say exactly who was part of the death squad and who was not.

33. As told by Basil Hatfield, son of John Wallace Hatfield, in Charlotte Sanders, "Hatfield Recounts How His Father Hauled the Bodies of Slain Brothers Back to the Home of Ranel McCoy," *Williamson Daily News.*

Chapter 9: Life After Death

1. Spears, "Mountain Feud," and Rice, 28.
2. Spears, "Mountain News Getting."
3. Staton, 128–31. Until recently, these indictments had been lost.
4. Sam Hill, "Report of the Adjutant General of Kentucky"; *Louisville Courier-Journal,* "Hatfields Arrive"; Jones, 59; Rice, 29; Howard, "Descendants of Tolbert McCoy"; Swain, 189; and Velke, 101. While the number of men indicated is generally agreed to be twenty-three, the exact number is no longer known and is sometimes put at twenty or twenty-seven. "I have searched for years for the men actually tried," said Pikeville genealogist Betty Howard. "The courthouse records are gone." Twenty-two names can be found in the evidence and subsequent events.
5. G. Elliott Hatfield, 35, 177, n. 3.
6. Ibid., 71–72; Jones, 276; and Howard, "Descendants of Larkin Smith." The two had no children until 1888. Hatfield and Spence (222–24) said that Nan was the daughter of L. P. Smith of Wayne County, not Rebel Bill Smith.
7. The story of Cap's fight with Reese is told by Crawford ("American Vendetta") and repeated in G. Elliott Hatfield (70–71). In a column of news from around the state, the Jan. 5, 1881, *Louisville Courier-Journal* ran a report from Catlettsburg dated Jan. 4, claiming that "Capt. Hatfield a well known bruiser" was killed in a "scrimmage" on Mate Creek. The report said that more than fifty shots were exchanged by the opposing parties and "a number" were wounded and that the clash was the result of an ongoing vendetta.
8. Jones, 76.
9. Spears, "Mountain Feud," and Hill, "Adjutant General."
10. Jones, 69–70, and Mutzenberg, 50–52.
11. Mutzenberg, 50.
12. Spears, "Mountain Feud," and Mutzenberg, 50–52.
13. Spears, "Mountain Feud." In Truda McCoy's version of this ambush (95–97), the perpetrators are Cap, Elias, and Wall Hatfield; Andy Varney; and Charley Gillespie. As she told it, the three young men were on their way to have corn ground at the mill at the mouth of Blackberry Creek when they were ambushed near a "patch of sumac . . . in the bend of the road about a quarter mile above Randall's house." Her sources were Randall's son Sam's wife, Martha McCoy, who she said was at Randall's house at the time of the ambush, and Bushy Scott, "when he was an old man" (225), in 1921–22, nearly four decades after the event.
14. Spears, "Mountain Feud"; Truda McCoy, 96; and Sam McCoy, 64.
15. Spears, "Mountain Feud," and Mutzenberg, 50–52. According to Sam McCoy (64), upon realizing that they had ambushed the wrong men, the

Hatfields fled, swearing that "if Scott died, which they thought he would for some time, that Randolph's blood should stain the ground."

16. This account comes from Sanders, "Hatfield Recounts." The newspaper mistakenly called Cap's intended target Ryan.

17. Sam McCoy, 64–65, 124, 152–62; Truda McCoy, 316; and Sanders, "'Squirrel Huntin' Sam' McCoy." This episode is unique to McCoy's account. Sam Jr. would be the couple's only child, as America, the first of Sam's four wives, was destined to die young. He would have ten children with his next wife, Vandora. Sam said that Ellison reprimanded Johnse when he aimed his rifle at the McCoys, but given the timing, Ellison would have already been dead. I have put Elias in Ellison's place, as he is the most likely candidate.

Chapter 10: Taking Names and Keeping a List

1. *New York Times*, "Three Desperadoes Trapped." The story ludicrously dubs the three murderers part of the "Hatfield-McCoy gang," as if the two opposing families were one.

2. Donnelly, 16, and Beulah Cantley, *"Uncle Dan, What a Man,"* iv.

3. Bill Wintz, "The Bruen Lands Feud."

4. *New York Herald*, "Murderers Turn Lynchers," and Dan Cunningham, *Memoirs of Daniel W. Cunningham: The Criminal History of Roane and Jackson Counties, West Virginia*, 14.

5. Cunningham, *Memoirs*, 10.

6. The name of the town of Jeffreys was later changed to Kenna.

7. Prichard, 71–72, and Randall Osborne and Jeffrey C. Weaver, *The Virginia State Rangers and State Line*, 201.

8. Cunningham, "Horrible Butcheries," 25, n. 1, and *Memoirs*, 14. See also Wintz.

9. The dialogue here is taken from Samuel Hopkins Adams, "Dan Cunningham: A Huntsman of the Law," *McClure's Magazine*, 216–17. Writing in 1904, Adams had access to Cunningham and his diaries, which are unfortunately now lost. Wade Counts's name is sometimes spelled "Waid" (Shirley Donnelly, *Beckley Post Herald*, "Testifying Was Dangerous Business," and Cunningham, *Memoirs*).

10. Cunningham, "Horrible Butcheries," 25, n. 1.

11. Ibid.; Cunningham, *Memoirs*, 49; George W. Atkinson and Alvaro F. Gibbens, *Prominent Men of West Virginia*, 469; and PoliticalGraveyard.com, "Index to Politicians: Thomas W. Harvey," www.politicalgraveyard.com/bio/harvey .html. Some sources say that Cunningham was made a deputy U.S. marshal in 1884, appointed by Marshal George W. Atkinson. Atkinson, a

successful Internal Revenue agent from 1879 to 1881 who arrested many moonshiners, was appointed a U.S. marshal in 1881 and served until 1885. He was elected to Congress in 1888 and served as governor of West Virginia from 1897 to 1901. Of Cunningham, Ludwell H. Johnson III (in Cunningham, "Horrible Butcheries," 25) wrote, "He returned in 1887 as a Deputy U.S. Marshal dedicated, he tells us, to bringing his brother's killers to justice." This is apparently based on Adams, 217. Johnson (Cunningham, 25, n. 1) said that Cunningham was appointed marshal in 1884. Cunningham wrote, "About one year after Robert Duff's throat was cut at the Lynn Camp School house...I began working for the Government as Deputy U.S. Marshal" (Cunningham, *Memoirs,* 48). This would be in 1888, but all other evidence points to the 1884 date.

12. Adams, 220.

Chapter 11: A Double Whipping

1. Ely, 21, 269–78, 286–87, 326–27, 342–60.

2. Marilynn Marchione, "Disease Underlies Hatfield-McCoy Feud," *Washington Post;* Mary Holley and Ron McCoy (phone interviews with author); Atuk O. Nuzhet et al., "Pheochromocytoma in von Hippel–Lindau Disease," *Journal of Clinical Endocrinology and Metabolism,* 117; and Carole Bartoo, "Genetic Clues to Famous Feud," *Vanderbilt Reporter.* In 2002, scientists at Vanderbilt University isolated a gene that they believe encodes a tendency to violence in those who possess it. Furthermore, they suggested that Randall McCoy might have had the VHLD (von Hippel–Lindau disease) gene.

3. Sanders, "Ollie McCoy," and Deborah McCoy Autry (phone interview, Nov. 3, 2011). Lark's family would later say that he had killed so many men that his conscience bothered him; he could not go to sleep unless a white cloth was put over his eyes. And when one daughter-in-law (who called him a "vile-tempered man") tried to convert him to her brand of Christianity, she said, "he picked up a chair, and I thought he was going to hit me with it." In the end, however, she managed to convert him.

   In more McCoy on McCoy violence, in 1921, the eighty-three-year-old retired county judge John J. McCoy, "the oldest survivor of the McCoy faction," was killed at his home in Martin County, Kentucky, in a knife fight with his cousin Tom McCoy, who cut his throat from ear to ear. *New York Times,* "Kentucky Feudist Is Slain."

4. Sam McCoy, 67–68; Spears, "Mountain Feud"; Truda McCoy, 112; and Staton, 124.

5. Crawford, "American Vendetta," and Spears, "Mountain Feud."

6. Mutzenberg, 50–52; Swain, 189; and Sam McCoy, 63.

7. Hatfield and Spence, 126; Truda McCoy, 120–21, 227, n. 13; Mutzenberg, 52; Donnelly, 18; and Brewster Rawls (interview, Feb. 2, 2012).

8. Mutzenberg, 52–54; Truda McCoy, 227, n. 13; and Hatfield and Spence, 153, 228.

9. Spears, "Mountain Feud"; Donnelly, 17–18. Most histories do not name Wallace's wife but identify her as a sister of Jeff and Nancy McCoy. In Truda McCoy (227, n. 13), the book's editor, Leonard Roberts, wrote that Wallace "is alleged to have forged a marriage license," but he and Victoria Daniels did legitimately marry on Aug. 30, 1886. A record of the marriage, performed by Alex Varney (who, though not ordained, was an accepted and prolific administrator of vows in the valley), is in *Logan County, West Virginia, Marriages, Book 1, 1872–1892* (edited by Donna Brown), albeit somewhat disguised: Wallace is listed as "Walls, Thos," son of Henry and Betty Walls. Staton (149) spelled the name "Wallas" in a Pike County grand jury indictment. He is listed as twenty-five, she as twenty-one, though other records show her to be sixteen. Exactly who Wallace married has often been confused. Donnelly (18), oddly, referred to her as the "Staton girl" and got comically confused when identifying not Wallace but the recently murdered Tom Wolford as the man who lived with her.

10. Spears, "Mountain Feud"; Truda McCoy, 312; and Donnelly, 18.

11. Spears, "Mountain Feud"; Howard, "Descendants of Richard Daniels"; and *Louisville Courier-Journal*, "Hatfields Arrive." Mutzenberg (52–54) said that "the wife and mother of one Daniels were accused of furnishing information to the McCoys" and that "Daniels' [sic] wife was a sister of Jeff McCoy." Thus, it would be Daniels's own mother who was the supreme gossip and his wife who was not much better. In Truda McCoy (227, n. 13), editor Leonard Roberts wrote that Wallace whipped his wife "after he and the other masked men whipped Mary and her mother-in-law," which would mean that there were three adult women in the house, a claim made nowhere else but combining information in various accounts. In reality, the women present were Mary McCoy Daniels and her daughter Victoria (born 1869). Donnelly and Spears both described a home invasion in which only Cap Hatfield and Tom Wallace were involved. Other accounts present them as the ringleaders of a mob, often said to be in disguise but still identified by the women. Some of these accounts maintain that Bill Daniels was away at the time of the attack.

12. *Louisville Courier-Journal*, "Hatfields Arrive"; Staton, 196. Much is made of this cow-tail whip in Hatfield-McCoy lore. Spears wrote that Cap "carried in his hand the tail of a cow, which he cut from an unfortunate brute some

time before, just to see her jump, and had then hung it up and dried it."
Donnelly (18) wrote: "One day the Hatfields killed a cow and the subject of
the way Bill Daniels's wife and girl were gossiping must have come up for
an airing at the butchering. With a stroke of imagination that bordered on
sadistic genius, Cap thought of a useful purpose to which he might put that
cow's tail."

13. *Old Pond Hatfield-McCoy Newsletter*, "Letter from Anderson Hatfield."
According to Donnelly (18), who called this "the outstanding case of cor-
poral punishment suffered by any women [in the feud]," Cap "mortally beat
Mrs. Bill Daniels with the cow's tail." Mutzenberg (52–54) wrote that
"Mrs. Daniels subsequently died from her injuries; the old lady was rendered a cripple for life." But Spears ("Mountain Feud") reported that Mary
"afterward partially recovered" and that Victory "is in good health now."
He noted, however, that Mary's "lungs were affected, and she will probably
die of consumption inside of a year." According to Howard ("Descendants
of Richard Daniels"), Mary Daniels went on to have four more children
from 1889 to 1896.

14. *Logan Banner*, "Devil Anse's Grandson Reminisces."

15. Prichard, 59, and Atkinson, 720–21. The younger John B. Floyd came
from a storied family. His grandfather and uncle were former Virginia governors, and his father, George, had served as the secretary of state for the
territory of Wisconsin before the war and then sold his Virginia estate, in
Burkes Garden, to buy ten square miles of land in Logan County. A coal,
salt, timber, and iron magnate, George had served as a colonel in the Confederacy. Using his mines as hideouts, his men were able to make raids and
then vanish underground again. George Floyd was also a mentor to Elias
Hatfield's son Henry, the future fourteenth governor of West Virginia.

16. G. Elliott Hatfield, 69, 72–73, and Swain, 95–96, 113. In 1852, Mayor
Thomas Dunn English engineered the change of the town's name from
Lawnsville to Aracoma, but it was the Logan County seat and home of the
county courthouse, so most people continued to refer to it as Logan Courthouse. The town incorporated in 1884 and changed its name to Logan in
1907.

17. John L. Spivak Papers.

18. Mutzenberg, 52–54; Swain, 189; and Spears, "Mountain Feud." Naturally,
the McCoys had a different version of events. According to them, after the
attack on the Daniels women, Devil Anse saw Jeff McCoy, who had not taken
part in the feud, on a road and greeted him cordially. He was apologetic about
the beating, which had been well publicized, and lamented the fact that Cap
was causing trouble. Understanding that amends needed to be made, he

offered up Wallace. Jeff agreed to come get Wallace to take him to the Pikeville jail. But, according to this account, Devil Anse was double-crossing
Jeff. The meeting, which took place at Johnse's house on Grapevine Creek,
was a trap. Jeff was seized, handed over to Wallace, and taken down the
creek to Cap's place on the Tug. "It is said that Cap nearly laughed himself sick
when he saw Jeff driven into his yard and learned how neatly the old man had
worked on the unsophisticated mind of McCoy," wrote Spears. Cap got his
rifle and told Wallace to drive Jeff down the road until he was opposite the
Daniels cabin, where they could shoot him in front of his sister.

19. Jones, 77; Donnelly, 27; and Hatfield and Spence, 221, 225.

20. Spears, "Mountain Feud"; Jones, 78; and Mutzenberg, 54–55. Hurley, who
either escaped in the hubbub or was released after the killing, was of little
interest to Cap and Wallace.

21. Spears, "Mountain Feud"; Mutzenberg, 52–56; and Swain, 189–90. While
most accounts said that Cap killed Jeff McCoy, Cap denied it, and Donnelly (27) noted that "whether it was Tom Wallace's gun or Cap Hatfield's —
no one knows." Several houses still exist near the junction of Thacker
Creek and the Tug Fork, and I can attest to the continuing ferocity of the
neighborhood. In the spring of 2010, the day before the annual Hatfield-
McCoy reunion, two forest rangers, Craig Kadcravek and Terry Elkins,
helped me and my daughter Hazel, who was assisting me in my research,
find this spot. We parked Terry's SUV off a dirt road beside train tracks
and bushwhacked down an overgrown path to the river's edge and out onto
the silty delta of the creek mouth. Soon two riders on an ATV were peer-
ing at us from the riverbank, far enough away to be out of hailing distance
but close enough for them to get a good look at us. They drove to a collection of houses upriver. Pretty soon a hidden marksman began firing a pistol
into the water dangerously close to us. The salvo — at least half a dozen
shots — was more than enough to make a point.

22. *Old Pond Hatfield-McCoy Newsletter*, "Letter from Devil Anse to P. A. Cline,"
and Hatfield and Spence, 127.

Chapter 12: The Enforcers

1. Index to Order Books, County Court, Pike County, Kentucky; G. Elliott
Hatfield, 79; *Louisville Courier-Journal*, "Back to Pikeville"; L. D. Hatfield,
35; and Spears, "Mountain Feud." Many accounts call Cline the Pike
County prosecuting attorney, but this is incorrect.

2. Waller, 41–46, and "Last Will and Testament of Jacob Cline," Cline Family
website, www.clinefamilyassociation.com/will_of_jacob_rich_jake_cline.

3. John Ed Pearce, *Days of Darkness: The Feuds of Eastern Kentucky*, 22.

Considered a humane man, Governor Blackburn (who served from 1879 to 1883) nonetheless stood accused of one of the more nefarious plots of the Civil War, an attempt to infect President Lincoln and start a yellow fever pandemic in the North using the clothes of yellow fever victims. Though the plot was never proven, much evidence confirmed its existence. In any case, it would have failed because yellow fever can be spread only by mosquitoes. National Park Service, "Fort Donelson: The Battle," www.nps .gov/fodo/planyourvisit/the battleforfortdonelson.htm.

4. Mutzenberg, 56–60, and Swain, 190. Knott served as Kentucky's twenty-ninth governor, from Sept. 1883 to Aug. 1887.

5. Spears, "Mountain Feud"; Swain, 190; Jones, 75–78; Hatfield and Spence, 128; Pearce, 66; G. Elliott Hatfield, 74–75; and Truda McCoy, 227, n. 13. Some say it was Jake and Lark who caught Tom Wallace, but both Mutzenberg (52–56) and Spears said it was Jake and Bud, not Lark. Sink resigned as deputy sheriff soon after but passed the bar the next year.

6. Donnelly, 27, and Jones, 157. Some say Lark McCoy killed Wallace. Others say Wallace lived to a ripe old age and fathered his last child in 1921.

7. Thomas, 59.

8. *New York Times,* "Vigilantes Take a Hand Disposing of a Band of Murderous Robbers," and Adams, 217, 220. Adams said that Cunningham returned as a deputy U.S. marshal; however, in *Memoirs,* Cunningham indicated that this occurred later. *New York Times,* "A Gang of Murderers."

9. Atkinson, 915–18. Alf Burnett was born July 9, 1850.

10. Adams, 217, and *Charleston Daily Mail,* "Death Ends Eventful Career of 'Uncle Dan' Cunningham."

11. Robert was the son of Cunningham's sister Keziah, who was twelve years Dan's senior and had married George H. Duff in 1856. Their sister Caroline also married a Duff, George's brother Isaac, in 1861.

12. Cunningham, *Memoirs,* 38.

13. Arndt Stickles, *Simon Bolivar Buckner: Borderland Knight,* 165–70, 186–90, 346, 353–75.

14. Jones, 84.

15. Ibid., 84–85; Mutzenberg, 79–80; Pearce, 66; and Spears, "Mountain Feud." Spears wrote that "Governor Buckner offered five hundred dollars each, for Bad Anse, Cap, and Johnse Hatfield, Tom Mitchell (under the name of Chambers), and Tom Wallace." Jones (85) said only that a five-hundred-dollar reward was offered for Devil Anse. According to Mutzenberg, Buckner wrote in a Jan. 30, 1888, letter to Wilson that he "offered suitable rewards for four of the number, represented as being the leaders of the party and most responsible for their conduct."

16. *New York Times,* "Vigilantes Take a Hand."
17. Ibid.; James P. Mylott, *A Measure of Prosperity: A History of Roane County,* 52–55. Mylott said it was a "forty-four caliber pistol," but the fact that it was a Winchester plays a continuing part in Cunningham's version of events.
18. Cunningham, *Memoirs,* 35–37. According to the *New York Times* ("Vigilantes Take a Hand"), Coon was from Tyler, Texas, and called himself Jesse James.
19. Adams, 218–19, and Cunningham, *Memoirs,* 48.

Chapter 13: Diplomacy Failed

1. Hatfield and Spence, 294, 297.
2. Creelman, "Bloody Border War."
3. Tom Atkins, "Franklin Phillips—No Outlaw," *Old Pond Hatfield-McCoy Newsletter,* 43–47.
4. Ely, 45–55; Prichard, 60, 69; and Baker and Hall, "Organization and History." Dils adamantly denied any wrongdoing and, it is said, was in Washington, DC, pursuing an audience with Lincoln in order to plead his case when the president was assassinated.
5. Pearce, 66; Mutzenberg, 56–60; Hill; Spears, "A Mountain Feud"; Atkins, "Franklin Phillips," 48, and Swain, 190. One account claimed that Phillips's first marriage was annulled because he and his wife were first cousins, but this seems unlikely. After the Civil War, first-cousin marriage became increasingly frowned upon, based on the (still controversial) theory that it affects the health of offspring. However, Kentucky was not among the thirteen states and territories that had passed prohibitions against first-cousin marriage by the 1880s, and it would not do so until 1943.
6. Mutzenberg, 74, 79, from Jan. 30, 1888, letter from Buckner to Wilson; Crawford, *American Vendetta,* 26–27; Jones, 84–86; and Pearce, 66.
7. Spears, "Mountain Feud"; Mutzenberg, 56–60; and Swain, 191.
8. From Transcripts of Records, U.S. Supreme Court, 1887, as recorded in Jones, 86–87. Spellings per the original source.
9. Jones, 88–89.
10. Mutzenberg, 80. Many variant accounts of the sequence of arrests exist. Reporting in 1888, Spears ("Mountain Feud") said that Tom Chambers's house was raided on Dec. 9 and that Selkirk McCoy and Mose Christian were taken on Dec. 20. I have used this account, despite the fact that Jones (88) said that Selkirk McCoy was put in prison on Dec. 12, and cited the courthouse records; they do not, however, mention Mose Christian, who was captured with Selkirk. To give yet another report, Governor Buckner said in a Jan. 30 letter to Governor Wilson—based on adjutant general

Sam Hill's investigation, also in 1888—that in "the latter part of Dec. (1887), Frank Phillips . . . having sent the required fee, and being unable to hear anything from your Excellency, went into West Virginia in company with two others, and . . . succeeded in capturing Tom Chambers, Selkirk McCoy and Mose Christian."

11. Jones (88), though he said the prisoner was Selkirk McCoy, not Tom Chambers. Sanders, "'Squirrel Huntin' Sam' McCoy" Phillips letter from Jones (89), who cited the original in the West Virginia State Archives, in Charleston, but as of Oct. 2011, archivists could not locate the letter. Spelling per the original. Also, Pearce, 66–67.

12. Spears, "Mountain Feud," and Pearce, 66.

13. *Wheeling Intelligencer,* "New Developments in the Hatfield-M'Coy Feud."

14. Based on Hill, "Adjutant General"; Mutzenberg, 60–61; and Spears, "Mountain Feud."

15. Spears, "Mountain Feud"; Jones, 90–91; Pearce, 66–67; and Logan County Courthouse Law Order Book B, 471.

16. Jones, 91–92.

17. John R. Spears, "Murderous Mountaineers," *New York Sun.*

18. Coleman A. Hatfield, as quoted in Hatfield and Spence, 125, 166–68. Elsewhere Elias comes across as reluctant to be involved in the feud, as when Anse has to use threats to get Elias to join him to take back Johnse from the McCoys after his capture. However, Coleman A. Hatfield argued that it was Elias who now "rekindled the smoldering feud fires."

19. "Confession of Ellison Mounts," Nov. 5, 1888.

20. Ibid., and *Weston Democrat,* "The Hatfield-McCoy Vendetta."

21. Hatfield and Spence, 164–66, 169, and Anderson, 145. When Jim Vance was about fifteen, his family "lost tremendous tracts of land," according to Margaret Hatfield (interview transcript, 4). Vance "didn't own land until he was up in his sixties, 'til Devil Anse took the Grapevine Tract back from Perry Cline and his associates. . . . Jim Vance was an old, bitter man, and he blamed the Clines and the McCoys for the loss of all that land and he was determined to make them pay for every rock, clod, and gravel, and every deer."

22. Sam McCoy, 68–69; Mutzenberg, 60–61; Pearce, 67; and Hatfield and Spence, 169.

Chapter 14: A House Burning

1. *Louisville Courier-Journal,* "The Beautiful."

2. Hatfield and Spence, 169. No two versions of the most infamous event of the feud are exactly alike. As recently as 2003, new details appeared about the ill-fated house raid. According to Coleman C. Hatfield, who got it from

his father, Coleman, who got it from Cap, the raid was originally attempted on New Year's Eve.

3. Anderson, 138–40. Her uncle John Vance once got into a dispute over a woman in Sugar Hill, Kentucky, and was beaten with a fire poker by two men. His brother Homer shot them, killing one, and then for good measure shot the woman they were arguing over in the face. She lived, but he had blasted out all of her teeth. The brothers each got twenty-one years in prison for the murder.

4. Hatfield and Spence, 169.

5. Crawford, *American Vendetta*, 179–80.

6. G. Elliott Hatfield, 180; "Confession of Ellison Mounts"; Crawford, *American Vendetta*, 57–58; and Howard, "Descendants of French Ellis."

7. Crawford, *American Vendetta*, 180; Pearce, 67–68; Spears, "Mountain Feud"; Jones, 95; Hill; and Waller, 79, 253. In Truda McCoy (228–29, n. 15), editor Leonard Roberts noted that most sources list nine or ten participants in the raiding party. Only Truda, who said there were fifteen, included Devil Anse. Roberts noted that Donnelly, who listed nine names, interviewed a woman who lived in the valley above Randall's house and whose mother had lived there at the time of the raid and watched the mysterious party return under a full moon; she counted fourteen. According to Roberts, Charley Gillespie, who was the first to be caught, named everyone involved, "10 including himself." However, according to Crawford's transcription of Gillespie's confession (180), he actually said, "There were just nine of us." Spears identified Elliott Hatfield as a son of Ellison, and Bob as a son of Cap. In Crawford, Gillespie named "Ellis," as if he were a Hatfield, but Spears said it was French Ellis, while another source said it was his cousin Doc Ellis.

8. Crawford, *American Vendetta*, 180.

9. "Confession of Ellison Mounts."

10. Ibid., and Staton, 160. See Gillespie's confession in Crawford, *American Vendetta*, 179–85. Though Gillespie claimed that he and Indian were stationed on the road as guards and "never went near the house until the house was burning and all was on their way back to Hatfields [*sic*] house," he nonetheless gave legal authorities a thorough description of the assault on the house. He claimed that his account came from Cotton Top Mounts, with whom he shared a horse on the way back, but by that point, Cotton Top was losing consciousness from his wounds.

11. Staton, 159; Hill, "Adjutant General"; Spears, "Mountain Feud"; and Truda McCoy, 141.

12. "Confession of Ellison Mounts"; Jones, 98; Crawford, *American Vendetta*,

179–85; Spears, "Mountain Feud"; and Mutzenberg, 62–63. Spellings of the name of McCoy's daughter Alifair abound: "Alafair" (Staton); "Alfaro" (Crawford); "Allaphare" (Spears); "Allifair" (Mutzenberg, Jones); "Alifair" (Truda McCoy; Waller); "Alifaire" (L. D. Hatfield).

13. Spears, "Mountain Feud." L. D. Hatfield uniquely claimed that Alifair "was taken for Bud and killed" (34–35), but Bud was already dead. Perhaps he meant Bill; however, Bill was either dead or had been sent into hiding out west.

14. *Louisville Courier-Journal*, "Death by Law"; Crawford, *American Vendetta*, 184; and Truda McCoy, 113.

15. Truda McCoy, 228–29, n. 15, and "Confession of Ellison Mounts." Cotton Top, who was also known as Big Man, confessed to the shooting, but whether he or Cap actually fired the fatal shot remains a matter of dispute. According to Truda, Melvin said that "all the McCoys said that Cap Hatfield killed Alifair." Cotton Top called the sister Addie. In his Oct. 29 confession, he said, "Addie asked her if she were killed; her only answer was one word, 'Yes.'" In his Nov. 5 confession, he said, "I heard her sister ask her if she was dead. She muttered something, but I could not understand it, but the other sister said, 'Farewell, Alifair.'"

16. Spears, "Mountain Feud"; Crawford, *American Vendetta*, 182; Truda McCoy, 228–29, n. 15; and Donnelly, 11. Mitchell bound his hand up and returned to the fight, aiming and firing his Winchester with one hand. Cap found great mirth in Guerilla's loss of fingers and the fact that he cried "like a baby over the loss."

17. Spears, "Mountain Feud," and *Weston Democrat*, "Hatfield-McCoy Vendetta."

18. *Louisville Courier-Journal*, "Death by Law"; Spears, "Mountain Feud"; and Hill.

19. Crawford, *American Vendetta*, 183; Spears, "Mountain Feud"; Mutzenberg, 63–65; and Hill. Coleman C. Hatfield claimed that most of the action—"the shots that wounded the Hatfield party, Randal McCoy's escape . . . and the killing of Calvin and Allifair" (Hatfield and Davis, 170)—took place in under a minute. *Weston Democrat*, "Hatfield-McCoy Vendetta."

20. *Weston Democrat*, "Hatfield-McCoy Vendetta," and "Confession of Ellison Mounts."

21. Crawford, *American Vendetta*, 183–88. Many versions of their parting depredations would later appear in print. Adjutant general Sam Hill reported that before they left the burning house, the gang closed what little remained of the door shutters that had not been shot away, "with the evident purpose of burning the remaining members of the family." Mutzenberg (66) wrote: "The insensible mother they had dragged back into one of the rooms, that she, too, might perish by fire."

Chapter 15: The Death of a Soldier

1. The granddaughters found the manuscript, and in 1993 they printed a small batch of books for a family reunion, bringing lost feud details back to light. In 2011, I bought the last copy of the paperback version that a Google search could produce. A WorldCat search shows seven copies in libraries.

2. Staton, 159–61, and Spears, "Mountain Feud." These graves, on property now owned by John Vance, a descendant of Jim Vance, are marked by old headstones and a monument erected by McCoy descendants in 1975. According to Vance, the grave sites were moved when the road behind his house was built, in 1959. "The first road was built in 1959. There is a coal mine on the level where my garden is, that was mined in 1959. The mine is still open on the one side after all these years," Vance wrote to me in an e-mail on Sept. 12, 2012. "The monument was placed in 1975, I was told by several older neighbors that when they hunted on the property that there were no indications of a graveyard being here. The property was surveyed in 1957 and the graves are marked in a different place than they are now. My thoughts are that when the monument was placed they put the rocks where they wanted them."

3. Spears, "Mountain Feud."

4. *Louisville Courier-Journal*, "A Murderous Gang," and Mutzenberg, 67–68.

5. *Wheeling Intelligencer*, "A Terrible Story of a Family Feud and Murder," and Mutzenberg, 67. "It seemed," wrote Mutzenberg, who tended toward sanctimony, "beyond the possibility of belief that such horrors could occur in our day of enlightenment, in a land which boasts of a superior civilization and culture."

6. *Welch Daily News*, "Hatfield Heirloom Warms," and Sam McCoy, 79.

7. Sam McCoy (72) and Mutzenberg (68–69) cast Phillips as a hero, having a "superiority of cunning and courage." Spears ("Mountain Feud"), by contrast, called him a "cool-headed desperado."

8. Sam McCoy, 76; Mutzenberg, 81; and Howard, "Descendants of Elliott 'Doc' Rutherford." Bud Rutherford is sometimes called Ben. Hill and Swain (193) gave Jan. 8 as the date Phillips crossed the Tug.

9. Sam McCoy, 73–74.

10. *Wheeling Register*, "Outlawry: The Story of the Border War in Logan County"; Spears, "Mountain Feud"; Mutzenberg, 69; and Sam McCoy, 73–74. Sam gave a different version of what went on at the Vance cabin.

11. "Confession of Ellison Mounts," and *Weston Democrat*, "Hatfield-McCoy Vendetta."

12. Mutzenberg, 69; L. D. Hatfield, 31–32; Spears, "Mountain Feud"; and Swain, 192. Some, like Spears, say that instead of leading the men over the

hill, Mary Vance had just gone from the house to a hideout on the mountain to deliver breakfast to her husband and maybe others and that she was carrying an empty pail, which made her mission obvious.

13. Spears, "Mountain Feud," and Sam McCoy, 75, 164.

14. Spears, "Mountain Feud"; *Louisville Courier-Journal*, "Hatfields Arrive"; Sam McCoy, 75–76; Swain, 192; and Mutzenberg, 70. Spears said that Cap made a run for it without firing a shot. Swain said that Cap and Jim held the attackers at bay "for several minutes" until "a flanking movement . . . enabled one of them to shoot Vance . . . and the latter advised Cap to make his escape."

15. In Oct. 2010, Scotty May and Alvin Harmon, descendants of Ellison Hatfield, took me up to what is now known as Devil Anse rock. We talked to Elmer Hatfield and then rode ATVs up a narrow trail so steep that at one point we reared back dangerously on two wheels. Examining the boulder, we saw chinks that might have come from bullets and that are now filled with moss. And we saw initials carved into the rock. May and Harmon told me that there used to be just *D.A.*, but a cousin later added an *H*.

16. Spears, "Mountain Feud."

17. Sam McCoy, 75. According to Squirrel Huntin' Sam, Mose Maynard and Dave Plymale hit him three times in the hip.

18. Sam McCoy, 75–76; Thomas Henshaw, *The History of Winchester Firearms, 1866–1992*, 30–32; and Jim Supica, "A Brief History of Firearms," National Firearms Museum.

19. *Wheeling Intelligencer,* "Devil Anse Tells the True History"; Spears, "Mountain Feud"; and Sam McCoy, 76. Spears noted that Crazy Jim "had been neither a faithful nor a kind husband" and in "Murderous Mountaineers," he said that after his killing, his wife, Mary, in reference to the mistress he had brought home, lamented: "Poor old man: he's dead now. If it hadn't been for a woman he'd have been alive yet, and so would Allifair, I reckon." Mutzenberg had only disdain for the "dying desperado" who'd given "the heartless order to Ellison Mounts to shoot the innocent Alifair" and "incited Cap to the burning of the McCoy home" (71). In L. D. Hatfield's 1945 account (32), which he claimed derived from "reliable sources" and was not a "reflection on either side," the McCoys approached wounded Jim Vance and—here Hatfield allegedly quotes Devil Anse—"shot his brains out." Then, he continued with a flourish, "Bud McCoy took some of Vance's brains on his finger and polished his boots with them and then licked his finger." While newspaper journalists would take the blame for sensationalizing the feud, family members did their part as well.

20. Spears, "Mountain Feud"; Mutzenberg, 70; and L. D. Hatfield, 32–33. Swain (192) said Cap "fled across mountain ranges until he had reached the

Hatfield fortress at the mouth of Huff's Creek." Wrote Anderson (140), "Very few know the exact place he was buried." This Jim Vance is not buried in Snake Hollow, where a number of Vances rest in a hidden hillside cemetery that contains an aged stone marked J VANCE. In June 2012, I was able to locate Vance's grave (GPS coordinates: N37°36.506 W82°05.340) with the help of locals Scotty May and Dean May.

21. Jones, 109–10; Spears, "Mountain Feud"; and Sanders, "Beautiful Beech Creek Valley." G. Elliott Hatfield (211) spelled it "Doc." The Hatfields would claim that Wall, confident in his innocence, had written to Jim McCoy and Frank Phillips offering himself and his two sons-in-law up for arrest and telling them that they were willing to come to Pikeville to be tried.

22. Spears, "Mountain Feud"; Sam McCoy, 72–73; G. Elliott Hatfield, 211.

23. Hill and Mahon v. Justice, "Statement of the Case."

24. Jones, 108; New York Times, "A Deadly Inter-State Feud."

25. Louisville Courier-Journal, "Prospects for a Rise."

26. Buckner's letter to Wilson, Jan. 30, 1888, in Mutzenberg, 74–83.

27. Wheeling Register, "Outlawry."

Chapter 16: Bad Frank and the Battle of Grapevine Creek

1. Louisville Courier-Journal, "Two Sides to a Story," and Wheeling Intelligencer, "The Seat of War."

2. Spears, "Mountain Feud"; Sam McCoy, 68, 77–79; and Louisville Courier-Journal, "The Legislature." According to Governor Buckner's letter of Jan. 22, 1888, to Governor Wilson (Mutzenberg, 82) and to the Louisville Courier-Journal ("Hatfields Arrive"), the number of men with Phillips was eighteen. Truda McCoy (173) said that number was twenty-four. The murder indictment resulting from the raid included twenty-eight names. Truda McCoy named Ben Rutherford, but according to Howard in "Descendants of Reuben Rutherford, Sr.," this should be Bud. Also among them were George McCoy, Will Thompson (Trinnie McCoy's husband), Burbage King, and Dave Stratton. Whether or not Squirrel Huntin' Sam was along is hard to say. While his memoir usually depicted him at the forefront of the action and included quirky personal observations, Sam was cagey here, uncharacteristically terse and distant, suggesting that he was not present. However, men involved in murder may understandably be less than forthcoming. The murder indictments that resulted from the raid would include him.

3. Wheeling Register, "Border Vendetta"; Spears, "Mountain Feud"; Jones, 107–8; G. Elliott Hatfield, 135–36; and Logan Banner, "Last Survivor of Hatfield-McCoy Feud Tells of Battle of Grapevine Creek." According to Governor Buckner's Jan. 22 letter (Mutzenberg, 82) and to the Louisville

Courier-Journal ("Hatfields Arrive"), there were twelve Hatfields present, including Cap and Devil Anse. Truda McCoy (174) listed nine: those two and Bill Dempsey; Lee White; Charley Gillespie; Tom Mitchell; French Ellis; and, most notably, Johnse Hatfield, who had probably already set out for Colorado, and Jim Vance, who was, in fact, already dead. The *Wheeling Intelligencer* ("Seat of War," from a correspondent in Catlettsburg, Kentucky) would go against its statesmen and accuse these men of "organizing for a raid over on Peter Creek, in Kentucky, the scene of their New Year's night deeds, to murder people, burn property and kill stock."

4. Spears, "Mountain Feud." Harrison told his story to the *Logan Banner* ("Last Survivor") at the age of ninety-one. He confused some details, placing Jim Vance, who was already dead, at the scene (as did Truda McCoy) and conflating his death with the events of this day. He reported that Devil Anse was there, and so did Governor Buckner in his Jan. 22 letter to Governor Wilson. The Appalachian practice of passing out moonshine even at a time when you need your wits about you continues. While researching in the area, I was offered a tot before heading up a dangerous ridge on an ATV.

5. *Wheeling Intelligencer,* "Seat of War."

6. Spears, "Murderous Mountaineers," "Mountain News Getting," and "The Story of a Mountain Feud" (*Munsey's Magazine*), 508; Mutzenberg, 72–73; Sam McCoy, 77; *Louisville Courier-Journal,* "Bloody War in Pike County"; and Truda McCoy, 173. In Hill's report to Governor Buckner ("Adjutant General"), he stated that "Phillips and party . . . were again fired upon (without warning this time); and in the fight which ensued, one Dempsey, of the Hatfield party, was killed, and Bud McCoy, of the Phillips party, was severely wounded."

7. Jones, 278, n. 4, and Howard, "Descendants of Larkin Smith."

8. Mutzenberg, 73. This contradicts his earlier statement that "at this time, the heavy repeating Winchester rifle had come into general use. While other modern inventions found no market there, the most improved guns and pistols might have been found in homes that had not learned the use of a cook stove" (54).

9. Coleman A. Hatfield in Hatfield and Spence, 178.

10. While Spears ("Mountain Feud") said Dempsey was shot "through the body," most accounts say he was shot in the leg.

11. *Louisville Courier-Journal,* "Pike County's Troubles"; Spears, "Mountain Feud"; *National Police Gazette,* "He Held Life Cheaply"; Mutzenberg, 72–73; Jones, 107; and G. Elliott Hatfield, 180, n. 4. Spears, whose version was a source in the *National Police Gazette* article and elsewhere, repeated the theme that Cap left garb after fleeing. L. D. Hatfield (33) said: "Dempsey was lying on the

ground in a semi-conscious condition when Jim McCoy and Frank Phillips approached him. He thought it was some of his own friends and asked for a drink of water and Frank Phillips said, 'I'll give you water,' whereupon he raised his rifle and shot Dempsey in the head, killing him instantly."

12. Truda McCoy, 177.

13. *National Police Gazette,* "He Held Life Cheaply"; Spears, "Mountain Feud"; Mutzenberg, 73; and Swain, 192–93, who called this "the last serious fight between these two factions." According to Charlie Harrison, the Hatfields hid out in the woods for several hours. Then Devil Anse asked who wanted to cross the gap to see if it was safe to come down. It was quiet. Harrison said he would go. "Leave your gun here," Devil Anse told him. "If you're captured with a gun, they'll hang you sure." Harrison had full confidence in Devil Anse, as he later explained: "I doubt if the bravery of Devil Anse has ever been surpassed. Though he was a careful and deliberate thinker, he would fight a mountain lion. He was a smart man and hard to fool." Still, Harrison said he would take his gun just the same. "When I reach the ridge on the other side, I'll hoot like a horned owl, and you'll know it's safe to come across the gap." *Logan Banner,* "Last Survivor."

14. Hatfield and Spence, 178–79, and Jones, 108, 111.

15. Mutzenberg, 73; Hatfield and Spence, 179–80; and *Wheeling Intelligencer,* "New Developments in the Hatfield-M'Coy Feud."

16. Spears, "Mountain Feud"; Waller, 198–99; and *Louisville Courier-Journal,* "Hatfields Arrive."

17. Crawford, *American Vendetta,* 77–79.

18. The original of this arrest warrant is in the papers of Governor Simon Buckner in the Archives Research Room, Hatfield and McCoy Feud reference file. Nancy C. Hatfield and Richard Blankenship joined Thompson in making the complaint. John Phillips was also among those indicated for the murder of Bill Dempsey; he was either Frank's brother or his uncle. (He had both an uncle and a brother by that name.) Sam McCoy (68) said that the brother had no part in the Hatfield-McCoy "troubles."

19. Sam McCoy, 79.

20. *Louisville Courier-Journal,* "No Troops for Pike" and "The Legislature," which concludes: "From the best advices received here, the man who fired that shot was Sheriff Phillips, of Pike County, who, strange to say, is related by blood to the Hatfields, whom he is now making war to the death upon."

21. *Louisville Courier-Journal,* "Contest of the States."

22. *Wheeling Intelligencer,* "The New York *World,*" and *Louisville Courier-Journal,* "No Troops for Pike."

23. *Wheeling Intelligencer,* "The War Is Over."

24. *Louisville Courier-Journal,* "Peace Reigns in Pike" and "Innocents at Home."

25. *Louisville Courier-Journal,* "Peace Reigns in Pike," and Ely, 61.

26. Governor Buckner's letter to Governor Wilson of Jan. 30, 1888, as reproduced in Mutzenberg, 75–76. According to *Mahon v. Justice,* "Statement of the Case": On Jan. 30, Wilson informed Buckner that he declined to issue his warrant for the arrest of Plyant Mahon in compliance with the requisition made upon him because he had become satisfied, upon investigation of the facts, that Mahon was not guilty of the crime he was charged with in the indictments. On Feb. 1, Wilson demanded that Buckner release Mahon from the Pike County jail and grant him safe conduct back to West Virginia. Buckner declined to comply on the ground that Mahon was in the custody of the judicial department of the commonwealth and that the question of his release on the grounds alleged in the demand was one that the courts alone could determine, and was not within the purview of his powers as governor.

27. *Cincinnati Enquirer,* "Still Buying Winchesters," and *Louisville Courier-Journal,* "Pike County's Troubles."

28. Hill; *Louisville Courier-Journal,* "Two Sides to a Story"; and *Wheeling Intelligencer,* "The Vendetta."

29. Mutzenberg, 77–78.

30. Ibid., 82–83.

31. *Louisville Courier-Journal,* "Hatfield-McCoy Mess." The article named Tom Chambers, Andy Varney, Selkirk and L. D. McCoy, Mose Christian, David Mahon, D. D. Mahon, and Plyant Mahon. Jones (109, 278, n. 6) noted that there was confusion over the arrest of Tom "Guerilla" Mitchell, alias Tom Chambers, apparently unaware that it was his stepfather, Tom Chambers, who had mistakenly been arrested and jailed in Pikeville.

32. *Wheeling Intelligencer,* "The Hatfild [*sic*] M'Coy Feud." The *Intelligencer* called Mahon "Mahan." Ely (61) referred to the "Big Sandy Criminal Court."

33. *Louisville Courier-Journal,* "Two Sides to a Story," and Hill (see Kentucky Documents 1888 for complete correspondence). Hill missed a few other essentials too, dating the start of the feud to Devil Anse's interception of Tolbert McCoy as he was carrying Johnse to jail. He did not mention the romance between Johnse and Roseanna or speculate on Tolbert's motivations for arresting Johnse. He maintained that this confrontation led to the Election Day fight of 1882 (which, he reported, "'Big' Ellison Hatfield . . . provoked") and thus the death of Ellison and the murders of the McCoy brothers. Hill described the murder of the boy Bud, blaming it on Devil Anse. Hill was clearly charmed by Wall, saying, "I think if Anson Hatfield and his two boys were brought to justice that would be an end to it"—the exact case that Wall was making for himself. Five days later, the state sen-

ate passed a resolution requiring Buckner to turn over his official correspondence with Governor Wilson as well as the report from Hill.

34. Like Kentucky, West Virginia braced for a border war with a certain evident pride. "The difficulty grows out of an old war feud, the Hatfields being Confederates and the McCoys Unionists," noted the *Huntington Advertiser* ("It Is to Be Hoped That the Deplorable Necessity for Sending Troops . . . "). "The people of this State will sustain Governor Wilson in his determination to protect the lives and property of our citizens from the assaults of Kentucky desperadoes. The prompt and gallant action of many of the military companies offering their services to settle the disturbance is a matter of pride and gratification."

Chapter 17: Disorder in the Courts

1. *Louisville Courier-Journal,* "Signs of Enterprise."
2. A major front-page story covering the event appeared in the *Louisville Courier-Journal* on the morning of Friday, Feb. 17, 1888 ("Hatfields Arrive"), and included photos and drawings of the mountaineer captives.
3. Mose Christian was the grandson of Perry Cline's aunt Margaret Cline Mounts.
4. Index to Order Books, County Court, Pike County, Kentucky, 181.
5. The reporter gave Randall McCoy's age as fifty-five. In fact, he was sixty-three. *Louisville Courier-Journal,* "Hatfields Arrive."
6. *Louisville Courier-Journal,* "Hatfields Arrive," and Ely, 332.
7. *Louisville Courier-Journal,* "Enjoying Prison Life."
8. *Wheeling Intelligencer,* "The Inter-State War."
9. Ibid., "Eustace Gibson's Mission" and "West Virginia Wins," and *Louisville Courier-Journal,* "Wants Her Citizens."
10. Jones, 129, and *Louisville Courier-Journal,* "Holcombe at the Jail."
11. Although West Virginia argued this, it is not strictly true, since Jim Vance was not wanted in the murder of the three McCoy brothers and was not known to be involved in the raid on the Randall McCoy house until after he was killed.
12. *Louisville Courier-Journal,* "In Favor of Kentucky."
13. *Wheeling Intelligencer,* "Kentucky Is Winner."
14. Spears, "Mountain Feud"; G. Elliott Hatfield, 180–81; Waller, 198–99; and *Louisville Courier-Journal,* "Hatfields Arrive."
15. *Louisville Courier-Journal,* "Back to Pikeville."
16. Ibid., "Hatfields Arrive."
17. Ibid., "Back to Pikeville."
18. Spears, "Mountain Feud."

19. Jones, 145.
20. *Wheeling Intelligencer,* "Argument Begun in the Famous Hatfield-McCoy Cases in the United States Supreme Court."
21. The decision and dissent are adapted from the original, which can be found in its entirety at www.supreme.justia.com/us/127/700/case.html; *Wheeling Intelligencer,* "The Hatfield-M'Coy Case."
22. *Mahon v. Justice* and Kathryn Selleck, "Jurisdiction After International Kidnapping: A Comparative Study," *Boston College International and Comparative Law Review,* 249–50. In the landmark 1829 case *Ex Parte Scott,* Susannah Scott, wanted in England for perjury, was arrested in Brussels by an English police officer and carried to England. Scott argued that the English court did not have jurisdiction to try her because she had been illegally arrested and wrongly brought into the country. The court ruled that it could not consider the circumstances of her arrival in the jurisdiction, saying only that if Belgian law gave Scott a cause for a grievance, she could pursue it there, but that this circumstance would not affect the English court's jurisdiction over Scott.

Chapter 18: The Lawmen

1. *Louisville Courier-Journal,* "Middleton's Murder," "A Boy Resents an Insult to His Mother," "A Very Bad Man," and "Shot to Pieces."
2. Atkinson, 915–18, and Velke, 3. Burnett's partners in the Eureka Detectives were William Baldwin, Tom A. Campbell, I. Hammond, and W. J. Hotchkiss. The partners all listed their place of residence as Charleston, except for Campbell, who hailed from Wellston, Ohio.
3. Mutzenberg, 93; Atkinson, 915; Velke, 3, 43–44, 51–53, 105; and *Acts of the Legislature of West Virginia at the Nineteenth Regular Session Commencing Jan. 9, 1889.* G. Elliott Hatfield made mistakes when writing about the detectives, placing the Eureka detectives in competition with Dan Cunningham, whom he called a Baldwin-Felts detective. Thomas Felts would not become a partner of William Baldwin's until 1900, and the name of the agency, Baldwin's Detectives, would not incorporate Felts's name until 1910. Baldwin, who worked at Eureka beginning in 1885, later established an agency in Virginia and hired Felts in 1892. Cunningham was working for Baldwin by 1902 while still a deputy U.S. marshal.
4. Spears, "Mountain Feud"; Truda McCoy, 231; and Velke, 105.
5. Mutzenberg, 88–89, and James M. Callahan, *History of West Virginia, Old and New,* 76–77. Mutzenberg identified Keadle as the sheriff of Mingo County, but his timing was off. Keadle was not appointed sheriff until 1895, when Mingo County was created. Records show that he was a printer

who in 1887 established a newspaper in Logan Courthouse, the *Logan Dem ocrat,* which became the *Logan Banner* in 1888. Following this success, Keadle was appointed deputy revenue collector for southern West Virginia in 1889.

6. Spears, "Mountain Feud"; *Wheeling Intelligencer,* "Hatfields and M'Coys"; and G. Elliott Hatfield, 137–38. Nancy McCoy Hatfield, a canny survivor who was nothing if not flexible in her loyalties, would also be accused of spying for the McCoys and helping them track down Ellison Mounts. Truda McCoy learned of Frank Phillips's relationship with Nancy from Phillips's daughter Elsie Ford. Polly Adams told Truda (229, n. 17): "Nancy was as pretty a woman as you ever laid eyes on, but she was a crackerjack. She was the best thing you ever saw if she liked you, but if she didn't like you—look out!"

7. Spears, "Mountain Feud," and Harry Leon Sellards Jr., *Hatfield and Phillips Families of Eastern Kentucky and Southwestern West Virginia,* 274. "When Phillips learned of her duplicity he simply laughed at her and continued his unlawful relations," wrote the *National Police Gazette* in 1893 ("He Held Life Cheaply"). "Because he was a hero in her eyes and kind to her as well, she was faithful to him thereafter."

8. *Wheeling Intelligencer,* "Hatfields and M'Coys," and Waller, 188. Some sources say it was Campbell and Burnett who captured Stratton, though the *Intelligencer* said that Burnett was sick for several days, making it unclear whether he was one of the two men who captured Stratton.

9. Spears, "Mountain Feud"; Swain, 341–42; Atkinson, 469; Waller, 142, 188, 200, 219–20; and G. Elliott Hatfield, 87–89.

10. Cunningham, *Memoirs,* 42, and "Warren Miller" entry in *West Virginia Legislative Hand Book,* 727.

11. There was a minor triumph, however. About a year after Cunningham's friend Robert Duff was killed, the Skean clan moved into Mud Sock (now Mt. Alto) and started making whiskey. But Mud Sock's law-abiding citizens soon flushed out Skean and his cohorts, who went back to Kentuck. Cunningham followed them there, captured Frank Skean's son Peter, and took him to Parkersburg for trial, thus breaking up what he called the "Mud Sock whiskey crowd."

12. Cunningham, "Horrible Butcheries," 36–37, and G. Elliott Hatfield, 197. Original text changed from "handing at his side" to "hanging at his side."

13. Adams, 218, 220; Spears, "Murderous Mountaineers"; Cunningham, "Horrible Butcheries," 37; and G. Elliott Hatfield, 135. Spears said the third detective was T. M. Brown, not Treve Gibson. Cantley reported Cunningham telling stories with pious asides, such as "I never felt like I was alone in

my journeys, but always relied on a higher power to guide my footsteps and to protect me from evil" (22) and, later, upon escaping the Hatfields, "God answered my prayers again" (24). Adams is confusing on this point, quoting Cunningham on the decline of his enemies: "The hand of God has been laid on these men in dreadful forms." Adams commented, "Thus the faith of Dan Cunningham shines out in his diary" (219). But then he quoted Cunningham again—"God will not let me be killed while one of Nathan's murderers is above ground"—and commented, "That is the one tenet of his creed; otherwise he is not a religious man" (220). By most evidence, it seems that he was.

14. In Cantley's account (22), the detectives killed two of the McCoys in the gunfight. Cantley tended to overdramatize events.

15. Cunningham, "Horrible Butcheries," 37; Spears, "Murderous Mountaineers"; and G. Elliott Hatfield, 86. Hatfield called him Wild Bill Napier and said that he "looked, talked and liked to eat like Buffalo Bill, his patron saint" and came from "the Southwest, where bad men were really bad, and the notches on the young cannons in his holsters proved it." He told a story, repeated from Crawford, of Napier hiding for two days inside a hollow log to avoid being captured by the Hatfields. (The Nov. 8, 1888, *Wheeling Intelligencer* put that at a more reasonable "several hours.") Other writers called him Kentucky Bill. In an 1892 *New York Times* article, Kentucky Bill was identified as William Napier. Harrison (*Logan Banner,* 1957) called him Kentucky Wild Bill. The *Intelligencer* said Kentucky Bill was John L. Napier, originally from Wayne County, though he obtained his nickname while in Colorado, and said he was connected with a Louisville detective agency.

16. Cunningham, "Horrible Butcheries," 36–37. In G. Elliott Hatfield (87–94), Cunningham was against the Hatfields from the start. In Truda McCoy, he switched in the opposite direction, from a hunter of Hatfields to a hunter of McCoys. In all Cunningham-originated accounts, however, he started out against the McCoys and then decided that he was morally obligated to pursue the Hatfields.

17. Spears, "Murderous Mountaineers," and *Louisville Courier-Journal,* "The Hatfield-M'Coy Feud." In the *Atlanta Constitution* ("Cunningham's Historic Hunt for the Hatfields"), Adams said that the Eureka agency had learned that Gillespie was hiding out at an aunt's house on a remote mountainside in Tazewell County, Virginia, where the Gillespie family was well established.

18. The *Cincinnati Enquirer* ("Hatfield-M'Coy: Origin of the Deadly Feud") described the capture differently, giving young Gillespie more bravado: "With a revolver a few inches from his heart, Gillespie was ordered to throw up his hands, but he coolly remarked: 'You've got me dead to rights:

shoot if you want to, but recollect a Hatfield never throws up his hands. Treat me like a man, though, and I'll go quietly with you.'"

19. *Wheeling Intelligencer,* "The Hatfield Gang"; *Louisville Courier-Journal,* "Hatfield-M'Coy Feud." The *Louisville Courier-Journal* identified Tom Campbell as Lon Campbell.

20. *Wheeling Intelligencer,* "The Hatfield Gang"; *Louisville Courier-Journal,* "Hatfield-M'Coy Feud"; *Cincinnati Enquirer,* "Hatfield-M'Coy"; *Atlanta Constitution,* "Cunningham's Historic Hunt"; and Cunningham, "Horrible Butcheries," 37. n. 19. The *Enquirer* identified the man who captured Gillespie not as Dan Cunningham but as Detective Campbell. The mistake was perpetuated by G. Elliott Hatfield (137), who confused matters further when he used Cunningham's first name and credited the arrest to "Detective Dan Campbell and his partner, Treve Gibson."

21. Spears, "Murderous Mountaineers."

22. Howard, "Descendants of Tom Chambers."

Chapter 19: Yellow Journalists on the Bloody Border

1. Creelman, "Bloody Border War," and Deed of Conveyance between Sarah McCoy and Randolph McCoy and Thomas G. Farley, May 4, 1889.

2. Spears, "Murderous Mountaineers" and "Mountain News Getting."

3. Spears, "Mountain Feud." Smith was married to Frances McCoy, the daughter of a Peter Creek Union soldier and a cousin of Harmon McCoy. The *Wheeling Intelligencer* ("Visiting the Hatfields") reported that the "indictment against Dave Stratton will be *nollied,*" meaning he would be set free without a trial.

4. Crawford, *American Vendetta,* 7, 12, 54, 90–92, 103, 115.

5. Ibid., 48–94, 98–102, 108–10, 115–16.

6. Ibid., 55–58, and *New York Sun,* "Sport in Wood and Field."

7. Crawford, *American Vendetta,* 59, 73, 84–85, 116.

8. Ibid., 65–66, 82–86, 101–2.

9. *New York World,* "A Bloody Vendetta," and Crawford, *American Vendetta,* 91–92, 121–22. The headline for Crawford's story in the *World,* "An American Vendetta: Mountaineers Who Have Been Killing Each Other for 25 Years," clearly asserted that the feud had taken root in the Civil War.

10. The 1880 federal census showed one Jeff Skean in Logan County, with a wife, Arminda, and two children. In 1888, he would have been thirty-five, and Arminda thirty-one. Cunningham, "Horrible Butcheries," 37–38, n. 20, and *Memoirs,* 33, and U.S Census of 1880, Magnolia, Logan, West Virginia, Jeff Skean household, sheet 301B, family 0.

11. G. Elliott Hatfield, 137.

12. Harrison remembered Kentucky Bill only as a McCoy partisan. Recounting his story in 1957 at the age of ninety-one to the *Logan Banner* ("Last Survivor"), Harrison confused and compressed some episodes. I have tried to correct this confusion and provide the most likely chain of events regarding Kentucky Bill.

13. *Atlanta Constitution,* "Cunningham's Historic Hunt"; Cunningham, "Horrible Butcheries," 38; G. Elliott Hatfield, 137–38; Staton, 170–71; and Spears, "Murderous Mountaineers." Some accounts give the date of this capture as Oct. 1. The *Weston Democrat* ("Hatfield-McCoy Vendetta") gave Oct. 29, 1888, as the date of the capture. In this report, Mitchell was shot and knocked down by Gibson but still managed to get away, the "leaves being so dry that he could not be tracked." This report also said that the detectives took Mounts to Pikeville, "where he was lodged in jail and the detectives paid $500, the amount offered by the Kentucky authorities for his arrest." Staton told a variation of this incident. According to him, it was John T. Vance, Devil Anse's future son-in-law (he would marry Nancy Hatfield in May 1889), who guided Cunningham and Kentucky Bill (whom he called "Pinkerton, or Wild Bill") to a place called Johnnie Cake, where a secret trail leading to the Hatfield hideout on Pigeon Creek crossed the main trail at the head of Mate Creek. Staton said that Mounts was accompanying Guerilla Mitchell to the doctor to have his wounded hand treated. Mounts and Mitchell were shocked to see that Vance had betrayed them. Afterward, Cap volunteered to kill him and proceeded to do so. However, records show that John T. Vance lived to the age of eighty-one and died Dec. 3, 1939 (West Virginia, Deaths Index). The *New York Times,* picking up a report from Charleston, titled its story of the arrest of Mounts "Rough-and-Tumble Battle" and simply merged the two fighting families into one menacing "Hatfield-McCoy gang," the Hatfields being the gang's "West Virginia contingent." The *Times* said that Chambers was "shot in the hand," though that was most likely the wound from the New Year's Day raid, and that he had shot Napier, as opposed to Gibson.

Chapter 20: The Trial

1. *Weston Democrat,* "Hatfield-McCoy Vendetta."
2. "Confession of Ellison Mounts." I found a reproduction of this previously lost confession in Matewan. An envelope reproduction attached to it is addressed to Governor Buckner and postmarked Sept. 4, 1889.
3. Hatfield and Spence, 178–79. The town of Brownstown is now called Marmet.
4. This incident is recorded in Cantley (24) and G. Elliott Hatfield (89–92).
5. Jones, 155–56; G. Elliott Hatfield, 138, based on Jones; and Velke, 107.

Possibly confusing an encounter with Cap Hatfield, Cantley (26) says that Cunningham and Gibson found Messer sitting on a log with a Winchester across his lap in the woods near the homes of the Hatfields. He put up no fight, perhaps figuring that they could not make it out of the woods with him. He had reason to believe that. In a handwritten memoir (now lost), Cunningham gave an alternative version, saying that Gibson found Messer on Big Ugly Creek in Lincoln County. However, the owner and editor of that memoir, the former William and Mary history professor Ludwell H. Johnson III, noted that "Cunningham and Treve Gibson were equally responsible for Messer's capture" (Cunningham, "Horrible Butcheries," 38, n. 21).

6. Jones, 157–58. "They flashed their badges from courthouse to blacksmith shop," according to Jones, "and let it be known that they were planning an early raid on the Hatfield domain." This sounds out of character for the well-trained, disciplined Eureka detectives, especially Cunningham, who was known to be introspective and sly.

7. Ibid. The Logan merchant U. B. Buskirk, who carried the news of the capture of the three detectives to Charleston, believed they got caught because they talked too much.

8. James C. Klotter, "A Hatfield-McCoy Feudist Pleads for Mercy in 1889," *West Virginia History*, 327, and Jones, 157.

9. *Logan County Banner*, "We Want Peace and Not Destruction of Property by Fire." Jones (158) mistimed this event, which did not occur in Jan. but in Mar. of 1889. In July, Devil Anse and Vicey would sell more land, 239 acres on Mate Creek (owned in partnership with Asa McCoy, the son of Uriah and Aunty Betty, and Asa's wife, Nancy, the daughter of Preacher Anse), to Cotiga Development Company of Pennsylvania for eight hundred dollars.

10. Jones (159–63) and Mutzenberg (45–46) provided detailed descriptions of the trials; so did L. D. Hatfield (35). These accounts were based on a story in the *Cincinnati Enquirer* ("Hatfield-M'Coy") and on the testimony in Case No. 19594, *Valentine Hatfield v. Commonwealth*, Kentucky Court of Appeals, Nov. 9, 1889.

11. Mutzenberg, 45–46; Cunningham, "Horrible Butcheries," 38; and G. Elliott Hatfield, 139.

12. Anderson, 130. Mose Christian would later be hanged for killing a salesman on Barrenshea Creek. Christian beat the man to death with rocks and then hid the bloody rocks in a tree trunk near a church. Decades later, the tree would be cut down to reveal the bloodstained rocks.

13. Jones, 162, from Case No. 19594, *Valentine Hatfield v. Commonwealth*, Kentucky Court of Appeals.

14. *Southwestern Reporter*, 309–10.

15. *Wheeling Intelligencer,* "The Hatfield Feud"; Jones, 162, 166; Mutzenberg, 89–90; L. D. Hatfield, 36–38; and Ely, 332–33.

16. *Southwestern Reporter,* 311–12.

17. *Wheeling Intelligencer,* "Hatfield Feud."

18. *Southwestern Reporter,* 310, and Mutzenberg, 89–90.

19. *Charleston Sunday Gazette-Mail,* "Feud's Lore, Gore Aimed at Tourists."

20. *Southwestern Reporter,* 310–12.

21. The *Wheeling Intelligencer* identified him as "Dan" Stratton, "a bitter enemy of old Anse." Dave Stratton was a political rival of the Hatfields and part of Frank Phillips's posse.

22. *Wheeling Intelligencer,* "'Devil Anse' Hatfield: Arraigned in the United States Court at Charleston" and "Devil Anse Tells"; Bourland, "Biography of Henry Solomon White"; Jones, 172, 184; G. Elliott Hatfield, 147–50; Donnelly, 31–34; and David Turk, "History—How Much Did It Cost to Find Billy the Kid?" John Jay Jackson was the brother of Judge James Monroe Jackson and Jacob B. Jackson, the governor of West Virginia from 1881 to 1885. For expenses for the escort, White claimed $103.20 (at ten cents a mile plus incidentals). The attorney general disputed the need for so many guards and ruled that $93.20 was denied because Devil Anse was acquitted.

23. *Wheeling Intelligencer,* "'Devil Anse' Hatfield." Devil Anse said that they were all good friends after the war until Floyd Hatfield and Randall McCoy—who he said were married to sisters but who were not—got into an argument over "a sow and pigs." The account was filled with other errors, including his naming the man killed as a result of the trial Stratten (later Stratton) instead of Staton. He also confused Roseanna McCoy and Nancy McCoy.

Chapter 21: The Bitter End

1. *Detroit Free Press,* "Surprised in Camp."

2. *Wheeling Intelligencer,* "That Lincoln County War."

3. No one knows if the original photograph still exists. The best reproduction I have seen is at the Big Sandy Cultural Center in Pikeville. Also, Jones, 175–76, 182–83, and *Louisville Courier-Journal,* Feb. 18 and Feb. 20, 1890. Mounts made no mention of a wife, but on Christmas Day in 1882 in Logan County, one Ellison Hatfield, a nineteen-year-old son of Harriet Hatfield, married a thirty-six-year-old neighbor named Rebecca Justice. Cotton Top and his younger brother George were the sons of the unmarried Harriet Hatfield and her cousin Ellison Hatfield. Later, their mother married a man named Daniel Mounts, and the boys usually went by that surname. Rebecca

Justice died while Cotton Top was in jail. U.S. Census, 1870 and 1880, and West Virginia, Marriages, 1853–1970; also, *Wheeling Intelligencer,* "Hatfield Feud."

4. Truda McCoy, 232, n. 23, and Mutzenberg, 93.

5. Matewan.com, "Matewan, West Virginia." Matteawan, New York, is now known as Beacon.

6. Jones, 181; Swain, 193–94; and Donnelly, 28. Some say the package, addressed to "Devil" Anse Hatfield, was what gave him his nickname. Others say he already had it.

Chapter 22: After the Hanging

1. *Charleston Sunday Gazette-Mail,* "Feud's Lore"; Sanders, "Beautiful Beech Creek Valley"; and L. D. Hatfield, 35.

2. Jones, 185–89.

3. Ibid., 189–91, and Howard, "Descendants of Rebecca Browning."

4. Thomas, 264–65. Thomas heard this story from Lark's son Bud. She said he said it was "Vicey or Nancy" who was sick; however, Vicey was thirteen years older than Lark, so he could not have witnessed such a scenario when Vicey was small, and Lark did not have a daughter named Nancy. Vicey was briefly married to James Wolford and had a daughter named Nancy. She and Nancy might conceivably have moved back home with Lark.

5. Jones, 191–93, and Howard, "Descendants of Perry A. Cline." Prichard (76) said that the letter followed the death of Perry Cline, but, in fact, it preceded it. Hatfield did not hold out hope for peace until the death of Cline.

6. Hatfield and Spence, 237–38.

7. Andrew Chafin interview transcript, 1, 15–16, 21, and Waller, 79, 253.

8. Andrew Chafin interview transcript, 5, 7, 10; *Huntington Advertiser,* "Story of the Hatfields and McCoys"; Waller, 253; and Crawford, *American Vendetta,* 121.

9. Andrew Chafin interview transcript, 1–4, 8–9; Brad Chafin interview with author; and *Montgomery News,* "Hatfield Brothers Killed in Shootout."

10. Andrew Chafin interview transcript, 4, 8–10, and *Huntington Advertiser,* "Story of the Hatfields and McCoys." While Lee was at work, Anse would borrow his shotgun to go hunting. "It was the first pump gun in Logan County," Lee said. "I paid twenty-two dollars for it from Sears Roebuck in Chicago. That was twenty-two days of work."

11. Andrew Chafin interview transcript, 4–5.

12. G. Elliott Hatfield, 197–98; Sanders, "Emma Hatfield Reminisces"; and Ada Hatfield journal.

13. Andrew Chafin interview transcript, 2. Andy Chafin did not like to talk about the feud, but in the fall of 1972, when he was eighty-six, his family

finally persuaded him to tell the story. They recorded the conversation on a tape recorder under the table. The tape was misplaced and not transcribed until 2002. Also, interview with Chafin's grandson Andy Chafin, Sept. 12, 2012. While Dan Cunningham would say that more men died after the hanging of Cotton Top Mounts than before (most of them simply murdered and disappearing in the woods), Chafin's account is the only eyewitness evidence to support this claim.

14. Hatfield and Spence (237–38) mistakenly called Treve Gibson "Treve Brown."
15. Coleman A. Hatfield, as quoted in Hatfield and Spence, 238–39.

Chapter 23: The Last Murders and Manhunt

1. Hatfield and Spence, 239; G. Elliott Hatfield, 211, 224–25; Howard, "Descendants of Valentine Hatfield"; *West Virginia Marriages Index, 1785–1971*; and *Register of Marriages Within the County of Logan*, 64–65. His previous wife was Rebecca Browning. It is unclear how Johnse's marriage to Rebecca Browning ended or whether his new wife, Roxie Browning, was related to his previous wife. There were many Browning families in the area.

2. Truda McCoy, 173; C. Coleman Hatfield in Hatfield and Spence, 230–31; Waller, 41; and Howard, "Descendants of Nathaniel Chafin."

3. Hatfield and Spence, 230–31; G. Elliott Hatfield, 159; and John G. Morgan, *West Virginia Governors: 1863–1980*, 88–89.

4. Hatfield and Spence, 228–32. Mutzenberg and G. Elliott Hatfield (based on Mutzenberg) said that these wounds were inflicted not by John Rutherford but by Elliott Rutherford, who was also shooting at Cap. As they told it, Joe Glenn then shot and killed Elliott. Coleman A. and Coleman C. Hatfield gave a different account—one that's been passed down within the family—and greater detail. I have relied primarily on their version of this clash. Jones (205–6) and Hatfield and Spence (231) correctly located this incident in Matewan, as per the *Cincinnati Enquirer* article "Bad 'Cap' Is Grimly Awaiting. . . ." Mutzenberg and G. Elliott Hatfield placed it in Thacker, as was mistakenly reported in the *Cincinnati Enquirer* article "In Cold Blood." Waller (*Feud*, 242) referred to it incorrectly as the "1896 Williamson incident."

5. Mutzenberg, 94–98; G. Elliott Hatfield, 159; and Howard, "Descendants of Elliott 'Doc' Rutherford." Mutzenberg, who said Cap claimed that he walked into an ambush, called Cap's version a "total contradiction of the statements made by all the eye-witnesses" (96). Coleman A. Hatfield (in Hatfield and Spence, 232) said that five men were shooting at his father: Reece Halsey, Ed Hopson, Elliott Rutherford, Lewis Rutherford, and John Rutherford. The *New York Times* ("Pardon for a Feudist") confused matters by reporting, "On election day, 1896, Johnson Hatfield, after drinking too much moonshine,

killed Rutherford McCoy, Jr. He was captured and sentenced to serve three months for this last killing." Not only was Johnse not involved, but there was no Rutherford McCoy Jr.

6. Hatfield and Spence, 231–33; Howard, "Descendants of Elliott 'Doc' Rutherford"; Coleman A. Hatfield in Hatfield and Spence (233). Coleman A. Hatfield's written and recorded commentary was passed on to his son Coleman C., who died in 2008. This fast-paced getaway is in contrast with the accounts of Mutzenberg and G. Elliott Hatfield. "Every man upon the voting ground appeared dazed, dumbfounded, paralyzed with astonishment and fear," wrote Mutzenberg (95). "No one dared attempt the arrest of the fugitives." "Cap coolly turned to them and said it was 'too bad,'" wrote G. Elliott Hatfield (159), and then he "took the boy's hand and strolled leisurely out of town unmolested."

7. Cincinnati Enquirer, "Bad 'Cap'" and "Scot Free Is 'Devil Anse' Hatfield," and G. Elliott Hatfield, 158.

8. Cincinnati Enquirer, "Barkers Beside Their Pillows Couldn't Guard the Mountain Terrors" and "Scot Free."

9. Cincinnati Enquirer, "Barkers" and "In Cold Blood"; Mutzenberg, 96; Charlotte Sanders, "Sheriff Keadle Had a Prize Prisoner in 1897," Williamson Daily News; Waller, Feud, 79, 253; Henry Clay Ragland, History of Logan County, W. Va., chapter 21; and Robert Y. Spence, "Henry Clay Ragland." G. Elliott Hatfield, who adhered to Mutzenberg, wrote, "Dusk fell over the hills, a harvest moon hung in the sky like a huge lantern to light the way" (160). In fact, the last full moon was on Oct. 29, and the next would not be until Nov. 20. Hatfield and Spence (233–34) told a different version of the story. In theirs, Cap decided to make for the home of family friend Dan Christian. After sleeping out in the woods overnight, he and Little Joe ate their first meal in two days at Christian's and hid in the attic. Meanwhile, a posse raided Cap's home but learned nothing from Nan, who had not even heard about the gunfight. Although Cap believed he had acted in self-defense, he knew that the Rutherfords would be out for revenge and that he needed to get out of the area fast. He had Christian hide him and Little Joe in his wagon and take them down to Thacker, where they jumped a train at night. When it reached Huntington, Cap found the town's sheriff and surrendered.

10. Cincinnati Enquirer, "Scot Free."

11. Sanders, "Sheriff Keadle"; Hatfield and Spence, 234; G. Elliott Hatfield, 160–61; and Mutzenberg, 98. According to Mutzenberg, Cap was tried on only one of the charges, fined, and sentenced to jail for a year. Two other indictments, both for murder, were pending in court for the following

term, and Cap did not like his chances. He preferred to be killed by a Winchester than made an example of on the scaffold.

12. Andrew Chafin interview transcript, 10–14. While Chafin mentioned Uncle Melvin Browning, Coleman C. Hatfield said he stayed the night with George F. Browning, his cousin.

13. Mutzenberg, 99–101.

14. G. Elliott Hatfield, 163, 182. It was believed that Cap's brothers Johnse, Elias, and Troy, and his allies, all heavily armed, were rallying around him and prepared to fight. It was even said that Randall McCoy, looking like Davy Crockett in homespuns and a wide-brimmed hat with a dangling squirrel's tail and bearing an old-fashioned, muzzle-loading rifle, had come from Kentucky to join in the hunt, and Keadle had welcomed him. But McCoy had retired from the fighting and remained in Pikeville.

15. Mutzenberg (100–102) claimed that Randall McCoy was leading the group up the path. Some say that the Devil's Backbone was over on Beech Creek.

16. Ibid., 103–6.

17. Ibid., 103–8, and Hatfield and Spence, 234. According to Mutzenberg (107), after the first blast, "it was seen that more than half of the 'Devil's Backbone' was torn up and blown down the mountain-side into a small arm of the Tug River, changing the course of the stream." Mate Creek, which empties into the Tug at Matewan, runs near the Devil's Backbone, but its course does not seem to have been altered.

Chapter 24: The Last Dance: Cunningham Gets His Hatfield

1. G. Elliott Hatfield, 156.

2. Jones, 204; Sellards, 274; and G. Elliott Hatfield, 156. Becoming a better man was not something that came easily to Bad Frank. In 1894, he had a daughter, Pearlie, by his wife, Mary. He divorced Mary and married Nancy McCoy Hatfield in Sept. of 1895. In Oct. of 1896, he had another child by Mary, Roy. The last of his nine known children, Goldie, was born in Sept. of 1897 to Nancy.

3. G. Elliott Hatfield, 157: "Data on Frank Phillips's death from unpublished manuscript by Henry P. Scalf."

4. Sellards, 274, and G. Elliott Hatfield, 157–58, based on an unpublished manuscript by Henry P. Scalf.

5. Hatfield and Spence, 221, and G. Elliott Hatfield, 225.

6. *Atlanta Constitution,* "Cunningham's Historic Hunt"; Cantley, 26; Hatfield and Spence, 251; and Howard, "Descendants of French Ellis."

7. Hatfield and Spence, 251.

8. Cantley, 27. Not surprisingly, Coleman Hatfield (in Hatfield and Spence, 250–51) gave an alternative version of events. Johnse was "kidnapped by

six men," he claimed. As Johnse and Ank Damron passed through a railroad cut beside the Tug River, three armed men blocked their way, and three more blocked their retreat. No shots were fired, as only Damron was armed. Three days later, Squirrel Huntin' Sam (Sam McCoy, 80) visited Johnse in jail. He refused to help Johnse escape but told him he would do anything he could to prevent a mob from forming and harming him. Sam conferred with Big Jim McCoy, who said there was some "strong talk" in town and would not commit to being against it.

9. Hatfield and Spence, 235–37. Mutzenberg (101) says Cap and two others killed "Charles McKenney, a cousin of the McCoys, a lad of only eighteen," whom they "riddled with buckshot."

10. Hatfield and Spence, 251–52, drawing on writings by and interviews of Cap's son Coleman; Andrew Chafin interview transcript, 6; and Charlotte Sanders, "Feud Was Revived in 1899 After the Killing of 'Doc' Ellis," *Williamson Daily News*, based on the *Bluefield Daily Telegraph* of July 4, 1899. In both the Hatfield and Spence and *Daily Telegraph* versions, Elias Hatfield was boarding the train as a passenger, heading to Wharncliffe, according to the latter. Though Elias was Devil Anse's son, the *Daily Telegraph* referred to him as Elias Hatfield Jr., presumably to differentiate him from Devil Anse's brother Elias. In Hatfield and Spence (252), Coleman A. Hatfield said the gun was a "new Winchester." In Sanders's and Chafin's accounts, it was a pistol. In Hatfield and Spence (251), the bullet ricocheted off Ellis's gold cuff link.

11. Hatfield and Spence (252–53) said, "Atkinson arrived in Williamson, accompanied by a man named Boggs, and convinced Elias to surrender." Later, they said Atkinson did this "as a lawyer"; however, by this time, Atkinson, who served as the governor of West Virginia from 1897 to 1901, was already in the executive office.

12. Velke, 107–11, from Jones, 117, 193.

13. *New York Times*, "Hatfield Feud Renewed."

14. Jones, 217. According to the *Southwestern Reporter*, on Dec. 6, 1906, Alex Messer was briefly released on parole. However, he was arrested again after he was found carrying a gun and "molesting people." He failed to live up to promises to reform and, in 1907, returned to prison, where he stayed for the rest of his life.

On July 11, 1904, the *New York Times* ("Pardon for a Feudist") reported that the McCoys signed the petition only because Johnse had not taken part in the New Year's Day raid, though he actually had. Rice (120) said Thorne himself was attacked while touring the prison, which is incorrect.

15. *Louisville Courier-Journal*, "Hatfield Dies Tied to a Tree," and L. D. Hatfield, 38.

Coda

1. Hatfield and Spence, 222.
2. Mutzenberg, 108. For a good description of the gunfight, see Donnelly, 15, 19–20; *Montgomery News,* "Hatfield Brothers Killed"; Velke, 107–11, 158; and G. Elliott Hatfield, 212.
3. Spivak, "Interview with Cap Hatfield."
4. Donnelly, 15–16, and Charlotte Sanders, "Hatfields Produced Mingo's 2nd Sheriff," *Williamson Daily News.* Greenway and his wife, Cora Lee, had five sons, all of whom became prominent citizens of Williamson. Wirt was a Republican mayor of the town for sixteen years. W.E. served as postmaster and county sheriff, the latter post beginning in 1932, after his father's last stint as sheriff. Shayde also served as postmaster. Anthony worked in the sheriff's department, and Neenie ran a bookstore.
5. Joseph Platania, "Three Sides to the Story."
6. Ibid., and West Virginia Archives, "Henry Drury Hatfield" and "Inaugural Address of Governor Henry D. Hatfield."

Epilogue: Mine Is the Vengeance

1. Velke, 180 d–e, and Howard, "Descendants of French Ellis."
2. Donnelly, 20–21.
3. Hatfield and Spence, 221; G. Elliott Hatfield, 225, 235; Swain, 194; Donnelly, 15–16; Mutzenberg, 109; Klotter, 328; Cantley, 28; and Margaret Hatfield interview transcript.
4. Donnelly, 22–23.
5. *New York Times,* "Randall McCoy, Feudist, Dies"; Truda McCoy, 215; and Tyree, "Funeral of Sarah McCoy."
6. Sanders, "Ollie McCoy" and "Tom McCoy Ordained as Minister," and Hoffman, 9.
7. Cunningham, "Horrible Butcheries," 25; Kenneth R. Bailey, "Dan Cunningham"; and *Temptation to Lawlessness,* 25–45.

SELECTED BIBLIOGRAPHY

~

Writings on the Hatfield and McCoy feud come in a great array of forms. The sources below include everything from feud-dedicated newsletters to well-researched hybrid novel/nonfiction works (such as Spivak's and Judge Staton's) to family reminiscences to standard academic references. Some early sources, such as the report of Kentucky adjutant general Sam E. Hill to the governor of Kentucky, inform quite a few later works. The reporting of Spears and Crawford in 1888 is seminal. Charles Mutzenberg's 1917 chapter on the feud, which is partly based on Hill, is frequently referred to by other authors. After 1949, Virgil Carrington Jones's feud history became the standard reference, and later works by Otis K. Rice and Altina Waller added much to the discussion. Truda McCoy and G. Elliott Hatfield offer detailed and partisan accounts, with excellent geneaologies, and Coleman C. Hatfield's books contribute more stories with details, color, and opinions. A number of the works borrow without attribution from earlier accounts but are not without their own merits. In particular, Swain contains a chapter entitled "Truth About the Hatfield-McCoy Feud" with a note stating: "An attempt will here be made to give the cold facts as they have been gathered after an exhaustive investigation during which much of this information was gleaned from living actors who participated in this unhappy Feud" (183). However, he copied verbatim from Mutzenberg. L. D. Hatfield did too, sometimes amusingly putting Mutzenberg's dialogue in the vernacular.

Adams, Samuel Hopkins. "Dan Cunningham: A Huntsman of the Law." *McClure's Magazine* 23 (June 1904): 215–20.

Andersen, Kurt. "Appalachia: Hatfields and McCoys." *Time,* Dec. 14, 1981.

Anderson, Helen Vance, and John Vance. *Tug River Memories.* Privately published. Hardy, KY: Barbara Vance, 2004.

Atkins, Tom. "Franklin Phillips—No Outlaw." *Old Pond Hatfield-McCoy Newsletter* 3, no. 1 (Spring/Summer 2000): 40–50.

————. *Old Pond Hatfield-McCoy Newsletter* 3, no. 2 (Fall/Winter 2000): 36–41.

————. *Old Pond Hatfield-McCoy Newsletter* 3, no. 4 (Fall/Winter 2001): 7–8.

Atkinson, George W., and Alvaro F. Gibbens. *Prominent Men of West Virginia: Biographical Sketches of Representative Men in Every Honorable Vocation, Including Politics, the Law, Theology, Medicine, Education, Finance, Journalism, Trade, Commerce and Agriculture.* Wheeling, WV: W. L. Callin, 1890.

Ayers, Edward L. *In the Presence of Mine Enemies: The Civil War in the Heart of America, 1859–1863.* New York: W. W. Norton, 2003.

Bailey, Kenneth R. "Dan Cunningham." *e-WV: The West Virginia Encyclopedia.* www.wvencyclopedia.org/articles/1697.

Baily, Rebecca J. *Matewan Before the Massacre: Politics, Coal, and the Roots of Conflict in a West Virginia Mining Community.* Morgantown: West Virginia University Press, 2008.

Baker, Robert, and Brian E. Hall. "Organization & History of the 39th Kentucky Mounted Infantry Regiment and Company 'F.'" Blue Gray Historical Group. Last modified Feb. 28, 2007. www.bluegrayhistoricalgroup.org/39thktymtdinfhis.htm.

Bartoo, Carole. "Genetic Clues to Famous Feud." *Vanderbilt Reporter.* www.mc.vanderbilt.edu/reporter/index.html?ID=5470.

Block, Lawrence. *Gangsters, Swindlers, Killers, and Thieves: The Lives and Crimes of Fifty American Villains.* Oxford: Oxford University Press, 2004.

Bolgiano, Chris. *The Appalachian Forest: A Search for Roots and Renewal.* Mechanicsburg, PA: Stackpole Books, 1998.

Broadstone, Michael A., ed. *History of Greene County, Ohio: Its People, Industries, and Institutions.* Indianapolis, IN: B. F. Bowen and Co., 1918.

Callahan, James M. *History of West Virginia, Old and New.* Vol. 2. Chicago: American Historical Society, 1923.

Cantley, Beulah. *"Uncle Dan, What a Man": By a Loving Grandaughter* [sic]. Charleston, WV: Boda, 1976.

Chafin, Andrew. "Andrew Chafin Interview: Thanksgiving, 1972." Typescript. Transcription by Andy Chafin, Brad Chafin, and Betty Avril, Jan. 2002. West Virginia Collection, West Virginia University.

Chafin, Andy. Personal interview with author, Sept. 12, 2012.

Clark, Thomas D. "Kentucky Logmen." *Journal of Forest History* 25, no. 3 (July 1981): 144–57.

Cline, Cecil, and Harry Dale Cline. *Clines and Allied Families of the Tug River Region of Kentucky and West Virginia: A Historical and Genealogical Study of the Pioneer Settlers and Their Descendants.* Baltimore, MD: Gateway Press, 1998.

Selected Bibliography

Cole, Merle T. *A Comprehensive History of the West Virginia State Police, 1919–1979.* Electronic publication. Merle T. Cole, 1998. www.statepolice.wv.gov /about/Documents/wvspHistory.pdf.

———. "Soldiers of the New Empire: The Gaujot Brothers of Mingo County." *West Virginia Historical Society Quarterly* 16, no. 2 (Apr. 2002).

Crawford, Theron Clark. *An American Vendetta: A Story of Barbarism in the United States.* New York: Belford, Clarke and Co., 1889.

———. "An American Vendetta." *New York World,* Oct. 7, 1888.

———. "American Barbarians." *New York World,* Oct. 14, 1888.

———. "The Land of the Vendetta." *New York World,* Oct. 21, 1888.

Creelman, James. "Bloody Border War." *New York Herald,* Feb. 9, 1888.

———. "West Virginia's Savages." *New York Herald,* Feb. 13, 1888.

Cunningham, Dan. *Memoirs of Daniel W. Cunningham: The Criminal History of Roane and Jackson Counties, West Virginia.* New River Notes Books, 2005. Also found as *Murders of Roane and Jackson Counties* [bound typescript], Feb. 24, 1928, in the West Virginia State Archives.

———. "The Horrible Butcheries of West Virginia: A True Story of the Hatfields and McCoys, Including Anse Hatfield's War History." Edited and with an introduction by Ludwell H. Johnson III. *West Virginia History* 46, nos. 1–4 (1985–1986): 25–43.

Dabney, Joseph Earl. *Mountain Spirits: A Chronicle of Corn Whiskey from King James' Ulster Plantation to America's Appalachians and the Moonshine Life.* Asheville, NC: Bright Mountain Books, 1974.

Darwin, Charles. *The Descent of Man and Selection in Relation to Sex.* Vol. 2, *Sexual Selection.* 2nd ed. New York: American Home Library Company, 1902.

Dizney, Elijah F. "Mountain Feuds." *Berea Quarterly* 13, no. 1 (Apr. 1909): 7–18.

Donnelly, Shirley. *The Hatfield-McCoy Feud Reader: Stories About the Famous Feud.* Parsons, WV: McLain Printing Company, 1972.

Doolittle, Jerome. *The Southern Appalachians.* New York: Time-Life Books, 1975.

Dorman, John Frederick. "Petitions from Kentuckians to the Virginia Legislature." *The Kentucky Genealogist* 11, no. 1 (Jan.–Mar. 1969).

Dotson, Grace. "Abner Vance, The True Story." *The Appalachian Quarterly* (Sept. 2003): 40–42.

Dunaway, Wilma. *The First American Frontier: Transition to Capitalism in Southern Appalachia, 1700–1860.* Chapel Hill: University of North Carolina Press, 1996.

Ely, William. *The Big Sandy Valley: A History of the People and Country from the Earliest Settlement to the Present Time.* Catlettsburg, KY: Central Methodist, 1887.

Fox, Richard K. *Devil Anse, or The Hatfield-McCoy Outlaws: A Full and Complete History of the Deadly Feud Existing Between the Hatfield and McCoy Clans.* New York: Richard K. Fox, Publisher, 1889.

Gladwell, Malcolm. *Outliers: The Story of Success.* New York: Little, Brown, 2008.

Hamilton, Emory L. *The David Musick Tragedy.* From *Indian Atrocities Along the Clinch, Powell and Holsten Rivers.* Unpublished manuscript, 219–25.

Hanmer, James Williams. "The Making of an American Myth: The Hatfields and the McCoys." MA thesis, San Jose State University, 1997.

Harkins, Anthony. *Hillbilly: A Cultural History of an American Icon.* New York: Oxford University Press, 2004.

Harris, John T., ed. "Warren Miller." In *West Virginia Legislative Hand Book and Manual and Official Register, 1917.* Charleston, WV: Tribune Printing Company.

Hatfield, Coleman C., and F. Keith Davis. *The Feuding Hatfields and McCoys.* Chapman, WV: Woodland Press, 2008.

Hatfield, Coleman C., and Robert Y. Spence. *The Tale of the Devil.* Chapman, WV: Woodland Press, 2007.

Hatfield, G. Elliott. *The Hatfields.* Revised and edited by Leonard Roberts and Henry P. Scalf. Pikeville, KY: The Big Sandy Valley Historical Society, 1988.

Hatfield, L. D. *The True Story of the Hatfield and McCoy Feud.* L. D. Hatfield, 1945. Kessinger Publishing, in reprint.

Hatfield, Margaret. Transcript of interview with Margaret Hatfield, June 11, 1992, for the film *West Virginia.* West Virginia History Film Project. West Virginia Division of Culture and History. www.wvculture.org/history /wvmemory/filmtranscripts/wvhatfield.html.

Hatfield, Philip. *The Other Feud: William Anderson "Devil Anse" Hatfield in the Civil War.* Charleston, WV: CreateSpace, 2010.

Henshaw, Thomas. *The History of Winchester Firearms, 1866–1992.* Clinton, NJ: Winchester Press, 1993.

Hill, Sam. "Report of the Adjutant General of Kentucky." Kentucky: National Guard History eMuseum. Last modified May 29, 2008. www.kynghistory .ky.gov/history/3qtr/addinfo/hatfieldmccoy.htm.

Hoffman, Margaret. "Hatfields, McCoys Bury the Hatchet." *Panorama: Sunday Dominion Post,* Aug. 1, 1976.

Howard, Betty P. "What Was the Cause of the Hatfield-McCoy Feud?" *Kentucky Explorer* 25, no. 4 (Sept. 2010): 34–37.

———. "Rebecca Scott." *Medical Leader,* Mar. 10, 2007.

———. "Pauline Cecil." *The Medical Leader,* June 2, 2007.

Johnston, David E. *A History of the Middle New River Settlements and Contiguous Territory.* Huntington, WV: Standard PTG and Pub. Co., 1906.

Jones, Virgil Carrington. *The Hatfields and the McCoys.* Chapel Hill: University of North Carolina Press, 1948.

Karr, Carolyn. "A Political Biography of Henry Hatfield." *West Virginia History* 28, no. 1 (Oct. 1966): 35–63.

Katz, William Loren. "1876: The Year When Things Went from Bad to Worse for Indians and Blacks." *History News Network,* Jan. 23, 2012.

Kephart, Horace. *Our Southern Highlanders: A Narrative of Adventure in the Southern Appalachians and a Study of Life Among the Mountaineers.* Knoxville: University of Tennessee Press, 1976. Originally published in 1913.

Klotter, James C. "A Hatfield-McCoy Feudist Pleads for Mercy in 1889." *West Virginia History* 43, no. 1 (Fall 1981).

Lawson, W. B. "The Hatfield-McCoy Vendetta; or Shadowing a Hard Crowd." *Log Cabin Library,* Oct. 18, 1894, 2–29.

Leyburn, James G. *The Scotch-Irish: A Social History.* Chapel Hill: University of North Carolina Press, 1962.

Litsey, E. Carl. "Kentucky Feuds and Their Causes." *Frank Leslie's Popular Monthly* 53, no. 3 (Jan. 1903): 161–72.

MacCorkle, William Alexander. *The Recollections of Fifty Years.* New York: G. P. Putnam's Sons, 1928.

Maddox, Ed. "Hatfield McCoy Feud Select Bibliography." Pikeville, KY: Pike County Society for Historical and Genealogical Research, 2001.

Maynard, Lee. *Crum: The Novel.* Morgantown, WV: Vandalia Press, 2001.

McCoy, Homer Claude. "The Rise of Education and the Decline of Feudal Tendencies in the Tug River of West Virginia and Kentucky in Relation to the Hatfield and McCoy Feud." MA thesis, Marshall College, 1950.

McCoy, Sam, Hobert McCoy, Orville McCoy, and Leonard Roberts. *Squirrel Huntin' Sam McCoy: His Memoir and Family Tree.* Pikeville, KY: Pikeville College Press, 1979.

McCoy, Truda Williams. *The McCoys: Their Story.* Edited by Leonard W. Roberts. Pikeville, KY: Preservation Council Press, 1976. Written in the 1930s.

McKinney, Gordon B. "Industrialization and Violence in Appalachia in the 1890's." In *An Appalachian Symposium,* edited by J. W. Williamson. Boone, NC: Appalachian State University Press, 1948.

Messerer, E. P. "The Sportsman Tourist: Days and Nights in West Virginia." *Forest and Stream* 51, no. 7 (Aug. 13, 1898): 122.

Morgan, John G. *West Virginia Governors: 1863–1980.* 2nd ed. Charleston, WV: Charleston Newspapers, 1980.

Mounts, Willard. *The Rugged Southern Appalachia.* Denver: Ginwill Publishing Company, 1997.

Mutzenberg, Charles G. *Kentucky's Famous Feuds and Tragedies: Authentic History of the World Renowned Vendettas of the Dark and Bloody Ground.* New York: R. F. Fenno and Co., 1917.

Mylott, James P. *A Measure of Prosperity: A History of Roane County.* Charleston, WV: Mountain State Press, 1984.

Nuzhet, O. Atuk, et al. "Pheochromocytoma in von Hippel–Lindau Disease: Clinical Presentation and Mutation Analysis in a Large, Multigenerational Kindred." *Journal of Clinical Endocrinology and Metabolism* 83, no. 1 (1998): 117–20.

O'Brien, Frank M. *The Story of the Sun: New York, 1833–1918.* New York: George H. Doran Company, 1918.

Osborne, Randall, and Jeffrey C. Weaver. *The Virginia State Rangers and State Line.* Lynchburg, VA: H. E. Howard, 1994.

Otterbein, Keith F. "Five Feuds: An Analysis of Homicides in Eastern Kentucky in the Late Nineteenth Century." *American Anthropologist* 102, no. 2 (June 2000): 231–43.

Otto, John Solomon. "Forest Fallowing Among the Appalachian Mountain Folk: An Ethnohistorical Study." *Anthropologica* 30, no. 1 (1988): 3–22.

Pearce, John Ed. *Days of Darkness: The Feuds of Eastern Kentucky.* Lexington: University Press of Kentucky, 1994.

Pike County, Kentucky, 1821–1987, Historical Papers 6. Pikeville, KY: Pike County Historical Society, 1987.

Platania, Joseph. "Three Sides to the Story: Governor Hatfield and the Mine Wars." WVGenWeb Project. www.wvgenweb.org/wvcoal/sides.html.

Plumb, William T., Jr. "Illegal Enforcement of the Law." *Cornell Law Quarterly* 24 (1938–1939): 337–93.

Prichard, James M. "The Devil at Large: Anse Hatfield's War." In *Virginia at War 1863,* edited by William C. Davis and James I. Robertson Jr. for the Virginia Center for Civil War Studies. Lexington: University Press of Kentucky, 2009.

Ragland, Henry Clay. *History of Logan County, W. Va.* Chapters 13–22: The Genealogical Section. Transcribed by Tom Steele, June 30, 1998. www.freepages.genealogy.rootsweb.ancestry.com/~ptsonline/history/ragland.htmlrootsweb.ancestry.com/~ptsonline/history/ragland.html.

Rakes, Paul H., and Kenneth R. Bailey. "'A Hard-Bitten Lot': Nonstrike Violence in the Early Southern West Virginia Smokeless Coalfields, 1880–1910." In Bruce Stewart, *Blood in the Hills: A History of Violence in Appalachia.* Lexington: University Press of Kentucky, 2012.

Rasmussen, Barbara. *Absentee Landowning and Exploitation in West Virginia, 1760–1920.* Lexington: University Press of Kentucky, 1994.

Rice, Otis K. *The Hatfields and the McCoys.* Lexington: University Press of Kentucky, 1982.

Ridenour, Martha. "Perry Anderson Cline." Unpublished essay in possession of Big Sandy Heritage Center.

Roesch, Helen Blankenship. "Hatfields of Southwest Virginia, Kentucky." Henry P. Scalf Papers, University of Pikeville.

Sanders, Charlotte. *Williamson Daily News,* Sept. 12, 1989 (special feud anniversary edition).

———. "Beautiful Beech Creek Valley Not Always Peaceful," pp. 10–11a.

———. "Condit's Mother Sided with Hatfields."

———. "Drinking Was Popular with Both Hatfields and McCoys," p. 14a.

———. "Emma Hatfield Reminisces About 'Uncle Anderson,'" p. 9a.

———. "Ex–Mingo County Sheriff Tom Chafin Remembers."

———. "Feud Was Revived in 1899 After the Killing of 'Doc' Ellis," p. 18a.

———. "Few Were Aware of Phillips' Connection with Famous Feud," p. 17a.

———. "Hatfield Recounts How His Fathers Hauled the Bodies of Slain Brothers Back to the Home of Ranel McCoy," p. 61a.

———. "Hatfields Produced Mingo's 2nd Sheriff," p. 16a.

———. "Hog Trial Is Part of Feud Legend."

. "'Johnse' Hatfield Earned Reputation as a Mountain Romeo."

———. "Ollie Jane McCoy Smith Going Strong at 87."

———. "Ranel McCoy's Century-Old Well Still Exists on Blackberry Fork."

———. "Sheriff Keadle Had a Prize Prisoner in 1897," p. 29a.

———. "'Squirrel Huntin' Sam' McCoy Played Active Role in Feud," p. 18a.

———. "Tierney Woman Recalls Life with 'Devil Anse.'"

———. "Tom McCoy Ordained as Minister," p. 3a.

Scalf, Henry. *Kentucky's Last Frontier.* Pikeville, KY: Pikeville College Press of the Appalachian Studies Center, 1972.

Sellards, Harry Leon, Jr. *Hatfield and Phillips Families of Eastern Kentucky and Southwestern West Virginia.* Deland, FL: Sellards, 1993.

Selleck, Kathryn. "Jurisdiction After International Kidnapping: A Comparative Study." *Boston College International and Comparative Law Review* 8, issue 1, art. 9 (1985). www.lawdigitalcommons.bc.edu/iclr/vol8/iss1/9iclr/vol8/iss1/9.

Shapiro, Henry D. *Appalachia on Our Mind: The Southern Mountains and Mountaineer in the American Consciousness, 1870–1920.* Chapel Hill: University of North Carolina Press, 1978.

SHG Resources. State Handbook and Guide. "Early History of Logan County, West Virginia." www.shgresources.com/wv/counties/logan/.

Southeastern Reporter. Vol. 30. June 7–Sept. 27, 1898: 183–96. St. Paul, MN: West Publishing, 1898.

Spears, John R. "The Dramatic Story of a Mountain Feud." *Current Literature: A Magazine of Record and Review* 1 (July–Dec. 1888): 409–17. New York: Current Literature Publishing Co., 1888. Originally published in the *New York Sun*.

———. "The Moonshiner's Still." *New York Sun,* Oct. 21, 1888, p. 6.

———. "A Mountain Feud: A Remarkable Story of Murder and Outrage." *New York Sun,* Oct. 7, 1888, p. 8.

———. "Mountain News Getting." *New York Sun,* Oct. 21, 1888, p. 6.

———. "Murderous Mountaineers." *New York Sun,* Oct. 21, 1888, p. 6.

———. "The Story of a Mountain Feud." *Munsey's Magazine* 24 (Oct. 1900–Mar. 1901): 494–509.

Spence, Robert Y. "Henry Clay Ragland." *e-WV: The West Virginia Encyclopedia.* Last updated Oct. 22, 2010. www.wvencyclopedia.org/articles/1961.

Spivak, John L. *The Devil's Brigade: The Story of the Hatfield-McCoy Feud.* New York: Brewer and Warren, 1930.

Staton, Willis David. *Hatfields and McCoys: True Romance and Tragedies.* Huntington, WV: Aegina Press, 1993. Manuscript was completed in 1947.

Steele, Paul Curry. *Anse on Island Creek and Other Poems.* Charleston, WV: Mountain State Press, 1981.

Stewart, George R. *Names on the Land.* Boston: Houghton Mifflin, 1967.

Stickles, Arndt. *Simon Bolivar Buckner: Borderland Knight.* Chapel Hill: University of North Carolina Press, 2001.

Sturgill, Roy L., and Luther F. Addington. *Crimes, Criminals, and Characters of the Cumberlands and Southwest Virginia.* Bristol, VA: Quality Printers, 1970.

Supica, Jim. "A Brief History of Firearms." National Firearms Museum. www.nramuseum.com/gun-info-research/a-brief-history-of-firearms.aspx.

Swain, G. T. *History of Logan County, West Virginia.* Kingsport, TN: Kingsport Press, 1927.

Tapp, Hambleton, and James C. Klotter. *Kentucky: Decades of Discord, 1865–1900.* Frankfort: Kentucky Historical Society, 1977.

Thomas, Jean. *Big Sandy.* New York: Holt, 1940.

Thomson, Oliver. *The Great Feud: The Campbells and the Macdonalds.* Stroud, UK: Sutton, 2000.

Thurmond, Walter R. *The Logan Coal Field: A Brief History.* Morgantown: West Virginia University Library, 1964.

Titon, Jeff Todd. "Old Regular Baptists of Southeastern Kentucky: A Community of Sacred Song." *1997 Festival of American Folklife Program Book.* www.folklife.si.edu/resources/festival1997/baptists.htm.

Turk, David. "History—How Much Did It Cost to Find Billy the Kid?" U.S. Marshals Service. www.justice.gov/marshals/history/billythekid.htm.

Tuten, Belle S., Stephen D. White, and Tracey L. Billado. *Feud, Violence and Practice: Essays in Medieval Studies in Honor of Stephen D. White*. Farnham, England: Ashgate Publishing, 2010.

United States Department of Agriculture. *Fourth and Fifth Annual Reports of the Bureau of Animal Industry for the Years 1887 and 1888*. Washington, DC: Government Printing Office, 1889.

Vanderbilt Magazine. "Tumors May Have Fueled Hatfield-McCoy Feud." Fall 2007.

Velke, John A., III. *The True Story of the Baldwin-Felts Detective Agency*. Privately published, 2004.

Waller, Altina L. *Feud: Hatfields, McCoys, and Social Change in Appalachia, 1860–1900*. Chapel Hill: University of North Carolina Press, 1988.

———. "The Hatfield and McCoy Feud." Matewan 2000. www.matewan.com/History/HM%20story.htm.

Weaver, Jeffrey C. *45th Battalion Virginia Infantry, Smith and Count's Battalions of Partisan Rangers*. Lynchburg, VA: H. E. Howard, 1994.

———. *The Civil War in Buchanan and Wise Counties: Bushwhackers' Paradise*. Lynchburg, VA: H. E. Howard, 1994.

Webb, James. *Born Fighting: How the Scots-Irish Shaped America*. New York: Broadway Books, 2004.

Wilson, Janet. "Kissing Cousins." *ARTnews* 94 (1995). 116–30.

Wintz, Bill. "The Bruen Lands Feud." *e-WV: The West Virginia Encyclopedia*. Last updated Jan. 7, 2011. www.wvencyclopedia.org/articles/672.

Woods, Roy C. "History of the Hatfield-McCoy Feud with Special Attention to the Effects of Education on It." *West Virginia History: A Quarterly Magazine* 22, no. 1 (Oct. 1960).

Newspapers and Serials

Atlanta Constitution: Apr. 7, 1901, "Cunningham's Historic Hunt for the Hatfields: The Story of a Famous Southern Feud and How It Was Ended," p. A4.

Baltimore Herald: July 25, 1890. " 'Kentucky Bill' Heard From," p. 8.

Beckley Post Herald: Mar. 4, 1970. "Testifying Was Dangerous Business," Shirley Donnelly.

Bluefield Daily Telegraph: Morning, Sept. 1, 1915. "Hatfield-M'Coy Feud Started over Old Sow and Pigs," pp. 1, 6; Morning, Sept. 8, 1915. "Devil Anse Stirred 'Em," p. 5; Sept. 11, 1926. "What We Were Doing: Twenty Years Ago Today," p. 6.

Charleston Daily Mail: Morning, Aug. 25, 1929. "Police Veterans Spring Surprises," p. 3; Evening, Feb. 5, 1942. "Death Ends Eventful Career of 'Uncle Dan' Cunningham," pp. 1–2.

Charleston Sunday Gazette-Mail: Sept. 24, 1967. "The Mystery of Stillhouse Run," p. 8m; May 2, 1976. "No Feuding: Hatfields, McCoys Shake Hands in Rain at Monument Dedication," pp. 1, 10; July 31, 1994. "Feud's Lore, Gore Aimed at Tourists."

Chicago Daily Tribune: Feb. 18, 1888. "The Hatfield-M'Coy Feud," p. 7.

Cincinnati Enquirer: Jan. 30, 1888. "The Bloody Feud: Between the Hatfields and McCoys," p. 1; Jan. 31, 1888. "Still Buying Winchesters," p. 1; Oct. 7, 1888. "Devil Ance: The Outlaw King of Kentucky," p. 1; Oct. 14, 1888. "Hatfield-M'Coy: Origin of the Deadly Feud," p. 9; Nov. 6, 1896. "Bad 'Cap' Is Grimly Awaiting...," p. 1; Nov. 7, 1896. "Barkers Beside Their Pillows Couldn't Guard the Mountain Terrors," p. 1; Nov. 7, 1896. "In Cold Blood," p. 1; Nov. 8, 1896. "Scot Free Is 'Devil Anse' Hatfield," p. 1.

Daily News (Bowling Green, KY): June 4, 2000. "Hatfields, McCoys Bury the Hatchet."

Daily State Journal (Parkersburg, WV): Feb. 1, 1888. "The Hatfield-McCoy War: A Tale of Horror and Outrages Rarely Equaled," p. 1.

Evening Times: Sept. 22, 1906. "The Story of a Kentucky Feud," p. 1.

Floyd County Times: Dec. 3, 1959. "Rev. Dyke Garret, the Minister Who Baptized Devil Anse Hatfield," Henry P. Scalf, p. 2.

Huntington Advertiser: Jan. 14, 1888. "A Second Battle," p. 3; Feb. 4, 1888. "It Is to Be Hoped That the Deplorable Necessity for Sending Troops...," p. 2; Feb. 18, 1888. "The Complications Resulting from the Hatfield-McCoy Vendetta...," p. 2; Sept. 22, 1975. "The Story of the Hatfields and McCoys According to A. M. (Lonnie) Lee," p. 4.

Huntington Herald-Advertiser: Sept. 18, 1938. "Cutting of the Mingo Oak," Henry King, www.wvculture.org/history/parks/mingooak02.html; Sept. 25, 1938. "Cutting of the Mingo Oak," H. R. Pinckard, www.wvculture.org/history /parks/mingooak01.html; Jan. 2, 1966. "Hatfield-McCoy Feud Created Legends That Are Still Growing," George Hanna.

Huntington Herald Dispatch: Aug. 8, 1982. "The Hatfield-McCoy Feud 100th Anniversary," Dave Peyton.

Kansas City Journal: Feb. 1, 1888. "The Kentucky Vendetta: The True History of the Hatfield-McCoy War."

La Crosse Tribune: Oct. 21, 1913. "Governor's Uncle a Vaudeville Artist."

Logan Banner: Oct. 18, 1957. "Last Survivor of Hatfield-McCoy Feud Tells of Battle of Grapevine Creek," Eleanor Brewster; May 4, 1986. "Devil Anse's Grandson Reminisces," p. 1.

Logan County Banner: Apr. 4, 1889. "We Want Peace and Not Destruction of Property by Fire," p. 4; Apr. 11, 1889. "The Flat Top Fight" and "Notice," p. 2.

Los Angeles Times: June 11, 2000, "Hatfields, McCoys Unite to Put Famous Feud to Rest," Eric Slater, p. A-1.

Louisville Courier-Journal: Jan. 18, 1880. "Curious Facts"; Jan. 1, 1888. "The Beautiful," p. 2; Jan. 8, 1888. "A Murderous Gang," p. 2; Jan. 25, 1888. "Bloody War in Pike County," p. 1; Jan. 26, 1888. "No Troops for Pike," p. 5; Jan. 30, 1888. "The Legislature: Pike County Legislation," p. 1; Jan. 30, 1888. "Pike County's Troubles," p. 1; Jan. 31, 1888. "Peace Reigns in Pike," p. 2; Feb. 1, 1888. "Innocents at Home," p. 1; Feb. 2, 1888. "Hatfield-McCoy Mess," p. 1; Feb. 7, 1888. "Two Sides to a Story," p. 1; Feb. 9, 1888. "Middleton's Murder," p. 1; Feb. 10, 1888. "Wants Her Citizens," p. 6; Feb. 17, 1888. "The Hatfields Arrive," p. 1; Feb. 20, 1888. "Enjoying Prison Life," p. 2; Feb. 27, 1888. "Holcombe at the Jail," p. 6; Mar. 2, 1888. "Gossip," p. 7; Mar. 3, 1888. "Signs of Enterprise," p. 6; Mar. 4, 1888. "In Favor of Kentucky," p. 1; Mar. 6, 1888. "Back to Pike," p. 3; Mar. 6, 1888. "The Hatfield Case," p. 4; Mar. 7, 1888. "The Appeal Taken," p. 8; Mar. 8, 1888. "Bullet Riddled," p. 1; Mar. 9, 1888. "A Boy Resents an Insult to His Mother," p. 2; Mar. 10, 1888. "Prospects for a Rise," p. 8; Mar. 10, 1888. "A Very Bad Man," p. 1; Mar. 11, 1888. "Shot to Pieces," p. 5; Mar. 17, 1888. "Back to Pikeville," p. 1; Oct. 13, 1888. "The Hatfield-M'Coy Feud," p. 5; Feb. 18, 1890. "Death by Law," p. 1; Feb. 20, 1890. "Mounts on the Scaffold," p. 1.

Milwaukee Journal: Nov. 9, 1975. "Hatfields, McCoys Bury the Hatchet," pp. 1, 25.

Montgomery News: Oct. 20, 1911. "Hatfield Brothers Killed in Shootout."

Morgantown Dominion Post: May 13, 1975. "Hatfields Mourn, Too, for a McCoy," p. 3-A.

National Police Gazette: Feb. 11, 1888. "The Hatfields and M'Coys," vol. 51, no. 543, p. 2; Nov. 17, 1888. "Devil Ance's Pal," vol. 53, no. 583, p. 7; Feb. 8, 1890. "Editorial Notes," vol. 55, no. 648, p. 2; Jan. 7, 1893. "He Held Life Cheaply," vol. 59, no. 801, p. 6; Apr. 21, 1894. "Hatfield-M'Coy Romance," vol. 63, no. 868, p. 7.

New York Herald: Jan. 11, 1888. "Murderers Turn Lynchers," p. 7; Jan. 25, 1888, "Interstate War," p. 3.

New York Sun (also see Spears in bibliography): Oct. 7, 1888. "An Article Filling . . . ," p. 14; Nov. 4, 1888. "It Will Be Nip and Tuck," p. 15; Nov. 4, 1888. "Politics on the Big Sandy," p. 4; Nov. 4, 1888. "Sport in Wood and Field," p. 8; Nov. 8, 1888. "Logging on the Big Sandy," p. 3; Nov. 11, 1888. "Ways of Mountain Lovers," p. 8; Nov. 29, 1889, "East Kentucky in Terror," p. 5.

New York Times: Aug. 13, 1882. "General Telegraph News: Offenses Against the Laws," p. 2; Oct. 19, 1887. "Vigilantes Take a Hand Disposing of a Band of

Murderous Robbers," p. 1; Jan. 13, 1888. "A Deadly Inter-State Feud: Three of the Hatfield Gang Killed by the M'Coys," p. 3; Mar. 26, 1888. "A Gang of Murderers," p. 1; July 26, 1888. "A Battle with Outlaws," p. 2; Nov. 3, 1888. "Rough-and-Tumble Battle," p. 2; Nov. 18, 1888. "For a Crime Six Years Old," p. 5; Oct. 28, 1889. "Taken from Jail and Lynched," p. 1; June 4, 1890. "Charged with Murder," p. 2; Oct. 15, 1892. "Three Desperadoes Trapped: Detectives Fool Members of the Hatfield-M'Coy Gang," p. 1; Dec. 7, 1895. "Shot Dead by Jealous Boy," p. 1; Apr. 3, 1896. "Robert K. McCoy Probably Shot," p. 1; May 3, 1896. "The Great Interstate Strife of the Last Decade," p. 26; Nov. 7, 1896. "Capt. Hatfield Arrested," p. 1; Mar. 11, 1900. "Hatfield Must Go to Prison: Murderer of a Woman in a Feud to Serve Life Sentence," p. 2; Mar. 30, 1902. "Hatfield Feud Renewed," p. 1; July 11, 1904. "Pardon for a Feudist," p. 7; Feb. 23, 1908. "Hatfield Dies Tied to a Tree," p. 1; Feb. 24, 1908. "Hatfield-M'Coy Feud Has Had 60 Victims," p. 5; Mar. 3, 1908. "Not a Feudist," p. 6; Mar. 29, 1914. "Randall McCoy, Feudist, Dies"; July 9, 1921, "Kentucky Feudist Is Slain: Oldest Survivor of McCoy Faction Is Killed in Knife Fight," p. 12.

New York Tribune: Apr. 8, 1869. Editorial. 1, p. 2.

New York World (also see Crawford in bibliography); Feb. 8, 1888. Evening, "A Fight to the Death," p. 1; Oct. 7, 1888. "A Bloody Vendetta," p. 4.

Ohio Democrat: Dec. 8, 1888. "Given a Dosed Apple," p. 3.

Old Pond Hatfield-McCoy Newsletter. South Williamson Kentucky: Old Pond, Hatfield-McCoy Historical Association and Tug Valley Genealogical Society. Vol. 1, No. 1 Spring/Summer 1998; Vol. 1, No. 4 Fall/Winter 1998, "Letter from Anderson Hatfield to P. A. Cline, Dec. 26, 1886"; Vol. 3, No. 1 Spring/Summer 2000; Vol. 4, No. 2A Fall/Winter 2001; Vol. 5, No. 1 Spring/Summer 2002.

Paducah Sun: July 1, 1903. "A Relic of Feudism," vol. 10, no. 156, p. 1.

Raleigh Herald: Thursday morning, Aug. 27, 1908. "Moonshiners Are Captured," p. 1; Thursday morning, Feb. 18, 1909. "Dan Cunningham," p. 1.

Social Economist: Mar. 1895. "Homicides, American and Southern," Van Buren Denslow, p. 35.

Sunday World-Herald (Omaha): Nov. 9, 1975. "Hatfields, McCoys Bury Hatchet," pp. 1, 6a.

Sunny South: Apr. 7, 1901. "Cunningham's Historic Hunt for the Hatfields: The Story of a Famous Southern Feud and How It Was Ended," p. 4.

Washington Post: June 1, 2003. "The Fiend in Gray," Jane Singer, p. W18; Apr. 5, 2007. "Disease Underlies Hatfield-McCoy Feud," Marilynn Marchione, www.washingtonpost.com/wp-dyn/content/article/2007/04/05/AR2007040501135.html.

Wayne County News: Feb. 24, 1891. "I Ask Your Valuable Paper."

Welch Daily News: Mar. 27, 1992. "Hatfield Heirloom Warms Local Clan," Cathy Patton.

Weston Democrat: Nov. 10, 1888. "The Hatfield-McCoy Vendetta."

Wheeling Intelligencer: Jan. 9, 1888. "A Terrible Story of a Family Feud and Murder," p. 1; Jan. 10, 1888. "Bunnie and Baby in the Hands of the Jury," p. 1; Jan. 10, 1888. "Named for Gen. Logan," p. 3; Jan. 12, 1888. "Roane County Vendetta," p. 3; Jan. 13, 1888. "A Family Feud," p. 1; Jan. 16, 1888. " 'Bunnie' at Home," p. 1; Jan. 20, 1888. "A Terrible Crime," p. 1; Jan. 20, 1888. "The Vendetta," p. 1; Jan. 25, 1888. "The Seat of War," p. 1; Jan. 27, 1888. "The Vendetta of Pike County, Ky., and Logan County, W. Va.," p. 1; Jan. 28, 1888. "The New York *World,*" p. 1; Jan. 30, 1888. "The Legislature: Pike County Legislation," p. 1; Jan. 31, 1888. "The War Is Over," p. 1; Feb. 1, 1888. "From the Frontier," p. 1; Feb. 2, 1888. "Hatfield-McCoy Mess," p. 1; Feb. 2, 1888. "New Developments in the Hatfield-M'Coy Feud"; Feb. 6, 1888. "The Hatfild [*sic*] M'Coy Feud," p. 1; Feb. 9, 1888. "Eustace Gibson's Mission," p. 1; Feb. 11, 1888. "West Virginia Wins," p. 1; Feb. 18, 1888. "Old Man Hatfield: His Story of the Famous Feud," p. 1; Mar. 5, 1888. "Kentucky Is Winner," p. 1; Mar. 19, 1888. "West Virginia Forests," p. 4; Apr. 17, 1888. "The Inter-State War," p. 1; Apr. 19, 1888. "The Hatfield-M'Coy Case," p. 1; Apr. 24, 1888. "Argument Begun in the Famous Hatfield-McCoy Cases in the United States Supreme Court," p. 1; June 29, 1888. "Hatfields and M'Coys," p. 1; Oct. 8, 1888. "Visiting the Hatfields," p. 1; Oct. 17, 1888. "The Hatfield Gang," p. 1; Sept. 6, 1889. "Sentenced for Life: Wall Hatfield Convicted of Murdering the Three McCoys"; Oct. 21, 1889. "The Hatfield Feud," p. 1; Nov. 21, 1889. " 'Devil Anse' Hatfield: Arraigned in the United States Court at Charleston," p. 1; Nov. 23, 1889. "Devil Anse Tells the True History," p. 1.

Wheeling Register: Jan. 17, 1888. "Outlawry: The Story of the Border War in Logan County," p. 1; Jan. 26, 1888. "Border Vendetta," p. 1; Apr. 25, 1888. "The Hatfield Case," p. 1; Sept. 12, 1888. "They Were Not Tried: The Hatfields Still in the Pike County Jail," p. 1.

Williamson Daily News (for the special feud anniversary edition, see Sanders in bibliography): Mar. 20, 1998. "The Hatfields, the McCoys and the Railroad"; Mar. 7, 1999. "Mr. Collector: Store Manager Has Vast Collection."

Documents

Blackburn, Ron G., and Betty Howard. "Ephraim Hatfield Genealogy Chart" and "William McCoy Genealogy Chart."

Bourland, Charles R., Jr. "Biography of Henry Solomon White (1840–1931)." Unpublished manuscript.

Dec. 17, 1890, letter from Governor Simon Bolivar Buckner to the Sheriff of Pike County, fixing the execution date of Ellison Mounts.

Feb. 18, 1890, note from William Harmon Maynard confirming execution of Ellison Mounts.

Hatfield, Anderson. Letter to Perry Cline, Dec. 26, 1886. University of Kentucky Collections.

Hatfield, Ada. "The Legend of the Hatfields." Unpublished journal in possession of Hester Keatley.

Howard, Betty. Annotated Genealogies ("Descendants of . . ."): Nathan Chafin, Tom Chambers, Michael Charles, Perry A. Cline, William Floyd Coleman, Richard Daniels, William Daniels, French Ellis, Richard Ferrell, William "Yankee Bill" Francis, Ephraim Hatfield, Thompson Hatfield, Valentine Hatfield, Nehemiah Hurley, Samuel King, Samuel McCoy, Tolbert McCoy, Alex Messer, Mary Polly Phillips, Elliott "Doc" Rutherford, and Larkin Smith.

"Inaugural Address of Governor Henry D. Hatfield." Mar. 14 [sic], 1913. Compiled by the West Virginia State Archives and located at the West Virginia Division of Culture and History, Charleston.

Kentucky. Arrest warrant for Anderson Hatfield et al. Sept. 20, 1884. Original located at Big Sandy Cultural Center.

Kentucky. Birth Records, 1852–1910. Ancestry.com.

Kentucky. Court of Appeals of Kentucky. "Hatfield v. Commonwealth." Southwestern Reporter 55 (Feb. 19, 1900–Apr. 16, 1900): 679–81.

Kentucky. Court of Appeals of Kentucky. "Hatfield v. Commonwealth, Mayhorn et al. v. Same." Southwestern Reporter 12 (Aug. 26, 1889–Mar. 10, 1890): 309–11.

Kentucky. Court of Appeals of Kentucky. "Mounts v. Commonwealth." Southwestern Reporter 12 (Aug. 26, 1889–Mar. 10, 1890): 311–12.

Kentucky. Kentucky State Penitentiary (Frankfort) Register Book. Entry for Valentine Hatfield, committed for murder, with death date of Feb. 13, 1890. Kentucky Historical Society.

Kentucky. Lawrence Circuit Court indictment against Anderson Hatfield, Johnson McCoy, Wm. McCoy, et al. for grand larceny of a cart of dry goods. Oct. 13, 1865. Kentucky Historical Society.

Kentucky. Order Book Lawrence Circuit Court. Oct. 13, 1865. Kentucky Historical Society.

Kentucky. Petition and Amendment: George Hatfield v. Peter Cline and others, 1866. Kentucky Historical Society.

Kentucky. Pike County Circuit Court Cases 2177 and 2183. Public Records Division, Kentucky Department for Libraries and Archives, Frankfort (KDLA).

Kentucky. Pike County Will Book B, pp. 271–72. "Last Will and Testament of Frank Phillips." July 6, 1898.

Kentucky (Pikeville). "Confession of Ellison Mounts." Nov. 5, 1888. Reproduction of confession given in the presence of county attorney J. Lee Ferguson, found at Depot Museum, Matewan, West Virginia.

Kentucky Senate. Tuesday, Mar. 6, 1888. Legislative Document No. 2, including the Report of the Adjutant General of Kentucky of Feb. 6, 1888.

"Last Will and Testament of Jacob Cline." Transcribed by Cindy Nichols. www .clinefamilyassociation.com/will_of_jacob_rich_jake_cline.

Logan County Courthouse Law Order Book B, 1878–1886.

Mahon v. Justice. Appeal from the Circuit Court of the United States for the District of Kentucky. No. 1411. Argued Apr. 23–24, 1888–Decided May 14, 1888.

"Plaintiffs Bill of Exceptions: Court of Kentucky vs. Anderson Hatfield and other defendants."

Ridenour, Martha. "Perry Anderson Cline." n.d.

Scalf, Henry P. Henry P. Scalf Papers. University of Pikeville.

Spivak, John L. John L. Spivak Papers. West Virginia Collection, West Virginia University Library.

———. Nov. 10, 1929. "Interview with Reese Chambers."

———. Nov. 10, 1929. "Interview with Smith Hatfield."

———. Nov. 11, 1929. "Interview with Cap Hatfield."

———. Jan. 22, 1930. "Letter from J. S. Cline to John L. Spivak."

———. n.d. "Anse Runs an Election."

———. n.d. "Anse Goes to Law."

United States Census. 1870. FamilySearch.

United States Census. 1880. FamilySearch.

Unpublished journal in possession of Hester Keatley.

West Virginia. Deaths Index, 1853–1973. Ancestry.com.

West Virginia. Logan County Court. "Last Will and Testament of Jacob Cline." Transcribed by Cindy Nichols and published at www.clinefamilyassociation .com/will_of_jacob_rich_jake_cline.

West Virginia. Logan County Court. "Warrant Issued by Justice J. M. Jackson Against Frank Phillips, et al., and Returned by J. R. Thompson, a Constable of Said County." Papers of Governor Simon B. Buckner, Kentucky State Archives.

West Virginia. Marriages, 1853–1970. FamilySearch.

West Virginia. Requisition from Governor E. W. Wilson to the Governor of
Kentucky for the arrest and return of Frank Phillips and the men wanted in
Logan County for the murder of Thomas Dempsey, and appointing Alf.
W. Burnett as the agent to receive them. Jan. 23, 1888. Papers of Governor
Simon B. Buckner, Kentucky State Archives.

West Virginia. Requisition from Governor E. W. Wilson to the Governor of Kentucky requesting the release and return of Valentine Hatfield, Thomas Chambers, Andrew Varney, and others unlawfully jailed in Pike County. Feb. 25,
1888. Papers of Governor Simon B. Buckner, Kentucky State Archives.

West Virginia. West Virginia State Supreme Court of Appeals. "Ellison v. Torpin et al." *Report of Cases Argued and Determined in the Supreme Court of Appeals
of West Virginia* 44 (Nov. 11, 1897–Apr. 16, 1898): 414–28.

INDEX

~

Page numbers in *italic* refer to photographs.

Index

Index

Index

Index

428

Index

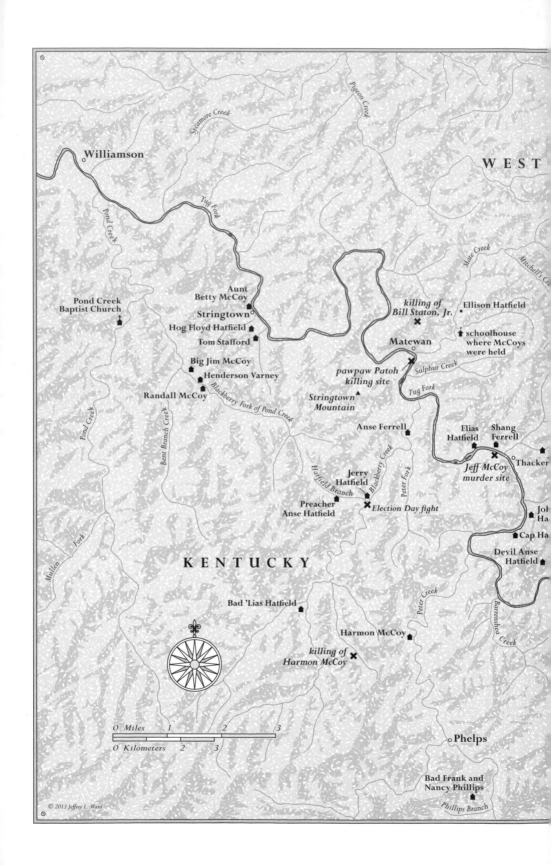